Regulation versus Litigation

T0351795

National Bureau of
Economic Research
Conference Report

Regulation versus Litigation
Perspectives from Economics
and Law

Edited by **Daniel P. Kessler**

The University of Chicago Press

Chicago and London

DANIEL P. KESSLER is professor of buisness and law at Stanford
University, a senior fellow at the Hoover Institution, and a research
associate of the National Bureau of Economic Research.

The University of Chicago Press, Chicago 60637
The University of Chicago Press, Ltd., London
© 2011 by the National Bureau of Economic Research
All rights reserved. Published 2011
Printed in the United States of America

20 19 18 17 16 15 14 13 12 11   1 2 3 4 5
ISBN-13: 978-0-226-43218-2 (cloth)
ISBN-10: 0-226-43218-1 (cloth)

Library of Congress Cataloging-in-Publication Data

Regulation versus litigation : perspectives from economics and law /
edited by Daniel P. Kessler.
        p. cm.— (A National Bureau of Economic Research conference
report)
    Includes bibliographical references and index.
    ISBN-13: 978-0-226-43218-2 (hardcover : alk. paper)
    ISBN-10: 0-226-43218-1 (hardcover : alk. paper) 1. Administrative
procedure—United States. 2. Industrial laws and legislation—
United States. 3. Trade regulation—United States. 4. Actions and
defenses—United States. 5. Administrative procedure—Economic
aspects. 6. Actions and defenses—Economic aspects. 7. Social
control. I. Kessler, Daniel P. II. Series: National Bureau of Economic
Research conference report.
    KF5407.R44 2010
    342.73'066—dc22

                                                        2010016561

Relation of the Directors to the
Work and Publications of the
National Bureau of Economic Research

1. The object of the NBER is to ascertain and present to the economics profession, and to the public more generally, important economic facts and their interpretation in a scientific manner without policy recommendations. The Board of Directors is charged with the responsibility of ensuring that the work of the NBER is carried on in strict conformity with this object.

2. The President shall establish an internal review process to ensure that book manuscripts proposed for publication DO NOT contain policy recommendations. This shall apply both to the proceedings of conferences and to manuscripts by a single author or by one or more co-authors but shall not apply to authors of comments at NBER conferences who are not NBER affiliates.

3. No book manuscript reporting research shall be published by the NBER until the President has sent to each member of the Board a notice that a manuscript is recommended for publication and that in the President's opinion it is suitable for publication in accordance with the above principles of the NBER. Such notification will include a table of contents and an abstract or summary of the manuscript's content, a list of contributors if applicable, and a response form for use by Directors who desire a copy of the manuscript for review. Each manuscript shall contain a summary drawing attention to the nature and treatment of the problem studied and the main conclusions reached.

4. No volume shall be published until forty-five days have elapsed from the above notification of intention to publish it. During this period a copy shall be sent to any Director requesting it, and if any Director objects to publication on the grounds that the manuscript contains policy recommendations, the objection will be presented to the author(s) or editor(s). In case of dispute, all members of the Board shall be notified, and the President shall appoint an ad hoc committee of the Board to decide the matter; thirty days additional shall be granted for this purpose.

5. The President shall present annually to the Board a report describing the internal manuscript review process, any objections made by Directors before publication or by anyone after publication, any disputes about such matters, and how they were handled.

6. Publications of the NBER issued for informational purposes concerning the work of the Bureau, or issued to inform the public of the activities at the Bureau, including but not limited to the NBER Digest and Reporter, shall be consistent with the object stated in paragraph 1. They shall contain a specific disclaimer noting that they have not passed through the review procedures required in this resolution. The Executive Committee of the Board is charged with the review of all such publications from time to time.

7. NBER working papers and manuscripts distributed on the Bureau's web site are not deemed to be publications for the purpose of this resolution, but they shall be consistent with the object stated in paragraph 1. Working papers shall contain a specific disclaimer noting that they have not passed through the review procedures required in this resolution. The NBER's web site shall contain a similar disclaimer. The President shall establish an internal review process to ensure that the working papers and the web site do not contain policy recommendations, and shall report annually to the Board on this process and any concerns raised in connection with it.

8. Unless otherwise determined by the Board or exempted by the terms of paragraphs 6 and 7, a copy of this resolution shall be printed in each NBER publication as described in paragraph 2 above.

Contents

Acknowledgments

A great many institutions and people contributed to the research reported in this volume. I gratefully appreciate the generous financial support of the Smith Richardson Foundation in the form of a grant to the National Bureau of Economic Research. Martin Feldstein, James Poterba, and Andrei Shleifer provided invaluable guidance and intellectual encouragement throughout the process. Carl Beck and Brett Maranjian organized our group's meetings flawlessly. David Pervin, our editor at the University of Chicago Press, helped me and the contributors navigate the publication process and refine the chapters. Two anonymous referees provided numerous helpful suggestions for revision. Finally, Helena Fitz-Patrick made the production of the book—an editor's least favorite job—wonderfully smooth and efficient.

Introduction

Daniel P. Kessler

Modern capitalist societies take two approaches to controlling market failures. One approach relies on relatively specific rules developed and enforced by administrative agencies. In this approach, bureaucrats with technical expertise monitor private parties to ensure compliance. The bureaucrats operate in a larger framework that requires advance notice of and opportunities to comment on any rule changes. In addition, the bureaucrats are subject to political oversight by the executive and/or legislative branches, which limit (for better or worse) the scope of what they can do. This constellation of characteristics defines what is often described as "regulation."

Another approach relies on broad standards that are enforced by courts. In this approach, private parties may contract with one another about their rights and responsibilities; when parties fail to contract, either because their interaction is inadvertent, or because the costs of contracting are too great relative to the benefits, the courts apportion rights and responsibilities between them. The courts are staffed by judges—generalist lawyers who may or may not have expertise in the subject matter underlying the parties' dispute. The judges are sometimes answerable to voters, but often appointed for life and answerable to no one. The courts' decisions are not subject to notice requirements, but can be appealed to another court. This constellation of characteristics defines what is described as "litigation."

The purpose of this volume is to explore the trade-offs between these two approaches. In particular, the chapters will seek to determine the circumstances in which one approach dominates the other; to identify

Daniel P. Kessler is a senior fellow at the Hoover Institution, professor of business and law at Stanford University, and a research associate of the National Bureau of Economic Research.

general principles that should guide assignment of activities to regulation-versus litigation-based systems of social control; and to investigate which aspects of regulation- and litigation-based systems work well or poorly in practice.

Previous Research on Regulation versus Litigation

The study of regulation and litigation has a long history in law and economics, starting with Ronald Coase's (1960) provocative hypothesis that many types of externalities could be controlled by contract, with the remainder handled by tort law. In Coase's world, informational difficulties and transaction costs are minimal, and disputes (when they arose) would be subject to adjudication by the courts. As Andrei Shleifer points out in his contribution to this volume, this position is consistent with the broader Chicago School suspicion of regulation as an efficient mechanism.

Subsequent work focused on situations that differed from Coase's ideal. This work highlighted the various factors that determined whether regulation or litigation would be preferred from the perspective of social welfare, depending on which of Coase's assumptions failed to hold. Although largely in the theoretical law-and-economics tradition, this growing literature painted a considerably more nuanced picture than did Coase. Isaac Ehrlich and Richard Posner (1974) focused on the trade-offs between rules, which were traditionally enforced through regulation, and (more general) standards, which were traditionally enforced through litigation. Donald Wittman (1977) observed that litigation—which is based on enforcement that takes place after an injury or violation occurs—could be less attractive than regulation when monitoring and assigning responsibility for injuries was more costly than monitoring levels of precaution. Steven Shavell (1984b) proposed a more general framework that balanced the influence of several factors, including informational advantages of a public enforcer, diffuseness of injured parties, limited ability to impose liability on injurers, and high administrative costs of courts.

The liability insurance crises of the 1980s stimulated a wave of empirical research that sought to evaluate regulation versus litigation in the real world. In a comprehensive review of both the theoretical and empirical literature, Don Dewees, David Duff, and Michael Trebilcock (1996) systematically compared the performance of litigation and regulation in terms of the systems' compensation and deterrence goals. Robert Litan and Cliff Winston (1988) examined litigation's deterrent effects in the realms of environmental pollution, occupational accidents, and design and production of defective consumer products. Peter Huber and Robert Litan (1991) reported the results of a series of case studies that compared the performance of regulation and litigation in industries such as aviation, pharmaceuticals, auto manufacturing, and chemicals.

Most (although not all) of these empirical studies questioned the efficacy of litigation. Several cited the unpredictability of the United States' decentralized system of state courts to explain why signals from the tort system often failed to translate into increases in safety. In fact, some claimed that the liability system actually had adverse effects on safety, particularly for long-lived durable goods. Graham (1991), for example, argued that the possibility that courts would interpret design improvements as an admission that a prior design was defective creates a disincentive for safety-enhancing innovation. Others focused on the deadweight burden from the substantial administrative costs imposed by the adversarial nature of the civil justice system. As summarized by Huber and Litan (1991, 15), "the documented direct linkages between liability and safety thus far are weak. In most of the sectors examined, other factors—primarily regulation and bad publicity—seem in the aggregate to provide much more important incentives to providers to improve the safety of products and services."

However, the failures of litigation were most striking in markets for health services. Paul Weiler and coauthors (1993) reported the results of the landmark Harvard Medical Practice Study, which analyzed the medical records of a random sample of 30,000 patients hospitalized in New York in 1984. They found that the sensitivity and specificity of the liability system were quite poor: only one in fifteen patients who suffered an injury due to medical negligence received compensation, and five-sixths of the cases that received compensation showed no evidence of negligence. Daniel Kessler and Mark McClellan (1996) found that these incentives translated into "defensive medicine"—use of precautionary treatments with minimal expected medical benefit out of fear of legal liability. In particular, in a population of elderly Medicare beneficiaries with cardiac illness, they found that direct liability reforms such as caps on damages reduced health spending, but had no effect on patient health outcomes.

The 1990s brought a new phenomenon: the use of litigation to impose regulation. In this scenario, executive-branch agencies or even private parties sue alleged wrongdoers and obtain settlements that govern the defendant's future behavior through a system of highly specific rules. The potential importance of the overlap between regulation and litigation was not a new issue. Although regulatory compliance was not a universal defense to negligence, it was in some cases admissible in tort as evidence. In addition, regulation and litigation were often viewed as substitutes, with optimal regimes containing some of each, depending on the two mechanisms' relative costs (Shavell 1984a).

However, the use of litigation as a means to force companies to accept regulation outside of the normal political process raised several new questions about litigation's dynamic costs and benefits (Viscusi 2002; Moriss, Yandle, and Dorchak 2009). On one hand, to the extent that litigation-inspired regulation addressed risks that, because of political market failures, were unacknowledged, then it might improve welfare. On the other hand, to the extent that litigation-inspired regulation allowed attorneys general to usurp the authority of the legislature, or allowed the plaintiffs' bar to extort funds from business to be shared with government officials, then it might reduce welfare.

The Current Volume

The current volume is a collection of eleven chapters, three of which are theoretical and eight of which are empirical. Although the three theoretical chapters offer distinct perspectives on how the trade-offs between regulation and litigation should be understood, they share some common themes. They agree in broad terms on the sorts of characteristics that determine whether a system should be viewed as regulation- or litigation-based. In addition, they agree that the two methods of social control are best viewed as the extremes of a continuum.

The taxonomy that Richard Posner proposes in his contribution makes this point clear. According to him, a regime can be characterized in four dimensions: the extent to which it relies on ex ante versus ex post metrics; on rules versus standards; on experts versus generalists for design and implementation; and on public versus private means of enforcement. In practice, every regime will be somewhere in the middle on each dimension. Litigation-based systems often have regulatory qualities, and vice versa; regulatory agencies often have provisions for court-like hearings when the agency's interpretation of rule is disputed; and courts bind themselves with rules, such as the judge-made rule entitling criminal suspects to a probable cause hearing within forty-eight hours of arrest.

Andrei Shleifer argues that Posner's four dimensions can be collapsed into one: the extent to which courts function well or poorly. By putting the focus on courts, Shleifer's chapter is very much part of the Coasean tradition, while at the same time highly critical of its sometimes unrealistic assumptions. He makes the point that regulation is ubiquitous in modern societies because courts fail. His analysis, however, extends beyond the usual enumeration of the magnitudes of the burdens imposed by transaction costs and imperfect information. He also proposes a political economy model that links the rise of the regulatory state to income inequality—and explains how this rise may be efficient. When enforcement is mostly private, the side with greater resources is likely to have a substantial advantage in court. This advantage may not only exacerbate the preexisting inequality, but also lead to a biased standard of care that reduces (distribution-neutral) social welfare.

Fredrick Schauer and Richard Zeckhauser explore a specific failure of litigation: its dependence on particular cases. They argue that making policy on the basis of cases is problematic because aberrational, rather than representative, cases tend to be the subject of lawsuits. The fact that litigated cases are nonrepresentative is well known (e.g., Priest and Klein 1984). However, as Schauer and Zeckhauser point out, failures of rationality (or, in Coasean terms, costs of information) may nonetheless preclude parties from correctly translating nonrepresentative case outcomes into decision rules to govern behavior in ordinary situations. More importantly, the cognitive availability of unrepresentative cases may lead judges to focus on the wrong issues; rules will be made to deal with the wrong events in the world. And although this is a particular problem with litigation, they observe as well that many legislatively or administratively created rules and regulations, such as Megan's Law and the Brady Bill, are also spurred by unusual cases, and thus often suffer from their case-inspired origins.

The eight empirical chapters include case studies in public health, financial markets, medical care, and workplace safety. However, these chapters have broader implications beyond the particular cases they examine.

The two chapters in public health deal with tobacco and guns. Joni Hersch and W. Kip Viscusi provide an assessment of the consequences of the tobacco Master Settlement Agreement (MSA), which took effect a bit over a decade ago. State attorneys general and tobacco companies entered into the MSA to resolve a series of lawsuits in which the states sought to recoup their cigarette-related Medicaid costs. The MSA imposed numerous regulatory requirements as well as financial payments from the cigarette manufacturers to the states. Unlike damages payments in most tort cases, the MSA payments were based on future sales, not past behavior; this had the effect of making the payments economically equivalent to an excise tax, and shifting their burden from tobacco-company shareholders to future smokers. This payment structure had the ironic effect of increasing states' dependence on future tobacco sales for their revenues, even as they had sued cigarette manufacturers over the dangers of smoking.

The tax and regulatory components of the MSA also may have potential anticompetitive effects. The MSA's restrictions on cigarette advertising have led to a plummeting of advertising expenditures, which may impede new entry into the market and the introduction of new products. Likewise, there may be anticompetitive effects arising from the requirement that new entrants are subject to the MSA payments despite having no past wrongful conduct. Potential new entrants were not represented in the negotiations that led to the MSA. Although Viscusi has written extensively on political and economic consequences of the MSA, his contribution with Hersch is more comprehensive in scope and provides the most up-to-date examination of the agreement that exists, including an analysis of the recently-passed Family Smoking Prevention and Tobacco Control Act.

Philip Cook, Jens Ludwig, and Adam Samaha evaluate the likely effects of the U.S. Supreme Court's decision in *D.C. v. Heller,* 118 S. Ct. 2783 (2008). In that decision, the Court struck down the District of Columbia's handgun ban, recognizing for the first time an individual constitutional right to own a gun. While the immediate effect of the opinion is to invalidate an unusually stringent regulation in a city that is also an enclave of the federal government, the reach of the decision is not yet clearly defined. Cook, Ludwig, and Samaha predict that the decision will ultimately increase the prevalence of handguns in jurisdictions that currently have restrictive laws, and as a result, increase the burden of crime due to more lethal violence and more burglaries. They note, however, that if the ruling is understood as providing people an entitlement to own handguns for self-defense, then from that starting point it is plausible that the "ban on bans" is justified, but so are reasonable restrictions that raise the price of handguns.

These two chapters are both about "regulation through litigation." The MSA imposed regulation through litigation; the Heller decision limited it. Both chapters are also critical of the phenomenon, primarily on grounds that judicial intervention in matters that have been traditionally the province of the legislature constitutes an end-run around the political process. However, as both chapters acknowledge, evaluating such end-runs in general is difficult. To do so would require a political economy model that considered the extent to (and circumstances under) which the judiciary should be allowed more or less latitude to limit regulation than to impose it; this is an important topic for future research.

The contributions of Tomas Philipson, Eric Sun, and Dana Goldman and of Adam Gailey and Seth Seabury address another general issue in the study of regulation versus litigation: whether duplicative control by regulation and litigation leads to advantages over and above those that could be obtained with either system alone.

Philipson, Goldman, and Sun conclude that the answer to this question in the realm of prescription drug safety is no. In the United States, drug safety is governed jointly by the Food and Drug Administration, which oversees premarket clinical trials, and the liability system, which allows patients to sue manufacturers for injuries. They examine the adoption of the National Vaccine Injury Compensation Program, which sharply reduced vaccine manufacturers' liability in 1988. They find that the Program reduced vaccine prices without affecting vaccine safety, consistent with the hypothesis that duplicative control by regulation and litigation is inefficient.

Gailey and Seabury conclude that the answer to this question in the realm of workplace safety is yes. They examine how workers' compensation rules affect the impact of employment protection statutes on the labor market outcomes of the disabled. They estimate whether statutorily-required "reasonable accommodation" of workers' disabilities reduces the workers' compensation costs of workers who become disabled due to a workplace injury. Put another way, they test whether the costs of the litigation-based system of protection from workplace discrimination might be at least partially offset by savings in the regulation-based workers' compensation system.

Based on their analysis of March Current Population Surveys from 1996 to 2007, they find that the interaction between workplace discrimination law and workers' compensation leads to lower costs than would be expected from the two mechanisms considered independently. Changes to the California Fair Employment and Housing Act that required greater accommodations of workers' disabilities led to increased rates of employment for workers' compensation recipients as compared to other disabled workers.

Alison Morantz examines the performance of the workers' compensation system more generally. Her chapter shows how a regulatory system can become more litigious than the litigation system itself. The "great compromise" of worker's compensation, whereby workers relinquished the right to use their employers for negligence in exchange for no-fault compensation for occupational injuries, was one of the great triumphs of regulation over litigation in the twentieth century. As Morantz observes, with the joint support of workers and employers, every state adopted a workers' compensation law between 1910 and 1948. Today, participation in the workers' compensation system is required in most states.

Yet in recent years, the workers' compensation system has been criticized for becoming increasingly like the litigation system it was originally intended to replace. In response, some large employers in the state of Texas—the only state that has preserved an elective statutory scheme—have begun opting out of the workers' compensation system and permitting their employees to sue them for workplace injuries in tort.

Based on a unique survey of large, multistate "nonsubscribers" to Texas workers' compensation, Morantz documents the remarkable turnabout in the system's appeal to large firms since its inception almost 100 years ago. Although workers' compensation may have once offered the advantages of regulation, from the perspective of most surveyed corporations, it now suffers from many of the shortcomings of litigation. According to Morantz, Texas nonsubscribers reported that opting into the tort system *reduced* costs, litigation, delays in claim reporting, and delays in employees' return to work relative to workers' compensation. She also reports several additional interesting findings. Virtually all surveyed nonsubscribers compensated injured employees, regardless of fault, for occupational injuries. Unlike workers' compensation, however, most of these "home-grown" occupational-injury plans did not impose any maximum weekly dollar amount or waiting period on the receipt of wage replacement benefits. On the other hand, such plans typically imposed stricter reporting guidelines, capped total benefits, allowed the employer to direct medical treatment, and excluded payouts for permanently-disabling injuries. Most surveyed firms also sought to limit their tort exposure by resolving disputes through mandatory arbitration.

The contributions of John Coates, Stephen Parente, and Tom Chang and Mireille Jacobson investigate the relative advantages of regulation and litigation in settings that have been previously unexamined. John Coates compares the law governing mergers and acquisitions (M&A) in the United States and the United Kingdom. One dimension of M&A law is the treatment of "break fees"—payments that the target of a merger offer agrees to make to a prospective acquirer in the event the target is ultimately acquired by someone else. Break fees have two competing effects on shareholders' interests: although they may encourage prospective bidders to participate in an auction, they may also enable managers to favor bidders who will enrich the managers at shareholders' expense. Break fees are routinely restricted as part of the corporate law doctrines of the United States and the United Kingdom. In the United States, courts review break fees in ex post litigation, applying a general common-law standard of fiduciary duty; the United Kingdom caps such fees with a bright-line rule set by a regulatory body.

Based on his analysis of 2,579 bids for U.S. and UK corporations from 1989 to 2008, Coates finds that the break fees are statistically significantly lower in the United Kingdom than in the United States. In addition, he finds that the number of deals with competing bids is higher in the United Kingdom, and the number of completed bids is lower. Although he cautions against drawing any welfare conclusions, his results suggest that a regulatory approach to M&A has at least some gross (if not necessarily net) social benefits, in the form of stronger competition for targets conditional on an M&A bid, but may come at the cost of reduced M&A activity.

Steve Parente evaluates the performance of a new regulatory mechanism to detect prescription drug misuse. As he and many others have pointed out, prescription drug misuse generates large negative externalities. Most efforts at controlling misuse, however, are based on ex post approaches implemented by generalized law enforcement agencies. Parente proposes a medical-claims-based algorithm that compares a prospective drug purchaser's observable characteristics to those that have been historically associated with misuse. He finds that several commonly-observable characteristics are significant predictors of misuse. He concludes with a discussion of how point-of-service fraud detection and intervention systems used by banks and credit card vendors could be adapted to this setting.

Tom Chang and Mireille Jacobson examine the use of a cap-and-trade mechanism to regulate hospitals' provision of essential services. They study California's mandate that all general acute care hospitals retrofit or rebuild in order to maintain their structural soundness after an earthquake. They demonstrate that the mandate has important unintended consequences for the availability of hospital services and the provision of charity care. They propose an alternative regulatory mechanism: a system in which each California hospital would be required to provide a given number of earthquake-safe beds, but then be allowed to pay a neighboring hospital to satisfy their requirement. They show that this cap-and-trade system could achieve the goal of insuring a minimum number of operational hospital beds after an earthquake at a much lower cost than the existing mandate.

References

Coase, R. 1960. The problem of social cost. *Journal of Law and Economics* 3:1–44.

Ehrlich, I., and R. Posner. 1974. An economic analysis of legal rulemaking. *Journal of Legal Studies* 3:257–86.

Dewees, D., D. Duff, and M. Trebilcock. 1996. *Exploring the domain of accident law: Taking the facts seriously.* New York: Oxford University Press.

Graham, J. D. 1991. Product liability and motor vehicle safety. In *The liability maze,* ed. P. W. Huber and R. E. Litan, 120–90. Washington, DC: The Brookings Institution.

Huber, P. W., and R. E. Litan, eds. 1991. *The liability maze.* Washington, DC: The Brookings Institution.

Kessler, D. P., and M. B. McClellan. 1996. Do doctors practice defensive medicine? *Quarterly Journal of Economics* 111:353–90.

Litan, R. E., and C. Winston, eds. 1988. *Liability: Perspectives and policy.* Washington, DC: The Brookings Institution.

Moriss, A. P., B. Yandle, and A. Dorchak. 2009. *Regulation by litigation.* New Haven, CT: Yale University Press.

Priest, G. L., and B. Klein. 1984. The selection of disputes for litigation. *Journal of Legal Studies* 13:1–55.

Shavell, S. 1984a. A model of the optimal use of liability and safety regulation. *RAND Journal of Economics* 15:271–80.

———. 1984b. Liability for harm versus regulation of safety. *Journal of Legal Studies* 13:357–74.

Viscusi, W. K., ed. 2002. *Regulation through litigation.* Washington, DC: AEI-Brookings Joint Center for Regulatory Studies, the American Enterprise Institute for Public Policy Research, and the Brookings Institution.

Weiler, P. C., H. Hiatt, J. P. Newhouse, W. G. Johnson, T. Brennan, and L. Leape. 1993. *A measure of malpractice: Medical injury, malpractice litigation, and patient compensation.* Cambridge, MA: Harvard University Press.

Wittman, D. 1977. Prior regulation versus post liability: The choice between input and output monitoring. *Journal of Legal Studies* 6:193–211.

Regulation (Agencies) versus Litigation (Courts)
An Analytical Framework

Richard A. Posner

1.1 Introduction

Economic analysis of law treats common law fields, especially tort law—which provides legal remedies for physical, mental, or financial injuries caused by negligence, medical malpractice, nuisance (which includes pollution), defamation, defective products, misrepresentation, or other wrongful conduct—as forms of regulation. The emphasis is thus on the deterrent effect of the threat of liability, rather than on the compensatory role of liability; compensation is thought better provided for by insurance. Common law is thus conceived of as regulation by judges—by judges not only because common law remedies are obtained by means of lawsuits against injurers but also because common law doctrines are made by judges.

My objective in this chapter is to compare common law (including federal common law; i.e., the body of common law made by federal judges—indeed, my primary concern is with federal regulation) with administrative regulation as methods of social control. More precisely, my objective is to compare common law regulation with administrative regulation, while giving due recognition to the fact that administrators often use common law methods of regulation and that judges sometimes use methods similar to those of

Richard A. Posner is a Judge in the U.S. Court of Appeals for the Seventh Circuit, and a Senior Lecturer at the University of Chicago Law School.

I thank Daniel Kessler, and two anonymous referees, for helpful comments on an earlier draft of this piece. I have decided to spare the reader the burden of footnotes and references. Much of the key literature on which I build is cited in the editors' introduction; of particular note is Steven Shavell, "Liability for Harm versus Regulation of Safety," *Journal of Legal Studies* 13:357–74 (1984). See also the discussion and references in chapter 13 ("The Choice between Regulation and Common Law") of my book *Economic Analysis of Law,* 7th ed. (Aspen Publishers, 2007).

administrative agencies. (The principal example is the "regulatory decree," under which courts will administer rules, often agreed to by the parties— governing institutions, such as school systems or prison systems—that have been determined to have violated constitutional law.) Nevertheless, judges are considerably more comfortable with the common law approach, and agencies that rely on common law methods to regulate are generally thought to have forgone the distinctive advantages of administrative regulation. So there is some utility to contrasting "litigation" with "regulation" as alternative methods of social control, while recognizing the overlap.

But besides noting the overlap, I need to point out an intermediate position between common law and administrative regulation. In common law adjudication, the judges make as well as apply the doctrine. In administrative regulation, the judges play a limited role of deferential judicial review of the administrative agency's decision. But in between is the judicial enforcement of statutes that are not administered by a regulatory agency. For example, although the Federal Trade Commission has antitrust enforcement authority, most antitrust cases are brought by public officials or private firms in federal courts that interpret and apply the antitrust laws without the intervention of an administrative agency. The judges' role is nominally interpretive but owing to the age and vagueness of the antitrust statutes in fact resembles common law lawmaking. But for simplicity I will focus on the contrast between pure common law adjudication and administrative regulation.

My analysis is normative; the question I address is what the better method—litigation or (administrative) regulation—would be, from the standpoint of economic efficiency, for regulating a particular activity. I leave to other work (some in this volume) positive questions about the choice between litigation and regulation, such as the political and cultural forces (including legalistic and individualistic traditions, and the influence of the legal profession, which has been said to be the American counterpart of European aristocracy and elite bureaucracy) that shape American government. No competent student of regulation thinks that the line between common law and regulation has been drawn primarily on the basis of comparative economic advantage.

From a normative economic standpoint the goal of regulation, whether by courts or by agencies, is to solve economic problems that cannot be left to the market to solve—such as problems created by positive or negative large externalities that market forces cannot internalize because transaction costs are too great for the Coase theorem to apply. Even so, it is still necessary to consider whether public control is justified, because the costs may exceed the benefits from internalizing the externalities, or because an intermediate form of regulation between pure market forces and public control may be superior to both; I refer to industry self-regulation, illustrated by board certification of physicians, hazing-type medical education to instill norms and create a "high commitment" environment ("professionalism"), contracts between patients and physicians and between consumers and producers, rulemaking and standards-setting by trade or professional associations, and arbitration or mediation to resolve disputes. If public control is not superior to private ordering, the next question—the positive one—is why the private alternative has been rejected.

1.2   Characterizing the Differences between Regulation and Litigation

Regulation and litigation tend to differ along four key dimensions: (a) regulation tends to use ex ante (preventive) means of control, litigation ex post (deterrent) means; (b) regulation tends to use rules, litigation standards; (c) regulation tends to use experts (or at least supposed experts) to design and implement rules, whereas litigation is dominated by generalists (judges, juries, trial lawyers), though experts provide input as witnesses; and (d) regulation tends to use public enforcement mechanisms. Litigation more commonly uses private enforcement mechanisms—private civil lawsuits, handled by private lawyers although the decision resolving the litigation is made by a judge (with or without a jury), who is a public official (the jurors are ad hoc public officials).

1.2.1   Ex Ante versus Ex Post

The first method is illustrated by speed limits, the second by personal-injury suits for negligence. As in this example, the two types of regulation are frequently conjoined. The regulation of highway safety is a complex mosaic of ex ante regulation (including speed limits and other safe driving rules, federal safety design standards, standards for the design and maintenance of highways, and the licensure of drivers) and ex post regulation (such as suits for negligent driving, product liability suits for defects in the design or manufacture of motor vehicles, and criminal prosecutions for drunk or other reckless driving).

Ex ante regulation can, as I said, be judicial as well as administrative, as in preventive detention, injunctions, and regulatory decrees, and ex post regulation can be administered by agencies as well as courts, such as the Federal Trade Commission and the National Labor Relations Board, which operate mainly by trial-type proceedings conducted after a violation of the laws administered by the agency has occurred.

Ex ante: pros. The ex ante approach promotes clarity of legal obligation and therefore presumably better compliance (fewer inadvertent violations) by laying down rules in advance of the regulated activities. Ex ante regulation is activated before there is a loss, unlike a lawsuit; it can be centrally designed and imposed (for example, by a single agency such as the Food and Drug Administration, as opposed to a decentralized judicial system); and it is enforceable by means of light penalties, because the optimal penalty for creating a mere risk of injury is normally lighter than the optimal penalty for causing an actual injury. This means, however, that ex ante and ex post regulation actually are inseparable; because compliance with rules is never 100 percent, there must be a machinery for punishing violators, though the machinery may involve penalties meted out by the regulatory agency itself, with judicial involvement limited to judicial review of the penalty proceeding. But while rules involve heavy fixed costs (i.e., designing the rule in the first place), if they are very clear and carry heavy penalties compliance may be achieved without frequent enforcement proceedings, so marginal costs may be low. Rules are therefore attractive when the alternative would be vague standards, resulting in frequent actual or arguable violations and hence frequent enforcement proceedings.

As this discussion shows, ex ante regulation and rules have an affinity. Ex ante regulation enables exploitation of the economizing properties of rules as preventives. With vague standards, the regulatory emphasis shifts to seeking deterrence by proceedings to punish violators.

But the affinity between ex ante regulation and rules requires a qualification. Consider the criminal penalties for the sale of illegal drugs. The underlying criminal prohibition is a flat, clear rule, but compliance is achieved almost entirely by threat of punishment, which is ex post. Contrast that with the regulation of legal drugs, where, although there is ex post enforcement, including products liability suits, the emphasis is on testing new drugs in advance for safety and efficacy and refusing to allow drugs to be sold that flunk the tests.

Ex ante: cons. Ex ante regulation narrows the information base because when it takes the form of rules, it buys precision at the cost of excluding case-specific information that the promulgators of the regulation either did not anticipate or excluded in order to keep the regulation simple (i.e., to keep it a rule). Standards (such as negligence) versus rules (such as a numerical speed limit) allow much more information to be considered in particular cases. In doing so, however, standards not only reduce predictability; they also, as noted before, veer into ex post regulation, because vague standards beget disputes that require litigation over alleged violations to resolve. In addition, ex ante regulation, like preventive care in medicine, can burden much harmless activity, such as safe driving in excess of the speed limit. (Compare screening the entire population for medical conditions that afflict only a few people.) This is related to the fact that rules exclude relevant circumstances for the sake of clarity.

When ex ante regulation takes the form of licensure rather than merely prohibition—compare a requirement of a building permit to a speed limit—costs of compliance may soar, along with an increased risk of bribery if the permit is highly valuable.

Ex post: pros. Ex post regulation may require only rare interventions (again compare screening for medical conditions with treatment if and when a condition produces symptoms) and zero in on the limiting case in which a rule or standard achieves 100 percent compliance, though there may of course be costs of compliance. Ex post regulation economizes on administrative expense because intervention is sporadic, and utilizes both case-specific information (including information about causation and victim fault, and other information obtained after regulation is promulgated and in the context of a particular injury) and adversary procedure, which may increase accuracy. There is more information, including up-to-date and case-specific information, and it is screened and weighed more carefully because it is presented in a contested proceeding. In its private (as distinct from public) and adversary character, litigation as a regulatory approach borrows the methods of competitive markets.

The information advantage of ex post regulation is especially pronounced when the ex post standard is strict liability, meaning that the injurer is obligated to pay damages even if he or she could not have avoided at reasonable cost inflicting the injury. An example is an injury caused by the use of explosives, viewed as an ultrahazardous activity, in building a tunnel. Potential injurers have a strong incentive to balance the costs and benefits of the hazardous activity in order to decide whether or on what scale or in what circumstances engaging in the activity is cost-justified, and they have ready access to the necessary information.

The earlier example of illegal drugs illustrates the case in which ex post regulation does not refine a preexisting rule or standard. The laws are clear and their enforcement is concerned simply with punishing violations. The enforcement is also, however, largely ineffectual. For although the penalties are stiff, the expected cost of punishment is for many potential offenders low relative to the expected profits of drug trafficking because of the ease of concealment of illegal activity—a general problem with "victimless" crimes, since there is no one to complain to the authorities. But this is a case where both ex ante and ex post regulation are failures, and the best solution would be decriminalization coupled with excise taxation—though that could be considered a form of ex ante regulation, though remote from the usual examples.

Ex post: cons. Ex post regulation, typified by common law adjudication, with its heavy emphasis on standards (such as negligence and good faith) in preference to rules, involves high costs per case compared to adjudicating a speeding ticket. This is partly because of the additional information generated by a proceeding focused on a specific injury inflicted in particular circumstances. More information cannot only make a proceeding more costly but also create more uncertainty and as a result more variance in outcome; uncertainty also makes it more difficult to monitor the performance of the judge or other regulator to make sure he or she is competent and honest. Furthermore, a point related to the fact that the optimal penalty when an injury has occurred is greater than when a risk has been created that has not yet materialized, the injurer may not have sufficient resources to pay the penalty. There are also problems of proof when the cause of an injury must be proved. The problems are illustrated by cases in which exposure to radiation increases the incidence of cancer, but it is impossible to determine whose cancers were due to the radiation and whose would have occurred anyway. This particular problem, however, can be solved, at least in principle, by class actions that amalgamate claims of probabilistic injury of all persons who had been exposed to the hazard in question.

Since deterrence is unlikely to be 100 percent effective, ex ante regulation is strongly indicated when the regulated activity can give rise to catastrophic injury. The greater the injury if deterrence fails and the likelier deterrence is to fail, the stronger the case for ex ante regulation. Even if 99 percent of building collapses, but only 10 percent of drug offenses, can be prevented by ex post regulation (suits for negligent design or construction in the first case, criminal punishments in the second), the social cost of the 1 percent of building collapses may exceed the social cost of the 90 percent of drug offenses. If it also exceeds the cost of prevention by the enactment and enforcement of building codes, then ex ante regulation is justified in the building's case. Reinforcing this conclusion is the fact that positive correlation between the gravity of the injury and the likelihood that deterrence will fail. They are positively correlated because the limited solvency of potential injurers is likely to make the expected cost *to them* of the injury (for remember that we are assuming a grave injury) lower than the expected social cost.

A similar example is public inspections of restaurants and food-processing plants versus relying entirely on threat of negligence suits to prevent food poisoning. In the case of restaurants, the owners would often be judgment-proof, so in the absence of a system of public inspections people would be very reluctant to patronize a small or new restaurant. In the case of food-processing plants, carelessness can result in mass injuries the costs of which to the victims might exceed the ability to pay of the negligent food processor.

This point also helps to explain the different regulatory systems for new drugs and for medical procedures. A drug sold to millions of people can, if it is unsafe, wreak enormous harm, whereas individual cases of medical malpractice injure only one patient. Moreover, it is feasible to test every new drug, and thus determine safety in advance, but infeasible to require physicians to seek approval from a regulatory agency for every procedure they perform. Consistent with this analysis, ex ante regulation is the dominant mode of regulation of new drugs, while ex post regulation in the form of medical malpractice suits is the dominant mode of regulation of medical treatment. Medical education and apprenticeship (residency) also play a major role in preventing malpractice, but that is not the focus of the training.

Thus far I have assumed that the cost of an injury can be determined. But often it cannot be, at least satisfactorily. Examples are death, disfigurement, disability, emotional injury, and many forms of environment damage, including reduction in species diversity. Economists have developed methods of estimating such costs, but they are crude approximations at best to the underlying loss in utility or welfare, and can be elided by ex ante regulation that averts the loss entirely—although a determination of how much to spend on such regulation should, from an efficiency standpoint, depend on an estimate of the cost of the losses that it will avert.

A timely example of a situation in which difficulty of measuring costs, combined with difficulty of estimating causal responsibility and aggregating claims, argues strongly against ex post regulation is the economic downturn triggered by the financial collapse of September 2008. It is quite impossible to see how ex post regulation could protect the economy from the macroeconomic consequences of an unregulated business cycle.

A related point is the limited feasibility of ex post regulation as a control over official misfeasance, other than corruption. Although the successive Federal Reserve chairmen Alan Greenspan and Ben Bernanke committed mistakes that played a substantial role in the financial collapse, it is unlikely that the mistakes would have been averted if Federal Reserve chairmen were suable for the consequence of unsound monetary policy or bank regulation.

A broader problem that this example illustrates is the difficulty of ex post regulation as a means of deterring individual as distinct from corporate or other institutional conduct. Individuals are rarely wealthy enough to be worth suing, although physicians, other professionals, and wealthy businessmen are exceptions; and while they can be required to (and will often choose voluntarily to) buy liability insurance, this creates a moral hazard problem when insurers are unable, or are forbidden, to calibrate premiums to the risks of liability created by particular insureds. If all victims of unlawful conduct are fully compensated, there is no social loss. But because of loss limits in insurance policies, and uncompensated losses even in an efficient system of private law (the resources consumed when a person is injured—for example, in the medical care that he or she receives—are a deadweight loss that compensation does not restore), the reduction that liability insurance brings about in the deterrent effect of threat of litigation is a social loss.

1.2.2 Rules versus Standards

I elaborate here on the comparison that I made earlier between rules and standards as regulatory techniques. I noted the (loose) association between rules and ex ante regulation on the one hand and standards and ex post regulation on the other.

A rule abstracts from a number of relevant facts (as in a numerical speed limit, which ignores other circumstances bearing on the danger caused by driving). A standard, such as "due care," or "unreasonable restraint of trade," or "recklessness," is open-ended because it directs the judge or jury or other regulator to consider the particular circumstances in which a violation is alleged.

Rules: pros. Rules tend to be simple and clear, which reduces enforcement costs and facilitates monitoring of the court or other agency that applies the rules to particular facts. The simplicity of rules and the ease of monitoring compliance with them make them especially attractive for societies in which the judiciary is prone to incompetence and corruption.

Rules: cons. Yet often rules are not really simple and clear, because of pressure for exceptions and the boundary issues created by exceptions; it may be unclear whether a particular case falls within the general rule or within one of its exceptions. The answer to such a question is usually found by considering the purpose behind the rule and the exception in question, and that is the sort of analysis employed when standards are being applied.

Rules tend also to be crude, because they exclude relevant facts (such as, in the speed-limit example, traffic conditions, weather and time of day, emergencies, and driver skills). Thus, they rest on a narrower information base than standards. That exclusion also makes them somewhat arbitrary, and as a result counterintuitive. "Being careful" is intuitive; driving below 50 mph is not, which is why speed limits have to be posted. Rules, in contrast to standards, tend also to separate rule creation from application: legislatures promulgate rules, courts apply them. Common law courts both create and apply standards, and there are efficiency gains from vesting both functions in the same organization.

Standards: pros. Standards are the inverse of rules, so that the disadvantages of rules become the advantages of standards. They are flexible, intuitive, and generate and utilize more information, including information generated after the standard was initially adopted (that is a serious problem with rules—they exclude from consideration factors the significance of which was not realized when a rule was promulgated). They also facilitate merging the maker with the applier of the standard—it is often the same entity; namely, the same court.

Standards: cons. Similarly, the advantages of rules show up on the other side of the ledger as the disadvantages of standards. They are vague, costly to administer because open-ended, and difficult to monitor compliance with by the court or other body that enforces the standard. The more courts are distrusted, whether because of suspected corruption, incompetence, or a lack of resources for determining facts accurately, the more attractive rules become as the sources of the law applied by the courts. One therefore expects and finds a secular trend toward increased reliance on standards relative to rules.

Notice that despite the association of rules with legislatures and rulemaking with administrative agencies, rules can be judicial (an example is the judge-made rule entitling a criminal suspect to a probable-cause hearing within forty-eight hours of arrest), and standards can be administrative (examples are police discretion in enforcing speed limits and the use of broad standards such as "unfair labor practice" and "unfair or deceptive acts or practices" by the National Labor Relations Board and the Federal Trade Commission, respectively). Also, standards can be ex ante, as in the safety and efficacy standards used by the Food and Drug Administration to decide whether to approve a new drug. And rules can be ex post; for example, when a rule is declared by a court for the first time in a case in which the parties did not anticipate it; nevertheless it binds them, as well as others who may have violated the rule before it came into existence. Indeed, judicial rulemaking is characteristically ex post.

1.2.3   Agencies versus Courts

Agencies: pros. Agencies are specialized, and this facilitates the development of expertise in technical subjects (examples are traffic safety departments prescribing speed limits and the Food and Drug Administration regulating pharmaceuticals). They usually have large staffs and flexible powers—often they are authorized to use both ex ante and ex post regulation. They are less hobbled by precedent than are courts. Agency members have more political legitimacy than judges do because they do not enjoy life tenure, and thus have less need to avoid being thought "activist" and to demonstrate continuity with past political settlements. Judges are reluctant to innovate, or at least to seem to innovate, lest they be accused of crossing the line that separates applying law from making law, the latter considered in orthodox jurisprudence and political theory a legislative rather than a judicial function. Judges are forever denying that they make policy—something that agencies do unapologetically. In fact, the difference is merely one of degree.

Agencies: cons. Agencies are subject to far more intense interest-group pressures than courts. The agency heads are political appointees and their work is closely monitored by congressional committees. The fact that agency members are specialized, and that they are less insulated from the political process than judges are, makes them targets for influence by special-interest groups; hence the term "regulatory capture." Historically, the missions of regulatory agencies have often been anticompetitive, as capture theory implies: interest groups seek to influence agencies to insulate the groups' members from competition, as by blocking new entry. Execution of valid regulatory policies is often thwarted by the dependence of regulators on information supplied by the regulated entities and by the perverse incentives created by "revolving door" behavior. The large staffs of most regulatory agencies result in the typical agency-cost problems of bureaucracies that are not disciplined by marketplace competition. And regulation is really dual agency-court regulation, because agency rulings are appealable to courts. Regulation can, as in the case of Social Security disability benefits, beget four tiers of adjudication: in the Social Security case they are an administrative law judge in the Social Security Administration, review by an appellate body within the Administration, further review by a federal district court, and appeal from that court to a federal court of appeals. There are no economies from such multitiered regulation.

Courts: pros. Courts are relatively immune to interest-group pressures (at least federal courts, whose judges have secure tenure, and some state courts), nonbureaucratic, decentralized, and semiprivatized (because of the major role played by the litigants' lawyers). They bring to the table an outsider's perspective on issues that regulators, afflicted with tunnel vision, might botch. Judges are also less mission-oriented than regulators. Being generalists, and coming from diverse professional as well as personal backgrounds, they are less likely to identify with particular policies and therefore bring a more balanced approach to issues than regulators committed to a particular policy do. If an agency were established to eradicate drug trafficking, and was given the authority to try violators of the drug laws, it would give short shrift to procedural safeguards for accused violators. Federal judges have greater prestige, better working conditions, better salary and (particularly) benefits, more job security, and far more autonomy (in particular, insulation from political and interest-group pressures) than regulators, and all these advantages result in a higher average quality of judicial than of regulatory appointees.

Courts: cons. Judges in the Anglo-American judicial systems are among the last generalists in an increasingly specialized government and society, and this is a source of weakness as well as of strength. The judges' lack of specialized knowledge, their limited staffs, limited investigatory resources, cumbersome and to a degree antiquated procedures, commitment to incremental rulemaking, and delay in responding to serious social problems—courts cannot act until a case is brought, which often is long after the activity giving rise to the case began—are impediments to effective regulation, especially of technical subjects. These problems are aggravated by the heavy use—idiosyncratic by world standards—of juries in civil cases. When technical issues are committed to courts, such as issues concerning medical malpractice, product-design defects, and patents on drugs or software, the results often are unsatisfactory. The costly practice of "defensive medicine," a response to the threat of malpractice liability, is an example of costs resulting from the commitment of technical issues to generalist judges and jurors bound to make many errors. But it is unclear whether the costs of defensive medicine outweigh the benefits of tort liability in creating increased incentives to exercise care in medical treatment. And the poor performance of the Patent and Trademark Office *and* of the semispecialized Court of Appeals for the Federal Circuit (which has a monopoly of patent appeals), suggests that specialization of courts or agencies is no panacea even in highly technical fields.

1.2.4   Public versus Private Enforcement Mechanisms

The common law litigation system, as indeed any private-law system, depends on private individuals and firms to activate the system. The award of monetary damages as the standard outcome of a successful private suit provides the incentive for a private party to sue. The common objection that because of the expense of litigation, victims of small harms (though they may be great harms when cumulated over all victims) is overcome or at least diluted by the class-action device, which allows the aggregation of small claims to create a prospective damages award large enough to motivate a suit. Penalties of various sorts can also be annexed to compensatory damages in order to increase the private motivation to sue.

Nevertheless, litigation is very costly in the United States, and quite slow as well; and the existence of criminal laws is proof (if any is needed) that damages awards (or injunctions, the other common remedy awarded to a plaintiff who prevails in a private suit) are not always an adequate device for controlling behavior. Limited liability (shareholders generally are not personally liable for the debts, including debts created by legal judgments, of their corporation) and liability insurance blunt the deterrent effect of damages liability; and the criminal law, because of the procedural protections that it accords defendants, has limited applicability to negligent or otherwise undesirable business behavior. Hence the creation of regulatory mechanisms that do not require recourse to litigation, although judicial review of the result of the regulatory proceeding is typically available. The rise of the federal administrative agency, which began with the creation of the Interstate Commerce Commission in 1887, reflected a desire to increase the role of expert knowledge in regulation and to counteract what was widely and to a degree correctly believed to be stubborn judicial resistance to modern social-welfare policies. But it also reflected a desire to provide cheaper and more expeditious remedies for perceived wrongs administered by civil servants. Gained was a degree of expertise, expedition, and procedural and remedial flexibility; lost was the superior ability of most judges (at least federal judges) to agency administrators, their greater sensitivity to rule-of-law values, and the energy and initiative of private persons and firms affected by regulation.

The 1970s saw the beginning of a bipartisan deregulation movement that continued until the financial collapse of 2008 and resulted in a substantial curtailment of federal regulation, including the abolition of some regulatory agencies, such as the Interstate Commerce Commission and the Civil Aeronautics Board, and the shrinkage (sometimes by Congress, sometimes by the agencies themselves) in the scope and powers of other regulatory agencies. The fields affected included air and surface transportation (including pipelines), natural gas, wholesale electricity, telecommunications, broadcasting, and banking and finance generally, including securities regulation. But the deregulation movement (which crashed along with the financial crash) did not reflect a preference for courts over agencies, or indeed institutional considerations at all, but rather a shift in economic policy in favor of competition over both administrative and judicial regulation, a shift that influenced the courts as well in such fields as antitrust and securities regulation.

Moreover, the deregulation movement was limited to commercial competition, and coincided with increased regulation of employment (with particular emphasis on discrimination), health and safety, and the environment. Neither general dissatisfaction with administrative regulation nor with judicial regulation powered changes in the scope and emphasis of regulation.

1.3   Litigation and Regulation in Practice

1.3.1   Pure versus Mixed (Hybrid) Systems (Corner versus Interior Solutions)

A pure system of regulation would be only administrative regulation or only litigation; a mixed system combines the two modes of control. There are virtually no pure regulatory systems, because most regulatory decisions by administrative agencies are subject to judicial review. That is a more limited form of judicial intervention than a proceeding that begins in court rather than in an agency, but on the other hand it is common to provide parallel administrative and judicial remedies for the same harms, as in the case of antitrust, where one can bring a suit in federal court or file a complaint with the Federal Trade Commission, which can decide to institute an administrative proceeding, with eventual judicial review. A different kind of dual regulation is found in employment discrimination. A person complaining of discrimination in violation of federal law can file a suit in federal court. Alternatively the Equal Employment Opportunity Commission (EEOC) can file a suit in federal court on the person's behalf; in neither case is that adjudication within the commission itself, unlike the antitrust example.

Nearest to a pure system of administrative regulation is a system in which compliance with a regulatory rule or order precludes a subsequent lawsuit (preemption). The financial industry has the closest approach to a pure regulatory regime. Medical malpractice approaches a pure litigation system, except that there is some regulation of hospital and physical practices, and of course there is licensure of physicians and other health-care providers. Antitrust approaches a pure litigation system too, despite the merger guidelines published by the Department of Justice and the Federal Trade Commission (FTC). The guidelines provide a basis for advance determinations by the agencies whether to approve proposed mergers, but are nonbinding. A parallel is the federal sentencing guidelines, which are administrative guidelines that influence but do not bind federal criminal sentencing.

Pure: pros. A pure system is cheaper, simpler, operates much more quickly, and provides better guidance. The need for speed, well illustrated by the response of the Federal Reserve and the Treasury Department to the sudden financial collapse in September 2008, can be a compelling reason for a regulatory system in which courts play little or no role. Thus, while failing firms normally are subject to liquidation or reorganization in a bankruptcy court (part of the federal court system), commercial banks that fail are "resolved" in administrative proceedings by the Federal Deposit Insurance Corporation.

Pure: cons. When time is not of the essence, a pure system of administrative regulation has many disadvantages. For one thing, it increases the incentives for, and therefore the likelihood of, regulatory capture by interest groups; the interest group has only to "buy" an agency, and not the courts as well—and the federal courts are very difficult to "buy." Also, a pure system of either kind (agency or court) sacrifices complementarities, because courts and agencies are complements as well as substitutes. Agency action subject to judicial review melds specialist with generalist perspectives and mission-directed policy with sensitivity to rule-of-law factors.

Mixed: pros. A mixed system, as just mentioned, exploits complementarities between agencies and courts. Sentencing judges fine-tune sentencing guidelines; antitrust judges fine-tune Justice Department or FTC merger guidelines; and judges review the rulings of administrative agencies for compliance with statutes and with principles of fair procedure, which are subjects that judges are more familiar with and more scrupulous in giving appropriate weight to than mission-oriented administrators are apt to be. A mixed system is also (as I have suggested) less susceptible to capture by interest groups because in a mixed system the interest group has to "buy" both the agency and the courts. (This is a traditional argument for trial by jury rather than trial by judge: it is harder to bribe twelve "judges" than one.) The mixed system also provides a back-up or fail-safe regulatory capability. In the case of drug safety, for example, when the Food and Drug Administration fails to prevent the sale of an unsafe drug, the tort law of products liability provides an alternative, ex post control over its sale.

More generally, a violation of a regulation might create a calculable injury to particular persons—allowing them to sue for damages provides a remedy tailored to the social cost of the violation. More interesting is the case (illustrated by the example of drug safety in the preceding paragraph) in which the regulation is complied, but with injury results, and it is apparent ex post that the regulation was inadequate. Allowing a suit for damages not only compensates the injured person but also provides an incentive for the persons or firms subject to the regulation to take additional precautions.

Mixed: cons. A mixed system conduces to delay and uncertainty of outcomes and imposes costs of duplication.

1.3.2   Competitive Regulation

Often more than one agency regulates the same activity. Both the Justice Department and the Federal Trade Commission enforce the federal antitrust laws, and in addition state attorneys general enforce state antitrust laws modeled on the federal laws and applicable to many of the same enterprises. Private suits can also be brought to enforce both the federal and the state antitrust laws. To complicate the picture still further, state attorneys general can bring federal antitrust suits on behalf of their states. Regulatory competition increases the likelihood that a violation will be detected and punished, but also increases compliance costs for the firms subject to the dual or multiple regulatory regime.

"Regulatory arbitrage" refers to the unedifying practice of firms' configuring their businesses in such a way as to bring them within the regulatory jurisdiction of an agency likely to favor the firm, perhaps because the agency is supported by fees of the firms it regulates and therefore, to increase its budget, seeks to entice firms by an implicit promise of light regulation. Thus, a bank might decide to seek a state rather than federal charter because it thought the state banking commissioner would be more tolerant of the bank's loan policies than a federal banking regulator, and the commissioner might welcome the newcomer because of the effect on the commissioner's budget of having a new fee-paying "client."

It is difficult to generalize about the choice between monopoly and competitive regulation. In the case of safety regulation, it is common to allow states to impose stricter safety standards than the federal regulators, although the federal regulation will invariably be deemed to preempt state regulation that contradicts the federal so that, if applicable, it would impose inconsistent duties on the regulated firms.

A competitive system should not be confused with a mixed (regulation plus litigation) system. In the mixed system, the different regulators (administrative agency and court) are stacked vertically; the parallel in business is to the hierarchy in a firm. In a competitive system, two agencies (or two judiciaries) may find themselves empowered to regulate the same activity, and the hope is that the competitive setting will keep each one on its toes.

Competition among federal agencies, as in the banking and antitrust areas, is rare. Regulatory competition primarily involves overlapping federal and state jurisdiction, and the primary reason for this competition is simply the constitutional status of the states. They are not merely bureaucratic subdivisions of the national government but instead quasi-sovereignties that make and administer their own laws until Congress or the federal courts intervene to prevent actual conflicts with federal law.

1.3.3   Comparative Analysis

There are significant differences in regulatory institutions and procedures across countries and also across states of the United States and between federal and state governments. For example, civil-law courts are much like U.S. regulatory agencies (bureaucratic, rule-bound), and state courts are on average more politicized than federal courts. In general, rules are more important, and standards less important, in civil-law than common-law countries. Hence, mixed systems in civil-law countries are likely to involve fewer agency-court complementaries than in common-law countries.

1.4   Reforming Existing Regulatory Regimes: Transition Costs

Suppose some new area of activity is sought to be brought under regulation; or there is dissatisfaction with the scope or implementation of an existing regulatory system. The choice is often between seeking to reform the existing system or creating a new system. In the usual case this comes down to a choice between tinkering with an existing agency (its powers, resources, leadership, or staff) and creating a new agency.

Tinkering with the existing agency: pros. This has the advantage of speed, economy, avoiding turf warfare (the creation of a new agency is likely to step on bureaucratic toes by taking powers from or competing with other agencies), and avoiding an increase in the complexity of government. Also, it is easier to rescind changes in an existing agency, if they prove unsound, than to abolish an entire agency, which will have developed a constituency in Congress or among interest groups.

Tinkering with the existing agency: cons. Agency staff, having civil service protection against being fired, may be bold in resisting change and may resist it effectively, with assistance from members of Congress and interest groups. Giving an agency new responsibilities may reduce its ability to perform its old responsibilities and create tension between staff assigned to old responsibilities and staff assigned to the new ones. Seniority considerations may give "old timers" significant positions in administering new programs with which they are unsympathetic.

Creating a new agency: pros. Creating a new agency is a strong signal of a new departure and may attract committed leaders and staff from outside the existing governmental bureaucracy. Exclusively committed to the new programs that gave rise to the new agency, leaders and staff will be judged by the success of the programs and will not be able to bury them in a bureaucracy that has many other programs and constituencies to attend to.

Creating a new agency: cons. These are the converse of the pros of tinkering with an existing agency. Creation of the agency will be time-consuming and involve struggle with existing agencies and their backers in both Congress and industry, will be difficult to reverse, and will increase the complexity of government.

1.5 Conclusion

The costs and benefits of the different control institutions and techniques have changed over time. The optimal and actual mixture has therefore changed. For example, diseconomies of scale in litigation (a court system is pyramid-shaped to maintain uniformity, and if there is too much litigation too many layers of review are required, creating unacceptable delay and confusion) may require the creation of regulatory alternatives to litigation. And the rise of public finance as a consequence of more efficient methods of taxation has made regulation, which is more costly to the government than litigation (largely financed by the litigants themselves), more feasible. Rising information costs because of greater technological complexity may also increase the gain to expertise and hence the comparative advantage of specialized agencies relative to generalist courts.

2

Efficient Regulation

2.1 Ubiquitous Regulation

American and European societies are much richer today than they were 100 years ago, yet they are also vastly more regulated. Today, we work in jobs extensively regulated by the government, from hiring procedures, to working hours and conditions, to rules for joining unions, to dismissal practices. We live in houses and apartment buildings whose construction—from zoning, to use of materials, to fire codes—is heavily regulated. We eat food grown with approved fertilizers and hormones, processed in regulated factories, and sold in licensed outlets with mandatory labels and warnings. Our cars, buses, and airplanes are made, sold, driven, and maintained under heavy government regulation. Our children attend schools that teach material authorized by the state, visit doctors following regulated procedures, and play on playgrounds that are certified based on government-mandated safety standards.

Government regulation is extensive in all rich and middle income countries. It transcends not only levels of economic development, but also cultures, legal traditions, levels of democratization, and all other factors economists use to explain differences among countries. There is surely a lot of variation across countries, but it pales by comparison with the raw fact of ubiquity. Why is there so much government regulation?

To a student of traditional Pigouvian (Pigou 1938) welfare economics, such extensive government regulation makes perfect sense. Markets fail,

Andrei Shleifer is professor of economics at Harvard University, and a research associate of the National Bureau of Economic Research.

I am grateful to Nicola Gennaioli, Oliver Hart, Joshua Schwartzstein, and Holger Spamann for helpful comments.

a Pigouvian would say, because of externalities, asymmetric information, and lack of competition, and governments need to regulate them to counter these failures. Regulation is ubiquitous because market failures are.

This view, however, has lost much ground over the last half century, under relentless intellectual pressure from the law and economics tradition originating with Coase (1960). This tradition holds that competition is merciless in driving firms toward efficiency, that markets exhibit tremendous ingenuity in dealing with potential failures, that contracts enforced by courts get around most externalities, and that even when for some reason contracts do not take care of all harmful conduct, tort law addresses most of the rest. The space left for efficient regulation is then very limited. From the efficiency perspective, the ubiquity of regulation is puzzling.

In fact, it is even more puzzling than the Coasian logic would suggest. In Coase's view, contracts are a substitute for regulation. If potential externalities can be contracted around, no regulation is necessary. Yet, contrary to this prediction, we see extensive government regulation of contracts themselves. Employment terms are delineated in contracts, yet these contracts are heavily regulated by the government. Purchases of various goods—from homes, to appliances, to stocks—are governed by detailed contracts, yet these contracts too are restricted by government mandates. The regulation of contracts goes much beyond mandatory disclosure, which suggests that asymmetric information is not at the heart of the problem. The fact that contracting itself is so heavily regulated severely undermines both the Pigouvian and the Coasian theories of regulation. The Pigouvian theory is undermined because market failures or information asymmetries do not seem to be necessary for regulation, yet those are seen by the theory as the prerequisites for government intervention. The Coasian position is undermined because free contracts are expected to remedy market failures and eliminate the need for regulation, yet regulation often intervenes in and restricts contracts themselves, including contracts with no third-party effects. The puzzle of ubiquitous regulation remains.

These considerations have led many economists to accept the position that regulation is driven not by efficiency but by politics. Under the most prominent version of this theory, proposed by Stigler (1971), industries or other interest groups organize and capture the regulators to raise prices, restrict entry, or otherwise benefit the incumbents. Alternatively, regulation is just a popular response to an economic crisis, introduced under public pressure whenever market outcomes are seen as undesirable, regardless of whether there are more efficient solutions (Hart 2009). Yet the political theories are not entirely persuasive, as they fail to come to grips with the fairly obvious facts that opened this chapter; namely, that regulation is ubiquitous in the richest, most democratic countries, with most benign governments, and seems to support the highest quality of life. Extensive regulation seems to be embraced in nearly all corners of these societies, which seems inconsistent with the view that regulation is inefficient.

In this chapter, I revisit the case for efficient regulation. My basic point is simple. The case against regulation relies on well-functioning courts. Courts are needed both to enforce contracts and to provide remedy for torts, and hence are central to the basic private mechanisms for curing market failures. Insofar as courts resolve disputes cheaply, predictably, and impartially, the efficiency case for regulation is difficult to make in most areas. Efficient regulation would be an exception, not the rule. But when litigation is expensive, unpredictable, or biased, the efficiency case for regulation opens up. Contracts accomplish less when their interpretation is unpredictable and their enforcement is expensive. Liability rules would not cure market failures if compensation of the victims is vulnerable to the vagaries of courts. In short, the case for efficient regulation rests on the failures of courts.

In what follows, I show that this approach explains the ubiquity of regulation, but also its growth over the last century. The approach also helps shed light on the patterns of regulation and litigation across activities, as well as across jurisdictions. I am not suggesting that regulation is universally desirable; regulators often suffer from far deeper problems than courts. The point is that there are trade-offs between the two. Indeed, if the approach is correct, it suggests that the growth of regulation reflects an efficient institutional adaptation to a more complex world.

2.2   Perfect Courts

To fix ideas and to illustrate the arguments, consider the example of workplace safety regulation, an important area of government intervention in markets. Workplace safety is especially informative because the traditional objection to the Coase theorem, namely that contracting is impractical because many parties are involved (as with pollution), does not apply. Nor is it plausible that asymmetric information between firms and their workers, who are specialists and interact over time, limits contracts (or has third-party effects). Indeed, the puzzle of ubiquitous regulation is most dramatic in areas, such as workplace safety, where there are no obvious limitations on or externalities from contracts and tort law is well developed.

The explosion of workplace safety regulation is indeed puzzling from the Coasian perspective. To begin, market forces should work in this area, even with spot labor markets and without complex contracts. Because wages adjust in risky occupations, employers have an economic incentive to control accident risks so as to reduce the wage premium they have to pay. Firms would also want to establish reputations as safe employers to attract better workers, and to pay them less. Competition for labor provides strong incentives to take care of safety.

Extensive contracting opportunities are available as well. Employees, through collective bargaining agreements or even individual employment contracts, can require firms to take safety precautions. Firms can likewise require certain levels of care from their employees by specifying that they follow safety procedures. Private insurance is available to both workers and firms to insure the damages to health and property resulting from accidents. Insurance companies can then demand, as part of the insurance contract, that firms and workers take specific precautions. With knowledgeable firms, knowledgeable workers, and knowledgeable insurance companies, one might think correct incentives could be worked out. Moreover, the parties interact over time, and are able to learn where the risks are, mitigate them, and adjust their contracts accordingly. It seems compelling, in this context, that private solutions provide parties with correct incentives to take efficient precautions.

Should one of the parties fail to follow the terms of the contract, the other can go to court. Indeed, it can do so even before an accident occurs if contractual terms regarding precautions are violated. After an accident, likewise, the victim can demand in a lawsuit a contractually specified compensation. Courts can then enforce the contracts, by requiring the insurance company or the firm to pay, or alternatively by finding that the worker had not taken contractually agreed-upon precautions. No government authority beyond courts is needed.

If the necessary contracts are too elaborate to negotiate up front, insurance companies and industry associations can produce recommendations for safety standards, and contracts can incorporate those. An individual firm, a union, or even a worker bears few incremental costs of figuring out what is appropriate by opting into industry standards. Standardization also reduces the costs of compliance by creating standard safety equipment, standard safety procedures, and so forth.

Finally, even if contracts do not cover some eventualities, tort law deals with accidents not covered by contracts. Courts develop precedents and guidelines for addressing questions of liability and damages, and can also rely on industry standards for reaching conclusions. As the law develops over time, these precedents and other rules developed by courts cover more and more situations, leaving ever smaller uncertainties. Indeed, as courts complete the law, there will be no need for actual litigation as parties will know what to expect and settle before trial.

With so many protective mechanisms for both workers and firms available through markets and courts, and so many incentives for efficient precautions provided by these mechanisms, why would anyone need regulation?

Once the puzzle is framed in this way, it becomes clear where to look for the answer. Start with the forces of competition on the spot markets, without contracts or insurance. It is probably true that, in the world of well-heeled and well-established firms, with access to capital markets and expectation of long-run survival, the savings from taking efficient precautions outweigh the immediate costs. But many firms operate in a very different world, in which capital is scarce, downward pressure on prices is relentless, and incentives to cut costs today are strong. In such a competitive world, the firm may face huge pressure to undersupply precautions relative to the efficient level and to accept incremental accident risks. Should an accident happen, the firm might be able to fight its liability in court, settle for a small sum with a desperate victim, or go bankrupt. To hold the firm accountable for causing accidents, there need to be effective courts. The incentive to undersupply precautions is even greater when competitors undersupply them and so face lower short-run costs, perhaps because they come from different countries. Competition without courts and contracts does not do much for safety.

If competition does not lead firms to take efficient precautions, it must be contracts, including insurance contracts, as well as tort rules, that do the job. But those fundamentally rely on courts. Suppose for concreteness that the firm and its employees have agreed on a contract that delineates the precautions that need to be taken, and suppose further that the firm has taken out an insurance policy compensating workers who are hurt. After that, an accident happens. Neither the insurance company nor the firm wants to pay the victim, so the victim has to sue for damages. Most accidents occur because of some combination of bad luck and lack of precautions on the parts of both the employer and employee (or, to make it more complex, an employee other than the one who got hurt). Each litigant blames the other, often sincerely. And even if the "true" facts of the case are clear to an omniscient observer, and even if the litigants know what happened, they each have a story for why it is not their fault, but the other party's. The insurance company likewise has a story for why the particular accident is not covered, or if covered, not to the full extent of the damages. A court, or some substitute such as an arbitration board, has to ascertain the facts and interpret the contract or apply the law. The question then becomes how cheaply, predictably, and impartially the court can do so.

Consider this question in steps. Begin with courts as assumed in law and economics. In those courts: (a) verification is relatively straightforward and inexpensive; (b) judges are motivated to exert effort to enforce contracts and laws; (c) judges are knowledgeable enough to verify the facts; and (d) judges are impartial. I argue later that all four of these assumptions are dubious descriptions of reality, and that the failure of each gives rise to a distinct argument for regulation. But for now consider this extreme.

One might think that, under these assumptions, courts could easily verify which contractual terms apply. But even here several issues hamper adjudication and make it uncertain. First, judges do not witness the accident and so they need to figure out what happened. They can only do so imperfectly. The litigants have different perceptions of what had happened, even if they are honest, and the judge needs to piece the story together. Second, the contract may not cover the exact facts of the dispute: in an accident, both litigants are often at fault. Moreover, language is often unclear, and vulnerable to alternative interpretations. What are best efforts, for example? The litigants then disagree on how the contract allocates the costs of an accident. The judge has to decide what the contract means and how tort law applies.

This leads to a third set of issues; namely, that both contractual interpretation and tort liability are governed by multiple conflicting principles, and judges need to pick which ones to apply. Judges reason by analogy to precedents, and a case is often similar to multiple precedents with conflicting results. Lawyers argue that the precedent favoring their clients is the closest one. Judges then decide. It might be difficult to tell in advance which of the potentially governing precedents the judge will pick, especially when the facts are close to the line.

With factual, contractual, and legal uncertainty, the judge must exercise at least some discretion in resolving a dispute. Aspects of such discretion have been called fact discretion, referring to the judge's flexibility in interpreting facts, and legal discretion, referring to room to maneuver in applying the law to the facts. Pistor and Xu (2003) aptly call this "incomplete law." Posner (2008) refers to this as "open area" uncertainty. Posner recognizes the existence of such uncertainty, but seems to believe that this open area is usually small. I return to this issue later.

Even assuming that judges are unbiased, knowledgeable, and properly motivated, judicial discretion imposes risk on the litigants. The litigants can settle and avoid the risk, but the prospect of such a settlement distorts incentives and contracts (Gennaioli 2009). Judicial discretion, which follows from legal, contractual, and factual uncertainty, is an essential feature of litigation, and one from which many consequences follow.

Recent research has begun to uncover systematic evidence of judicial discretion. A large empirical literature discussed by Posner (2008) documents the effect of the judges' political party affiliations on their decisions. Chang and Schoar (2007) use a sample of 5,000 Chapter 11 filings by private companies in the United States, and find that in their motion-granting practices, some bankruptcy judges are systematically more procreditor than others. Niblett (2009) examines interpretation of very standard arbitration clauses in contracts by California appellate courts. He finds that judges make arbitrary distinctions in their contract interpretation even in the simplest of cases; for instance, focusing on the size of the print or the location of the arbitration clause in the contract. This evidence is noteworthy because the cases Niblett selects are so similar.

Beyond judicial decision making, there is also the problem of enforcement. A firm, especially a small firm, might not have the money to pay to compensate the employee, might not have bought insurance, and might even go bankrupt. In fact, such a firm might ex ante choose to skimp on precautions and go bankrupt after an accident occurs. This problem, identified by

Summers (1983) and Shavell (1984), plagues contract and tort law enforcement. Even without bankruptcy, damage payments for negligence might be high, especially when they are jacked up to compensate for imperfect detection (Becker 1968). Although such penalties may provide strong incentives for firms to take precautions, they may also deter socially useful activity when courts make unavoidable mistakes in assigning liability. Firms reluctant to bear such risks may exit, or not enter in the first place. This aspect of imperfect enforcement leads to inefficiency because it reduces desirable business activity (Schwartzstein and Shleifer 2009).

These aspects of the legal process interact prominently with the effectiveness of competition. A firm facing significant price competition seeks to reduce costs. It knows that, should an accident occur, the trial may take some time and it may wiggle out of paying under either contract or tort. It can also settle with the victim of an accident, who may need money and be less patient. If all goes badly in court, it can go bankrupt and still avoid paying. Facing competitive pressure today, such a firm might take fewer precautions or buy less insurance. When justice is not certain, competition leads firms to economize on worker safety measures.

All these problems arise in even the simplest of circumstances. Their effect is to make contract enforcement expensive and unpredictable, leading workers and firms to bear unnecessary risks. This of course is just the beginning of the story: we need to return to our four assumptions about judges.

2.3   What Do Judges Do?

I have argued that judicial work is quite complex, and judicial outcomes uncertain, even in relatively simple circumstances, and with well-intentioned, hard-working, and unbiased judges. Reality, of course, is less idyllic. Several of the assumptions I made must be revisited.

The first assumption—that verification is straightforward and inexpensive—is typically false. To protect the system from manipulation, legal procedure is itself heavily regulated, burdensome, and expensive. Discovery is extensive, invasive, and expensive, including both the collection of records and the examination of witnesses. Judges consider multiple cases at once, so cases drag on for years, consuming resources and postponing compensation of the victim. Djankov et al. (2003) examine the regulation of legal procedure and efficiency of courts in 109 countries by focusing on the simplest cases: the eviction of a nonpaying tenant and the collection of a bounced check. Based on surveys of legal experts in these countries, they find that the judicial procedures governing such litigation are extremely cumbersome and time consuming, yielding highly uncertain payoffs to plaintiffs.

Beyond the slowness and expense of court operations, the facts are often complex. Witnesses lie or shade the truth. Courts must rely on representations by attorneys, who are paid for advocacy just short of deception. When issues are complex, courts rely on experts to interpret contracts and testify as to appropriate precautions, remedies, and damages. These experts also lie or shade the truth when they are hired by the litigants. In some areas, even with expert advice, it might take a judge an enormous effort to understand liability and damages.

Part of the reason is that disputes are highly idiosyncratic, and consequently so is litigation. There are two sides to most arguments. Legal scholars tend to think that most cases are routine, and the law can be easily applied to established facts, but litigants obviously do not think so. The court needs to familiarize itself with the details of each case, and assess whether particular conduct crosses the threshold of liability, be it negligence, gross negligence, recklessness, or some other standard. This threshold typically depends on many factual circumstances, including those that are extremely difficult, perhaps impossible, to verify, such as intent and knowledge of the defendant. To sort out these issues, the court often cannot rely on documents, but must instead interview witnesses and decide who to believe when the evidence is conflicting. The point, again, is that litigation is both expensive and uncertain, which reduces the effectiveness of contract and tort law in providing socially correct incentives.

The second assumption is that judges are motivated to understand the issues of the case. In reality, judges face weak incentives (see Posner 2008). Judges cannot be fired. They do not receive promotions with sufficient likelihood to elicit effort, and promotion need not depend on diligence. Judges are not paid for performance. Some judges are elected, but it may be not diligence but humoring the community that improves their election chances. The weak incentives of judges to work hard are particularly important when the cost of verification is high, as when the facts are complex. And when judges do not bother to verify, litigants bear the risk of judicial error. Firms might fail to take precautions, for example, hoping to confuse the judge.

The third assumption about judges is that they are knowledgeable enough, at least with the assistance of court experts, to get to the bottom of the relevant issues. This is a tall order, especially in the modern world. Judges are trained as lawyers, not safety experts. Their work is fundamentally general: they consider large numbers of cases in multiple areas of law. In a complex case, judges must rely on lawyers and experts. The goal of lawyers and experts, however, is to seek judicial favor, not enlightenment. It would often take a rather brilliant judge to get to the bottom of the issue when persuasion takes this form.

The fourth assumption is the most interesting; namely, that judges are impartial. Judicial partiality may derive from many sources, including political biases, intrinsic preferences over litigants, incentives such as those coming from reelection, or vulnerability to persuasion by the litigants, appropriate or not. Partiality would not be problematic if judicial discretion were minimal. But when discretion in finding fact, interpreting contract, or applying legal rules is substantial, it can massively amplify the effects of partiality.

Start with judicial preferences over litigants, or over their lawyers. Legal realists such as Frank (1930) thought that these are crucial in shaping the outcomes of trials. These preferences might be over individuals, but also over issues, perhaps because of the political preferences of judges. Some judges sympathize with workers injured in accidents and believe that, absent overwhelming evidence of worker malfeasance, companies should pay. Other judges feel that workers employed in dangerous occupations accept the risks and are put on notice to be extra-careful, so absent overwhelming evidence of company malfeasance, they should not collect. When the facts of the case are uncertain, and judges exercise discretion over which testimony or expert analysis to accept, these biases, even if relatively minor and even unconscious, can translate into substantially biased decisions.

Recent research has begun to unravel, at least theoretically, the crucial interaction between judicial preferences and fact discretion. Gennaioli and Shleifer (2008) argue that the selection of "relevant" facts is the crucial mechanism by which judges satisfy their biases, especially because, as we discuss later, the finding of fact is rarely vulnerable to appeal. Once the facts are found, the application of the law to the facts is typically uncontroversial. Likewise, when contractual terms are uncertain, judges can interpret contracts to favor the party, or the issue, to which they are sympathetic, perhaps by choosing one of the several conflicting principles of contractual interpretation (Gennaioli 2009). In either case, adjudication is biased. And when the contracting parties do not know the judge's preferences up front, they bear substantial risks that they can mitigate by taking inefficient actions and signing inefficient contracts that protect them from judicial discretion in the first place.

Many legal scholars do not like this kind of argument. Some, like Posner (2008) see judicial biases as relatively minor (except on the highly political Supreme Court) because judges are selected from a relatively uniform population: "The pool from which our judges are chosen is not homogeneous, though neither is it fully representative; it is limited as a practical matter to upper-echelon lawyers, almost all of whom are well-socialized, well behaved, conventionally-minded members of the upper middle class" (155). Posner is surely correct, but it is far from clear how much such selection limits the variety of views. Politicians who appoint judges wish to be confident that judges agree with them on particular issues. Such selection may well bias away from moderation. For example, a politician moderately concerned with worker safety might not choose a judge who is centrist on that issue but rather one who is far left of center, just to be sure. Similarly, lawyers who accept judgeships often give up considerable income as private attorneys. In part, they do so to win the respect of their peers, but in part because, like academics, they have strong beliefs about influencing the world. As with academics, such beliefs are not always conducive to moderation.

Another argument is that review by appellate courts constrains trial judges. If judges were automatically applying unambiguous law to unambiguous facts, this argument would compel. But, as I already indicated, much of the time judges are interpreting incomplete contracts in light of uncertain facts, or else applying uncertain law. In such circumstances, the role for appeal is more limited, especially since appellate courts do not review the facts except for "egregious error." Fact discretion gives trial judges enormous flexibility. Indeed, appellate review may cause a trial judge to further distort his rendition of facts, so as to render the application of the law to those facts uncontroversial and thus invulnerable to appeal (Gennaioli and Shleifer 2008).

In many jurisdictions, judges are elected, which raises the question of whether this mechanism bolsters impartiality. The electoral process for judges, like that for other local officials, selects individuals whose views are representative of the communities they serve. Berdejo and Yuchtman (2009) examine judicial elections in the state of Washington, and find that judges increase sentences prior to elections, in line with voter preferences for harsher criminal sanctions. More generally, if the community is large and diverse, the median voter is likely to be fairly centrist. On the other hand, when a community is neither large nor diverse, the views of its median voter might be quite biased relative to a broader group. The United States Congress is full of representatives diligently articulating the parochial views of their constituents.

The final source of judicial bias is historically the most important one, and that is judicial vulnerability to persuasion or subversion. Such vulnerability follows from litigants having different access to resources. Defendants in workplace accident cases have access to substantial financial resources, including better lawyers, while the victims might be poor, in part because they are injured. Some adaptations, such as contingency fees for attorneys, ameliorate this problem, but probably only in selected cases. If judges do not correct for the inequality of weapons, litigants with more resources have a substantial advantage in court.

Better resources may take the form of better lawyers and court tactics, of delay when plaintiffs cannot wait and settle for less, but they may also take the form of bribes. Corruption may be only modestly relevant for the U.S. courts today (how one thinks of this depends in part on the distinction between bribes and campaign contributions), but bribing judges was evidently common in nineteenth century United States, and is pervasive in large parts of the world today. Corruption helps the richer litigants, and would lead to fewer precautions and excessive injuries.

Judicial bias interacts with the evolution of law over time, and the consequent predictability of the legal rules themselves. It is one of the core beliefs of law and economics that common law is fairly complete and provides unique legal answers to most patterns of case facts. A stronger version of this thesis holds that common law converges to efficient legal rules (i.e, these answers encourage efficient behavior). Yet recent scholarship begins to question the belief in convergence to efficiency, both theoretically and empirically. Plausible models do not suggest that sequential decision making by appellate courts with preferences over the shape of the law brings the law to efficient rules (Gennaioli and Shleifer 2007a, 2007b). From time to time, judges overrule existing precedents because their preferences are different from those of their predecessors. Such overruling undermines convergence. More frequently, judges do not overrule the existing precedents, but rather distinguish cases from precedents, based on possibly material (and sometimes immaterial) facts, with the result that they reach different conclusions—which of course reflect their own preferences—based on these new facts. Such distinguishing can refine and complete the law over time, but need not do so. Even if there is improvement on average, the law need not converge or become predictable (Gennaioli and Shleifer 2007b).

Recent empirical evidence casts doubt on the proposition that common law converges to efficient rules over time, even in relatively simple situations. Niblett, Posner, and Shleifer (2009) look at the evolution of the Economic Loss Rule, a well-known common law doctrine limiting tort claims when plaintiffs only suffer financial losses, using the universe of state appellate court decisions in a very homogeneous group of construction disputes. The authors find that, over the last thirty years, different U.S. states treated the Economic Loss Rule in construction disputes very differently, and have achieved no agreement on the scope of its applicability and exceptions. Nor is there evidence of convergence over time in the acceptance of this rule or of its exceptions. Legal certainty looks like a myth even in standard situations after decades of legal evolution.

Posner (2008) recognizes all these concerns with the exercise of judicial discretion, but in the end appeals to judicial professionalism:

> To regard oneself and be regarded by others, especially one's peers, as a good judge requires conformity to the accepted norms of judging. One cannot be regarded as a good judge if one takes bribes, decides cases by flipping a coin, falls asleep in the courtroom, ignores legal doctrine, cannot make up one's mind, bases decisions on the personal attractiveness or unattractiveness of litigants or their lawyers, or decides cases on the basis of "politics" (depending on how that slippery word is defined). (61)

I think that Posner is exactly right. So long as a judge does not take bribes, acts deliberately, refers to precedents and legal principles, renders decisions with only modest delays, does not flirt with lawyers, and is not overtly and exorbitantly political, he will be regarded as professional and remain unchecked. The open area uncertainty referred to by Posner is vast.

2.4   The Efficiency Case for Regulation

The implication of this analysis is that the case for efficient regulation is essentially the case for the failure of courts. When courts are expensive, unpredictable, and biased, the public will seek alternatives to dispute resolution in courts. The form this alternative has taken throughout the world is regulation. Indeed, each of the problems with litigation discussed in the previous section gives rise to a separate argument for efficient regulation.

Begin with the point that litigation is idiosyncratic, so the facts relevant to the establishment of liability are costly to verify. Regulation tends to homogenize the requirements for appropriate conduct by both employees and firms. Such homogenization is often excessively rigid, but it reduces enforcement costs because the items that need to be verified are standardized. Does the factory floor have the required number of fire exits? Is there proper spacing between machines? Are the workers wearing helmets? Even if the determination of violation and of damages is left to courts, regulation may reduce the costs of litigation because it effectively provides a judge with a checklist of items that need to be verified, as opposed to leaving open the scope of issues to be debated to the litigants. By narrowing the range of issues to be debated, regulation may render outcomes, and hence behavior, more predictable.

What about incentives? In contrast to judges, the incentives of regulators can be manipulated by their superiors, or even by legislation. Regulators can be forced to specify precautions, to verify whether they are taken, and to investigate in detail after an accident occurs. Unlike judges, regulators can be asked to go through checklists of items to be verified, and incentivized to follow these rules. This possibility of compelling the regulators to investigate and check, perhaps by rewarding them for finding violations, was one of the crucial New Deal arguments for regulation (see Landis 1938; Glaeser, Johnson, and Shleifer 2001).

Unlike the generalist judges, regulators also tend to be specialized, and are expected to understand more. Courts, of course, can also be specialized (Posner 2008), but perhaps not to the same extent as regulators. In principle, such specialization lowers the costs of understanding the facts in a given situation, as well as of applying the rules to the facts. Specialization of the regulators is the central efficiency argument in their favor, particularly in areas such as finance and the environment, where the issues are enormously complex (Landis 1938).

Finally, one can make a case for regulation as a mechanism for reducing the vulnerability of law enforcers to subversion. Unlike judges, regulators are experts, and hence might be less vulnerable to persuasion by the skilled but disingenuous litigants. In some situations, because they have limited job security, they may also be less susceptible to corruption than the judges (I am skeptical that this argument is general). Historically, inequality of weapons has been the crucial factor behind the rise of the regulatory state in the United States. The mechanism was democratic politics at the end of the nineteenth and the beginning of the twentieth century. As industrialization changed the economic landscape, the country saw a sharp rise of industrial and railroad injuries. Evidently, workers could not find adequate compensation for these injuries in courts, because companies exercised what many saw as undue influence on judges. As muckraking journalists exposed the problem, it became a political issue in several presidential campaigns, including those of Theodore Roosevelt and Woodrow Wilson. Regulation became a central feature of Wilson's *New Freedom* program. Glaeser and Shleifer (2003) summarize these historical developments, and argue that the rise of regulation was indeed a political—and efficient—response to the failure of courts to adjust to economic changes in the country.

Regulation can take a variety of forms (at the extreme, the government can take ownership of firms if it believes nothing short of complete control can get around the consequence of market or contractual failure—think about the ownership of Air Force One). In some instances, the government can lay down the rules for required precautions and conduct inspections, and impose penalties up front for both failure to comply before an accident occurs, and after an accident happens if the failure to comply is recognized only then. In other instances, the government can lay down the regulations, such as disclosure rules and procedures for dealing with conflicts of interest, but then leave the enforcement to private action in court, as in the case of many financial regulations. The purpose of such regulations, very much in the spirit of the present argument, is to reduce the costs of litigation, so that both courts and litigants know more precisely what constitutes liability. A particular version of this approach is the regulation of contracts, which makes perfect sense as a strategy of facilitating enforcement by courts when judges exercise discretion, but not if all contracts are interpreted equally predictably.

This, in sum, is the argument. I should stress that the analysis is not in any way intended as an endorsement of all regulation and of its expansion. At the level of implementation, all the complaints leveled at judges apply to regulators as well. Enforcement effort, expertise, and absence of bias in the public sector can all be fairly questioned. Regulators are public sector employees, and as such often lack incentives for hard work, know less than they ought to, exhibit policy preferences inconsistent with efficiency, and are vulnerable to subversion by those they regulate. Academic studies and news stories are replete with accounts of regulatory failures.

With respect to the creation of rules, there are even deeper concerns about regulators than about judges. After all, judges are supposed to be relatively impartial, and legal rules evolve slowly over time, which makes them less vulnerable to improper political influence than regulations (Ponzetto and Fernandez 2008). Regulators, in contrast, might pursue a highly political agenda, and create regulations that further the incumbent government's goals, or create opportunities for bribe-taking by officials. Djankov et al. (2002) examine the rules for entry regulation by new firms in eighty-five countries. They find little evidence that these rules further efficiency, but more evidence that they are correlated with poor government performance and corruption. Perhaps more importantly, as Stigler (1971) argued, regulators might be captured by the industry to a much greater extent than judges possibly can, since judges do not have long-term relationships with firms. The regulators' behavior may end up considerably more biased against consumers than that of the judges.

The choice between regulators and courts, then, is one between imperfect alternatives, in which the virtues and failings of each must be compared. But this in no way detracts from my basic point: the case for efficient regulation rests on that against efficient courts. And historical trends in the best-governed countries suggest that this efficiency case often wins the day.

2.5 Institutional Choices

The comparative perspective on regulation and litigation yields a range of empirical predictions. Some of these turn on the comparative efficiency of the two approaches to enforcing efficient conducts. Other predictions focus on institutional choices shaped by considerations other than efficiency, such as politics, history, and culture.

To begin, the analysis may shed some light on the choice between courts and regulators for a given activity in a country. Courts appear to be particularly appropriate in relatively nontechnical yet idiosyncratic situations, such as the interpretation of individual contracts (even if some aspects of these contracts are restricted by regulation) or the determination of liability in torts or fault in crimes. In these situations, flexibility is of great value ex ante, and application of reasonably broad standards is of value ex post. Such situations are difficult to homogenize through regulation, and indeed are typically addressed by courts (see Posner, chapter 1, this volume).

On the other hand, when similar problems recur often enough that repeated utilization of courts is too expensive or unpredictable, regulation might be a socially cheaper alternative. This would be so if the regulator is the ultimate decision maker, but even if in the end the judge must decide, regulation can delineate the issues that must be addressed. It might be more efficient for the legislature to specify the rules than for courts to sort out the threshold of liability in distinct situations. This argument makes the strong prediction that regulation should be more efficient in the more common situations. Mulligan and Shleifer (2005) test this prediction. They find, in cross-sections of both U.S. states and countries, that higher populations are associated with more extensive regulation. They argue that the regulation of a particular area requires a fixed setup cost, which can be amortized over a higher number of disputes that comes with more people. With small populations, litigation, while idiosyncratic, is rare enough that fixed costs are not worth paying. This approach might also explain why we see regulation in areas such as workplace safety, where contracts and torts are readily available: disputes occur often enough that standardized regulation is cheaper, and more predictable, than idiosyncratic litigation.

Regulation would also be more common in situations where facts are complex, and fact finding requires expertise and incentives. As the society develops, this criterion might apply to a growing range of activities. This observation might explain the basic fact of growing regulation over time. It might also explain why we see regulation in financial markets or in complex industrial activities. Indeed, as I mentioned earlier, expertise and motivation of the regulators were the crucial arguments for the expansion of regulation in the United States (Landis 1938).

Finally, regulation might be particularly relevant in situations of inequality between the injured plaintiffs and the injurer. The rise of regulation might be intimately tied to specialization and the rise of large corporations as organizational forms. Thus, while courts or similar methods of dispute resolution might work when disputants have comparable resources, they fail when inequality of weapons becomes overwhelming. This, too, might account for the ubiquity of regulation, including the regulation of contracts between parties with different resources, in the modern world. In fact, if we go back to the introductory paragraph, this might be the reason for regulation of so many basic aspects of consumption and employment.

When it comes to a comparison of patterns of social control across countries, many additional considerations come into play (see Djankov et al. 2003). Different societies might have different levels of expertise, and hence comparative advantage, at regulation, or litigation, or perhaps other forms of social control. For example, as Glaeser and Shleifer (2003) have argued, poor countries might experience severe failures of all public administration, including both regulation and litigation. In these countries, free markets might be the best approach, even when market failure is pervasive. In more developed countries, in which the capacity to administer laws and regulations is higher, stronger government intervention, whether through courts or regulators, becomes more attractive.

One crucial determinant of the actual choices is specialization. In a series of papers written with Simeon Djankov, Florencio Lopez-de-Silanes, and Rafael La Porta (e.g., La Porta, Lopez-de-Silanes, and Shleifer 2008), I have argued that countries from common and civil law legal traditions exhibit different regulatory styles. Relatively speaking, common law countries tend to rely on private orderings and courts, while civil law countries, particularly French civil law ones, rely more heavily on regulation. We see these differences empirically across a broad range of activities, from the regulation of product and labor market, to the regulation of legal procedure, to military draft. Such specialization in the forms of social control might be efficient, as each legal tradition perfects its approach, or it might be just a consequence of hysteresis. Whatever the ultimate cause, we see substantial variation in the reliance on regulation and litigation across legal traditions.

More recently, Aghion et al. (2009) found that another factor shaping a nation's reliance on regulation is trust. High trust appears to be a substitute for regulation. In high trust societies, individuals do not expect to be mistreated by other individuals or firms, and hence support a lower level of restrictions on others in the form of regulation. In low trust societies, in contrast, individuals do expect to be mistreated by others, and hence support greater restraint of business activity through regulation. Aghion and colleagues argue further that these approaches to regulation are self-fulfilling: when levels of regulation are low, people choose to act civically because civic behavior opens up more attractive entrepreneurial opportunities, which would otherwise have been limited by regulation.

These aspects of institutional choice, like Stigler's emphasis on politics, are part of a broader picture of institutional evolution. Yet one point remains central in conclusion: efficiency should not be ignored in considering which institutions survive. In the rich countries in particular, the case for efficiency of courts as opposed to regulators is often tenuous.

References

Aghion, P., Y. Algan, P. Cahuc, and A. Shleifer. 2010. Regulation and distrust. *Quarterly Journal of Economics,* forthcoming, August.

Becker, G. S. 1968. Crime and punishment: An economic approach. *Journal of Political Economy* 76 (2): 169–217.

Berdejo, C., and N. M. Yuchtman. 2009. Crime, punishment and politics: An analysis of political cycles in criminal sentencing. Harvard University. Unpublished Manuscript.

Chang, T., and A. Schoar. 2007. Judge specific differences in Chapter 11 and firm outcomes. MIT. Unpublished Manuscript.

Coase, R. H. 1960. The problem of social cost. *Journal of Law and Economics* 3:1–44.

Djankov, S., E. Glaeser, R. La Porta, F. Lopez-de-Silanes, and A. Shleifer. 2003. The new comparative economics. *Journal of Comparative Economics* 31:595–619.

Djankov, S., R. La Porta, F. Lopez-de-Silanes, and A. Shleifer. 2002. The regulation of entry. *Quarterly Journal of Economics* 117 (1): 1–37.

———. 2003. Courts. *Quarterly Journal of Economics* 118 (2): 453–517.

Frank, J. 1930. *Law and the modern mind.* New York: Brentano's.

Gennaioli, N. 2009. Contracting in the shadow of the law. Harvard University. Unpublished Manuscript.

Gennaioli, N., and A. Shleifer. 2007a. Overruling and the instability of law. *Journal of Comparative Economics* 35 (2): 309–28.

————. 2007b. The evolution of common law. *Journal of Political Economy* 115 (1): 43–68.

————. 2008. Judicial fact discretion. *Journal of Legal Studies* 37 (1): 1–36.

Glaeser, E. L., S. Johnson, and A. Shleifer. 2001. Coase versus the Coasians. *Quarterly Journal of Economics* 116 (3): 853–99.

Glaeser, E. L., and A. Shleifer. 2003. The rise of the regulatory state. *Journal of Economic Literature* 41 (2): 401–25.

Hart, O. 2009. Regulation and Sarbanes-Oxley. *Journal of Accounting Research* 47 (2): 437–45.

La Porta, R., F. Lopez-de-Silanes, and A. Shleifer. 2008. The economic consequences of legal origins. *Journal of Economic Literature* 46 (2): 285–332.

Landis, J. M. 1938. *The administrative process.* Westport, CT: Greenwood Press.

Mulligan, C., and A. Shleifer. 2005. The extent of the market and the supply of regulation. *Quarterly Journal of Economics* 120 (4): 1445–73.

Niblett, A. 2009. Inconsistent contract enforcement. Harvard University. Unpublished Manuscript.

Niblett, A., R. A. Posner, and A. Shleifer. 2009. The evolution of a legal rule. NBER Working Paper no. 13856. Cambridge, MA: National Bureau of Economic Research, March.

Pigou, A. C. 1938. *The economics of welfare,* 4th ed. London: Macmillan and Co.

Pistor, K., and C. Xu. 2003. Incomplete law—A conceptual and analytical framework and its application to the evolution of financial market regulation. *Journal of International Law and Politics* 35 (4): 931–1013.

Ponzetto, G. A. M., and P. A. Fernandez. 2008. Case law versus statute law: An evolutionary comparison. *Journal of Legal Studies* 37 (2): 379–430.

Posner, R. A. 2008. *How judges think.* Cambridge, MA: Harvard University Press.

Schwartzstein, J., and A. Shleifer. 2009. Litigation and regulation. NBER Working Paper no. 14752. Cambridge, MA: National Bureau of Economic Research, February

Shavell, S. 1984. Liability for harm versus regulation of safety. *Journal of Legal Studies* 13 (2): 357–74.

Stigler, G. J. 1971. The theory of economic regulation. *Bell Journal of Economics and Management Science* 2 (1): 3–21.

Summers, J. 1983. The case of the disappearing defendant: An economic analysis. *University of Pennsylvania Law Review* 132 (1): 145–85.

The Trouble with Cases

Frederick Schauer and Richard Zeckhauser

3.1 Introduction

The recent hearings on Judge Sonia Sotomayor's and Solicitor General Elena Kagan's nominations to the Supreme Court vividly exemplify the enthusiastic concurrence between the senators and the nominee that judges make neither law nor policy. Judges decide particular cases between particular litigants, the questioners and the responders agree, and in doing so they apply laws and policies made by the allegedly more representative legislative, administrative, and executive branches of government.

Thus goes the collusive charade played out before each Supreme Court nomination, one designed simultaneously to reassure and mislead the general public. Denying the law- and policy-making role of the courts is the standard mantra, and no nominee intelligent enough to find herself in that position would dare acknowledge at the hearing that judges serve, at least in part, as lawmakers and policymakers.

Most of us, of course, know better. Courts make law and set policy all the time, an inevitable consequence of the indeterminacy and open-endedness both of the common law and of the vague language in which many constitutional and statutory provisions are drafted. When the Supreme Court

Frederick Schauer is the David and Mary Harrison Distinguished Professor of Law at the University of Virginia. Richard Zeckhauser is the Frank Plumpton Ramsey Professor of Political Economy at the John F. Kennedy School of Government, Harvard University, and a research associate of the National Bureau of Economic Research.

The authors are grateful for the comments and advice of Ken Abraham, John Horton, and Peter Strauss. A referee provided a helpful review that led us to create the appendix and to greatly extend footnote 16.

concludes that tying arrangements[1] and resale price maintenance[2] violate the Sherman Act's prohibition on "[e]very contract, combination . . . , or conspiracy, in restraint of trade or commerce . . .",[3] for example, the Court is establishing antitrust policy no less than if those prohibitions had been explicitly set forth in the statute or adopted as formal regulations by the Federal Trade Commission. And so too with the determination of which types of searches and seizures will be deemed "unreasonable" and consequently in violation of the Fourth Amendment, of what forms of discrimination constitute denial of "the equal protection of the laws," and of which varieties of nondisclosure to investors will count as "device[s], scheme[s], or artifice[s] to defraud" for purposes of Section 17(a) of the Securities Act of 1933[4] and of Rule 10b-5 issued by the Securities and Exchange Commission.[5]

Policy-making by appellate judicial interpretation is well-known to the cognoscenti, and almost certainly to the senators and nominees who in publicly denying it tell a form of white lie to reassure a legally unsophisticated polity. But policy-making also occurs at the trial level when decisions in particular cases influence the nonlitigants who contemplate acting similarly to or differently from those whose behavior has previously been the subject of litigation. When a jury or judge convicts a particular defendant of negligent homicide for unintentionally killing someone while driving under the influence of barbiturates, for example, it is likely to affect the decisions and behavior of countless other drivers who might be considering taking barbiturates before getting behind the wheel or getting behind the wheel after taking barbiturates. More commonly, when a jury determines that a manufacturer of a chainsaw is negligent and responsible for user injuries as a result of not having fitted its products with a particular safety device or not having provided sufficiently vivid warnings of the dangers associated with using a chainsaw, the verdict, especially if accompanied by a large damage award, will affect the future conduct of chainsaw manufacturers as much (or more) as if the safety device or warnings had been required by an act of Congress or by the regulations of the Consumer Product Safety Commission or the Occupational Safety and Health Administration.

Our goal in this chapter is to examine policy-making in response to par-

---

1. See, for example, *Illinois Tool Works, Inc. v. Independent Ink, Inc.*, 547 U.S. 28 (2006); *Jefferson Parish Hospital District No. 2 v. Hyde*, 466 U.S. 2 (1984); *Northern Pacific Railway v. United States*, 356 U.S. 1 (1958).

2. See, for example, *Continental T.V., Inc. v. GTE Sylvania Inc.*, 433 U.S. 36 (1977); *Dr. Miles Medical Co. v. John D. Park & Sons*, 220 U.S. 373 (1911). Minimum resale price maintenance agreements are now subject to a so-called rule of reason rather than being per se invalid, *Leegin v. Creative Leather Products, Inc.*, 551 U.S. 877 (2007), but that does not detract from the fact that finding such agreements to be legally problematic, regardless of the degree of scrutiny, is a product of judicial law-making in the common-law style that the vague language of the Sherman Act has plainly (and intentionally) spawned.

3. 15 U.S.C. §1 (2006).

4. 15 U.S.C. §77q (2006).

5. 17 C.F.R. §240.10b-5 (2008).

ticular cases. When commentators refer to "regulation by litigation," this is what they typically mean, but we shall argue that the problem is not one peculiar to litigation, because much legislation and some administrative rule-making is shaped by particular cases—or highly salient examples— as well. Still, we focus initially on litigation, and suggest that litigation's focus on the particular litigants and their particular actions, while necessary and desirable for determining liability and awarding compensation, is a flawed platform for more broad-based policy-making. And this problem is not, we emphasize, a function of the errors that juries or judges may make in the decision of cases. Although such errors are often the subject of commentary and outrage, our claim is not dependent on the possibility of judge or jury error in deciding the case before the court. Rather, the argument is premised on the distinction between particular adjudication and the inherent generality of policy-making. This distinction would be of little moment were the particulars of particular litigation representative of the kinds of problems likely to arise in the future. But that is not the case. Instead, the goals and incentives of the litigation process are likely to contribute to aberrational rather than representative cases being the subject of lawsuits, and a collection of phenomena—most notably the availability heuristic—will cause the policy that emerges from litigation to be systematically based on an imperfect picture of the terrain that the policy is designed to regulate.

Yet although it is tempting and not wholly inaccurate to see the problem as one caused by litigation and thus intrinsic to it, in fact the problem is larger, and is a consequence of a focus on one or a few particular events, regardless of the setting in which the stories about those events may be told. Thus we will argue that even outside of the context of litigation, many regulatory policies also flow from experience with one or a few cases, and that the same problems that flow from case-based policy-making in litigation also flow from case-based policy-making with ex ante rule-making. The thrust of our argument is that the individual cases that receive sufficient attention to affect policy significantly are often both salient and, systematically, highly unrepresentative, and so the strategy of using such cases to provide the principles that inform policy is broadly misplaced.

3.2   The Generality of Policy

Policies are general, both by definition and necessity. Bobbie had a bowl of cereal for breakfast this morning, but it is her *policy* to have a bowl of cereal for breakfast *every* morning. Officer Smith may stop Susan Jones for driving at 47 miles per hour at a particular point on Main Street on a particular day, but it is a policy if all police officers are expected to stop all drivers driving more than 40 miles per hour at all points on Main Street. A policy is not an action. Rather, it is a course of action. Policies, by their very nature, are decisions about what is to be done in a multiplicity of cases involving a multiplicity of acts by multiple people at multiple times.

The observation that policy is general is banal, but the banality is worth emphasizing because doing so makes clear that policy-*making* involves setting a policy that will cover many acts by many actors in many places at many times. Good policy-making, therefore, involves making an aggregate determination of what ought to be done over a multiplicity of instances.[6] But in order to make this aggregate determination, the wise policymaker must be able to assess initially just what these instances in the future are likely to be. The optimal speed limit is not the speed limit that would be optimal for the worst driver, nor is it the one that would be optimal for the best driver. Rather, it involves determining what the full range of driving abilities covered by the policy will look like, as well as assessing the expected benefits and costs consequent upon applying alternative policies to that range. But although the assessment of benefits and costs is difficult and important, it is subsequent to the determination—our principal concern in this chapter—of just what the future array of applications of any policy will look like. Thus, it is a necessary condition of good policy-making that the policymaker be able to assess the current range of relevant behaviors (and their consequences) and the range of behaviors likely to exist under various different policy options.

3.3   Surveying the Field of Policy Applications

How, then, are policymakers expected to survey the range of applications of any policy, and predict the distribution of behaviors that one or another policy option will produce? There is of course no single method of empirical assessment and prediction that will apply for all policies or for all types of policies. Still, the goals of the assessment are clear. They are not merely to gauge what activities are now taking place, but also to assess what change in those activities will be brought about by some policy, or indeed by other changes in society. If a policymaker were contemplating, to take an issue recently in the news, a prohibition on the use of cellular telephones while driving, the policymaker would want to know, among other things, what percentage of drivers owned cellular phones, how many of those drivers used the phone while driving and in what fashion, how many accidents and of what kinds and with what consequences were caused by cellular phone use, and how cell phone use while driving will evolve in the future, say through Blue Tooth and other methods of hands-free calling, or, as is now the greatest concern, with the capacity to send and receive text messages. Finally, it is crucial to be able to predict with some accuracy what changes (and at what cost) in all of the foregoing would be brought about by various different

6. See generally Stokey and Zeckhauser (1978).

potential policy interventions. And we can imagine and understand similar exercises with respect to workplace safety, misrepresentation in the sale of securities, tobacco-related illnesses, environmental hazards, and much else. Whatever methods might be used to pursue an empirical survey of this type, it should be clear that assuming too quickly that any one event or practice is representative of all of the events or practices to be encompassed by some policy is a recipe not for accuracy but for distortion. To be sure, an accurate evaluation of expected benefits and costs will recognize that it is often (or at least sometimes) desirable to engage in strategic overregulation as regards the average case as the only or most effective way of controlling low probability events with serious negative consequences. Nevertheless, it is a mistake to assume that unrepresentative events or practices are in fact typical or representative, and making that kind of empirical error at the outset of a policy-making exercise is the path to ineffective and perhaps harmful policy.

3.4   When Easy Availability Makes for Bad Law

With this broad goal of empirical accuracy across multiple instances in mind, we are now in a position to evaluate litigation and ex ante rule-making along the dimension of fostering or impeding an accurate assessment of the terrain of potential policy application.[7] And from this perspective, litigation appears to present significant risks of distortion, and in at least two different ways.

At times, a court making a decision will announce a rule that is to be applied in cases other than the one actually before the court. Typically, this is a feature of appellate decision-making rather than decisions (by judge or jury) at trial, for an appellate court will justify its decision with an opinion that implicitly or explicitly announces a rule of decision to be applied in other cases. In part the extension of a decision beyond the immediate case is a function of the logic of reason-giving, for to give a reason is to make a claim about a type or category that is necessarily broader than the particular instance that the reason is a reason for.[8] And the extension of application beyond the immediate case is even more apparent when an appellate court explicitly announces a rule rather than simply giving a reason. That is because a rule, even more than a reason, necessarily and by reason of its generality encompasses instances other than the one that initially inspired the

---

7. Some of the existing literature describes the relevant choice as one between litigation and regulation (e.g., Viscusi 2002), but this strikes us as a poor characterization. Because the entire point of the inquiry is to understand and evaluate litigation as a regulatory strategy, the real question is about the relative merits of regulation by ex post litigation and regulation by ex ante rule-making; we will frame the issue in terms of litigation versus rule-making and not litigation versus regulation.

8. See Schauer (1995).

announcement of the rule.[9] When an appellate court, for example, upholds a trial court verdict against a franchisor that required its franchisees to purchase napkins and cleaning products from the franchisor as a condition of being allowed to use the franchisor's trademark and food recipes,[10] the appellate court will announce a rule regarding tying arrangements that represents a policy about some general category of tying arrangements, and not just about the particular tying arrangement at issue in this particular case. Maybe it will be a policy about all tying arrangements involving non-food products in the food industry, maybe about all tying arrangements in the food industry, maybe about all tying arrangements within a particular market structure, and maybe about all tying arrangements, but the rule will be about *all* of something, for that is just what a rule is and just what rules do.

There is considerable debate in legal theory over the extent to which the court that announces such a rule is or should be constrained by the rule in subsequent and different cases. Some argue that the rule announced in the first case exerts genuine pressure on the determination of a subsequent and different case that lies within the linguistic contours of the rule announced in the first case, and others claim that it is the characteristic virtue of the common law that the so-called rules it announces are little more than weak guides, rarely if ever requiring a court to reach a result other than the one it would have reached on its all-things-considered best judgment about how the particular case should be resolved.[11] But even if this latter view is empirically and jurisprudentially correct, the rule announced in the first case will still be a rule that lower courts are expected to follow, and, more importantly, will still be a rule that primary actors and their lawyers will look to in trying to predict what will happen in a case that appears to be encompassed by the rule.

Once we realize, therefore, that the rule announced by an appellate court is a policy, and, further, that the rule is a policy that will affect numerous agents other than the ones before the court, all of the aforementioned considerations about assessing the terrain of policy application come into play. The question, then, is whether the decision of a particular case involving a particular dispute between particular parties is the optimal or even a desirable vehicle for announcing a rule and a policy that will affect the behavior of parties other than the ones whose dispute prompted making the rule, and thereby will influence actions at least somewhat at variance with the actions that were adjudicated in the initial case.

There is a view, and one embodied in much of American constitutional

9. See Schauer (1991).
10. This is a frequently-litigated scenario. See, for example, *Queen City Pizza, Inc. v. Domino's Pizza, Inc.*, 124 F.3d 430 (3rd Cir. 1997); *Ungar v. Dunkin' Donuts of America, Inc.*, 531 F.2d 1211 (3rd Cir. 1976); *Siegel v. Chicken Delight, Inc.*, 448 F.2d 43 (9th Cir. 1971).
11. The respective positions are described and analyzed in Schauer (2009, 108–18).

doctrine, that seeing a real "case or controversy" between real litigants is the best way for a court to understand the actual landscape that will be affected by one of its rulings.[12] By delving into the detailed facts of a genuine controversy, so it is said and so it has been held countless times, a court can truly know what the impact of its rulings is likely to be.[13]

With respect to making the best decision in the particular controversy, there is much to be said for the traditional view. A judicial decision will produce, typically, a real winner and a real loser, and only by serious immersion in the situation can the court appreciate the consequences of its decision, as well as understand the fit (or lack thereof) between an outcome and the relevant legal language and legal doctrine.

As a result of understanding, however, that at the appellate level the consequences and reach of a decision will extend beyond the particular parties and the particular decision, substantial new problems become apparent. If a court is making a decision whose influence goes beyond the particular case, and thus beyond the identical situation before the court, one might think that the court should, ideally, have some sense of the range of instances encompassed by its rulings. If the decision in this case is to have consequences for other cases, other disputes, and other actions, it seems plainly desirable for the court to know what those other cases, disputes, and actions are likely to look like before issuing a ruling that will affect them. One problem, however, is that the structure of appellate courts makes them especially ill-equipped to assess the full field of potential applications of any ruling, even though it is entirely appropriate, at the appellate level, for an appellate court to take account of the effect of a ruling on future cases. It would not be in the interests of the parties themselves to provide information about other potential cases, though they might provide it for strategic purposes.[14] Moreover, apart from cases in the Supreme Court, and to some

12. See, for example, Eisenberg (1988); Calabresi (1982). See also Shavell (1995, 379–423) ("appeals courts sometimes can learn about opportunities for lawmaking only from disappointed litigants").

13. In *Valley Forge Christian College v. Americans United for Separation of Church and State, Inc.*, 454 U.S. 464 (1982), for example, the Supreme Court noted that "a concrete factual context" will generate "a realistic appreciation of the consequences of judicial action." 454 U.S. at 472. See also *Baker v. Carr*, 369 U.S. 186 (1962) (concrete disputes "sharpen . . . the presentation of issues" and thus aid "the illumination of difficult constitutional questions"); Fletcher (1988) (a concrete case will inform a court of "the consequences of its decisions").

14. One such exception would arise in the common situation in which an undesirable claimant of constitutional rights has a strong incentive to show a court how many other and more desirable claimants would benefit from a ruling in favor of the undesirable litigant before the court. When groups such as the American Nazi Party and the Ku Klux Klan claim free speech rights under the First Amendment, for example, it is obviously in their interest to show how rulings in their favor would benefit less repulsive dissident organizations.

Participants in criminal proceedings may also seek to identify realms of applicability beyond the specific case. Thus, when the generally guilty claimants of criminal procedure rights under the Fourth, Fifth, and Sixth Amendments argue that their convictions should be overturned because of a violation of such rights, they similarly have an interest in informing the court of the existence of innocent or less culpable defendants who would be among the beneficiaries

extent even for Supreme Court cases, the information provided in amicus curiae submissions, even opposing ones, is likely to be highly selective and hence incomplete. And most significant is the absence of any way in which an appellate court, lacking an investigate arm and often even the rudiments of non-case-specific factual research capabilities, can actually go out and find the information it might need to understand the full import of one of its rulings.[15]

Even more serious, however, is the way in which the particular case, the particular facts, and the particular litigants are likely to dominate a judicial assessment of the relevant terrain. The particulars of the case are *available,* in the technical sense of that term,[16] and the risk is that their very availability will lead a court to assume, mistakenly, that future cases will resemble the cognitively available case now before the court.[17] Just as someone who has just learned about a death from a rattlesnake bite is likely to overestimate the number of deaths caused by rattlesnake bites compared to the number caused by bee stings,[18] so too can we expect a court immersed in the details of particular litigation with particular parties and particular facts to assume, possibly mistakenly, that other and future events within the same broad category will resemble the events involved in the case now before the court. The case before the court may indeed be representative of the full population of cases of that broad type, but the availability of this case may lead to an assumption of representativeness even when such an assumption is unwarranted.[19] Thus, although it is possible that the single case before the court accurately represents the larger array, and although it is possible that a court will properly assess the particular case as exemplary of many cases,

---

of such a ruling. Prosecutors may argue for consideration beyond the particular case either to achieve appropriate outcomes or to promote deterrence: "Let this defendant go, and precedent would require granting dozens of future captured terrorists their freedom. Moreover, terrorist acts will become more common."

Appellate judges could craft their opinions to explain how broadly or narrowly they believe they should apply in future cases. However, we expect such guidance to be limited for multiple reasons: (a) the availability of the facts and arguments in the current case makes them seem more general than they are, thus requiring less parsing of how the circumstances do and do not extend than might be desirable; (b) In many circumstances, it is difficult to conjecture what future cases might arise with facts that call for the same decision, or somewhat similar facts that call for a different decision; (c) the decision reflects the legal arguments presented by the lawyers as well as the facts. The judge may be reluctant to comment on precedent when the skill of present or future lawyers will affect the outcome. And finally, (d) the judge, particularly if he or she feels overloaded, may feel that his or her role is to decide present cases effectively, not to speculate on extensions to future cases.

15. An important analysis of the informational dimensions of regulation by litigation is Schuck (2005).

16. See Tversky and Kahneman (1973). Useful overviews include Plous (1993, 125–27, 178–80); Sherman and Corty (1984); Reyes, Thompson, and Bower (1980); Taylor (1982).

17. For an earlier and more rudimentary presentation of this argument, see Schauer (2006).

18. See Anderson (1991).

19. See Kahneman and Frederick (2002).

it is precisely the ease of recall[20] of the case before the court that may lead the court to assume from the ease of recall that the case is representative when in fact it is not.[21]

Litigation is also especially likely to exacerbate the availability problem because the judge or court is obliged not only to see the details of the case before it, but also, and more importantly, because the judge or court must *decide* that case. Whatever possibility a decision maker may have of ignoring the most available event and thus transcending the availability-produced mischaracterization of the larger array, that possibility is likely to decrease when the decision maker has a particular *task* to perform with respect to the available example. Because tasks narrow a decision maker's focus, and because tasks thus make it more difficult for those performing a task to see beyond what is necessary to perform that task,[22] a decision-making situation in which the primary task is to decide a particular case will narrow the focus of the decision maker on the facts of that case. That makes it less likely that the decision maker will perceive the broader set of facts necessary to perform the secondary task of establishing a precedent, setting forth a rule, making law, or making policy.

A good example of this phenomenon in practice is the United States Supreme Court's 1964 decision in *New York Times Co. v. Sullivan.*[23] The case dramatically changed American law with respect to libel actions brought by public officials, setting forth the rule that in all such cases the plaintiff would henceforth be required to show with "convincing clarity" not only that what was said or published about him was false, but also that it was published with knowledge by the publisher (or writer or speaker) of its falsity at the time of publication. In placing such a heavy burden on a public official libel victim, the Court set out a rule that has been followed by no other country in the world, a rule that has virtually eliminated official defamation suits in the United States.

Seeing such a result, it is logical to inquire how it came about. The answer is that it is in many respects a *celebrity case,* and one with a quite uncharacteristic fact pattern. And it is the combination of celebrity, or high salience, combined with the unusual fact pattern that led to an extreme change in policy. The plaintiff was the Montgomery, Alabama, city commissioner in

20. See Shah and Oppenheimer (2009).
21. See Schwarz and Vaughn (2002) *op. cit.,* pp. 103–19. In fact, the broad field of behavioral decision-making throws up other cautions about the dangers of inappropriate extrapolation. Individuals substantially underestimate the uncertainties in the world, and are overconfident about their ability to predict ranges of outcomes, expecting that the outcomes will lie closer to our experiences to date than they actually do. See Taleb (2007). Individuals often do not recognize that the world presents us with fat-tailed distributions (which produce many extreme outliers), not the normal distributions found in most textbooks. And courts are likely to be subject to the same bias, believing that the world will present us with situations that cluster reasonably closely, when in fact many deep outliers are to be expected.
22. See Bazerman and Chugh (2006); Chugh and Bazerman (2007).
23. 376 U.S. 254 (1964).

charge of the Montgomery police, and his libel suit was based on an advertisement placed in 1960 by a group of civil rights leaders in the *New York Times* charging Sullivan with, among other things, hostility to the civil rights movement in his treatment of civil rights demonstrators. The case arose in a context, therefore, in which it was highly questionable whether the plaintiff had suffered any reputational damage at all, in which the factual errors in the advertisement were largely trivial, in which the underlying substance of the issue was a matter of great national social and political importance at the time, in which only forty-three copies of the offending publication were sold in the entire state of Alabama, and in which the jury-awarded damages—$500,000 in 1964 uninsured dollars—were substantial. In short, this was both a celebrity case and an outlier case.

Despite the case's unusual nature, unusual even when compared to other libel cases brought by public officials against the media, the Supreme Court (and a Court highly protective of the civil rights movement) set out a rule—made law, if you will—that governed the full array of public official libel cases, even though most of the libel cases controlled by the rule bear little resemblance to the actual events that, but for the rule, would have generated libel litigation. Now it is possible that the so-called actual malice rule of *New York Times v. Sullivan* is the best rule, or at least a good rule, but the case nevertheless presents a good example of a rule whose content would almost certainly have been quite different had the case before the Supreme Court been more representative of the typical libel case—a newspaper accusing a local official of financial malfeasance, for example—involving a public official.[24]

3.5 Selection Effects and the Battle over Availability

The availability problem in litigation would be substantial even if the cases that prompted rule-making were ones that were randomly selected from the larger array, because there would still remain the problem of assuming from a small sample size—typically a sample of one—a set of characteristics for the full array.[25] But the problem is actually far larger, because the incentives to litigate (or refrain from litigating) are likely to make unrepresentative cases especially likely to be the ones that wind up before appellate courts.[26] If ordinary events are disproportionately unlikely to generate disputes, if ordinary disputes are disproportionately unlikely to generate litigation, if ordinary litigated disputes are disproportionately likely to settle, if ordinary trial court verdicts are disproportionately unlikely to be appealed, and if ordinary appellate cases are disproportionately unlike to generate the pub-

24. See Epstein (1986).
25. See Cohen (1969, 1992).
26. See Hadfield (1992); Heiner (1986); Roe (1996).

lished opinions that are the vehicles for appellate rule-making, then the result will be that the cases that prompt rule-making are likely to be especially unrepresentative of the events that the rules that emerge from appellate rule-making will encompass.

In the American legal system, all of the conditional "ifs" in the previous paragraph are likely to be satisfied, in large part because litigation is quite costly. And thus the cases that make it to the appellate level will represent an extreme selection. Karl Llewellyn famously referred to appellate cases as "pathological."[27] To illustrate, a tobacco manufacturer may settle two dozen cases, accept the trial court's verdict in a dozen more, but appeal the case in which the warnings to the particular smoker were especially obvious and in which the smoker persisted in smoking even after health problems emerged. And a plaintiff's attorney who represents numerous smokers (individually, and not part of a class action) who have incurred smoking-related illnesses will similarly, say, settle two dozen cases, accept as unfortunate another dozen dismissals or defendant's verdicts, and appeal the case in which a sympathetic and largely nonnegligent smoker was not, because of a grant of a motion to dismiss, or grant of a defendant's motion for summary judgment, or grant of a motion for a directed verdict, even allowed to present his case to a jury. Thus, the mere fact that a case is appealed suggests from that alone that the case lies outside the norm.

The outlier status of the decided case would not be a problem if that outlier case was decided in a way that focused either narrowly on that case or set forth a rule only for other outliers sharing similar characteristics. The problem, however, is that the availability problem makes the outliers look more representative than they are, and thus the court deciding an outlier case and setting forth a rule on the basis of it will underappreciate the outlier's outlier status. Indeed, because any legal rule will produce some number of compliers, and some number of withdrawers from the activity, a court's understanding of the nature of the issue or problem will be informed only by the violators and the parties whose violation is unclear.[28] We might expect that the clear violator cases will settle or not be litigated in the first place, but that does not solve the problem because the court will still have seen not a representative sample of uncertain cases, but only those on the line between clear violations and unclear violations. By not seeing the compliers, the withdrawers, or the ones on the fuzzy edges of compliance and withdrawal, the court will still see a field that is far less representative than the court is likely to perceive.

Although most of the foregoing analysis addresses appellate rule-making,

---

27. See Llewellyn (1930, 58). Llewellyn observed that litigated cases bear the same relationship to the underlying pool of disputes "as does homicidal mania, or sleeping sickness, to our normal life." And if we expand the pool from disputes to rule-governed events, Llewellyn's point becomes even stronger.

28. See Hadfield (1992).

policy-making, and lawmaking, in fact trial court verdicts have generated most of the controversy about regulation by litigation.[29] Whether it be the widely reported verdict against McDonald's for failing to warn customers about its especially hot coffee, or the verdicts and settlements in the tobacco litigation, or the extremely large punitive damage awards in some environmental and products liability cases, or the potential policy impact of litigation about guns, lead paint, breast implants, automobile insurance, fast food, and the managed health care industry, much of the concern about policy-making by litigation turns out not to be so much a function of rules set forth by appellate courts, but rather is directed at the opinion-free verdicts by juries at the trial level, verdicts (or settlements) that are often not appealed, and which, even when appealed, often have their behavior-influencing effects as soon as the verdict is issued, and without regard to any ultimate resolution of the controversy or opinion on appeal.

Because trial verdicts do not involve opinions and hence do not involve published statements of reasons,[30] it might seem as if the concerns about availability and selection effects (or, to make the same point positively, about their representativeness) drop out with respect to such judgments. In fact, however, the biased-sample problem may be even worse for trial verdicts than it is with appellate rulings. Large verdicts and settlements may be highly unrepresentative, but they are the cases that get reported in the general press and in industry-specific publications. Given the thousands of trial court decisions every year in this broad domain, only cases that are remarkable in some way will get noticed. Thus, the set of reported verdicts will be a distorted sample of the set of verdicts and an even more distorted sample of some larger class of lawsuits, disputes, injuries, or simple events.

Billion dollar awards, after all, get everyone's attention.[31] Restaurants considering what kinds of warnings to issue in conjunction with serving hot beverages, for example, are unlikely to know about hot beverage lawsuits that were dismissed, or that were settled for small amounts because of the nuisance value of the lawsuit. These restaurants are even more unlikely to be aware of an even larger number of hot beverage injuries that generated no litigation at all, to say nothing about the literally billions of hot beverages consumed every year that produce no injury whatsoever. So although a verdict against McDonald's as a result of a hot coffee spill will be especially available to public knowledge because of the various media incentives that lead to reporting of the unusual story and not the routine event—man bites dog versus dog bites man—what becomes known will be especially unrepresentative.

Nevertheless, the ease of access to the unrepresentative but highly publi-

29. A good survey is in Lytton (2008).
30. Even though the cases often involve published preliminary rulings by the trial judges, especially the rulings denying motions to dismiss or motions for summary judgment.
31. See the February 23, 2000, comments of Theodore Olson, available at: http://www .manhattan-institute.org/pdf/mics2.pdf.

cized verdict may still lead potential defendants to assume that such a verdict is more representative than it actually is.[32] And when potential defendants overestimate the likelihood of such exceptional verdicts, as the availability heuristic tells us they will, and when those potential defendants alter their day-to-day behavior based on an inflated view of the likelihood of liability, then the policy of potentially excess caution on the part of potential defendants is as much if not more a product of an availability problem as is a distorted rule emanating from an appellate court.

Just as the wise policymaker assesses the full field of potential applications of a policy before adopting it, so too would a wise primary actor considering serving very hot coffee, for example, want to survey the full field of potential applications of that practice in order to be able to determine, inter alia, what percentage of customers would spill hot coffee, how many of those would be injured as a result, how many of those would initiate a dispute, and what benefits the company would reap by offering very hot versus tepid coffee. But if the availability of a hot coffee verdict leads the same primary actor to overestimate the likelihoods of spilling, of injury, of litigation, and of an unfavorable verdict, then that actor's behavior will be no different from, and no more optimal than, its behavior in response to an administrative regulation that required a too-low temperature because of the administrator's mis-assessment of the likelihood of injury. Even if potential defendants could calculate accurately the likelihood of an extreme award,[33] they must also be concerned with the mind-set of potential plaintiffs. If potential plaintiffs believe large awards are possible, they will be more likely to bring suit, making it even more important for defendants to try to limit their exposure. And thus we suspect that coffee temperatures dropped across America after the McDonald's decision, even for defendants who knew the odds.

Although it may be hard to grasp the social disadvantages of corporate hyper-caution in the context of serving hot rather than very hot coffee, or of selling serviceable and reliable tires rather than ultra-high-performance tires for consumer use,[34] these disadvantages may be more apparent when the hyper-cautious actors are pharmaceutical companies, newspapers engaged in investigative reporting, or physicians refraining from performing risky but potentially life-saving operations, for in such cases the societal losses or public harms from inaction are more easily grasped.[35] But even if these

32. The point is made forcefully in the context of more and more consequential events in Posner (2004).

33. Which will, ideally, take into account the way in which juries will also know something about outlier previous awards, and thus will have outlier information about award size and possibly outlier information about a jury's belief that a defendant should have been on notice.

34. See, for example, *LeBoeuf v. Goodyear Tire & Rubber Co.,* 623 F.2d 985 (5th Cir. 1980).

35. Breast implants represent a case in which medical device manufacturers essentially gave up, establishing a $4.25 billion compensation fund for "injured" recipients in the biggest class action settlement in history, even though the best scientific studies showed no evidence of harm. As is commonly the case, the most salient lawsuits involved the most sympathetic plaintiffs. See the book by former *New England Journal of Medicine* editor Marcia Angell (1997).

harms are understood, hyper-caution is a concern because in many psychological and legal contexts errors of commission count far more heavily than errors of omission, implying that there is already a background tilt in the direction of insufficient action.

Still, our goal in this chapter is not to enter into the debate about the socially optimal degree of caution that a manufacturer or other primary actor should adopt, assuming that the actor conducts an accurate empirical assessment of the expected social costs of the Type I errors of engaging in too much harmful conduct and the Type II errors of failing to engage in sufficient beneficial conduct. Rather, our two aims here are only to argue: (a) that such an assessment, a prerequisite to any determination of the proper risk level, cannot proceed wisely if the frequency of various potential events is miscalculated or misestimated; and (b) that such miscalculation or misassessment is especially likely to occur when aberrational events are highlighted because of the incentives of those—especially but not only the institutional press who report and the plaintiff's bar who litigate—who would be in a position to provide information about litigation.

Although it seems likely that the problem of misassessment is especially likely with respect to nonrepresentative verdicts for plaintiffs, from our perspective the misassessment would be equally problematic where the informational availability of aberrational defendant's verdicts distorted the behavior of primary actors so that they underestimated the likelihood of liability. Did the extreme availability of the verdict of acquittal in the trial of O. J. Simpson, for example, lead potential spouse-killers to overestimate the possibility of acquittal? Might the well-known appellate reversal of the multibillion dollar jury verdict in the Rhode Island lead paint litigation case[36] cause manufacturers of other potentially toxic substances to underestimate the possibility of liability?

The problem we highlight is one that is likely to be exacerbated because of the incentives that determine the identity of litigation parties as well. In class action lawsuits, for example, it would be a foolish plaintiff's attorney who selected a representative plaintiff rather than one who is especially sympathetic. It is true that Rule 23(a)(3) of the Federal Rules of Civil Procedure requires the judge to determine that the class representative present claims that are "typical of the claims . . . of the class," but such a determination will take place on only one side of the range. Some potential class representatives will in fact be typical of some class of plaintiffs, others will be atypically sympathetic, and some will lie in between. But none, unless the plaintiff's attorney is an idiot, will be atypically unsympathetic, and thus a judge faced with determining representativeness from candidates only on the sympathetic side of the typicality distribution can be expected systematically to incline the class of all class representatives in the direction of

36. *State v. Lead Industries Ass'n, Inc.*, 951 A.2d 428 (R.I. 2008).

the atypically sympathetic. To the extent that this is so, the litigation-based policy-making that ensues from class action judgments is especially likely to suffer from judge or jury misassessments of the aggregate character of the class, thus compounding the perceptual misassessments that are the product of the way in which only exceptional and thus unrepresentative verdicts are publicized, and even beyond the extent to which only unrepresentative disputes are litigated and only unrepresentative suits get to verdict without dismissal or settlement.

3.6   On Case-Based Rule-Making

On the basis of the foregoing, it may be tempting to perceive litigation itself as the problem, but in fact that is not so. Litigation does indeed present an example of the problem, but the problem—or at least the availability/ unrepresentativeness problem—is one that comes with an overemphasis on specific cases in the policy-making process, whether the policy originates in a court of law, an executive agency, or a legislature, and whether it is formal policy or simply a prescribed practice. Overemphasis on unrepresentative specific cases in policy-making appears across a wide range of regulatory/rule-making institutions, and is hardly restricted to litigation-based policy-making.

A good indication of the increasing tendency toward case-driven ex ante rule-making is the proliferation of laws named after particular individuals, of which Megan's Law, requiring the registration with local authorities of released sex offenders, is perhaps the most famous. Megan's Law, first enacted by the California legislature and then copied in many other states, is hardly unique, however, and federal laws dealing with missing children and adults include Kristen's Act, Jennifer's Law, and Bryan's Law, while among the federal laws dealing with sex offenders are Aimee's Law, the Jacob Wetterling Crimes Against Children and Sex Offender Registration Act, and the Hillary J. Farias and Samantha Reid Date-Rape Drug Prevention Act. Although many of these laws deal with missing persons and sex offenders, there are also case-generated laws dealing with drunk driving, including the Burton H. Greene Memorial Act; with crime on campus, as with the federal Jeanne Clery Act and the Michael Minger Act in Kentucky; with physically abusive dating partners, the object of Idaho's Cassie's Law; with hit-and-run driving in Brian's Bill in Maryland; with conditions of release for violent offenders, exemplified by Jenna's Law in New York; and many others.

These and similar named bills were drafted in response to celebrity cases, many of them representing the extremes of the bad behavior that winds up being the subject of the law. The Brady Law, for example, is a prime piece of federal gun control legislation, and it is named after President Reagan's press secretary, severely and permanently injured by a bullet meant for the president. But although gun control is mostly targeted at professional criminals and domestic violence, it is the celebrity attack on President Reagan and the injury to James Brady that spurred the legislation. And although most of these laws were prompted by crimes committed against the particular victims whose names are now on the laws, New York's Son of Sam Law—after which many other state laws restricting profitable activities by convicted felons are named—draws its title from the nickname for David Berkowitz, the perpetrator of a particularly notorious series of murders in New York in the 1970s.

It is of course difficult to avoid feeling sympathy for the victims of horrendous crimes and for their families, and it is understandable that many of these families view a law targeted at the specific crime from which their loved ones suffered as a fitting and enduring memorial. Nevertheless, the more a law, of necessarily general application, is designed in view of a specific example or specific case, the more risk there is either that the problem that prompted the law is itself rare or that the law is designed to deal with cases resembling the prompting case even though the highly salient prompting case is in fact unrepresentative of the problems that the ensuing law will in fact cover. Legislators who enact such laws are thus engaged in a two-level game with their constituents. The legislators may recognize the case-based law as somewhat misdirected, but feel they have no choice but to respond to public outrage over a heinous act, and a law enshrining a victim, even an uncharacteristic victim, is often the easy path to follow.

Sometimes, of course, a celebrity case is in fact representative. Lou Gehrig was medically a very representative example of people afflicted with what is now known as Lou Gehrig's disease. And the Megan of Megan's Law may well be a representative example of the problem that the law was aimed at preventing. But not infrequently the celebrity cases will be unrepresentative, and it is unlikely that a regulatory agency or legislature that is prompted to act by a celebrity case will come up with a solution that does not address that very case, or cases just like it, and thus the celebrity status of the celebrity case may make it close to impossible for a regulator to produce a rule that implicitly understands the outlier status of the celebrity cases and thus ignores the problem.

Even when a law is not prompted by a specific event, it has increasingly become part of the law-making process for legislative hearings to feature victims and case studies rather than experts on the relevant fields. Using vivid examples is of course a good rhetorical and persuasion strategy, and it is no surprise, for example, that President Obama's speeches about health care reform have invariably described at least several scenarios involving more or less worthy citizens who through no fault of their own have found themselves in health-care related difficulties due to absent or inadequate health insurance. But no public speaker of the president's caliber—or, indeed, well below his caliber—is going to pick unsympathetic examples, even if the unsympathetic examples may in fact be more representative. Moreover, and most importantly, it is extremely unlikely that the ensuing legislation would fail to "solve" the problem for the exemplar individuals, even though any law and any policy will of course not solve every problem. By relying on specific examples in circumstances in which specific and possibly unrepresentative examples are made salient and thus dominate the process, legislation may increasingly resemble litigation in being beholden to the unrepresentative and distorting example.

3.7   The Lessons to be Learned—The Penumbra Problem

In trying to draw together the lessons to be learned, the metaphor of a shadow may be useful, and may illustrate the ideal situation for case-based policy-making. The policy can be thought of as a light beam, and the case a specific object. The policy should apply to all situations that fall directly in the shadow of the specific case, closely resembling the specific case in terms of the critical elements of some principle. The difficulty, we have argued, is that salient cases tend to get exaggerated, and thus to cast perceived shadows that are far larger than the real shadows created by a more careful extrapolation from any one case. The result is a policy applicable not merely in the actual shadow, but across a much broader range of situations, and where the lessons from the original case do not apply.

Thus it is not a case's actual shadow, but its penumbra, its space of partial but not complete illumination, which winds up defining policy. And because the danger is that a case-based policy will be applied to a case's penumbra and not just to its shadow, it can be useful to think of the area of misapplication as the *penumbra problem.*

We have argued that the availability heuristic is the principal cause of the penumbra problem. Because availability leads individuals to judge the frequency of an event by how readily one can bring an instance to mind, it influences the extrapolation process. When a case comes into mental focus easily, as with a salient litigation instance or a prominent case that prompts legislation, the availability heuristic tells us that there is a tendency to overestimate its relevance, and thus to think it applies much more broadly than it does. When this happens, future events merely falling in the penumbra will be mistakenly treated as if they were directly in the case's shadow.

The problem of the penumbra is exacerbated when we encounter the phenomenon of the *celebrity case.* Some situations gain prominence because of media attention, sometimes because of their extreme and thus newsworthy facts, and sometimes because of the celebrity of the people involved. Almost by definition, newsworthy events are outliers, and celebrities are unusual. Basing policy on celebrity cases thus typically assures that their shadow will cover relatively few situations, but celebrity cases, like real world celebrities, appear larger than life, and their shadows will be exaggerated.

Consider a recent celebrity case that gained international publicity even though no crime was committed, few people were involved, no money was lost, and no physical injury was suffered. In July 2009, Sergeant James Crowley of the Cambridge, Massachusetts, police department arrested Harvard Professor Henry Louis "Skip" Gates in his Cambridge home. Gates, an African American and probably America's leading professor of Afro-American studies, was, with the help of his driver, trying to force the door to his own house, which somehow had jammed. The two were reported by a passerby as possible burglars. Sergeant Crowley responded to the call, and a series of misunderstandings and missteps ensued, with charges of racism and unruliness flying. As the encounter became increasingly angry, an enraged Gates was arrested for disorderly conduct. Ultimately, the charges were dropped, with the Cambridge mayor, the Massachusetts governor, and the president of the United States all getting involved.

Commentators of varying political stripes chimed in, including the aforementioned three political leaders, all African Americans. The thrust of their comments was that this case provided an excellent learning opportunity for some of the most important lessons for achieving an effective and peaceful multiracial society. So far so good, but the difficulty was that different commentators tended (and intended) to draw extremely different lessons. To some, the case illustrated the ever-present dangers of racial profiling, if even a small, neatly dressed, middle-aged, cane-carrying extremely distinguished Harvard professor could be subject to such an indignity in his own home. To others, however, the most important facts were that Sergeant Crowley was a highly respected police officer, known to go by the book, and known not only as nonracist, but as someone who taught courses to other officers about avoiding racial profiling. And thus many people understood the event not as an example of racial profiling, but rather as an elitist attack on a dedicated police officer, or a reflexive response by black leaders—including the president—who tended to see racism in every case of disagreement between people of different races.

The charges against Gates were dropped, and Gates dropped his threat to sue, so there will be no formal legal precedent from these events. Nevertheless, Cambridge has appointed a distinguished commission whose recommendations will surely influence future policy, quite possibly in the form of administrative edicts or city ordinances. And Gates has stated his intention to create a television series about racial profiling, thus increasing the likelihood that the events will have a major influence on policy more broadly, and possibly on specific legislation.

Yet although the effects of this case are likely to be major, it is hard to imagine a more unrepresentative case to address the twin issues of racial profiling by the police and respect for the police in minority communities. Each of the two protagonists was an extraordinarily appealing and extreme outlier on his side of any conceivable profiling situation. Gates is a highly distinguished African American whose profession and appearance are extremely unthreatening. Crowley is a very well-respected police officer, as deeply engaged in combating racial profiling as any white officer. Moreover, the locale and circumstances of the arrest were highly unrepresentative of typical racial profiling situations. The police officer was legitimately responding to an act reasonably arousing suspicion, yet the professor was in his own home. And thus the case is far afield from the much more common occurrence in which a white police officer asks young black men just hanging out to move along, or in which a black person driving in a white neighborhood is stopped on general suspicion, thus explaining the facetiously-named crime of "driving while black."

In short, any policy that emerges from this celebrity case will be built on a highly unrepresentative foundation. That failing, we have argued, is common to most policies that are built on the salient cases that tend all too often to be the basis for regulatory policy, whether that policy emerges from litigation, from legislation, or from action by an administrative agency.[37]

Although the pressures of politics and the ever brighter spotlights of the media have increasingly caused ex ante rule-making, especially by legislatures and occasionally by administrative agencies, to be plagued by the pitfalls of the available but unrepresentative case, these pitfalls are more of an unfortunate tendency of some legislative and administrative policy-making processes than something that is endemic or necessary to the process. By contrast, however, litigation cannot escape these risks, because having a real and present controversy between real parties is a defining feature of litigation. In this respect, therefore, the problem of the distortingly available example is almost always a problem with regulation by litigation, but only sometimes—even if increasingly—a problem with ex ante rule-making.

Still, the lesson is not that litigation is inferior to ex ante rule-making as a regulatory strategy. Rather, it is that case-based regulation entails risks of regulatory mismatch between regulatory goals and regulatory targets wherever case-based regulation appears, and that it is as problematic when it influences legislative and executive policy-making as when it distorts the policy-making that is an inevitable part of the litigation process.

Our goal here, however, is not to compare the negative aspects of case-based policy-making to the various positive features that it may possess, or with which it may contingently be coupled. Litigation-based policy-making, for example, may occasionally or usually bring advantages of nonbureaucratization—private versus public regulation[38]—that will outweigh the disadvantages that a case-based approach to policy-making entail. Litigation may also at times be a useful spur to agency-based or legislature-based ex ante rule-making.[39] But some forms of so-called regulation by litigation may avoid some of the desirable procedural constraints incorporated in

---

37. We recognize the irony, apparent throughout this chapter, of using available and potentially unrepresentative examples of unrepresentativeness to illustrate the problem of unrepresentativeness.

38. See Shavell (1984).

39. See Jacobson and Warner (1999). See also Mather (1998); Wagner (2007).

congressional rules or the Administrative Procedure Act.[40] And regulation by litigation can at times be unnecessarily complex, costly, unpredictable, and lengthy.[41] Numerous other factors also incline one way or another in the litigation versus ex ante rule-making debate, and it is far from our aim to even survey all of those factors, let alone evaluate them in general or in the context of particular policy-making topics. In short, any cost-benefit analysis would have to tally many elements on the benefit and cost sides of the litigation and regulatory rule-making approaches. But we leave that tally to others.

Our conclusion, therefore, is not that regulation by litigation is superior to or inferior to regulation by ex ante rule-making. It is simply that case-based policy-making is, ceteris paribus, a risky strategy, and that any approach to regulation is less desirable insofar as it relies too heavily on potentially unrepresentative examples, and more desirable insofar as it avoids this problem. This chapter has sought to identify one large negative factor. Determining which form of regulation is—all things including this factor considered— more desirable is a more ambitious goal than we have had for this chapter.

Appendix
Toward a Formal Model of Case-Based Law

This chapter proceeds by logic, not formal analysis.[42] Nevertheless, it is worth inquiring what a formal model of case-based decision-making law might tell us.[43] Justifiable simplicity is a prime quality for a model. Thus, we start with the simple situation where all cases are arrayed along a single dimension, say the extent of a defendant's degree of misrepresentation in a securities case, a variable ranging from 0 to 1. Moreover, we posit, as is common in legal decisions, that only binary outcomes are possible; there are no shades of gray.

The framework sketched later posits either that there is agreement on the facts, such as the extent of misrepresentation and the size of an award should liability be established, or that no further investigation of facts is permitted.

40. See Center for Regulatory Effectiveness, "What is Regulation by Litigation?" at www .thecre.com/regbylit/about.html.

41. See Kagan (2001).

42. We thank John Horton for conducting the simulations contained in this appendix, and Ashin Shah for preparing the figure.

43. Our referee recognized, correctly, that our chapter provides its empirical evidence by example, as opposed to more traditional economic methods, such as regression analysis. Thus, he argues, we may have been subject to availability bias ourselves. Given that, he suggested that we consider the potential for a formal model of how case-based law might perform, a model that would help determine whether the "evolution of decisions helps to correct the problem" posed here. This appendix provides a response.

In effect, information on the case is held in common, though the outcome for that information is unknown. The "no further investigation" proviso applies in appellate cases, which are our primary concern. Thus, the fundamental uncertainty is how the court will decide.

Priest and Klein (1984) address a quite different situation, where the contending parties differ in their assessments due to imperfect information about what the other party knows. Thus, if the parties start with overoptimistic assessments that the facts will favor their side, they will proceed to trial. They only stop once sufficient information, as uncovered by discovery or through arguments at trial, makes their assessments converge sufficiently to make settlement more attractive to both parties, rather than incurring additional transactions costs.

Returning to our assumptions of common knowledge and a one-dimensional framework, the system would quickly yield definable outcomes. Lawyers would only contest situations where the degree of misrepresentation lay in an interval where among prior decisions the next highest misrepresentation level led to a decision for the defendant and the next lowest led to one for the plaintiff. For example, if to date the greatest misrepresentation level associated with a finding of not liable was 0.64, and the lowest misrepresentation level leading to a finding of liable was 0.72, only cases between those two values would be potentially contested. Calculating the likelihood of a potentially contested case turns out to be a complex matter. Hence, we turned to simulation. The results are given in table 3A.1.

Matters become more complex if there is a second dimension. In the securities case, that dimension might be the extent of reliance by the plaintiff. Nevertheless, the system would still yield results once the number of cases becomes large. Following the securities example, say that x and y define the degrees of misrepresentation and reliance, respectively, of the defendant and plaintiff. We posit them to be continuous variables that are independent. We also posit that these are scale-free parameters arrayed along the positive line. Thus, the trade-off between x and y in determining liability is always strictly positive, but its value at any point is not related to trade-off values elsewhere.

Figure 3A.1 illustrates for all points above the curve, the defendant is liable; for all points below, he is not. The point x_j, y_j is said to dominate point x_i, y_i if $x_j > x_i$ and $y_j \geq y_i$.

There are two decisive conditions. Condition A: If a defendant's case dominates any prior case where he has been found liable, he is sure to be found liable in the current case, since both fact conditions are at least as bad for him. Condition B: If a defendant's case is dominated by any prior case where he has been found not liable, he is sure to get off in this case, since both fact conditions are at least as favorable for him. The potential for litigation arises when neither Condition A nor Condition B holds. If so, relying solely on precedent, the outcome in this case cannot be determined.

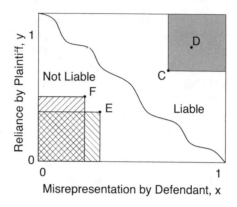

Fig. 3A.1   Relationship among reliance, liability, and wrongfulness

The figure shows a situation where there are four prior cases: C, D, E, and F. Here the relevant cases for precedent are C, E, and F. Case D dominates C, where less incriminating facts led to a finding of liability. Hence, C is the relevant precedent. Cases E and F, both of which found not liable, are both relevant, since neither dominates the other. The shaded portions of the figure represent regions where cases would not be contestable. In the unshaded area, however, it would be unclear whether liability would be found. Thus, cases that fell within that area are potentially contestable.

We conducted a simulation, drawing a random value from 0 to 100 for each unknown variable. These values can be thought of as the percentiles of the underlying density function, making no assumption about the form of that function. We then determine how likely it is that a new case will be potentially contestable.

Table 3A.1 shows the results for the one-, two-, three-, and ten-dimensional situations, where z is the third dimension.

The first crucial point to note is that moving up a dimension makes a potentially contestable case much more likely. With 100 prior cases, the likelihood jumps from less than 2 percent to more than 20 percent when we move from one to two dimensions. For three dimensions, the probability is almost 50 percent, and with ten dimensions it is almost a certainty. (In 1,000 trials, no case for the ten-dimensional case was resolved when there had been 100 prior cases.)

Of course, not all potentially contestable cases get contested, particularly if litigation costs are high. Condition A or Condition B may be almost satisfied, or the participants may think they can predict the court's trade-off rates in the contestable range. In either situation, if the outcome was fairly predictable, a case might not be contested.

But false reassurance should not be taken. We would argue that the real world presents a far more complex situation. There are dozens of dimen-

Table 3A.1   **The percent likelihood of a potentially contestable case (each entry based on 1,000 simulated histories)**

	Number of prior cases resolved		
	10	100	500
One-dimensional cases	17.9	1.8	0.3
Two-dimensional cases	57.5	20.6	10.2
Three-dimensional cases	80.4	48.8	29.7
Ten-dimensional cases	100	100	99.5

Notes: The cutoffs for determining liability were $x > 0.5$ in the one-dimensional case, $x + y > 1$ in the two-dimensional case, and $x + y + z > 1.5$ in the three-dimensional case. (For small numbers of cases, the cutoff matters. More extreme cutoffs—those closer to 0 or 1—give lower likelihoods of a contestable case. For any specific number of prior cases, when the numbers of cases gets large, the likelihoods converge for all cutoffs.) In the ten-dimensional case, the cutoff had a total value of 5 on the ten dimensions.

sions on which cases may differ. When there are many dimensions, potential contestability becomes extremely likely.

What of the possibility of giving weights to the different dimensions, and adding up the scores? Posit once again a radical simplification: there is no disagreement on the facts or the dimensions, and performance on each dimension can be readily measured quantitatively. This would still leave the problem of determining what weights are appropriate to apply to each dimension.[44] The lawyers could be expected to battle mightily over appropriate weights for a case until vast numbers of cases had been decided. Moreover, previously unexplored dimensions would continuously be introduced, particularly as the underlying world itself evolved. In real-world cases, of course, lawyers focus on the dimensions where the implicit scores are most favorable for their client, and may find it desirable to simply ignore some unfavorable dimensions. In effect they give zero weight to ignored dimensions, though the other side may stress its importance. And, of course, there would be disagreements on facts as well, although the general inability of appellate courts to correct lower court fact-finding will incline appellate decision-making to issues of law and not issues of fact.

The binary nature of many legal decisions plays a major role retarding the swift convergence of the case-law process. When a jury decides in favor of one party or another, it does not provide an estimate of how close the decision may have been. Indeed, it does not write an opinion. This dramatically reduces the information available to guide future cases. Appellate courts do provide opinions. But they too do not convey how close their decisions were.

44. Note, regression would not yield an answer, since our scale independence assumption implies that the weights would vary depending on the scores. If we assumed that x and y had some cardinal properties, as opposed to scale independence, then the court might draw inferences from trade-off rates away from current values, as say, through a regression analysis.

Indeed, it would be surprising if an appellate opinion gave the impression it could easily go the other way, even if the balance was close. Although appellate opinions typically speak with confidence, and equally typically set out their conclusions in strong rule-like fashion, the confidence of the opinions often masks the reality of underlying uncertainty, well captured in Justice Brandeis's remarked to Justice Cardozo that, in rendering an opinion, "[A]fter all, you only have to be 51 percent right."[45]

At worst, if there was a contrary consideration, if addressed in the opinion, it would have to be explained why it was not decisive, thus undercutting any ability to determine if the decision was close. In some appellate courts, most obviously the Supreme Court of the United States, the presence (or absence) of concurring or dissenting opinions will give some indication of whether a decision was a close one. But in many other appellate courts, such as panels of the federal courts of appeals, informal unanimity norms mask underlying disagreement and thus the degree of difficulty of the case.

Obviously, if both parties are willing to incur the costs of going to trial, or going to appeal, each must have thought it had a nontrivial probability of winning. Litigants in a future case, whether they are both private parties or if one is the government, as with regulatory or criminal proceedings, have limited information to guide them from past decisions. Say your case is a little stronger than that of a plaintiff who lost. If her case would have had a 60 percent chance of winning a priori, then you probably should go to trial, but probably not if it was 10 percent. But after the fact, if it was a jury decision, you get no information from the court itself beyond the decision. Moreover, juries have neither the ability nor the requirement to take guidance from prior jury decisions.

If an appeals decision determined the prior case, an opinion would have been issued, which could guide future cases, but opinions are usually crafted to justify the outcome chosen. And the whole process is made more difficult still because a case is not a case in the sense that the facts determine the decision. The decision in a case may well depend on how well it was argued by both sides. Thus, in judging one's own prospects, one must guess how relevant past cases would have come out had they been argued more effectively or differently by one side or the other, and how effectively your case will be argued by both sides.

The thrust of the argument we are making is that a formal model of the way the case system actually operates would show that the process would be extremely difficult for future parties to assess for a broad array of cases, quite apart from any role for the behavioral propensities that played a prominent role in our analysis. In a world where cases are complex to begin, where change is to be expected, and where case outcomes are usually binary, the guidance provided by precedent will often come extremely slowly. This is particularly true when opinions are not provided, or are crafted to justify the

45. See Rauh (1979, 12, 18).

choice in a close decision. Two unfortunate consequences result: many cases come to trial because outcomes could not be predicted and, after a decision is made, many participants feel the court system treated them unfairly.

References

Anderson, N. H. 1991. *Contributions to information integration theory, vol. I: Cognition.* Hillsdale, NJ: Lawrence Erlbaum Associates.

Angell, M. 1997. *Science on trial: The clash of medical evidence and the law in the breast implant case.* New York: W. W. Norton Co.

Bazerman, M. H., and D. Chugh. 2006. Decisions without blinders. *Harvard Business Review* 84 (1): 88–97.

Calabresi, G. 1982. *A common law for the age of statutes.* Cambridge, MA: Harvard University Press.

Center for Regulatory Effectiveness. n.d. What is regulation by litigation? Available at: www.thecre.com/regbylit/about.html.

Chugh, D., and M. H. Bazerman. 2007. Bounded awareness: What you fail to see can hurt you. *Mind and Society* 6:1–18.

Cohen, J. 1969. *Statistical power analysis for the behavioral sciences.* San Diego: Academic Press.

———. 1992. A power primer. *Psychological Bulletin* 112:155–59.

Eisenberg, M. A. 1988. *The nature of the common law.* Cambridge, MA: Harvard University Press.

Epstein, R. A. 1986. Was *New York Times v. Sullivan* Wrong? *University of Chicago Law Review* 53:782–818.

Fletcher, W. A. 1988. The structure of standing. *Yale Law Journal* 98:221–77.

Hadfield, G. K. 1992. Bias in the evolution of legal rules. *Georgetown Law Review* 80:583–617.

Heiner, R. A. 1986. Imperfect decisions and the law: On the evolution of legal precedent and rules. *Journal of Legal Studies* 15:227–51.

Jacobson, P. D., and K. E. Warner. 1999. Litigation and public health policy making: The case of tobacco control. *Journal of Health Politics, Policy and Law* 24:769–804.

Kagan, R. A. 2001. *Adversarial legalism: The American way of law.* New York: Oxford University Press.

Kahneman, D., and S. Frederick. 2002. Representativeness revisited: Attribute substitution in intuitive judgment. In *Heuristics and biases: The psychology of intuitive judgment* ed. T. Gilovich, D. Griffin, and D. Kahneman, 49–80. Cambridge, MA: Cambridge University Press.

Llewellyn, K. 1930. *The bramble bush: On our law and its study.* New York: Columbia University.

Lytton, T. D. 2008. Using tort litigation to enhance regulatory policy making: Evaluating climate-change litigation in light of lessons from gun-industry and clergy-sexual-abuse lawsuits. *Texas Law Review* 86:1836–76.

Mather, L. 1998. Theorizing about trial courts: Lawyers, policymaking, and tobacco litigation. *Law and Social Inquiry* 23:897–932.

Olson, T. 2000. *Regulation through litigation: Assessing the role of bounty hunters and bureaucrats in the American regulatory scheme.* New York: Manhattan Institute for Policy Research. Available at: http://www.manhattan-institute.org/pdf/mics2.pdf.

Plous, S. 1993. *The psychology of judgment and decision making.* New York: McGraw-Hill.

Posner, R. A. 2004. *Catastrophe: Risk and response.* New York: Oxford University Press.

Priest, G. L., and B. Klein. 1984. The selection of disputes for litigation. *Journal of Legal Studies* 14:215–43.

Rauh, J. L., Jr., M. Siegel, A. Doskow, and A. M. Stroock. 1979. A personal view of Justice Benjamin N. Cardoza: Recollections of four Cardozo law clerks. *Cardozo Law Review* 1:5–22.

Reyes, R. M., W. C. Thompson, and G. H. Bower. 1980. Judgmental biases resulting from different availabilities of arguments. *Journal of Personality and Social Psychology* 39:1–12.

Roe, M. J. 1996. Chaos and evolution in law and economics. *Harvard Law Review* 109:641–83.

Schauer, F. 1991. *Playing by the rules: A philosophical examination of rule-based decision-making in law and in life.* Oxford: Clarendon Press.

———. 1995. Giving reasons. *Stanford Law Review* 47:633–59.

———. 2006. Do cases make bad law? *University of Chicago Law Review* 73:883–918.

———. 2009. *Thinking like a lawyer: A new introduction to legal reasoning.* Cambridge, MA: Harvard University Press.

Schuck, P. H. 2005. Why regulating guns through litigation won't work. In *Suing the gun industry: A battle at the crossroads of gun control and mass torts,* ed. T. D. Lytton, 225–49. Ann Arbor: University of Michigan Press.

Schwarz, N., and L. A. Vaughn. 2002. The availability heuristic revisited: Ease of recall and content of recall as distinct sources of information. In *Heuristics and biases: The psychology of intuitive judgment,* ed. T. Gilovich, D. Griffin, and D. Kahneman, 103–18. Cambridge: Cambridge University Press.

Shah, A. K., and D. M. Oppenheimer. 2009. The path of least resistance: Using easy-to-access information. *Current Directions in Psychological Science* 18:232–36.

Shavell, S. 1984. Liability for harm versus regulation for safety. *Journal of Legal Studies* 13:357–74.

———. 1995. The appeals process as a means of error correction. *Journal of Legal Studies* 24:379–423.

Sherman, S. J., and E. Corty. 1984. Cognitive heuristics. In *Handbook of social cognition,* vol. 1, ed. R. S. Srull and T. K. Wyer, 189–286. Hillsdale, NJ: Lawrence Erlbaum Associates.

Stokey, E., and R. Zeckhauser. 1978. *A primer for policy analysis.* New York: W. W. Norton & Co.

Taleb, N. N. 2007. *The black swan: The impact of the highly improbable.* New York: Random House.

Taylor, S. E. 1982. The availability bias in social perception and interaction. In *Judgment under uncertainty: Heuristics and biases,* ed. D. Kahneman, P. Slovic, and A. Tversky, 190–200. Cambridge: Cambridge University Press.

Tversky, A., and D. Kahneman. 1973. Availability: A heuristic for judging frequency and probability. *Cognitive Psychology* 5:207–32.

Viscusi, W. K., ed. 2002. *Regulation through litigation.* Washington, DC: Brookings Institution Press.

Wagner, W. E. 2007. When all else fails: Regulating risky products through tort litigation. *Georgetown Law Journal* 95:693–746.

Tobacco Regulation through Litigation
The Master Settlement Agreement

W. Kip Viscusi and Joni Hersch

4.1 Introduction

For decades individual lawsuits by smokers against the cigarette industry were unsuccessful. In 1995 state attorneys general launched a series of lawsuits seeking to recoup the Medicaid-related costs associated with cigarettes. The prospects for such lawsuits were dim because the same demonstration of wrongful conduct required in individual tort cases would also be required for the states' claims. In addition, the states were seeking to recoup the value of a financial externality, which involves a more novel legal theory than does a standard torts claim.[1] However, because this litigation arose during a period of increased antitobacco sentiment as well as new legislation,[2] changing public sentiment might have been reflected in juror attitudes and would potentially have a negative effect on the companies' prospects in court.

The states' cigarette cases were resolved by the 1998 Master Settlement Agreement (MSA), which was notable in several respects. First, there was

W. Kip Viscusi is the University Distinguished Professor of Law, Economics, and Management at Vanderbilt University Law School, and a research associate of the National Bureau of Economic Research. Joni Hersch is professor of law and economics at Vanderbilt University Law School.

This chapter was presented at the NBER Regulation Versus Litigation Conference, September 11–12, 2009.

1. The existence of a financial externality from cigarettes is not a sufficient basis for a valid legal claim as there also must be wrongful conduct by the cigarette industry that led to the smoking behavior and the subsequent costs. Otherwise, automobile manufacturers and producers of all other risky products would be liable for accident costs irrespective of producer negligence or the presence of product defects.

2. For instance, states imposed new restrictions on locations, such as restaurants and hospitals, in which smoking is permitted. See Hersch, Del Rossi, and Viscusi (2004) and the State Tobacco Activities Tracking and Evaluation (STATE) System, available at http://apps.nccd.cdc.gov/statesystem/.

no apparent rationale for such a settlement of the states' lawsuits. There was no evidence at the time of the settlement that the litigation had failed and that it should be short-circuited by a negotiated settlement. The cigarette companies had not lost any of the state cases so it seems plausible that their unblemished record of success in the individual cases might have continued. Second, the MSA financial settlement was path breaking in that it did not involve a conventional damages payment, but instead imposed the equivalent of a per pack cigarette tax under the guise of a "settlement." These tax payments were only loosely related to the economic harms for which damages were being sought. Past cigarette sales, which will be strongly correlated with the cigarette-related Medicaid costs and thus the alleged damages in the case, had no effect whatsoever on the per pack MSA levy. Moreover, new entrants that begin selling cigarettes after the MSA by definition cannot be guilty of past wrongful conduct, but they also are subject to the de facto tax payments. Third, the MSA also imposed numerous sweeping regulatory restrictions, which were not the subject of the litigation of the alleged wrongful conduct by the industry. The litigation did not spur standard political processes into issuing regulations, but rather imposed regulations as part of the MSA. Unlike the normal promulgation of regulations, there was no legislative mandate granting authority to an agency to regulate, and there was no rulemaking process or public participation in the development and review of the regulation.

The MSA also may have had broader indirect effects by further fostering an antitobacco environment, affecting the prospects of the industry both in court and in the political arena. By imposing a de facto tax and a series of regulatory constraints, the MSA greatly expanded the degree of government intervention in the cigarette market. The early, unsuccessful attempts by the U.S. Congress to settle the state lawsuits against the cigarette industry ultimately led to the 2009 law giving the Food and Drug Administration (FDA) authority to regulate cigarettes. The MSA also influenced tort liability generally, both by providing billions of dollars in contingency fees to plaintiff attorneys and through an anchoring effect that set litigation damages award targets in the billions of dollars rather than millions. Thus, the MSA did not end the litigation against the industry but instead may have generated increased litigation costs.

The departure of the MSA from standard political processes for taxation and regulation raise a series of questions about whether the MSA outcome enhances or decreases economic efficiency. First, the regulatory restrictions and per pack levies jointly agreed to by the major cigarette manufacturers and the attorneys general were purportedly targeted at decreasing smoking but may have had anticompetitive effects. Second, the MSA has affected subsequent cigarette litigation. Third, how the settlement money—about $250 billion over twenty-five years—is being spent is of policy interest as well, given that the avowed rationale for the payments was to defray the health-related costs of cigarettes and to decrease youth smoking. In this chapter we analyze the terms of the settlement and assess the implications of the MSA on these dimensions. In making our assessment of the MSA, we follow the guidelines articulated in the introduction to this volume by Daniel Kessler, who suggests that an instructive reference point for judging the settlement and other such regulation through litigation efforts is whether they address some evident market failure, litigation failure, or political process failure so as to enhance economic efficiency.

4.2   The Master Settlement Agreement[3]

The Master Settlement Agreement of November 23, 1998 marked the end of the tobacco litigation launched by the state attorneys general against the cigarette industry.[4] Whether the lawsuits would have succeeded was never resolved as no trials were completed in any of the cases. The MSA settled possible claims for forty-six states. Previously, four states—Mississippi, Minnesota, Florida, and Texas—reached separate settlements with the tobacco industry. Because of the national scope of many of the requirements imposed by the MSA, our main focus is on the MSA itself rather than presenting parallel discussions of each feature of the individual state settlements.

4.2.1   Financial Externalities and the Litigation Focus

The cases on behalf of the states involved claims for the Medicaid-related costs incurred by the states. Thus, the damages did not pertain to the harms that cigarettes caused to smokers' health but rather focused on the Medicaid costs generated by the smoking behavior caused by the alleged wrongful conduct of the tobacco industry. The states' claims consequently focused on the gross cigarette costs to the states from one program, Medicaid, rather than on the net costs across all programs. Estimates in Viscusi (1995, 2002a) found that on balance cigarettes did not impose net financial costs at either the state or federal level, but rather yielded net cost savings.[5] However, the total net financial cost to society was not the focus of the litigation's damages claim.

---

3. For previous treatments of the MSA and regulation through litigation generally, see Bulow and Klemperer (1998); Wagner (1999); Viscusi (2002a, 2002b); and Cutler et al. (2002).

4. Because of the political sensitivity of the settlement, some states did not sign on to the agreement until after the November 1998 elections. One such example is Massachusetts, where antitobacco groups lobbied for more punitive settlement terms.

5. The national net financial costs per pack in 1995 U.S. dollars at a 3 percent interest rate were $0.58 total medical care, $0.01 sick leave, $0.14 life insurance, –$0.24 nursing home care, –$1.26 retirement and pension, $0.02 fires, and $0.43 taxes on earnings, for a net cost of –$0.32. While the financial externalities of smoking are not great and on balance are favorable, the health cost internalities are more substantial (Viscusi and Hersch 2008), but these were not the subject of the litigation.

In 1995, Mississippi filed the first financial claim against the cigarette companies for smoking-related Medicaid costs. Even though the cigarette industry had never advocated the net financial cost approach that takes into account the reduced costs due to smoking—such as lower retirement benefit expenses—nevertheless Mississippi's opening salvo in the cigarette litigation was its *Memorandum,* which explicitly targeted the net financial cost reasoning in the NBER working paper version of Viscusi (1995):

A credit to the cigarette industry for any monetary savings in elderly health care, as well as other savings resulting in the premature deaths of smokers, is utterly repugnant to a civilized society and must be rejected on grounds of public policy . . . The contention of entitlement to an "elderly death" credit is, on its face, void as against public policy. That policy and basic human decency preclude the defendants from putting forth the perverse and depraved argument that by killing Mississippians prematurely, they provide an economic benefit to the State. No court of equity should countenance, condone, or sanction such base, evil, and corrupt arguments. . . . The defendants' argument is indeed ghoulish. They are merchants of death. Seeking a credit for a purported economic benefit for early death is akin to robbing the graves of Mississippi smokers who died from tobacco-related illnesses. No court of law or equity should entertain such a defense or counterclaim. It is offensive to human decency, an affront to justice, uncharacteristic of civilized society, and unquestionably contrary to public policy.[6]

What is particularly noteworthy is that Mississippi's *Memorandum* attacked the net financial cost approach even before the defendants had put forth any arguments.[7] By framing the litigation in terms of the gross financial costs associated with Medicaid rather than any calculus involving net financial effects, the states clearly could enhance their prospective payoff.[8] All states adopted a similar approach although there were some differences in the calculations of the damages payments owed to the states.

In 1997 and 1998 there were legislative attempts by the U.S. Congress to settle the litigation at the national level through the imposition of cigarette tax payments and regulatory reforms. In this proposed legislation, which was

6. See Viscusi (2002a, 87). The extract paragraph is directly from *Memorandum in Support of the State's Motion for Ruling in Limine, or Alternatively, for Partial Summary Judgment,* in re Moore, Attorney General ex Rel., State of Mississippi Tobacco Litigation, Cause No. 94-1429, (August 11, 1995), pp. 3, 21, and 23. The Viscusi (1995) NBER study received no financial support from the tobacco industry, which was not aware of the study. To the best of Viscusi's knowledge, the study has never been presented in testimony on behalf of the tobacco industry.

7. For the state of Mississippi, which was the state that launched the litigation, the financial externalities from cigarettes were $0.02 medical care, –$0.03 nursing homes, –$0.05 pensions, $0.02 taxes on earnings, for a net financial externality of –$0.04. In addition, the Mississippi state cigarette excise tax was $0.18. See Viscusi (1999, 2002a).

8. The states also included the Federal share of Medicaid costs in the claim as well as other costs that the states did not actually incur. See Viscusi (2002a).

referred to as the Proposed Resolution, the cigarette industry had sought protections against punitive damages and class actions. No legislation was enacted because Congress' late drafts of the Proposed Resolution omitted such protections and escalated the tax payments. The tobacco industry withdrew its participation, decreasing support for the legislation in Congress.

After the failure of the Proposed Resolution, the cigarette companies settled the cases with four individual states and reached a broad agreement with the state attorneys general. This agreement, called the Master Settlement Agreement (MSA), put an end to the claims on behalf of the states. Not all states had filed claims. For example, the state of Alabama opposed the litigation and never filed a claim against the tobacco industry, but nevertheless participated in the MSA.[9] The MSA had no direct effect on individual lawsuits, class action lawsuits, or punitive damages. These efforts were not restricted by the MSA despite attempts by the cigarette industry to obtain protections in these areas.

4.2.2   Financial Characteristics of the Settlement

The financial stakes in the tobacco litigation settlements were quite substantial. In 1997 and earlier in 1998 before the MSA was finalized, four states reached separate agreements with the cigarette industry: $3.6 billion for Mississippi, $11.3 billion for Florida, $15.3 billion for Texas, and $6.6 billion for Minnesota, for a total of $36.8 billion. These four states had made the most progress in developing their cases.[10] In addition to the $36.8 billion in settlements for these four states, the MSA settlement in the remaining states was $206 billion. The combined undiscounted total of payments to all fifty states over the first twenty-five years is $243 billion. There are also about $7 billion in additional payments, including payments for a foundation and antismoking education as well as enforcement, making the total of all settlements about $250 billion.

While some of the payments were initial payments made in the first five

9. The reasoning for the state of Alabama was articulated by then-Deputy Attorney General and now Federal Judge William Pryor: "We recommend to the Governor and the Attorney General that the State of Alabama not file a Medicaid reimbursement suit. We do not believe that filing such a suit would serve the interests of the citizens of Alabama. First, such a suit would advance weak legal or equitable theories which, even if the State won the suit, would threaten to undermine Alabama law generally. Second, the State's burden of proving net harm is problematic, because widely respected economic studies conclude that there is no net harm to the State's treasury as a result of cigarette consumption. Third, this litigation would effectively raise taxes on tobacco companies without going through the ordinary legislative process. As a matter of judicial and political economy, if the State of Alabama wants to raise taxes on tobacco, the Legislature, not the judiciary, should do so" (Viscusi 2002a, 48).

10. The first state to file a lawsuit was Mississippi. The trial was about to begin in Mississippi at the time of the settlement. The amount of the settlement exceeded the damages sought in the case, much to the surprise of the defense attorneys litigating the case. The first of the state tobacco trials took place in Minnesota, but the settlement occurred before the trial was concluded. Texas and Florida had completed most of the depositions of experts before the settlement.

years of the agreement, the bulk of the payments consist of annual payments. Payments decline if cigarette sales decline, so the agreement does
function as an excise tax. The annual payment levels were set so that for the
$8 billion payment amount from 2004 to 2007, the MSA agreement would
impose a tax-equivalent charge of $0.33 per pack. Combined with the four
separate state settlements, the total tax equivalent is $0.40 per pack.

The first distinctive aspect of the MSA is that this settlement of the litigation did not involve settlement payments of the usual type. Financial
settlements in liability cases typically involve either lump sum payments or
structured payments to the claimant, where in each instance the payments
are being made by the defendant. Under the MSA, some of the minor costs,
such as the costs of the MSA executive committee and enforcement costs,
are borne directly by the companies, but the primary thrust of the settlement
terms is to impose the equivalent of an additional excise tax on cigarettes for
which payments would go to the states. In effect, the states used the MSA to
impose additional cigarette taxes rather than obtaining the authorization of
state legislatures. Specifically, the MSA imposes fees in perpetuity based on
cigarette sales so that the fees are tantamount to an excise tax. These costs
ultimately will be largely shifted to cigarette smokers.[11] The preferences of
the citizenry in the affected states were not reflected in the same manner that
they might have been if legislation were required. The decision to participate
in the MSA and the terms of the participation were the result of a series of
secret negotiations involving representatives of the affected companies and
the states, with a small group of attorneys general playing a pivotal role.[12]
The imposition of a tax equivalent through litigation rather than legislation
involved potential efficiency costs as well as the possible issue of propriety
of bypassing the usual legislative processes. Moreover, this type of intervention is an asymmetric and biased policy instrument, as such deals can boost
tax rates but not decrease them.

Settlement in the form of a tax equivalent rather than a lump sum payment has two principal economic ramifications. First, taxes raise the price
of the product, discouraging smoking behavior through the usual cigarette
demand curve effects. Second, because of the finite financial resources of
the affected firms, the total present value of the payments to the states could
be larger if the damages were paid in the form of a unit tax rather than a
lump sum penalty. Some antismoking advocates had favored a lump sum
damages payment to maximize the immediate harm to the industry, while
others placed greater weight on the objectives of discouraging smoking
behavior and maximizing the state's financial gain. The choice of the form
of payment influences the extent to which each of these objectives can be

---

11. Lillard and Sfekas (2009) examine the substantial tax shifting effects of the MSA.

12. None of the state legislatures were involved in ratifying the agreements, and at least in
some instances, notably Massachusetts, the actions of the state attorney general conflicted with
the views of the governor.

fostered, as there is an inevitable trade-off involved in the choice of the payment structure.

In a standard tort claim, the damages bear a direct relation to the harm. Thus, a lump sum damages payment for the recovery of costs incurred due to the defendant's wrongful conduct, once resolved through the legal process, provides a direct link between damages and harm. Replacing a lump sum payment with a tax that continues in perpetuity relaxes the relationship between damages and harm. The legal trigger for the payment of any damages is the wrongful conduct by the companies, such as that relating to claims of deceptive advertising and concealment of the product risks.[13] However, if this behavior was in the past and will not continue into perpetuity, as will the per unit tax equivalent feature of the MSA, then the penalty being levied is not directly related to the alleged wrongful conduct or even the time period in which the wrongful conduct is alleged to have occurred. Similarly, if all major manufacturers are not guilty of the same wrongful conduct, or if the manufacturers sold quantities of cigarettes before the MSA that are different from their current sales, then the imposition of uniform prospective per pack penalties on all firms is not warranted from an efficiency perspective. If the objective is to establish efficient prices, the per pack price should reflect the current marginal costs associated with the product.

The identical settlement tax treatment of products of different riskiness is inconsistent with the settlement tax being related to the Medicaid cost damages. Even if a new entrant or an existing firm were to market a completely safe cigarette, it would still have to pay the MSA fee for that product. The inconsistency of a cigarette tax with the damages claims in the litigation is also exemplified by the extreme case of potential new entrants that did not market cigarettes during the period of wrongful conduct. Even though these new entrants could not have generated any past damages, the MSA is structured so that new entrants will share in a variant of the penalty structure. To participate in the settlement revenues, states were required to adopt "Qualifying Statutes." These statutes required new entrants to pay a prorated damages amount based on their cigarette sales, where these per pack levies are the same as for cigarettes sold by the defendants in the state litigation. In this way the MSA provided a competitive shield so that firms that were not parties to the litigation could not have a cost advantage.[14] That new entrants are also subject to the tax is not surprising given that the terms of the MSA emerged from the bargaining power of the respective parties to

13. The states' damages claims assumed that all Medicaid-related costs of cigarettes were attributable to the industry's wrongful conduct. However, it is unreasonable to assume that smoking rates would be zero in the absence of possible wrong conduct.

14. Potentially, these new entrants could obtain reimbursement for these payments twenty-five years later if they could demonstrate that there was no wrongful conduct throughout the period. At least one new entrant, the South African firm Carolina Tobacco Company, claimed that the payments to the states threatened the firm's profitability.

the deal, which included the major cigarette producers but no representatives of potential new entrants or the smoking population.

The settlement did not emerge in the abstract but took shape only after the efforts in 1997 and 1998 to pass the Proposed Resolution were unsuccessful. A financial lesson from the Proposed Resolution experience was that information indicating that there would be a settled resolution of the state cases led to favorable stock price effects for the cigarette companies. The market expectations, and presumably the expectations of the companies as well, was that settling the state cases would eliminate the litigation threat as the companies had an unblemished record of success in individual smoker cases. While this may have been a reasonable expectation at that time, after the fact it proved to be quite wrong. If company executives were in fact cognizant of the adverse longer-term implications of the MSA but nevertheless favored the MSA to reap short-term benefits, that would reflect a possible agency problem.

4.2.3   The Political Economy of the Settlement Amounts

How the settlement funds would be divided among the forty-six MSA participants was determined by a political bargain of the participating parties, which are less broadly representative than the diverse interest groups that can have an input to legislation and regulation. The allocation of the MSA payments is summarized in table 4.1.[15] The first column of statistics is the percentage share of the state's medical costs calculated by Viscusi (1999, 2002a). These costs are calculated using state-specific information on smoking rates and medical cost structures including the state's Medicaid expenses, state expenditures on community hospitals, and other state medical costs. The sum of all states' expenses comprise the national medical costs that are being addressed by the MSA, where these calculations follow the states' procedures of assuming that the defense is liable for all such smoking-related costs.[16] Thus, the denominator is the total U.S. smoking-attributable state health costs, while the numerator is the state-specific value. These estimates are the actual economic costs calculated using the same procedure for each state and are not identical to the diverse approaches used by the handful of states that undertook such calculations at the time of the settlement.[17] All economic estimates reported here follow the practice in the economics literature of isolating the net incremental costs incurred by the states where the reference point is the nonsmoking smoker (i.e., a nonsmoker who has

---

15. The state-specific costs reported in table 4.1 are calculated by Viscusi (1999) using his economic cost calculation procedure, not that of the states.

16. If states had differed in whether the alleged wrongful conduct contributed to the costs, then the percentage of recoverable medical costs would need to be adjusted.

17. A critique of the state cost calculations appears in Viscusi (2002a), which shows that the states' calculations greatly overstated their smoking-related medical costs. The states' calculations also did not isolate the share of the costs attributable to wrongful conduct but rather included all costs.

Table 4.1   Ratio of the state settlement payment share to the state medical care cost share for states participating in the settlement

State	Percentage share of medical cost	Percentage share of settlement	Settlement share divided by medical cost share
Alabama	1.520	1.650	1.080
Alaska	0.280	0.350	1.263
Arizona	0.530	1.500	2.850
Arkansas	1.020	0.840	0.828
California	8.551	12.997	1.520
Colorado	1.229	1.396	1.136
Connecticut	1.948	1.890	0.970
Delaware	0.513	0.403	0.784
Georgia	3.154	2.499	0.792
Hawaii	0.212	0.613	2.886
Idaho	0.229	0.370	1.615
Illinois	5.609	4.739	0.845
Indiana	3.587	2.077	0.579
Iowa	0.983	0.886	0.901
Kansas	0.830	0.849	1.023
Kentucky	2.806	1.793	0.639
Louisiana	2.424	2.296	0.947
Maine	0.724	0.783	1.082
Maryland	2.048	2.302	1.124
Massachusetts	3.170	4.113	1.297
Michigan	3.326	4.431	1.332
Missouri	2.722	2.316	0.851
Montana	0.244	0.432	1.774
Nebraska	0.569	0.606	1.065
Nevada	0.521	0.621	1.191
New Hampshire	0.894	0.678	0.759
New Jersey	4.262	3.937	0.924
New Mexico	0.351	0.607	1.729
New York	15.170	12.995	0.857
North Carolina	3.491	2.375	0.680
North Dakota	0.211	0.373	1.764
Ohio	6.148	5.129	0.834
Oklahoma	1.199	1.055	0.880
Oregon	1.003	1.169	1.165
Pennsylvania	5.298	5.853	1.105
Rhode Island	0.736	0.732	0.995
South Carolina	1.422	1.198	0.842
South Dakota	0.256	0.355	1.389
Tennessee	2.874	2.485	0.865
Utah	0.220	0.453	2.058
Vermont	0.321	0.419	1.306
Virginia	2.766	2.082	0.753
Washington	1.498	2.091	1.396
West Virginia	0.978	0.903	0.923
Wisconsin	1.983	2.110	1.064
Wyoming	0.178	0.253	1.420

Note: Viscusi (2002a, table 3). Medical cost externality figures assume a 3 percent discount rate and cost levels for 1995.

the same personal characteristics as a smoker other than smoking status). With the exception of medical costs for Massachusetts, the states' calculations of the medical costs generally included the federal costs share as well as the state share and also did not account for the net incremental costs of smoking behavior.[18]

The second column of statistics in table 4.1 presents the percentage share of the settlement received by the different states. Interestingly, New York received a 12.995 percent share that is almost identical to that of California's 12.997 percent share, even though New York accounted for 15.17 percent of the national smoking-related Medicaid costs as compared to 8.551 percent for California. This disparity highlights the political influences on the MSA.

The best measure of how the states fared is represented by the statistics in the final column of table 4.1, which divides the payment share by the medical cost share. States with a value above 1 reaped a disproportionate share of the settlement. The state of Washington, which was represented by the lead MSA broker Christine Gregoire, then attorney general and subsequently governor, received a relatively high ratio of 1.396. The most prominent tobacco states fared particularly poorly, as North Carolina, Virginia, and Kentucky all had ratios in the 0.6 to 0.8 range. The state of Iowa, where the state's tobacco case had been dismissed, nevertheless had a ratio of 0.901, and the state of Alabama, where the state attorney general refused to file a case because he did not believe such cases had validity, had a ratio of 1.08. Factors other than the states' expected damages amounts in the litigation clearly influenced the distribution of the payments.

Using this sample of forty-six states, we estimate the determinants of the percentage share of the settlement and the states' relative gain from the settlement. Regression results are reported in table 4.2. The key explanatory variable is the state share of the medical costs, which should fully account for the division of the payments if the payments are distributed based on the rationale for the claims. In addition, we include the per pack cigarette excise tax that prevailed in the state in 1998 as a proxy for antitobacco political sentiments and political pressures to secure revenues from cigarettes.[19] One would expect that states with a stronger antismoking sentiment would be more aggressive in waging the litigation with respect to the Medicaid claims and in obtaining a larger share of the MSA. We also include a dummy variable for whether the state had a Republican governor in 1998. The regression results reported in the first column of table 4.2 indicate that the settlement share is strongly related to the medical cost share, but on less than a one-to-one basis. States with a higher cigarette excise tax fared better in terms of

---

18. Cutler et al. (2000) present estimates for the state of Massachusetts, where these calculations are consistent with sound economic principles.

19. These data are from Orzechowski and Walker (2008).

Table 4.2   **Regression estimates for settlement share and relative gain in settlement**

	Share of settlement	Relative gain in settlement[a]
Share of medical costs	0.934***	—
	(0.048)	—
Cigarette tax rate, 1998	1.472**	1.075***
	(0.619)	(0.320)
Republican governor	0.357	0.119
	(0.266)	(0.135)
Constant	–0.572	–0.259
	(0.297)	(0.151)
Adjusted R^2	0.90	0.18

Note: The dashes indicate that the share of medical costs variable was not included in the regression in the final column.

[a]Relative gain in settlement = (settlement share – share of medical costs) / (share of medical costs).

***Significant at the 1 percent level, two-tailed test.

**Significant at the 5 percent level.

the settlement share, but the political party of the governor did not have a statistically significant effect.[20]

The regression in the second column of table 4.2 reframes the issue in terms of the state's relative gain from the settlement calculated as the settlement share minus the share of medical costs divided by the medical cost share.[21] As expected based on the previous results, states with higher cigarette tax rates reaped a greater relative gain from the settlement based on what they should have received given their state-specific smoking-related medical costs. The major tobacco-producing states—North Carolina, Virginia, and Kentucky—have very low cigarette taxes, so these results are consistent with the earlier observation about the disproportionately small MSA payments to the tobacco states.

Because the details of the MSA negotiations were not made public, one can only speculate as to the source of the positive influence of state excise taxes. One prominent possibility is that the strong antitobacco states required more compensation to sign onto the agreement. A second possibility is that unlike the data in table 4.1 that reflect state differences in smoking rates, the negotiations were not based on total population size, but instead were based on actual medical expenditures reflecting state differences in smoking rates. Smoking rates are lower in states with higher excise taxes, so population-based compensation levels overcompensated the high excise tax states.

20. In exploratory regressions we examined other possible determinants of the state settlement share, such as whether the state is a major tobacco producer. However, most of these tobacco-related political factors are already reflected in the state's cigarette excise tax rate.

21. Thus, the dependent variable is the data in the third column in table 4.1 minus one.

4.2.4   Regulatory Components of the MSA

In addition to the financial structure that generates payments to the states, the MSA included additional regulatory provisions. Government regulatory agencies routinely issue regulations, including regulations affecting cigarettes, but these efforts are constrained by legislative mandates and a formal rule-making procedure. There is an opportunity for public participation and for affected interest groups to influence both the enabling legislation and to have an input into the rule-making process. Moreover, conventional regulatory mechanisms have greater flexibility in that regulations can be increased, decreased, or altered. However, as with taxes, the MSA could only increase regulatory restrictions and not decrease them.

The MSA includes several restrictions pertaining to marketing and advertising. The MSA banned the targeting of youths in advertising and cigarette marketing, which led to subsequent debate over which publications were youth-oriented and which were not.[22] Youths were no longer permitted to have access to free samples of cigarettes. In that same spirit, the MSA also banned the use of cartoons in advertising, such as the penguin that appeared in the Kool ads and Joe Camel in the Camel ads. A year before the MSA, R. J. Reynolds had voluntarily retired Joe Camel, who was the most prominent cigarette cartoon character.[23] The MSA also banned outdoor advertising, tobacco name brand merchandise, and payments for product placements in movies and television shows. The MSA imposed limits but not a ban on corporate sponsorship of events. The agreement also disbanded the two main trade associations, the Tobacco Institute and the Council for Tobacco Research, and prohibited the companies from lobbying against policies attempting to reduce youth smoking.

The various restrictions on advertising and marketing may have an effect on market concentration and on the introduction of new types of cigarettes, including those that may be less hazardous to health. We discuss these potential effects in the following.

4.3   The Levels and Allocation of the State Payments

4.3.1   Payments and Their Role in State Budgets

The MSA provides for substantial revenues for the states. In addition to a series of upfront payments ranging from $2.4 billion to $2.7 billion per year from 1998 to 2003, there are annual payments continuing into perpetuity. The annual payment amounts were $4.5 billion in 2000, $5 billion in 2001,

---

22. R. J. Reynolds in particular became embroiled in a controversy over the target age group for *Rolling Stone* magazine.

23. The role of Joe Camel with respect to youth smoking had been the subject of an FTC case that the agency dropped. Joe Camel retired just before his tenth birthday.

and \$6.5 billion in 2002 and 2003.[24] Including the four states that settled separately, the states received \$8 billion in payments in 2003 and a total of \$37.5 billion from 2000 to 2003 (McKinley, Dixon, and Devore 2003, 3).

While the proceeds from the MSA are substantial, they do not constitute a major part of states' budgets. Table 4.3 provides a breakdown by state of the MSA payments and the share these payments have of the total tax revenues for each state in 2003. For comparison, table 4.3 also presents comparable statistics for cigarette taxes. With the exception of Mississippi, the MSA payments constitute under 1 percent of the states' total revenues. Because the MSA payments are comparable to a \$0.40 per pack tax, the MSA revenues are sometimes less than the revenues from cigarette taxes.

Although the MSA provides for payments to the states that will continue indefinitely, some states obtained much of the future value of the funds by securitizing part of their share of the MSA payments. The principal impetus for these efforts is that many states faced budget deficits; cashing in on future payments might shortchange future residents but had the advantage of providing immediate political benefits. From fiscal year 2000 to 2005, total MSA-related payments to the forty-six states were \$52.6 billion, of which \$36.5 billion were annual MSA payments and \$16 billion were securitized proceeds (U.S. Government Accountability Office 2007).

Table 4.4 lists the securitized proceeds received by the states in fiscal years 2000 to 2005. The states with the largest securitized proceeds for fiscal years 2000 to 2005 are New York with \$4.2 billion, New Jersey with \$2.8 billion, California with \$2.5 billion, and Louisiana with \$1.1 billion. Some states have had multiple bond issues as they have securitized greater portions of their payments over time. Regression estimates show that the amounts securitized by the states are positively related to the state's share of the MSA payments.[25] State fiscal crises also have affected whether the state securitized (Sloan et al. 2005).

The value of the bond issues hinged on the ability of the cigarette companies to continue to make their MSA payments. Litigation that led to court awards that threatened the viability of the industry consequently reduced the value of the bonds so that the MSA led to an alignment of the interests of the cigarette industry and the states. After the \$10.2 billion verdict in the Illinois class action cigarette case, *Price v. Philip Morris Inc.*, Philip Morris was required to post a \$12 billion bond if it wished to appeal the case. Because this amount threatened the company's ability to pay its April 2003 MSA payments to the states, the value of the MSA tobacco bonds dropped by 20 percent (McKinley, Dixon, and Devore 2003, 26). Because of this threat to

---

24. These payments would continue to increase over time until reaching \$9 billion annually in 2018.

25. Specifically, a Tobit regression yields the following coefficient estimates, with standard errors reported in parentheses: Amount securitized (in \$ millions) = −1,584 (500) + 268 (73) Share of settlement + 1,236 (814) Cigarette excise tax in 1999.

Table 4.3   Cigarette tax revenue and MSA revenue in relation to state budgets in 2003

State	Total state revenues (in US $ billions)	MSA revenue (in US $ millions)	MSA percent share of state revenue	Cigarette tax revenue (in US $ millions)	Cigarette tax percent share of total state revenue
Alabama	19.10	109.22	0.57	61.16	0.32
Alaska	6.92	23.07	0.33	40.24	0.58
Arizona	17.93	99.61	0.56	216.94	1.21
Arkansas	11.81	55.96	0.47	86.74	0.73
California	195.55	862.59	0.44	1,040.62	0.53
Colorado	13.81	92.64	0.67	56.33	0.41
Connecticut	18.24	125.47	0.69	251.98	1.38
Delaware	5.04	26.73	0.53	35.22	0.70
Florida	55.21	546.50	0.99	426.55	0.77
Georgia	29.87	165.87	0.56	83.61	0.28
Hawaii	6.81	40.67	0.60	70.59	1.04
Idaho	5.49	24.55	0.45	25.06	0.46
Illinois	44.42	314.54	0.71	653.70	1.47
Indiana	24.55	137.85	0.56	343.66	1.40
Iowa	12.97	58.77	0.45	89.89	0.69
Kansas	10.40	56.34	0.54	119.41	1.15
Kentucky	18.38	119.02	0.65	21.44	0.12
Louisiana	19.44	152.42	0.78	117.93	0.61
Maine	6.80	51.99	0.76	95.97	1.41
Maryland	21.80	152.76	0.70	266.06	1.22
Massachusetts	30.37	272.96	0.90	438.74	1.44
Michigan	50.08	294.11	0.59	828.68	1.65
Minnesota	25.60	152.91	0.60	171.13	0.67
Mississippi	13.39	149.61	1.12	46.90	0.35
Missouri	22.02	153.72	0.70	105.04	0.48
Montana	4.61	28.71	0.62	16.74	0.36
Nebraska	7.29	40.21	0.55	60.86	0.83
Nevada	8.35	41.22	0.49	63.95	0.77
New Hampshire	5.21	45.00	0.86	95.76	1.84
New Jersey	46.08	261.33	0.57	612.09	1.33
New Mexico	9.85	40.30	0.41	20.56	0.21
New York	118.27	862.46	0.73	1,015.81	0.86
North Carolina	30.04	157.62	0.52	40.31	0.13
North Dakota	3.36	24.74	0.74	18.35	0.55
Ohio	49.90	340.44	0.68	548.77	1.10
Oklahoma	14.92	70.02	0.47	58.91	0.39
Oregon	19.25	77.56	0.40	224.18	1.16
Pennsylvania	49.46	388.37	0.79	887.86	1.80
Rhode Island	5.86	48.58	0.83	94 00	1.60
South Carolina	19.67	79.50	0.40	25.84	0.13
South Dakota	3.00	23.58	0.79	21.67	0.72
Tennessee	20.56	164.96	0.80	107.04	0.52
Texas	82.62	449.99	0.54	490.72	0.59
Utah	11.53	30.07	0.26	57.53	0.50
Vermont	3.64	27.79	0.76	44.39	1.22
Virginia	28.19	138.18	0.49	17.16	0.06
Washington	29.66	138.76	0.47	337.78	1.14
West Virginia	9.77	59.91	0.61	44.99	0.46
Wisconsin	25.17	140.03	0.56	298.47	1.19
Wyoming	3.40	16.78	0.49	6.85	0.20

Sources: Total revenue figures were obtained from the U.S. Census Bureau website (http://www.census.gov/govs/www/state03.html). The MSA revenues by state for 2003 were obtained from McKinley, Dixon, and Devore (2003). The cigarette tax revenues were obtained from Orzechowski and Walker (2008, table 8: Gross State Cigarette Taxes, 22).

Table 4.4   **Total amount of securitized proceeds received by states, Fiscal Years 2000–2005**

State	Total securitized proceeds (US $ millions)
Alabama	153.8
Alaska	203.0
Arkansas	58.3
California	2,485.0
Iowa	643.1
Louisiana	1,069.5
New Jersey	2,751.8
New York	4,200.0
Oregon	657.6
Rhode Island	545.9
South Carolina	785.9
South Dakota	278.0
Virginia	390.0
Washington	517.9
Wisconsin	1,275.0
Total	16,014.7

Source: U.S. Government Accountability Office (2006, table 3).

the solvency of Philip Morris, the prospects for securitization dimmed. California cancelled the sale of its bonds, and New York proceeded with its $4.2 billion sale only after pledging to make up any shortfall in the tobacco companies' payments with the state's general revenue funds (McKinley, Dixon, and Devore 2003, 18). Although the Illinois Supreme Court subsequently overturned the verdict in the *Price* case in 2006, this incident highlights the continued financial stake that the states have in the financial well-being of the cigarette industry. The MSA consequently bolstered the commonality of interests of the cigarette industry and the states, which reap the financial gains of cigarette excise taxes and settlement payments.

4.3.2   How the Payments Were Spent

Other than some modest payment amounts devoted to matters such as enforcement of the MSA, the settlement payments flowed into the states without any restrictions on their use. Thus, the allocation of MSA funds involves no interference with normal government processes for allocating revenues and does not usurp these government functions.

However, a concern does arise to the extent that the justification for the settlement amounts was to support tobacco-related expenses. The allocation of the payments by the states bore little relation to a prominent avowed objective—decreasing tobacco smoking, particularly among underage smokers. Table 4.5 summarizes the spending distribution of both the payments and the securitized proceeds. Note that these allocations are gross allocations, not net, so they may not necessarily indicate an increase in state spending in particular areas. Almost one-third of the funds were designated

Table 4.5   Amount and percentage of states' allocations of Master Settlement Agreement payments and securitized proceeds by category, Fiscal Years 2000–2005

Category	Dollars (US $ millions)	Percent
Health	16,807	30.0
Budget shortfalls	12,806	22.9
Unallocated	6,639	11.9
General purposes	3,955	7.1
Infrastructure	3,350	6.0
Education	3,078	5.5
Debt service on securitized funds	3,005	5.4
Tobacco control	1,943	3.5
Economic development for tobacco regions	1,490	2.7
Social services	961	1.7
Reserves/rainy day funds	810	1.4
Tax reductions	616	1.1
Payments to tobacco growers	521	0.9
Total	55,981	100.1

Source: U.S. Government Accountability Office (2007, table 2).

for health programs. While Medicaid is included among the targeted efforts, other funded programs included cancer prevention programs generally, drug addiction programs, the provision of adult health insurance, medical assistance for the disabled, and pharmaceutical assistance for the elderly (U.S. Government Accountability Office 2007, 8–9). As table 4.5 indicates, most of the funds were for deficit reduction, unallocated general revenues, general purposes, and other categories unrelated to smoking and health. Thus, with rare exceptions, the funds obtained from securitization were targeted to deficit reduction, economic development, education, capital projects, and other matters unrelated to smoking or health.

Many states had quite targeted allocations, as Tennessee allocated all the funds to general revenues to balance the budget, and Kentucky allocated 50 percent of the funds for economic assistance to tobacco farmers (McKinley, Dixon, and Devore 2003, 37, 59). Tobacco control efforts received only 3.5 percent of the funds, and this categorization is sufficiently broad that it overstates the amount actually targeted at antismoking efforts.[26] To the extent that funds were used for tobacco-related expenditures, these efforts are effective at reducing smoking. Gross et al. (2002) found that in 2001, the per capita level of spending targeted at tobacco control efforts was nega-

26. The relatively ambitious efforts by the state of Illinois in FY 2004 included "$1 million for the American Lung Association, $2.3 million for school-based health clinics, $5 million for grants to local health departments, $1.2 million to the Liquor Control commission for age enforcement, $0.5 million for MSA enforcement, $1 million for tobacco control research, and $5 million for tobacco-use prevention" (McKinley, Dixon, and Devore 2003, 34).

tively related to the percentage of smokers in the state and to whether the state was a tobacco-producing state.[27] Similarly, Sloan et al. (2005) found that the per capita settlement funds allocated to tobacco control followed expected patterns, with tobacco control expenditures negatively related to tobacco production and positively related to medical lobbies.

Because much of the funding has been used for nontobacco control expenses, antismoking groups have expressed dissatisfaction with how the funds have been allocated. Irrespective of state differences, the levels of expenditure for tobacco control are low. The Centers for Disease Control (CDC) established funding guidelines for tobacco-use prevention that few states have been able to meet. In 2000 the only state that met the guidelines was Mississippi, which was not part of the MSA. The states that met the guidelines in subsequent years were Hawaii, Indiana, and Maine in 2001; Maine, Massachusetts, and Mississippi in 2002; and Arkansas, Maine, and Mississippi in 2003. With the exception of Maine and Mississippi, there are no repeat players in meeting the minimum guidelines established by the CDC. The MSA funds have proven to be quite fungible, bearing little relation to the intended purpose of the funds.

One possibility is that there is no productive use for funds in fostering a reduction in smoking. While many smoking cessation interventions have failed, a new policy initiative in Massachusetts suggests that this need not always be the case. In particular, the provision of free smoking cessation assistance and drug treatment to Medicaid patients has substantially boosted the quit rates for this population.[28] While the efficacy of the initiative is still being assessed, the effect is consistent with other evidence with respect to the effect of insurance coverage on smoking status.[29]

4.4   The Effects of Advertising Restrictions

A particularly visible consequence of the MSA is that it bolstered the already stringent restrictions on the advertising and marketing of cigarettes. Table 4.6 reports the different expenditure categories from MSA year of 1998 and the most recent year for which data are available, 2005, based on data compiled by the U.S. Federal Trade Commission (2007). All data have been converted to 2005 U.S. dollars. The "Total" figures at the bottom of

27. Over the 1981 to 2000 time period that includes many years before the MSA, expenditures on tobacco control efforts have been found to reduce per capita cigarette sales. See Farrelly, Pechacek, and Chaloupka (2003). Marlow (2007) found that California's tobacco control expenditures accounted for much of the decline in that state's per capita cigarette sales since 1988.

28. Abby Goodnough, "Massachusetts Antismoking Plan Gets Attention," *New York Times,* December 17, 2009.

29. Viscusi and Hakes (2008) find that people who are not insured are less likely to quit smoking and more likely to be current smokers, controlling for smoking risk beliefs and a wide range of personal characteristics.

Table 4.6   Cigarette advertising and marketing, 1998 and 2005

Expenditure category	Expenditures (US $ thousands)	
	1998	2005
Promotional allowances and price discounts	3,449,404	10,623,755
Retail value added	1,863,606	732,536
Coupons	747,890	870,137
Newspapers	35,279	1,589
Magazines	337,038	44,777
Outdoor	353,123	9,821
Transit	48,116	0
Point-of-sale	348,352	182,193
Sampling distribution	17,297	17,211
Specialty item distribution	426,347	230,534
Public entertainment	297,786	214,227
Direct mail	69,220	51,844
Endorsements	0	0
Internet	150	2,675
Total	7,993,606	12,981,299

Source: U.S. Federal Trade Commission (2007, tables 2B and 2C).

Notes: Expenditure categories included in the total but not reported in the table are sponsorships, endorsements, and telephone. All data converted to 2005 U.S. dollars using the Consumer Price Index (CPI).

table 4.6 indicate an overall rise in advertising and marketing expenditures from 1998 to 2005. This jump in total advertising and marketing expenditures is frequently cited in the literature, in the press, and by the U.S. Congress as evidence that the MSA failed to influence advertising expenditures for cigarettes. However, advertising and marketing tallies that also include price discounts from the much higher post-MSA cigarette prices are a quite misleading measure of the temporal shifts. By far the three largest component categories in table 4.6 involve pricing effects rather than advertising, which is a reasonable marketing emphasis given the higher cigarette prices after the MSA. The largest components are promotional allowances and price discounts, which rose from $3.4 billion in 1998 to $10.6 billion in 2005. If these discounts had been at the wholesale level rather than the retail level, they would not have appeared in the advertising and marketing expenditure tally, so the fact that they are included at all in the expenditure totals is an accounting artifact. The second largest category in 2005 is coupons, which likewise represent a form of price discount. The third price-related component is the retail-value-added category. Almost all the retail-value-added component, or 99 percent in 2005, is from offers such as buy one pack, get one pack free. The remainder involves bonus items such as a T-shirt given away when the customer purchases three packs of cigarettes. Together, the three price-related marketing practices involve total expenditures in 2005 of $12.2 billion, which is 93 percent of all advertising and marketing expenditures. In contrast, in 1998 these categories accounted for 76 percent of all expenditures, as the advertising components had a larger share.

The net effects over the 1998 to 2005 period involve substantial declines in the advertising components. The three largest advertising categories in 2005 were specialty item distribution, public entertainment, and point-of-sale advertising, each of which accounted for about $200 million in expenditures. The overwhelming share of specialty items were nonbranded items such as lighters and sporting goods distributed with cigarettes. Sponsorships of events in adults-only facilities such as a bar night and sponsorships of general-audience entertainment such as fishing tournaments comprise the public entertainment category. Point-of-sale advertising consists of ads posted at the retail location, not including outdoor ads posted on the property.

Table 4.7 reports regression estimates of each expenditure category against a simple time trend variable and a 0–1 dummy variable for the post-MSA period. In most instances, data used for the regressions are available annually from 1975 to 2005 so that there are thirty-one observations per expenditure category. There are two matters of interest—whether there has been a general time trend in the spending category, and whether there has been a post-MSA shift in the level of spending.

As shown in table 4.7, promotional allowances and price discounts have been rising by $163 million annually, with an additional jump of $4.8 billion in the post-MSA period. There is no temporal trend in the retail-value-added component, but there is an increase of $1.9 billion after the MSA. The restrictions imposed by the MSA on marketing and advertising led to statistically significant post-MSA declines for outdoor advertising, transit advertising, point-of-sale displays, and specialty item distribution. For total advertising and marketing expenditures, there has been an annual temporal increase of $186 million, coupled with a post-MSA rise of $6 billion.

Along with the increase in product prices due to the MSA and subsequent state cigarette tax increases, the advertising restrictions led to a substantial shift in the marketing efforts for cigarettes. Constrained forms of marketing and advertising declined, while unconstrained forms often increased. Chief among these marketing efforts is the use of price discounts, which by their very nature are targeted to legal purchasers of cigarettes and are also responsive to the demand effects arising from the increased cost of cigarettes.

4.5   Market Structure

To the extent that the MSA restrained market competition, one might expect there to be a rise in market concentration.[30] Such an increase may

---

30. Data on market shares are drawn from the Maxwell Consumer Report, March 16, 1999, and the Maxwell Report dated March 9, 2000; March 3, 2001; February, 2002; March, 2003; February, 2004; and February, 2006. These are the year-end and fourth-quarter sales estimates for the cigarette industry in the respective preceding years. Reports include data for multiple years.

Table 4.7   Cigarette advertising and marketing regression

Expenditure category	Time trend	Post-MSA
Promotional allowances and price discounts	163,125***	4,765,772***
	(50,743)	(1,085,489)
Retail value added	13,604	1,875,498***
	(27,432)	(586,820)
Coupons	13,909***	438,279***
	(4,826)	(103,242)
Newspapers	−31,435***	223,472***
	(3,224)	(68,958)
Magazines	−16,509***	−65,246
	(3,434)	(73,452)
Outdoor	−2,404	−386,441***
	(2,435)	(52,094)
Transit	−490	−49,212***
	(434)	(9,275)
Point-of-sale	12,286***	−226,607***
	(2,594)	(55,497)
Sampling distribution	−7,305***	12,091
	(1,732)	(37,049)
Specialty item distribution	30,778***	−579,662***
	(5,134)	(109,829)
Public entertainment	7,496***	25,477
	(1,598)	(34,182)
Direct mail	3,126	1,691
	(2,333)	(49,899)
Internet	15.4	1,284***
	(12.3)	(264)
Total	186,199***	6,036,261***
	(30,141)	(644,773)

Source: Data used for the regressions are from the U.S. Federal Trade Commission (2007, tables 2B and 2C).

Notes: A constant is included in the regressions but is not reported. Expenditure categories included in the total but not reported in the table are sponsorship, endorsements, and telephone. All data converted to 2005 U.S. dollars using the CPI.

***Significant at the 1 percent level, two-tailed test.

boost price-cost margins and diminish the consumer surplus received by purchasers of cigarettes. An alternative hypothesis is that market concentration will not be affected, but that advertising limitations will freeze market shares. That there might be anticompetitive effects of the advertising restrictions is a concern that was raised after the fact by some economists, though it was not a prominent part of the policy debate.[31] It is noteworthy

31. Discussion of the possible anticompetitive effects appears in Viscusi (2002a) and in the Expert Report of Joseph E. Stiglitz (2005) in *Schwab et al. v. Philip Morris,* Civil Action No. 04-1945. U.S. District Court, Eastern District of New York.

that a classic textbook case of where industry collusion would be desirable is with respect to advertising expenditures, which tend to have a prisoners' dilemma type of structure (Viscusi, Harrington, and Vernon 2005, 102). While industry collusion to restrict advertising is illegal, collusion can be accomplished legally through a mechanism such as the MSA, in which the restrictions are instituted under the guise of decreasing smoking rather than reducing advertising costs to the industry. Whether the MSA was in fact a form of collusion is less important than whether it led to the anticompetitive effects associated with collusion.

The data reported in table 4.8 suggest that the most extreme fears of the effects of the advertising restrictions were not realized, although market shares of some firms shifted in the post-MSA period. Table 4.8 summarizes the market shares for the major tobacco companies from 1997 through 2005. Philip Morris, the clear market leader, had a 48 to 51 percent market share throughout the period and a 49 percent share both in 1998 and 2005. Lorillard likewise maintained a 9 to 10 percent share throughout this period, and Liggett remained an insignificant player in the market in the 1 to 3 percent range.

R. J. Reynolds experienced a modest decline in market share from 24 percent in 1998 to 22 percent in 2005. The company with which it merged, Brown & Williamson, dropped from a 15 percent market share in 1998 to 11 percent in 2003, but the spinoff of Brown & Williamson's discount brands complicates assessments of the effect of the MSA on market competition. The two growth categories were the "Others" grouping of generic cigarettes and Commonwealth Brands, which marketed six discount brands that it purchased from Brown & Williamson.[32]

The effects of the MSA on market concentration are modest. The bottom row of table 4.8 reports the Herfindahl Hirschman Index (HHI) values based on the cigarette industry categories shown in the table.[33] While the HHI values are relatively high, which would certainly be expected given that a single firm accounts for half the market, there is no evidence of an anticompetitive increase in concentration based on the change in the HHI. The HHI index in 1998 is 3327, which is a bit larger than the 2003 premerger value of 3222. After the R. J. Reynolds-Brown & Williamson merger, the HHI index rose modestly to 3271 and continued to increase to 3336 in 2005.

An instructive reference point is to ask what the pattern of HHI index values would have been if R. J. Reynolds and Brown & Williamson were treated as a single entity throughout the 1997 to 2005 period. If that industry structure had prevailed, the HHI index would have exhibited a decline from

32. The brands were Tuscany, which Commonwealth Brands calls its "premium" brand, and the generic brands USA Gold, Montclair, Malibu, Sonoma, and Riviera.

33. The HHI index is defined as follows. Letting s_i represent the fraction of industry sales by firm i, then HHI $= (100s_1)^2 + (100s_2)^2 + \ldots + (100s_n)^2$, where there are n firms in the industry. For purposes of our calculations, we treat sales by "Others" as being sales by a single firm.

Table 4.8 Year-end market shares and HHI

	1997	1998	1999	2000	2001	2002	2003	2004	2005
Philip Morris	0.487	0.494	0.496	0.505	0.510	0.490	0.504	0.475	0.487
R. J. Reynolds	0.242	0.240	0.230	0.230	0.223	0.231	0.215	0.288	0.282
Brown & Williamson	0.160	0.150	0.134	0.117	0.109	0.112	0.105	.	.
Lorillard	0.087	0.091	0.104	0.096	0.093	0.091	0.093	0.088	0.092
Commonwealth Brands	.	.	0.011	0.018	0.022	0.030	0.031	0.029	0.035
Liggett	0.013	0.013	0.012	0.015	0.022	0.024	0.026	0.023	0.022
Others	0.010	0.012	0.023	0.019	0.021	0.023	0.025	0.097	0.382
HHI Index	3291.71	3327.30	3284.82	3317.40	3317.68	3162.91	3221.77	3270.92	3335.90

Notes: The data on year-end market shares are obtained from the Maxwell Consumer Reports issued in March 1999, March 2000, March 2001, February 2002, March 2003, February 2004, and February 2006. The year-end market shares are reported in each Maxwell Consumer Report under the table entitled "Company Volume and Market Share." The dots indicate that Brown & Williamson no longer existed in 2004 and 2005, as it had merged with R. J. Reynolds.

4066 in 1997 to 3336 in 2005, indicating a substantial decrease in market concentration.

An additional aspect of market competition is the extent to which there are incentives to introduce new products such as safer cigarettes. Reduced yield cigarettes such as Eclipse have not made major inroads in the market. Consumers have continued to shift into the "light" cigarette segment, but the very low tar yield cigarette share has declined. From 1998 to 2005 the market share of cigarettes with 12 mg or less of tar rose from 56.8 percent to 58.4 percent, but there were declines from 22.9 percent to 18.7 percent for the 9 mg or less category, from 13.2 percent to 11.5 percent for the 6 mg or less category, and from 1.6 percent to 0.6 percent for the 3 mg or less category (U.S. Federal Trade Commission 2007, table 4A). Increases in cigarette prices coupled with the rise of higher tar generic brands contributed to these trends.

4.6   Legal Fees and Subsequent Litigation

The MSA had four principal ramifications for subsequent litigation against the cigarette industry. First, because the attorneys representing the states received billions of dollars in payments associated with the settlement, the financial resources of the plaintiffs' bar were enhanced, thus providing potential financial backing for additional litigation. Second, the tobacco industry's payment of a record-breaking amount of $250 billion to settle lawsuits launched by the states garnered substantial publicity and may have signaled to jurors that the companies were guilty of record-breaking wrongful conduct. Third, the settlement of the lawsuits in the billions gave jurors a new anchor value for damages in the billions rather than the millions.[34] Fourth, the Minnesota settlement provided for the public disclosure of the tobacco industry documents obtained during the discovery process, reducing litigation costs in future lawsuits. Thus, the settlement was not neutral in terms of its ramifications for other types of cigarette cases.

The states contracted out the tobacco cases on a contingency fee basis. Because these deals were not put out for open competitive bids and received little or no oversight, there is a strong possibility that the process was used to reward political allies with excessively lucrative arrangements that were not in the public interest. The attorneys representing Mississippi received 35 percent of the state's settlement amount as their fee, equal to $1.43 billion.[35] The attorney fee share of the Florida settlement amount was 26 percent, leading to a payout of $3.43 billion. The attorneys representing Texas in the litigation received 19 percent of the settlement amount, or $3.3 billion. At

---

34. Some observers have hypothesized that the subsequent large verdicts against other companies, such as GM, were also influenced by the anchoring effect of the MSA.

35. The state-specific figures discussed here are from Viscusi (2002a, 51). References are provided therein.

the low end, attorney fees were $111 million for the state of Missouri and $265 million for Ohio. Although no comprehensive tally of the amount of the fees is available, the U.S. Chamber of Commerce's partial tally in 2001 identified $11 billion in fees that had been received by attorneys.[36]

As part of the settlement with the state of Minnesota, the tobacco industry documents obtained during the course of the litigation were posted online and made available for future private suits and class actions against the industry (see www.tobaccodocuments.org). This measure consequently reduced the litigation costs that plaintiffs in future cases would have to bear by making the results of the discovery process in this case a public good.

Until the MSA the tobacco industry had a record of never having paid out an individual smoker liability claim. After the MSA the companies did not fare as well. In individual cases and class actions resolved after the MSA, cigarette companies were not only found to be liable for compensatory damages but also were found liable for punitive damages. Such awards greatly altered the legal landscape because awards of punitive damages require an assessment that the defendant's conduct displayed a reckless and callous disregard for the victim's safety.

Table 4.9 summarizes the results of the five largest punitive damages verdicts against the industry. Three of the cases were individual smoker cases but nevertheless involved enormous verdicts, chiefly in the punitive damages component. The punitive damages award is $150 million in *Schwarz v. Philip Morris Inc.*, $3 billion in *Boeken v. Philip Morris Inc.*, and $28 billion in *Bullock v. Philip Morris Inc.* The Florida cigarette class action *Engle v. R. J. Reynolds* had punitive damages of $145 billion, while the Illinois "light" cigarettes class action *Price v. Philip Morris* had punitive damages of $3.1 billion and compensatory damages of $7.1 billion.[37] The *Price* case verdict had broad ramifications with respect to the market for securitizing the MSA payments, as it threatened the solvency of Philip Morris and its continued participation in the MSA payment system. While these decisions were all appealed, the litigation landscape of the cigarette industry had undergone a dramatic shift. Rather than putting an end to litigation against the industry, the MSA increased it.[38] The protections against punitive damages and class actions that were part of the draft Proposed Resolution were not included in the MSA but would have proven to be valuable to the industry.

---

36. U.S. Chamber of Commerce, "Chamber Targets Excessive Legal Fees: Files 21 FOIA Requests on Tobacco Settlements," March 14, 2001.

37. Although the *Engle* class action verdict was overturned, the findings in the case regarding the addictive properties of cigarettes and wrongful conduct can be used in the thousands of individual *Engle* progeny cases that may follow. To date, plaintiffs in the few *Engle* progeny cases that have had some successes in these individual cases.

38. Sloan, Trogdon, and Mathews (2005) used daily stock market return data to estimate the effect on stock prices and the cost of equity capital. Unfavorable information reduced tobacco company returns.

Table 4.9   **Largest cigarette punitive damages verdicts**

| | Award (US $ millions) | | | |
Case name	Compensatory damages	Punitive damages	Total	Current status
Boeken v. Philip Morris Inc. (2001)	5.54	3,000.0	3,005.54	Punitive damages reduced to $50 million on appeal.[a]
Bullock v. Philip Morris Inc. (2002)	0.65	28,000.0	28,000.65	New trial ordered on the issue of punitive damages,[b] led to $13.8 million punitive damages award.[c]
Engle v. R. J. Reynolds Tobacco Co. (2000)	12.70	145,000.0	145,012.70	Reversed; the class was decertified and individual claims are being filed.
Price v. Philip Morris Inc. (2003)	7,100.00	3,100.0	10,200.00	Reversed by Illinois Supreme Court.
Schwarz v. Philip Morris Inc. (2002)	0.17	150.0	150.17	Punitive damages vacated and remanded for a new trial; compensatory damages upheld.

[a]Source: *Boeken v. Philip Morris Inc.*, 127 Cal. App. 4th 1640 (2005).
[b]Source: *Bullock v. Philip Morris USA, Inc.*, 159 Cal. App. 4th 655 (2008).
[c]Source: "Jury Awards $13.8 Million in Cigarette Suit," *New York Times*, August 24, 2009.

4.7 Policy Ramifications

4.7.1 Tax Policy Changes

The MSA also marked a pronounced shift in the treatment of the tobacco industry with respect to taxes and regulations. Although the MSA imposed a tax equivalent fee that generated revenues for the states, states also imposed substantial additional excise taxes. Table 4.10 summarizes the excise tax trends from 1998 to 2008.[39] Only five states did not boost the excise tax amounts over that decade. The absolute tax increase per pack is shown in the second to last column of table 4.10, and the percentage tax increase is shown in the final column. New York has been a leader in terms of the magnitude of the tax increase, as it raised excise taxes by $2.19 per pack, or 391 percent. Altogether there were twenty states that boosted the cigarette tax by $1.00 or more in addition to the MSA payments.

Raising cigarette taxes and cigarette prices will have the expected economic effects on demand. Price elasticity of demand estimates for cigarettes range from –0.4 to –0.7.[40] The average price per pack before the enactment

39. Trogdon and Sloan (2006) estimate that post-MSA cigarette taxes in 2002 were $0.10 higher.
40. Viscusi (1992) reviews dozens of cigarette demand studies, and Hersch (2000) provides recent demand elasticity estimates.

Table 4.10 **State cigarette tax changes, 1998–2008**

State	State cigarette tax, 1998 (US $ per pack)	State cigarette tax, 2008 (US $ per pack)	State tax increase, 1998–2008 (US $ per pack)	Percentage tax increase, 1998–2008
Alabama	0.165	0.425	0.260	157.6
Alaska	1.000	2.000	1.000	100.0
Arizona	0.580	2.000	1.420	244.8
Arkansas	0.315	0.590	0.275	87.3
California	0.370	0.870	0.500	135.1
Colorado	0.200	0.840	0.640	320.0
Connecticut	0.500	2.000	1.500	300.0
Delaware	0.240	1.150	0.910	379.2
District of Columbia	0.650	1.000	0.350	53.8
Florida	0.339	0.339	0	0
Georgia	0.120	0.370	0.250	208.3
Hawaii	0.800	1.800	1.000	125.0
Idaho	0.280	0.570	0.290	103.6
Illinois	0.580	0.980	0.400	69.0
Indiana	0.155	0.995	0.840	541.9
Iowa	0.360	1.360	1.000	277.8
Kansas	0.240	0.790	0.550	229.2
Kentucky	0.030	0.300	0.270	900.0
Louisiana	0.200	0.360	0.160	80.0
Maine	0.740	2.000	1.260	170.3
Maryland	0.360	2.000	1.640	455.6
Massachusetts	0.760	1.510	0.750	98.7
Michigan	0.750	2.000	1.250	166.7
Minnesota	0.480	1.493	1.013	211.0
Mississippi	0.180	0.180	0	0
Missouri	0.170	0.170	0	0
Montana	0.180	1.700	1.520	844.4
Nebraska	0.340	0.640	0.300	88.2
Nevada	0.350	0.800	0.450	128.6
New Hampshire	0.370	1.080	0.710	191.9
New Jersey	0.800	2.575	1.775	221.9
New Mexico	0.210	0.910	0.700	333.3
New York	0.560	2.750	2.190	391.1
North Carolina	0.050	0.350	0.300	600.0
North Dakota	0.440	0.440	0	0
Ohio	0.240	1.250	1.010	420.8
Oklahoma	0.230	1.030	0.800	347.8
Oregon	0.680	1.180	0.500	73.5
Pennsylvania	0.310	1.350	1.040	335.5
Rhode Island	0.710	2.460	1.750	246.5
South Carolina	0.070	0.070	0	0
South Dakota	0.330	1.530	1.200	363.6
Tennessee	0.130	0.620	0.490	376.9
Texas	0.410	1.410	1.000	243.9
Utah	0.515	0.695	0.180	35.0
Vermont	0.440	1.790	1.350	306.8
Virginia	0.025	0.300	0.275	1,100.0
Washington	0.825	2.025	1.200	145.5
West Virginia	0.170	0.550	0.380	223.5
Wisconsin	0.590	1.770	1.180	200.0
Wyoming	0.120	0.600	0.480	400.0

Source: Orzechowski and Walker (2008, 275–326).

of the MSA was $2.175 (Orzechowski and Walker 2001, 136). At that time the total state and federal excise tax amount averaged $0.63 per pack so that the MSA payments raised the tax equivalent penalty to about a dollar per pack. The MSA per pack cost raised cigarette prices by 18.4 percent, implying a 7 to 13 percent decrease in sales based on available demand elasticity estimates.

This range of effects is consistent with the overall estimated effect of the MSA, which includes the effect on prices and regulatory restrictions. Sloan and Trogdon (2004) found that the MSA reduced smoking rates by 13 percent for the age eighteen to twenty group and by 5 percent for older age groups.

The structure of cigarette taxes has also affected the mix of cigarette sales. The U.S. cigarette taxes are on a per pack basis rather than proportional to the product price. The higher cigarette taxes and MSA tax equivalents consequently have narrowed the relative price gap between premium cigarettes and lower end cigarettes, which has been to the advantage of producers of premium cigarettes.[41] To the extent that cigarettes taxes have a health-related objective, the per pack tax approach is appropriate as there is no evidence indicating that the health risks of premium cigarettes are greater. Indeed, the opposite may be the case, as many generic cigarettes have higher tar and nicotine ratings.

The MSA appears to have stimulated tax increases, but the increases were not uniform. The variability of taxes across jurisdictions creates potential problems of border effects. Consumers and possibly resellers of cigarettes may travel to purchase cigarettes if the price gap is sufficiently large. A noteworthy instance of such variability is that created by the combined New York State and New York City tax of $4.25 per pack. In addition to creating a price gap with respect to neighboring states, there is a price gap compared to cigarettes sold on Indian reservations, which by law are independent sovereign nations not subject to these taxes. Because of the increased attractiveness of such cigarettes to smokers in New York City, the City of New York sought an injunction in 2009 to prevent the sale of cigarettes by the Unkechauge Indian Nation.[42]

4.7.2   The Family Smoking Prevention and Tobacco Control Act

In many respects, the enactment of the 2009 Family Smoking Prevention and Tobacco Control Act marked the culmination of the tax and regulatory effort that began with the attempt to settle the state lawsuits against the industry. Various drafts of the Proposed Resolution would have provided legal protections for the industry against major stakes lawsuits such as class

---

41. "Tobacco Lights Up on Premium Blend," *Wall Street Journal,* July 27, 2009, C10.
42. See *City of New York v. Golden Feather et al.:* U.S. District Court for the Eastern District of New York.

actions and claims involving punitive damages. While this 1997 proposal included tax components, it also included detailed regulatory provisions. Among these provisions was a grant of authority to the FDA to regulate cigarettes. The proposal also sought to bolster the on-product warnings requirements for cigarettes and to impose advertising restrictions, including bans on descriptors such as "low tar" and "light" unless the cigarette could be shown to be safer for health. While the MSA included some advertising restrictions and a tax equivalent fee, these other components of the Proposed Resolution were not part of the MSA. An agreement with the states could not, for example, grant FDA authority to regulate cigarettes.

The combination of the MSA and the Family Smoking Prevention and Tobacco Control Act achieved the antismoking objectives of the Proposed Resolution. The 2009 law introduced a major increase in the degree of regulation of the cigarette industry. With the support of user fees that are expected to raise the price of cigarettes by about $0.06 per pack, the Food and Drug Administration will be regulating the labeling and content of cigarettes. Companies are not permitted to use artificial flavors such as cloves, though menthol is still permitted. Companies must submit the cigarette ingredients and nicotine information to the FDA for approval. The Act also imposes new labeling requirements so that the current series of four rotating warnings will be replaced by nine rotating warnings that must comprise 50 percent of the front and rear panels of the pack. The act also bans the use of descriptors such as "light" and "mild."

From the standpoint of efficient market operation, the FDA should foster a diversity of market choices with varying level risks, including lower risk cigarettes, coupled with information that enables consumers to have accurate assessments of the product risks. Whether the FDA regulatory regime will encourage or discourage the introduction of lower risk cigarettes is yet to be determined.[43]

One component of the Act that has already faced a legal challenge is the series of restrictions on advertising.[44] The increased limitations on advertising may violate the First Amendment protections afforded to commercial speech. A prominent rationale given in the Act for the restrictions on advertising was the Federal Trade Commission (FTC) figure of $13 billion

---

43. The FDA Commissioner Margaret Hamburg made the following comments regarding the focus of the new FDA Center for Tobacco Products: "We need to study the composition of tobacco products and understand both the addictive components of tobacco and the toxic chemical additives. We need to address how these substances are impacting health and ensure that there are not additional innovations by the tobacco industry that will put new products in the market that may be more addictive or more attractive to youth." "Margaret Hamburg Aims to Strengthen FDA Science," *Science*, vol. 325, August 14, 2009, 802.

44. The motion for a preliminary injunction challenging provisions of the act was filed on August 31, 2009, in *Commonwealth Brands, Inc. et al. v. United States of America et al.*, U.S. District Court for the Western District of Kentucky, Bowling Green Division, Case No. 1:2009cv00117.

in cigarette advertising and marketing in 2005. However, as shown earlier, most of these costs took the form of promotional discounts and price allowances. Additional advertising and marketing restrictions may impede new entrants and the introduction of new products. The 2010 decision by Judge Joseph H. McKinley Jr. ruled that some provisions of the Act, such as those prohibiting the use of color in packaging and marketing materials, were unconstitutional infringements on commercial speech, but other provisions, such as those pertaining to the introduction of more graphic warnings, were upheld.[45]

4.8 Conclusion

The state lawsuits against the cigarette industry introduced a wide range of novel legal and policy issues. If the states had prevailed, it would have been the first time that states were able to be reimbursed for financial externalities attributable to wrongful conduct that influenced consumption decisions. Although no cases were tried to verdict, the MSA represented the largest civil case damages payment in U.S. history. However, the settlement also took an unprecedented form, as it did not involve a lump sum payment or a structured settlement. Rather, it took the form of a cigarette excise tax and regulatory restrictions, all of which were negotiated privately by representatives of industry and state attorneys general. The MSA also established a commonality of financial interests of the cigarette industry and the states that may influence prospective tobacco policies.

The MSA served as a negotiated combination of tax equivalents and regulation that emerged from an out-of-court settlement that completely bypassed all traditional governmental inputs. Taxes are not the province of attorney general discretion but require the approval of state legislatures or the U.S. Congress and must also be signed into law. The enactment of new regulations likewise requires an enabling legislative mandate and involves a detailed governmental and public review process. For major regulations such as this, there must be a regulatory impact analysis, an opportunity for public comment, and internal administration review to ensure that the regulation is consistent with legislative requirements and societal interests. All of these checks on taxes and regulations were bypassed by the MSA.

Bargains in which the key parties are the attorneys general and the cigarette industry may not be reflective of the kinds of taxes and regulations that would emerge if the process had been more inclusive and open to public input. Chief among the possible economic efficiency effects is that the MSA might have anticompetitive effects by imposing per pack financial penalties

---

45. *Commonwealth Brands, Inc. et al. v. United States of America et al.,* U.S. District Court for the Western District of Kentucky, Bowling Green Division, No. 1:09-CV-118-M, January 5, 2010. The decision is likely to be appealed.

on new entrants that were not party to the litigation and by imposing limits on advertising and marketing, which would impede entry and the introduction of new products. Thus far, however, there is no firm evidence of significant adverse anticompetitive effects. Market shares have remained quite stable, as the MSA may have locked in market shares. Any anticompetitive effects will be more evident over time.

The other major critique of the MSA has been with respect to the allocation of the funds, as much less has gone to health care and antitobacco efforts than was anticipated. As with tax revenues generally, states have treated these funds as fungible, so there has not been the substantial increase in the allocation of funds to health and tobacco use prevention programs that many expected to result from the MSA. Whether such a targeting of funds should have been the appropriate policy objective is a different matter that involves comparison of the efficacy of such expenditures with other uses of the resources. Even though the states reaped the funds windfall because of the tobacco litigation, the allocation that best advances the interests of the citizenry may not be closely tied to antitobacco initiatives.

References

Bulow, J., and P. Klemperer. 1998. The tobacco deal. *Brookings Papers on Economic Activity 1998:* 323–94.

Cutler, D. M., A. M. Epstein, R. G. Frank, R. Hartman, C. King, III, J. P. Newhouse, M. B. Rosenthal, and E. R. Vigdor. 2000. How good a deal was the tobacco settlement?: Assessing payments to Massachusetts. *Journal of Risk and Uncertainty* 21 (2/3): 235–61.

Cutler, D. M., J. Gruber, R. S. Hartman, M. B. Landrum, J. P. Newhouse, and M. B. Rosenthal. 2002. The economic impacts of the tobacco settlement. *Journal of Policy Analysis and Management* 21 (1): 1–19.

Farrelly, M. C., T. F. Pechacek, and F. J. Chaloupka. 2003. The impact of tobacco control program expenditures on aggregate cigarettes sales: 1981–2000. *Journal of Health Economics* 22 (5): 843–59.

Gross, C. P., B. Soffer, P. B. Bach, R. Rajkumar, and H. P. Forman. 2002. State expenditures for tobacco-control programs and the tobacco settlement. *New England Journal of Medicine* 347 (14): 1080–6.

Hersch, J. 2000. Gender, income levels, and the demand for cigarettes. *Journal of Risk and Uncertainty* 21 (2/3): 263–82.

Hersch, J., A. Del Rossi, and W. K. Viscusi. 2004. Voter preferences and state regulation of smoking. *Economic Inquiry* 42 (3): 455–68.

Lillard, D. R., and A. Sfekas. 2009. Just passing through: The effects of cigarette taxes and the Master Settlement Agreement on cigarette prices. Cornell University. Working Paper.

Marlow, M. L. 2007. Do tobacco-control programs lower tobacco consumption?: Evidence from California. *Public Finance Review* 35 (6): 689–709.

McKinley, A., L. Dixon, and A. Devore. 2003. *State management and allocation of tobacco settlement revenue 2003.* Denver: National Conference of State Legislatures.

Orzechowski, W., and R. C. Walker. 2001. *The tax burden on tobacco: Historical compilation 2001,* vol. 36. Arlington, VA: Orzechowski and Walker.

————. (2008). *The tax burden on tobacco: Historical compilation 2008,* vol. 43. Arlington, VA: Orzechowski and Walker.

Sloan, F. A., E. S. Carlisle, J. R. Rattliff, and J. G. Trogdon. 2005. Determinants of states' allocations of the Master Settlement Agreement payments. *Journal of Health Politics, Policy, and Law* 30 (4): 643–86.

Sloan, F. A., and J. G. Trogdon. 2004. The impact of the Master Settlement Agreement on cigarette consumption. *Journal of Policy Analysis and Management* 23 (4): 843–55.

Sloan, F. A., J. G. Trogdon, and C. A. Mathews. 2005. Litigation and the value of tobacco companies. *Journal of Health Economics* 24 (3): 427–47.

Stiglitz, J. E. 2005. Expert report in *Schwab et al. v. Philip Morris,* Civil Action No. 04-1945. U.S. District Court, Eastern District of New York.

Trogdon, J. G., and F. A. Sloan. 2006. Cigarette taxes and the Master Settlement Agreement. *Economic Inquiry* 44 (4): 729–39.

U.S. Federal Trade Commission. 2007. *Federal Trade Commission cigarette report for 2004 and 2005.* Washington, DC: U.S. Federal Trade Commission.

U.S. Government Accountability Office. 2006. *Tobacco settlement: States' allocations of Fiscal Year 2005 and expected Fiscal Year 2006 payments,* GAO-06-502. Washington, DC: Government Accountability Office.

U.S. Government Accountability Office. 2007. *Tobacco settlement: States' allocations of payments from tobacco companies for Fiscal Year 2000 through 2005,* GAO-07-534T. Washington, DC: Government Accountability Office.

Viscusi, W. K. 1992. *Smoking: Making the risky decision.* New York: Oxford University Press.

————. 1995. Cigarette taxation and the social consequences of smoking. In *Tax policy and the economy,* vol. 9, ed. J. Poterba. 51–101. Cambridge, MA: National Bureau of Economic Research.

————. 1999. The governmental composition of the insurance costs of smoking. *Journal of Law and Economics* 42 (2): 575–609.

————. 2002a. *Smoke-filled rooms: A postmortem on the tobacco deal.* Chicago: University of Chicago Press.

————. 2002b. Tobacco: Regulation and taxation through litigation. In *Regulation through litigation,* ed. W. K. Viscusi, 22–52. Washington, DC: American Enterprise Institute–Brookings Institution.

Viscusi, W. K., and J. K. Hakes. 2008. Risk beliefs and smoking behavior. *Economic Inquiry* 46 (1): 45–59.

Viscusi, W. K., J. E. Harrington, Jr., and J. Vernon, eds. 2005. *Economics of regulation and antitrust,* 4th ed. Cambridge, MA: MIT Press.

Viscusi, W. K., and J. Hersch. 2008. The mortality cost to smokers. *Journal of Health Economics* 27 (4): 943–58.

Wagner, R. E. 1999. Understanding the tobacco settlement: The state as partisan plaintiff. *Regulation* 22 (4): 38–41.

5

Gun Control after *Heller*
Litigating against Regulation

Philip J. Cook, Jens Ludwig, and Adam Samaha

A well regulated Militia, being necessary to the security of a
free State, the right of the people to keep and bear Arms, shall
not be infringed.
—Second Amendment to the U.S. Constitution

And whatever else [the Amendment] leaves to future evaluation, it surely elevates above all other interests the right of law-
abiding, responsible citizens to use arms in defense of hearth
and home.
—District of Columbia v. Heller, 2008

5.1 Introduction

The economic justification for regulating firearms design, ownership,
or use is the existence of negative externalities. For many individuals, the
freedom to "keep and bear arms" brings private benefit in the form of the
enjoyment of the sporting uses of guns, as well as a heightened sense of

Philip J. Cook is Senior Associate Dean for Faculty and Research and ITT/Terry Sanford
Professor of Public Policy at Sanford School of Public Policy, Duke University, and a research
associate and co-director of the working group on the Economics of Crime at the National
Bureau of Economic Research. Jens Ludwig is the McCormick Foundation Professor of Social
Service Administration, Law, and Public Policy at the University of Chicago, a Non-resident
Senior Fellow in Economic Studies at the Brookings Institution, and a research associate and
co-director of the working group on the Economics of Crime at the National Bureau of Eco-
nomic Research. Adam Samaha is professor of law and Herbert and Marjorie Fried Teaching
Scholar at the University of Chicago.

This chapter was prepared for the September, 2009 NBER conference on Regulation and
Litigation, organized by Daniel Kessler. The research reported on here was supported in part
by a grant from the Joyce Foundation. Any errors and all opinions are of course our own.

security against intruders and other assailants; there may also be a public benefit if criminals are deterred by the risk that a victim will defend himself with lethal force. However, the widespread private ownership of guns comes at the price of increased availability of guns for criminal use, with a resulting intensification of criminal violence. The resulting increase in criminal homicide, including both routine and rampage shootings, lends support to the regulation of firearms commerce and use.

The effort to protect the public against gun violence is of course not limited to gun regulation. The misuse of guns is subject to criminal and civil sanctions, and the threat of these sanctions has some deterrent value. However, these sanctions have limited effectiveness and are costly to administer. Gun offenders typically have few assets and are hence judgment proof. The deterrent effect of criminal sanctions is muted by the limited capacity of the criminal justice system to deliver on its promises, and the youth, impulsivity, or intoxication of would-be offenders (Cook and Leitzel 1996). For these reasons there is a logical case for regulations designed to preempt criminal use (by reducing access by youths and criminals), to facilitate law enforcement efforts (by requiring record-keeping that facilitates investigation into shootings), to limit the likelihood of accidental misfires (through design regulations), and achieve other public purposes.[1]

The balance between benefit and cost differs widely across states, and in fact federal firearm regulations explicitly allow for and support such heterogeneity: the Gun Control Act of 1968 establishes a minimum standard for firearm regulation, and provides a framework to insulate the states from each other, so that it is feasible for some to choose a higher standard than the federal minimum. It is also true that much of the differentiation in the cost-benefit balance occurs *within* states, where residents of large cities tend to suffer relatively high rates of violent crime and have little interest in gun sports, while the reverse is true in rural areas and small towns. As a result, some of the most extreme regulations have been adopted by cities rather than states. Approximately forty states, out of concern for just that outcome of the local political process, have adopted preemption laws that reserve at least some gun regulation for the state legislature.

In the 1990s this regulatory system was challenged in court by a number of cities where gun crime was imposing great costs. Frustrated by their inability to change gun regulations through the legislative process, they initiated mass tort actions that were intended to impose higher standards through the "end around" of expanded liability. The theories in these suits asserted unsafe and hence defective design, or that the industry was creating a public nuisance through failure to police the supply chain by which guns were marketed (and often found their way into dangerous hands). As it turned out, this effort never got much traction in the courts and has been almost entirely unsuccessful. As the *coup de grace,* Congress enacted legislation in 2005 that

---

1. For a general treatment of the case for ex ante regulation see Shavell (1984, 2004).

provides immunity to the firearms industry in both state and federal courts for damages resulting from criminal misuse of guns (the Protection of Lawful Commerce in Arms Act).

The American system of firearm regulation is again threatened by litigation, but now the threat comes from the opposite direction. In June 2008 the U.S. Supreme Court struck down the District of Columbia's handgun ban (*D.C. v. Heller,* 118 S.Ct. 2783), recognizing for the first time an individual constitutional right to own a gun. While the immediate effect of this opinion is only to invalidate an unusually stringent regulation in a city that is also an enclave of the federal government, the domain of this new right has not yet been clearly defined. It will be subject to numerous tests in litigation during the years to come. Existing regulations governing firearms commerce and possession will be challenged by affected parties claiming they violate the new right that the majority of the Supreme Court has discovered in the Second Amendment. Litigation will seek to curtail, rather than extend, restrictions on the gun commerce, but this new scenario is once again an end-around the political process.

The "core right" established by the *Heller* decision is the right to keep an operable handgun in the home for self-defense purposes. If the Supreme Court extends this right to cover state and local jurisdictions through the Fourteenth Amendment, the result of this new litigation against regulation is likely to include the elimination of the most stringent existing regulations— such as Chicago's handgun ban—and could also possibly ban regulations that place substantial restrictions or costs on handgun ownership.

Our analysis is necessarily speculative, but we find evidence in support of four conclusions:

- The effect of *Heller* may be to increase the prevalence of handgun ownership in jurisdictions that currently have restrictive laws.
- Given the best evidence on the consequences of increased prevalence of gun ownership, we predict that these jurisdictions will experience a greater burden of crime due to more lethal violence and an increased burglary rate.
- Nonetheless, a regime with greater scope for gun rights is not necessarily inferior—whether the restrictive regulations in places like Chicago, California, Massachusetts, and New York City would pass a cost benefit test may depend on whether we accept the *Heller* viewpoint that there is a legal entitlement to possess a handgun. We develop this view by use of the Coase theorem applied to the subjective value of gun rights.
- In any event, the core right defined by *Heller* appears to leave room for some regulation that would reduce the negative externalities of gun ownership.

The remainder of the chapter is organized as follows. In the next section we characterize private gun ownership and uses, together with the existing system of firearm regulations in the United States. Section 5.3 discusses the initial wave of tort litigation against the gun industry that arose during the 1990s, while section 5.4 discusses the recent *Heller* decision and what it may, or may not, imply for existing firearm regulations at the federal, state, and local levels. Section 5.5 reviews what is at stake in the litigation against regulation, and provides an analysis from the welfare-economics perspective given alternative entitlements. Section 5.6 concludes.

5.2   Guns, Gun Violence, and Gun Regulation in America

Litigation in this area is motivated by concerns that existing regulations either go too far or do not go far enough.[2] Assessing these claims requires some understanding of the existing regulatory system. In what follows we first review what is known about guns and gun violence in America as a backdrop to discussing existing gun regulations.

5.2.1   Gun Ownership and Transactions

America has 200 to 300 million firearms in private circulation.[3] While there are enough guns for every adult to have one, in fact, gun ownership is concentrated in a minority of households. Survey data suggests that about 40 percent of males, 10 percent of females, and one-third of all households have one or more guns. Most people who own one gun own many. The most detailed national survey on the subject (the National Firearms Survey) found that gun-owning households average 5.2 guns in 2004, up substantially from the 1970s (Hepburn et al. 2007). The alternative to survey data are the administrative data on manufacturing and net imports, but these provide no guidance as to the rate of disposal of existing guns through breakage, confiscation, and off-the-books imports and exports.

One addition for many gun-owning households has been a handgun.

2. This section draws in part on material from Cook and Ludwig (2006).

3. This number can be estimated through two sources of data, from federal tax records on sales and from a survey. First, the number of new guns added each year is known from data kept by the federal government on manufactures, imports, and exports. The annual count of net additions can be cumulated over, say, the last century, with some assumption about the rate of removal through such mechanisms as off-the-books exports, breakage, and police confiscation (Cook 1991; Kleck 1997). The alternative basis for estimating the stock is the onetime National Survey of the Personal Ownership of Firearms (NSPOF) conducted in 1994; this is the only survey that attempted to determine the number of guns in private hands. (A number of surveys, including the General Social Survey, provide an estimate of the prevalence of gun ownership among individuals and households without attempting to determine the average number of guns per gun owner.) The NSPOF estimate for the number of guns in 1994 was 192 million, a number that is compatible with the "sales accumulation" method, assuming that just 15 percent of the new guns sold since 1899 had been thrown out or destroyed (Cook and Ludwig 1996). Since the survey, the annual rate of net additions to the gun stock has been about 4 to 5 million per year (ATF 2001, 2002), or 50 to 60 million by 2006. Given a continued removal rate of just 1 percent, the stock as of 2006 would be around 220 million. Hepburn et al. (2007) offer a wide range of estimates for the number of guns in circulation based on their 2004 survey—the answer is substantially higher if based on responses about individual ownership than household ownership.

The significance of this trend toward increased handgun ownership lies in the fact that while rifles and shotguns are acquired primarily for sporting purposes, handguns are primarily intended for use against people, either in crime or self-defense. The increase in handgun prevalence corresponds to a large increase in the relative importance of handguns in retail sales: in 2007, the Bureau of Alcohol, Tobacco, and Firearms (ATF) reported that handguns represented nearly 42 percent of new firearms manufactured in the United States.[4] (Just 23 percent of manufactures were handguns during the first half of the twentieth century [ATF 2000b].)

The prevalence of gun ownership differs widely across regions, states, and localities, and across different demographic groups. For example, while 10 percent of Boston households own a gun, 50 percent of Phoenix households own one. Residents of rural areas and small towns are far more likely to own a gun than residents of large cities, in part because of the importance of hunting and sport shooting. For the same reason gun ownership also tends to be concentrated among middle-aged, middle-income households (Cook and Ludwig 1996). These attributes are associated with relatively low involvement in criminal violence, and it is reasonable to suppose that most guns are in the hands of people who are unlikely to misuse them. On the other hand, gun owners are more likely than other adults to have a criminal record (Cook and Ludwig 1996).

The majority of guns in circulation were obtained by their owners directly from a federally licensed firearm dealer (FFL). However, the 30 to 40 percent of all gun transfers that do not involve licensed dealers, the so-called "secondary market" (Cook, Molliconi, and Cole 1995), accounts for most guns used in crime (see Wright and Rossi 1994; Sheley and Wright 1995; Cook and Braga 2001). Despite the prominence of gun shows in current policy debates, the best available evidence suggests that such shows account for only a small share of all secondary market sales (Cook and Ludwig 1996). Another important source of crime guns is theft—over 500,000 guns are stolen each year (Cook and Ludwig 1996; Kleck 1997).

The volume of gun transactions is impressively large, as indicated by the number of background checks submitted by licensed gun dealers. In 2008 there were 9.9 million checks, and since 1994 (when they were first required nationwide) there have been 97 million (http://www.ojp.usdoj.gov/bjs/pub/html/bcft/2008/bcft08st.htm). Note that there is not a one-to-one correspondence between checks and sales, since a single transaction can involve several guns. (It is also true that about 1.5 percent of background checks are denied.) Further, a large percentage of transactions do not involve a licensed dealer, as noted before, and hence are not subjected to a background check or included in the previous statistics.

The relatively active and open firearms market in the United States pro-

4. See http://www.atf.gov/firearms/stats/afmer/afmer2007.pdf.

vides a source of arms to criminals,[5] and also to traffickers who supply weapons to gangs in Canada and Mexico, where gun transactions and possession are more tightly regulated (Cook, Cukier, and Krause 2009).

5.2.2 Gun Violence

A great many Americans die by gunfire. The gun-death counts from suicide, homicide, and accident have totaled over 28,000 for every year from 1972 to 2006. In 2006, there were approximately 30,900 firearms deaths, a rate of 10.2 per 100,000 U.S. residents. All but 862 were either suicides or homicides. While homicides make the headlines, there were actually 4,100 more gun suicides than homicides. The remainder were classified as accidents, legal interventions, or unknown (http://webappa.cdc.gov/sasweb/ncipc/mortrate.html). Various points of reference help calibrate these numbers. In terms of Americans killed, a year of gun deaths in the United States is the equivalent of U.S. casualties during the entire Korean War. Another familiar reference is the highway fatality rate, which is about 50 percent higher nationwide than the firearms death rate.

It is criminal homicide and other criminal uses of guns that cause the greatest public concern. There are relatively few fatal gun accidents, and suicide seems more a private concern than a public risk. Fortunately the homicide rate (both gun and nongun) has been dropping rapidly in recent years, but from twentieth century highs in 1980 and 1991 of over 10 per 100,000. The rate was just 6.2 in 2006. Nearly 70 percent of homicides are committed with guns, mostly handguns (80 percent).

Homicide is not a democratic crime. Both victims and perpetrators are vastly disproportionately male, black or Hispanic, and quite young. With respect to the victims, homicide is the leading cause of death for minority youths. The gun homicide rate in 2006 for Hispanic men ages eighteen to twenty-nine was five times the rate for non-Hispanic white men of the same age; the gun homicide rate for black men eighteen to twenty-nine was 109 per 100,000, eighteen times the rate for white males in that age group. (Most male victims in the high-risk category are killed by people of the same race, sex, and age group [Cook and Laub 1998].) About 85 percent of the homicide victims in this group were killed with firearms. The disparity between the demography of gun sports and of gun crime is telling: sportsmen are disproportionately older white males from small towns and rural areas, while the criminal misuse of guns is concentrated among young urban males, especially minorities.

The costs of gun violence to society are more evenly distributed across the

5. The open market is also exploited by traffickers who supply gangs and violent individuals in Canada and Mexico (Cook, Cukier, and Krause 2009). These international spillovers have negative consequences for American interests, both directly and indirectly through our negotiating position with these countries.

population than victimization statistics would suggest. The threat of being shot causes private citizens and public institutions to undertake a variety of costly measures to reduce this risk, and all of us must live with the anxiety caused by the lingering chance that we or a loved one could become a victim. As a result, the threat of gun violence is in some neighborhoods an important disamenity that depresses property values and puts a drag on economic development. Gun violence, then, is a multifaceted problem that has notable effects on public health, crime, and living standards.

While quantifying the magnitude of these social costs is difficult, one contingent-valuation (CV) survey estimate found that the costs of gun violence were on the order of $100 billion in 1995 (Cook and Ludwig 2000). Most ($80 billion) of these costs come from crime-related gun violence. Dividing by the annual number of crime-related gunshot wounds, including homicides, implies a social cost per crime-related gun injury of around $1 million (Ludwig and Cook 2001).[6]

5.2.3   Self-Defense Uses

The same features of guns that make them valuable to criminals may also make guns useful in self-defense. Just how often guns are used in defense against criminal attack has been hotly debated, and remains unclear. Estimates from the National Crime Victimization Survey (NCVS), a large government-sponsored in-person survey that is generally considered the most reliable source of information on predatory crime, suggest that guns are used in defense against criminal predation around 100,000 times per year (Cook 1991). In contrast are the results of several smaller onetime telephone surveys, which provide a basis for asserting that there are millions of defensive gun uses per year (Kleck and Gertz 1995).

Why do these estimates for the number of defensive gun uses each year differ by more than an order of magnitude? One explanation is that the NCVS only asks questions about defensive gun use to those who report a victimization attempt, while the phone surveys ask such questions of every respondent. As a result the scope for "false positives" will be much greater with the phone surveys compared to the NCVS (Cook, Ludwig, and

---

6. Note that this estimate is intended to capture the costs of gun misuse and so ignores the benefits to society from widespread gun ownership, in the same way that studies of the social costs of automobile accidents ignore the benefits from driving. The figure comes, in part, from CV responses about what people say they would pay to reduce crime-related gun violence by 30 percent. One potential concern is that these estimates assume that societal willingness to pay to reduce gun violence is linear with the proportion of gun violence eliminated, which may not be the case. And in practice there remains some uncertainty about the reliability of the CV measurement technology. In any case, most of the estimated costs of gun violence to the United States appear to come from crime, since suicide seems more like a private concern, and the estimated costs of gun crime by Cook and Ludwig (2000) fits comfortably next to more recent CV estimates for the social costs of crime more generally (Cohen et al. 2004).

Hemenway 1997; Hemenway 1997a, 1997b). Moreover, as an expert panel of the National Academy of Sciences concluded, "fundamental problems in defining what is meant by defensive gun use may be a primary impediment to accurate measurement" (Wellford, Pepper, and Petrie 2005, 103; see also McDowall, Loftin, and Presser 2000). When respondents who report defensive gun use are asked to describe the sequence of events, many of the cases turn out to have involved something far less threatening than one might suppose (Hemenway 2004).

Whatever the actual number of defensive gun uses, the mere threat of encountering an armed victim may exert a deterrent effect on the behavior of criminals. A growing body of research within criminology and economics supports the notion that some criminals are sensitive to the threat of punishment (Cook 1980; Nagin 1998; Levitt 2001). It is therefore not surprising that the threat of armed victim response may also figure in criminal decisions: around 40 percent of prisoners in one survey indicated that they had decided against committing a crime at least once because they feared that the potential victim was carrying a gun (Wright and Rossi 1994). Whether that type of consideration actually affects crime rates is another matter, to which we return later.

Whether or not it enhances objective security, millions of households choose to keep a gun for self-defense. Many more keep guns for sporting purposes—hunting, target shooting, and collecting. The goal of gun policy in the United States has been to preserve these traditional uses of guns for most of the adult population, while reducing access and use by the highest-risk groups. Whether the current system achieves the proper balance between preserving access and preventing misuse remains, of course, the subject of considerable debate.

5.2.4   Gun Regulations

To see what may be at risk with the new interpretation of the Second Amendment, it is useful to review current regulations. While far less stringent that those in other wealthy nations (Hemenway 2004), most aspects of firearms commerce and possession are subject to federal and state regulations.

The primary objective of federal law in regulating guns is to insulate the states from one another, so that the stringent regulations on firearms commerce adopted in some states are not undercut by the relatively lax regulation in other states (Zimring 1975). The citizens of rural Montana understandably favor a more permissive system than those living in Chicago, and both can be accommodated if transfers between them are effectively limited. The Gun Control Act of 1968 established the framework for the current system of controls on gun transfers. All shipments of firearms (including mail-order sales) are limited to federally licensed dealers who are required to obey applicable state and local ordinances, and to observe certain restrictions on sales of guns to out-of-state residents.[7]

Federal law also seeks to establish a minimum set of restrictions on acquisition and possession of guns. The Gun Control Act specifies several categories of people who are denied the right to receive or possess a gun, including illegal aliens, convicted felons and those under indictment, people ever convicted of an act of domestic violence, users of illicit drugs, and those who have at some time been involuntarily committed to a mental institution. Federally licensed dealers may not sell handguns to people younger than twenty-one, or long guns to those younger than eighteen. And dealers are required to ask for identification from all would-be buyers, have them sign a form indicating that they do not have any of the characteristics (such as a felony conviction) that would place them in the "proscribed" category, and initiate a criminal-history check. Finally, dealers are required to keep a record of each completed sale and cooperate with authorities when they need to access those records for gun-tracing purposes (Vernick and Teret 2000; LCAV 2009). On the other hand, sales of guns by people not in the business are not subject to federal regulation; the seller, whether at a gun show or elsewhere, may transfer a gun without keeping a record of sale or doing any sort of background check on the buyer. This "private sale" loophole is more like a gaping barn door for the used-gun market.

In addition to these federal requirements, states have adopted significant restrictions on commerce, possession, and use of firearms. Eleven states require that handgun buyers obtain a permit or license before taking possession of a handgun, a process that typically entails payment of a fee and some waiting period (LCAV 2009). All but a few such transfer-control systems are "permissive," in the sense that most people are legally entitled to obtain a gun. In those few jurisdictions, including Massachusetts and New York City, it is very difficult to obtain a handgun legally, while Chicago and Washington, DC have prohibited handgun acquisition since 1982 and 1976, respectively. A variety of more modest restrictions on commerce have been enacted as well: for example, Virginia, Maryland, California, and New Jersey have limited dealers to selling no more than one handgun a month to any one buyer.

Gun Design

Federal law also imposes some restrictions on gun design, and in fact some types of firearms are effectively prohibited. The National Firearms Act of 1934 (NFA) was intended to eliminate gangster-era firearms, including

---

7. The McClure-Volkmer Amendment of 1986 eased the restriction on out-of-state purchases of rifles and shotguns. Such purchases are now legal as long as they comply with the regulations of both the buyer's state of residence and the state in which the sale occurs.

sawed-off shotguns, hand grenades, and automatic weapons that are capable of continuous rapid fire with a single pull of the trigger. The legal device for accomplishing that purpose was a requirement that all such weapons be registered with the federal government and that transfers be subject to a tax of $200, which at the time of enactment was confiscatory. While some of these weapons have remained in legal circulation, the NFA (now amended to ban the introduction of new weapons of this sort into circulation) appears to have been quite effective at reducing the use of automatic weapons in crime (Kleck 1991).

The Gun Control Act of 1968 included a ban on the import of small, cheap handguns,[8] sometimes known as "Saturday Night Specials." This ban was made operational through the development of the factoring criteria that assigned points to a gun model depending on its size and other qualities (Zimring 1975; Karlson and Hargarten 1997). Handguns that fail to achieve a minimum score on the factoring criteria, or do not meet size and safety criteria, cannot be imported. However, it is legal for domestic manufacturers to assemble guns, often from imported parts, that fail the factoring criteria, and that market "niche" has been well supplied. One study found that one-third of new domestically manufactured handgun models did not meet the size or quality requirements that are applied to imports through the factoring criteria (Milne et al. [2003]; see also Wintemute [1994]).

In 1994 Congress banned the importation and manufacture of certain "assault" weapons, which is to say military-style semiautomatic firearms. The Crime Control Act banned nineteen such weapons by name, and others were outlawed if they possess some combination of design features such as a detachable magazine, barrel shroud, or bayonet mount (Vernick and Teret 2000, 1197). The Act also banned manufacture and import of magazines that hold more than ten rounds. Existing assault weapons and large-capacity magazines were "grandfathered" (Roth and Koper 1999). In 2004, this assault weapons ban was allowed to expire.

Federal law leaves unregulated those types of firearms that are not specifically banned. Firearms and ammunition are excluded from the purview of the Consumer Product Safety Commission (Vernick and Teret 2000). There is no federal agency that has responsibility for reviewing the design of firearms, and no mechanism in place for identifying unsafe models that could lead to a recall and correction (Bonnie, Fulco and Liverman 1999). Some states have acted independently on this matter. For example, in 2000 the attorney general of Massachusetts announced that firearms would henceforth be regulated by the same authority available to his department for

---

8. An important loophole allowed the import of parts of handguns that could not meet the "sporting purposes" test of the Gun Control Act. This loophole was closed by the McClure-Volkmer Amendment of 1986.

other consumer products, and those deemed unacceptable would be taken off the market.[9]

Massachusetts is unique in asserting broad state authority to regulate gun design and gun safety. There are a handful of states in which the legislatures have acted to restrict the permissible design of new guns in a more limited way. The first important instance of this sort occurred in Maryland, with its ban on Saturday Night Specials. The Maryland legislature acted in response to a successful lawsuit against a manufacturer. In exchange for relieving manufacturers of small, cheap handguns from liability, the legislature created a process for reviewing handgun designs and specifying which models would be ruled out due to size and safety concerns. As of 2008 a total of eight states have some version of a Saturday Night Special ban in place (LCAV 2009). California has also been active in recent years, instituting among other measures its own ban on assault weapons and a number of safety requirements for handguns.

Gun Possession and Use

States and some localities also specify the rules under which guns may be carried in public. Every state except Vermont and Alaska places some restriction on carrying a concealed firearm. The trend over the past several decades has been to ease restrictions on concealed carry, replacing prohibition with a permit system, and easing the requirements to obtain a permit. Currently, adults who are entitled to possess a handgun can obtain a permit to carry after paying a fee in most states (LCAV 2009; Lott 2000).

There has also been some effort to regulate storage. Federal law beginning in 2005 requires that all handguns sold by licensed dealers come equipped with a secure storage device. Eleven states and the District of Columbia have laws concerning firearm locking devices. The Maryland legislature adopted a pioneering requirement, namely that all handguns manufactured after 2003 and sold in that state be "personalized" in the sense of having a built-in locking device that requires a key or combination to release. Massachusetts and the District of Columbia require that all firearms be stored with a lock in place.

Record Keeping

The primary purpose of some gun regulations is to assist law enforcement in solving crimes. In particular, federal law requires that all licensees in the chain of commerce (manufacturers, distributors, retail dealers) keep records of transfers and make them available to law enforcement for tracing purposes. For example, if a police department has confiscated a firearm that

---

9. The effect has been to ban "Saturday night specials" and require that handguns sold in Massachusetts include childproof locks, tamper-proof serial numbers, and safety warnings. The gun-safety regulations affect manufacturers as well as retailers.

may have been used in a crime, they can submit a trace request through the National Tracing Center of the Bureau of Alcohol, Tobacco, Firearms, and Explosives (ATF), which will attempt to trace the chain of commerce using the serial number and other characteristics of the gun. If all goes well, the retail dealer that first sold the gun will be identified, and will supply information from the form that the buyer filled out. This system is inefficient and error prone, and even if successful usually leaves the investigators far short of the information they really want, which is the identity of the most recent owner of the firearm (Cook and Braga 2001). A more direct system of national registration has been politically impossible to implement except in the case of weapons of mass destruction (National Firearms Act).

A few states have registration requirements. Notably, California requires registration of handgun transactions, even if they occur between private parties. That requirement complements a new regulation that all semiautomatic pistols sold in the state after 2010 be designed with a microstamp capability that will print the serial number, make, and model of the gun on the shell casing when the gun is fired. Shell casings are ejected from pistols and often left at the scene by the shooter, where they can be collected by investigators and, under the new law, used to initiate a trace even when the gun itself is not in custody.

Rulemaking versus Legislation

It should be noted that the regulations on gun commerce and possession are almost entirely the result of legislation rather than a regulatory rulemaking process. The latter places greater requirements on the decision makers to solicit alternative viewpoints and consider costs and benefits. Whether the federal courts will consider social costs and benefits in reviewing Second Amendment cases remains to be seen.

5.3   Tort Litigation Against the Gun Industry

The wave of mass tort litigation against the gun industry that occurred in the 1990s is now largely of historical interest, since it has accomplished very little except to confirm the political power of progun groups. However, the academic debate over these lawsuits may usefully inform our evaluation of the new wave of litigation inspired by the *Heller* decision.[10]

The suits against the firearms industry were inspired by and had strong parallels with the lawsuits so successfully brought by the state attorneys general against the tobacco industry. The cigarette manufacturers ultimately settled those suits, agreeing to some restrictions on their marketing practices and to pay the states over $240 billion in damages over the course of twenty-

---

10. For a more sanguine perspective of what this litigation accomplished, see Rostron (2006).

five years. One difference is that most of the plaintiffs in the case of the gun industry were cities rather than states. Another difference is that the firearms industry is much smaller and more diffuse than the tobacco industry, so that the financial stakes were much smaller. Indeed, the primary motivation for the plaintiffs was not to recover financial damages, but rather to force the industry to take greater responsibility for reducing the amount of damage done by its products.

The first of the local-government lawsuits against the gun industry was filed by the city of New Orleans on October 30, 1998 (*Morial v. Smith and Wesson Corp.*), which asserted, among other things, that the manufacturers neglected their duty to incorporate available safety features into the design of their products. The second lawsuit was filed by Chicago on November 12, 1998 (*City of Chicago and Cook County v. Beretta U.S.A., Corp*). Chicago's case focused on marketing practices, asserting that the industry had created a "public nuisance" by neglecting to take feasible measures that would help prevent the illegal sale of its products to Chicago residents or to traffickers who supply residents (Siebel 1999, 248–9; Vernick and Teret 1999). Following these actions by New Orleans and Chicago, thirty other cities and counties filed against the gun industry, claiming negligence in either its marketing practices or in the design of its products or both.[11]

Various theories of negligence were tried (Lytton 2005b). Some plaintiffs argued that the gun industry was responsible for negligent marketing practices, which did not do enough to keep guns out of the hands of prohibited users, or more failures to adequately supervise retail gun dealers. The gun industry was also charged with "oversupplying" gun dealers in states with relatively lax gun laws, with the claim that the industry knew the "extra" guns would wind up in jurisdictions with more restrictive regulations, or "overpromoting" weapons that only had legitimate military or law enforcement use. Chicago's case claimed that the unregulated secondary gun market is a "public nuisance" for which the gun industry has responsibility, while Cincinnati argued that the gun industry engaged in deceptive advertising—keeping a gun in the home was argued to increase the risk of injury to residents, rather than improve safety as the industry claimed.

Most of these arguments did not fare well in court. The New Orleans case was dismissed by the Louisiana Supreme Court after the state enacted a law barring such suits. Chicago's case was dismissed and then appealed.[12] As Lytton (2005b, 5) notes, of the city lawsuits the "great majority have been dismissed or abandoned prior to trial, and of the few favorable jury verdicts obtained by the plaintiffs, all but one have been overturned on appeal. A handful of claims have been settled prior to trial."

Then on October 26, 2005, President Bush signed the Protection of Law-

11. See www.vpc.org/litigate.htm.
12. See www.vpc.org/litigate.htm.

ful Commerce in Arms Act (PLCAA), which to a remarkable degree provided immunity to the firearms industry. This law did preserve the possibility of traditional tort actions against the industry—for example, injuries that result from defects in design or manufacture—but the industry is explicitly exempted from liability for injuries resulting from criminal misuse of its product. While Lytton (2005a) notes that the PLCAA might itself be subject to a variety of constitutional challenges, efforts to enhance gun regulation through litigation have failed for the most part. The *Heller* decision may add an additional legal barrier to this type of suit (Denning 2005; Kopel and Gardiner 1995).

5.4   The *Heller* Decision

For most of our country's history, the Second Amendment was absent from the Supreme Court's agenda.[13] When the Amendment came up, it was ineffectual. In the late 1800s, the Court confirmed that the Amendment could not be used against state regulation (*Presser v. Illinois,* 116 U.S. 252, 264–66). And in 1937, *United States v. Miller* concluded that the federal government was free to restrict possession of sawed-off shotguns (*U.S. v. Miller,* 307 U.S. 174, 178). This opinion seemed to connect Second Amendment rights to state-organized militias, rather than to individual preferences about gun ownership. The Court sought evidence that a short-barreled shotgun "has some reasonable relationship to the preservation or efficiency of a well regulated militia." Lower federal courts followed this notion and the Amendment was essentially a dead letter in litigation. Results involving state constitutions were not dramatically different. State supreme courts invoked state gun rights to invalidate only a few state regulations after World War II (Winkler 2007, 716–26).

The Second Amendment gained force in other locations, however. The gun rights movement made the Amendment a central rhetorical element in its organizing efforts. Many lawmakers were sympathetic. And by the late twentieth century, scholarship on the Amendment was booming. Some legal academics supported an understanding of federal gun rights beyond anachronistic state militias (e.g., Levinson 1989; Cottrol and Diamond 1991; Barnett and Kates 1996; Volokh 1998; see also Tushnet 2007). There were also judicial rumblings. In 1997, Justice Thomas suggested in a concurrence that the Amendment might have provided another basis for invalidating the Brady Act's mandate that local officials conduct background checks on handgun purchasers (*Printz v. U.S.,* 521 U.S. 898, 938–39). In 2001, the Fifth Circuit declared that the Second Amendment included a personal right to keep and bear arms unrelated to militia service, although the court upheld the regulation at issue (*U.S. v. Emerson,* 270 F.3d 203, 260–61). The Depart-

---

13. This section draws from Cook, Ludwig, and Samaha (2009).

ment of Justice then amended its litigation position and endorsed the Fifth Circuit's logic (Memorandum from the Attorney General 2001).[14]

In 2008, the Supreme Court changed its message, too. *District of Columbia v. Heller* became the first successful Second Amendment challenge in the Court's history. The case involved a police officer who wanted to keep an operable handgun in his home and to "carry it about his home in that condition only when necessary for self-defense" (p. 2788 and n.2). But the District is an urban jurisdiction where the gun rights movement has little traction. One local law prohibited possession of handguns by private citizens with only narrow exceptions. A second regulation required firearms to be either unloaded and disassembled or trigger-locked at all times. Exceptions were made for law enforcement officers, places of business, and otherwise lawful recreational activities, but the regulation reached people's homes. A third regulation involved firearms licensing by the chief of police. The *Heller* majority left unaddressed the issue of firearms licensing (p. 2819), but it concluded that the first two regulations infringed this plaintiff's right to have a handgun in his home for self-defense.[15]

It is quite possible to read the majority opinion for very little. The justices did not commit themselves to restraining state or local firearms laws under the Fourteenth Amendment (pp. 2812–13 and n.23). That is where much of the regulatory action takes place. Furthermore, the plaintiff's position in *Heller* was relatively strong. The regulations under attack were fairly broad, the argument came down to a qualified right to handgun possession in the home, and the dissenting justices thought the Amendment not even implicated without a militia connection (pp. 2823, 2847). Even under these circumstances, the gun rights position narrowly prevailed on a 5-4 vote. Perhaps a slightly different case would fracture the majority coalition. After all, it does not take special courage to oppose handgun bans. Opinion polls show large national majorities opposing such bans. Equally telling, a majority of Senators and House members signed an amicus brief arguing that the District's regulations were unconstitutional (Saad [2007] (reporting on Gallup polls); Brief for Amici Curiae 2008).[16] One can imagine the 5-4 vote going the other way had the District permitted a law-abiding citizen

14. When Emerson sought review by the Supreme Court, the Solicitor General abandoned the militia-related view of the Amendment. Brief for the United States (2002), n.3 (accepting, however, "reasonable restrictions designed to prevent possession by unfit persons or to restrict the possession of types of firearms that are particularly suited to criminal misuse").

15. Justice Scalia wrote the majority opinion, which was joined by Chief Justice Roberts and Justices Kennedy, Thomas, and Alito. The four dissenters joined two opinions: Justice Stevens' dissent focused on *Miller* and the history surrounding the Second Amendment's adoption (pp. 2823–46), while Justice Breyer's dissent rejected the plaintiff's claims even on the assumption that the Amendment includes a self-defense purpose (pp. 2847–48). Added together, the three opinions total approximately 50,000 words. Our discussion simplifies many nuances of the legal arguments.

16. There is a large literature on judicial behavior (Friedman 2005). Some scholars emphasize the role of formal law and institutional norms, but empirical studies often suggest other factors.

to store one handgun in the home, but required handgun training, registration, and a trigger lock at all times—except when and if self-defense became necessary.

Nevertheless, more significant lessons might be drawn from the decision. Its first notable feature is the virtual irrelevance of organized militias to the majority's view of gun rights. The text of the Second Amendment begins with the preface, "A well regulated Militia, being necessary to the security of a free State, ..." Whether or not this assertion is factually accurate, it could be made important to understanding the words that follow: "the right of the people to keep and bear Arms, shall not be infringed." But for the majority, the Amendment's preface cannot be used to limit or expand the meaning of the subsequent words (pp. 2792–97 and nn. 3–4). Instead, the militia reference is taken to indicate the purpose for codifying a preexisting right of "the people" to keep and bear arms (pp. 2800–02). Although the Amendment followed a debate over standing armies and state militias checking centralized tyranny, the majority contended that the codified right also was valued for self-defense. This self-defense function, not the prerequisites of a robust citizen militia, defines the scope of the right recognized in *Heller*.

Fencing off the Amendment's enforceable right from its militia-oriented preface is revealing. Some of the implications point toward judicial intervention. Private parties are now allowed to raise Second Amendment arguments in court without any relationship to a militia, state-run or otherwise. The content of the right is personal and nonmilitary. As well, incorporation into the Fourteenth Amendment might seem easier once the right is separated from any arguable connection to state militias. If the right is not about federal-state relations, it fits better with the individual rights the Court has been willing to enforce against state and local governments.[17] But another implication involves restraint. The Court's majority is not about to enforce a citizen's right to frighten the United States Armed Forces with overwhelming firepower. The majority's portrayal of the Second Amendment right seems, at most, tangentially related to people protecting themselves from the risks of centralized tyranny (p. 2817). Instead the majority's conception of the right is demilitarized and mainstreamed.

What, then, is the right recognized in *Heller*? Countless observers are struggling with this question. To make progress here, however, we can describe *Heller*'s minimum plausible content—the core right to which a majority of justices seem committed.

Whenever else it might include, this core right involves self-defense with

---

For the argument that justices vote their ideology, see Segal and Spaeth (2002). For an inquiry into strategic behavior, see Epstein and Knight (1998). The classic view of the Court as sticking close to national governing coalitions is Dahl (1957).

17. On the Court's selective incorporation of the Bill of Rights, see Chemerinsky (2006, 499–507).

a typical handgun in one's own home. The majority was not interested in a right to carry arms "for *any sort* of confrontation" (p. 2799), and declared that "self-defense . . . was the *central component* of the right" codified in the Amendment (p. 2801). In attempting to explain why the District's handgun ban was defective, the majority asserted that an inherent right of self-defense has been central to the understanding of the Second Amendment in American history, that handguns are now commonly chosen by Americans to provide lawful self-defense, and that "the need for defense of self, family, and property is most acute" in the home (p. 2817). For similar reasons, the majority immunized the plaintiff's handgun from the District's requirement that firearms in the home be kept inoperable at all times. If the plaintiff's handgun could never be made operable in his home, he would not be able to use it there for "the core lawful purpose" of self-defense (p. 2818). Hence the majority's core conception of the right is a law-abiding citizen with a functioning handgun in his own home for the purpose of defending it—perhaps only at the time of attack (pp. 2788, 2822). This conception matches the situation of the actual plaintiff in *Heller.*

In fact, limits were an important theme in the decision. The justices in the majority went out of their way to insulate certain forms of gun control not at issue in the case. They conceded that the Second Amendment right is "not unlimited" (p. 2816), and offered a list of "presumptively lawful regulatory measures" (p. 2817 and n. 26). To put it crudely, this nonexhaustive list includes regulation aimed at:

1. Atypical weapons
2. Abnormal people
3. Sensitive locations
4. Sales conditions
5. Safe storage
6. Concealed carry (perhaps)

Thus the majority sought to protect weapons "typically possessed by law-abiding citizens" for self-defense in the home (pp. 2815–18), asserting that a limitation to weapons in common use is consistent with a tradition of restricting "dangerous and unusual weapons" (p. 2817). Handguns are thereby covered in view of their current popularity in the market (p. 2818), while the majority strongly suggested that machine guns, M-16s, and sawed-off shotguns are not (pp. 2815, 2817). We do not know the extent to which regulation may validly influence which weapons become common. But this kind of limit fits with the majority's demilitarized vision of the Amendment.

The discussion of other regulations was even more brief: "nothing in our opinion should be taken to cast doubt on longstanding prohibitions on the possession of firearms by felons and the mentally ill, or laws forbidding the carrying of firearms in sensitive places such as schools and government buildings, or laws imposing conditions and qualifications on the commercial sale of arms" (pp. 2816–17). Later, in distinguishing founding era regulation of gun powder storage, the majority said that its logic does not suggest problems with "laws regulating the storage of firearms to prevent accidents" (p. 2820). Finally, the majority observed that most nineteenth-century cases had upheld prohibitions on concealed weapons (p. 2816).

Nevertheless, *Heller* has generated much litigation. So far, the lower federal courts have declined to strike down state or local gun laws based on *Heller* (Winkler 2009, 1565–66), in part because the Supreme Court has not yet ruled on the incorporation issue. Among the cases that may find their way to Supreme Court are challenges to Chicago's handgun ban and to New York City's stringent handgun permit system (Wise 2008). Some defendants are making long-shot objections to the federal machine gun ban and felon in possession convictions (e.g., *U.S. v. Whisnant,* No. 3:07-CR-32, E.D. Tenn. Sept. 30, 2008). And some jurisdictions are avoiding the costs and risks of litigation—which include paying the attorneys fees of prevailing plaintiffs (Lewis and Norman 2001, 442–64)—by repealing firearms regulation without a fight over incorporation. Chicago suburbs have repealed handgun bans after *Heller* (Horan 2008). In early 2009, San Francisco followed this course. It settled a gun rights lawsuit by agreeing to eliminate a lease provision for public housing tenants that prohibited storage of firearms and ammunition (Stipulation 2009). The question is how the legal uncertainty will shake out.

One potentially important issue involves incorporation. If Second Amendment norms restrain only the federal government and not state or local regulation, the policy space will be far less influenced by judicial review. The federal government has not been the principal source of the most stringent gun control measures, and state courts have not been especially aggressive in state constitutional challenges to such regulation. On the other hand, if the Supreme Court interprets the Fourteenth Amendment to include a Second Amendment right, the litigation threat becomes more important.

A fair guess is that the *Heller* majority is poised to incorporate.[18] The majority reserved the issue while noting that its nineteenth-century precedents had not employed the Court's more recent approach to incorporation (p. 2813, n. 23). In addition, the majority's understanding of the right is emphatically personal. This makes it difficult to resist application against the states with an argument that the Second Amendment was written to protect the militias of those same states. Moreover, the majority's discussion of Reconstruction Era sources indicates concern during that time for gun rights of freed slaves (pp. 2809–11). And if the question is whether the right is sufficiently "fundamental" to warrant enforcement against all

---

18. This is written in October, 2009, just as the U.S. Supreme Court agreed to hear the suit against Chicago's handgun ban, *McDonald vs. Chicago.*

levels of government, the *Heller* opinion intimates an affirmative answer (p. 2798). Finally, the Court would not have to totally repudiate a key precedent here, *Presser v. Illinois*. That case involved state restrictions on unauthorized military organizations parading as such, which is far from the demilitarized vision of gun rights endorsed in *Heller*. Still, it has been years since the Supreme Court seriously confronted an incorporation issue. The question involves high stakes and deep jurisprudential controversies, it is being litigated now, and the Court is likely to address it within the next few years.

5.5   What Is at Stake

The immediate effect of *Heller* is to ensure that most residents of the District of Columbia will have the legal right to keep a handgun in their home and have it ready to defend against intruders—a right that they have not had since 1976. Assuming that the courts extend this new "core" Second Amendment right to state and local jurisdictions, then handgun bans in Chicago and elsewhere will almost certainly be swept away, quite possibly along with other highly restrictive policies that stop just short of a ban, such as handgun regulation in Massachusetts and New York City. The elimination of legal barriers invites an increase in the prevalence of handgun ownership. Furthermore, it is possible that regulations that have the effect, if not the intent, of making handguns more expensive to acquire and possess will be subject to constitutional challenge. Included here could be such measures as the long-standing federal excise tax on firearms, federal and state design requirements intended to improve safety, licensing and registration fees required in some states, and a potential requirement that owners carry liability insurance. A constitutional limit on such regulations would reduce the effective price of guns in affected jurisdictions and thus provide a further impetus to handgun ownership.

There has been considerable research on the effects of gun prevalence on crime and public health. To understand the potential social costs of the *Heller* decision, we begin with a review of that evidence, and then discuss its application in the framework of welfare economics.

5.5.1   Effect of Gun Prevalence on Crime and Public Health

For some people, the ready availability of a firearm provides a sense of security against intruders, including the nightmare scenario of home invasion by violent criminals. That sense of security may be worth a great deal, whether or not it is based on a rational assessment of the chances that a handgun will be needed for this purpose, or if needed will actually be successfully deployed. One analysis of National Crime Victimization Survey data found that guns are sometimes used to defend against home invasions, but rarely: in only 3 percent of home invasions was a gun used in self-defense (32,000 instances per year during the period 1979 to 1987), despite the fact that about 20 percent of homes possessed a handgun (Cook 1991). It is also true that handguns kept in the home are sometimes used to threaten other family members or to act on a suicidal impulse. Further, other family members, including adolescents and children, may misappropriate them and do great harm. Someone deciding whether to keep a handgun in the home thus faces a situation of competing risks (Graham and Wiener 1995)—without a gun, there is a risk of being unable to defend against a criminal intrusion, while with a gun, there are multiple risks of accident and misuse. The magnitudes of these competing risks will differ widely depending on how the handgun is stored, as well as other factors—the crime rate in the community and household characteristics such as the presence of children in the home, and whether household members abuse alcohol and drugs, are inclined to violence, or suffer from depression or other mental illness.

Keeping guns in the home may also generate externalities for the community. Whether such externalities tend to be positive or negative is not clear a priori. There are several reasonable mechanisms, which depend in part on how would-be intruders evaluate potential targets. A burglar who knows that a particular residence has guns in it may avoid that residence for fear of encountering armed resistance. (Householders who post signs with a message like "this home is protected by Smith and Wesson" are counting on that mechanism.) If the burglars target nearby residences instead, then gun ownership displaces rather than prevents burglary, a negative externality of keeping a gun in the home. On the other hand, since guns are profitable loot, the incentive to burglars may go in the other direction; if the gun-owning household is specifically targeted, the displacement may be a positive externality to gun-less neighbors. In the more likely case that the burglar does not know which households possess guns, but has an impression of the likelihood that residents in the neighborhood are armed, then these same two mechanisms may operate at the neighborhood level rather than the level of the individual residence. In that case, the decision to keep a gun in the home, if it contributes to perceived gun prevalence in the neighborhood, will have a positive externality within the neighborhood (if guns deter burglary) or a negative externality (if guns induce burglary).

Burglars decide not only which neighborhoods and which homes in those neighborhoods to target, but also how careful to be in avoiding locations where someone is in the house. Burglaries of occupied dwellings may be safer if there are few guns, other things (such as alarms, dogs, and the vigilance of neighbors) held equal.

A variety of evidence has been cited in discussions of how gun prevalence affects residential burglary rates. Interviews with burglars or former burglars provide direct evidence on the deterrent effect, and also on the inducement to burglary of guns in the home. International comparisons are offered, usually comparing the percentage of residential burglaries that are "hot" in the United States with one or more other countries that have lower gun prevalence. And there have been several econometric studies of these relationships.

Interviews with burglars. Evidence directly relevant for judging the "deterrence" and "inducement" hypotheses comes from surveys of felons. For example, in one 1982 convenience sample of 1,823 state prisoners, 35 percent of respondents "strongly agreed" and 39 percent "agreed" that "one reason burglars avoid houses when people are at home is that they fear being shot." The fear of meeting armed householders also induced some burglars to carry a gun themselves: of the respondents who used a gun to commit the crime for which they were incarcerated, 50 percent reported that the possibility of encountering an armed victim was "very important" in their decision to employ a gun, while another 12 percent reported that this motivation was "somewhat important" (Wright and Rossi 1994).

At the same time guns are of considerable value to burglars, who typically prefer items that are easy to carry, easily concealed, and have high "pound for pound value" (Shover 1991). As one St. Louis burglar reported, "A gun is money with a trigger" (Wright and Decker 1994). Another respondent in the same study expressed a preference for working in neighborhoods with high proportions of white residents since households in these areas are likely to have "the basics," including guns: "White people hunt a lot more so than blacks."[19]

Nearly half of the respondents to the prison survey mentioned above report that they have stolen a gun during their lifetimes; of this group, 70 percent usually steal guns to sell or trade rather than to keep for themselves.[20]

International comparisons. Since the prevalence of household gun possession is substantially higher in the United States than Canada, Britain, and other wealthy nations, it seems reasonable to test the "deterrence" hypothesis by comparing residential burglary rates and patterns across these nations. As it turns out, relevant data are hard to come by. The Uniform Crime Reports do not provide a basis for estimating the number of "hot" burglaries, nor do the police-recorded data systems of other countries. Relevant survey-based estimates can be generated for the United States from the NCVS, but no other country has an annual crime survey of comparable quality.[21] There have been occasional crime surveys in other nations, which suggest that

19. See Wright and Decker (1994, 90). On the other hand, a burglar interviewed by Rengert and Wasilchick (1985) said that he shunned burglaries in neighborhoods in which the residents were of a different race because "You'll get shot if you're caught there" (62).

20. See Wright and Rossi (1994). The prevalence of gun theft in the Wright and Rossi convenience sample of prisoners is higher than in the nationally representative sample of prisoners interviewed as part of the 1991 Survey of Inmates of State Correctional Facilities, in which only 10 percent of respondents report ever having stolen a gun.

21. One attempt to generate internationally comparable survey-based results is the United Nations-sponsored International Crime Survey. This survey includes the United States, but is far smaller and in other ways inferior to the NCVS. More to the point, it does not include items that would permit the estimate of a hot burglary rate. For more details see ict-law.leidenuniv .nl/group/jfcr/www/icvs/Index.htm.

some other countries may have a higher percentage of residential burglaries involving occupied dwellings than for the United States. But there are severe comparability problems in the data, such as differences between the NCVS and the British Crime Survey in how burglaries are coded when it is not clear whether someone was home at the time of the break-in—that is, the respondent was not aware of the burglary, but believed in retrospect that he or she had been home at the time (Cook and Ludwig 2003).

More importantly, even if we had comparable data there would remain the fact that a variety of potential explanations are plausible for an observed difference in the percentage of residential burglaries that involve occupied dwellings. For example, when burglars are arrested the punishment is more certain and severe in the United States than in England and Wales. The difference in penalties provides an alternative explanation for why American burglars take extra care to avoid contact with victims. American and British households differ in a variety of other ways as well that are likely to affect the cost-benefit calculus facing burglars, including substantial differences in the proportion of households that have dogs or lack men. Without controlling for the other differences that may be important, attributing the disparity in hot burglary rates to one particular difference—gun prevalence—is entirely unpersuasive.

Econometric evidence. Cook and Ludwig (2003) analyzed two sorts of data, in both cases finding strong evidence that gun prevalence tended to induce burglary (on balance) rather than deter it. While the prevalence of gun ownership cannot be measured from administrative data sets, and surveys of gun ownership are unusual for subnational units, it turns out that there is an excellent well-validated proxy for prevalence—the percentage of suicides involving guns (Azrael, Cook, and Miller 2004; Kleck 2004). Burglary rates can be obtained from the Uniform Crime Reports (UCR) or from the National Crime Victimization Survey. We analyzed both types of data.

We first utilized a twenty-two-year panel of state-level UCR burglary data, finding that changes in burglary rates were positively related to lagged changes in the prevalence of gun ownership (confirming the results of a similar analysis by Duggan [2001]). The gun-prevalence elasticity of burglary rates is about 0.4 or 0.5. The lag was introduced in part to avoid problems of reverse causation. The positive association survived a number of specification checks. Our second analysis, of NCVS data, is unique in that we had access to the geo-coded microdata and could analyze the effect of county-level gun prevalence on the probability that a household would be burglarized, controlling for its socioeconomic characteristics and features of its location. Our analysis of data from 330,000 individual household interviews found that an increase in gun prevalence resulted in an increase in the probability of victimization (other things equal) and an increase in the chance that the respondent reported that guns were stolen as part of the burglary. (The basic result held up well through a variety of specification checks, including an instrumental variables analysis.) The likelihood that the home was occupied at the time of the burglary was not affected by the prevalence of guns.

Violent Crime

Firearms are the most lethal of the widely available weapons that are deployed in assaults, robberies, and self-defense. They are the great equalizer—with a gun, most anyone can threaten or actually inflict grave injury on another, even someone with greater skill, strength, and determination. With a gun, unlike a knife or club, one individual can kill another quickly, at a distance, on impulse. The logical and well-documented result is that when a gun is present in an assault or robbery, it is more likely that the victim will die. In other words, it is not just the intent of the assailant that determines the outcome, but also the means of attack. That conclusion about "instrumentality" has been demonstrated in a variety of ways, and is no longer controversial (Zimring 1972, 1968; Cook 1991; Wells and Horney 2002). Thus widespread gun use in violent crime *intensifies* violence, increasing the case-fatality rate. American "exceptionalism" in violent crime is not that we have so much of it, but that, because of widespread gun availability and use, it is so much more deadly than in other Western nations (Zimring and Hawkins 1997).

The likelihood that a gun will be used in crime is closely linked to the general availability of guns, and especially handguns. In jurisdictions where handgun ownership is common, the various types of transactions by which youths and criminals become armed are facilitated. The list of transactions includes thefts from homes and vehicles, loans to family members and friends, and off-the-books sales. In a high-prevalence area, then, transactions in the secondary market are subject to less friction and may well be cheaper than in markets where gun ownership is rare (Cook et al. 2008).

Cook and Ludwig (2006) analyzed the association between gun prevalence and homicide rates, both for a panel of the 200 largest counties, and a panel of the states. Our approach was similar to the analysis of UCR burglary rates described before, and we found strong evidence that an increase in gun prevalence has a positive effect on the homicide rate. A conservative estimate of the prevalence elasticity of homicide is 0.1. A back-of-the-envelope calculation suggests that the annual external cost of keeping a gun in the home amounts to at least $100 (differing widely according to the amount of violence in the community). We found that assault and rape were not affected by gun prevalence, confirming other evidence that gun prevalence has little or no effect on the *volume* of violence, but a considerable effect on the *intensity* of violence, and in particular the death rate in assault and robbery.

5.5.2   Drawing the Line in Gun Rights

In our view, the best evidence, reviewed earlier, indicates that private ownership of firearms creates negative externalities, in the form of increased residential burglary and homicide rates, with no discernible effect on other types of crime.[22] On the other hand, the private benefits of gun ownership, revealed by the choice of a large minority of people (mostly men) to a possess a gun, indicate that the perceived private benefits may outweigh any private risks and other costs. The exercise of that preference is protected by *Heller*, at least to an extent. In future Second Amendment decisions, the Court will begin to resolve the current uncertainty about what regulations of private ownership and transactions are acceptable. The *Heller* opinion states a presumption that a variety of common regulations are acceptable, but does not establish any principle for evaluating specific cases.

It is reasonable to suppose that regulations targeted on the negative externalities of handgun ownership shall be allowed if they do not impose too much of a burden on the core right of home defense.

The federal regulatory system is intended to limit gun sales by licensed dealers to adults who are legal residents and who are not disqualified by fact of a felony conviction, mental illness, conviction for domestic violence, and so forth. If the system were more successful in limiting access to this group, the problem of gun violence would be greatly reduced. For example, one study found that 43 percent of adults arrested for homicide in Illinois during the 1990s had at least one prior felony conviction, compared with just 4 percent of the general public (Cook, Ludwig, and Braga 2005). In fact, there is a great deal of leakage of guns from the entitled sector of the population to the proscribed sector. That leakage is the result of a variety of transactions, some legal under current laws, some not—private sales and loans, theft, straw purchases from dealers by qualified people under contract with a disqualified person, and so forth. An underground market for redistributing guns exists in some cities (Cook et al. 2007), and gun shows are ubiquitous.

Additional regulations that may help curtail this diversion of guns to the proscribed sector include those that would place limits on how owners could dispose of their guns, and create a record of transfers that did occur. For example, all licit transfers could be channeled through licensed dealers, with the usual requirement that the dealer conduct a background check of the intended recipient and keep a record of the transaction. Safe storage requirements could reduce theft (as well as creating a safer home for chil-

---

22. Just to be clear, we are referring here to the externalities associated with prevalence of gun ownership, rather than the much-debated topic of the consequences of liberal permit laws for gun carrying (Lott 2000; Donohue 2003).

dren), and owners could be required to report thefts. Straw purchases could be discouraged by limiting sales to one per month (as three states have done for handguns). The principle of holding the owner responsible for his gun could be furthered by requiring liability insurance, and by instituting some version of registration. (Note that there would be some utility in tracking gun transactions by requiring that dealers report all sales to a central location, even if the identity of the buyer were not reported but kept, as it currently is, in the dealer's records.) Gun shows could be regulated to limit illicit transactions, as they are in California.

Given that some diversion of guns will occur regardless of the regulations in place, there are additional measures that could limit criminal misuse by making guns a liability to criminals. The notion here is that if there were programs in place that had the effect of ensuring that gun use in robbery or assault increased the chance of arrest or the severity of punishment, then some violent criminals would substitute other weapons for guns or desist entirely—with the result that fewer victims would be killed, and fewer neighborhoods terrorized by gunfire. A case in point is a California requirement, scheduled for implementation in 2010. The law requires that new pistols be designed to microstamp a serial number on shell casings. Any casings left at the scene of a crime could then be traced to a specific gun, facilitating the identification of the shooter. Cash award programs for providing authorities with information on proscribed people who are involved with guns may also make guns a greater liability.

We do not necessarily endorse any of these regulations, but simply point them out as among the plausible possibilities for reducing the diversion of guns and of the incentive to misuse guns, and thereby reduce the negative externality of private ownership. None of these place much burden on the individual who wishes to keep a handgun for defense of the home, and hence all are in the spirit of the *Heller*-defined core right. Note that if the Court had chosen to develop the Second Amendment right as defense against government tyranny, rather than against crime, then regulations of this sort might be challenged as providing government authorities the means to confiscate guns. But the concern for tyranny, which many commentators have found reflected in the Second Amendment's text, did not figure in the decision of the *Heller* majority.

5.5.3   *Heller* Meets Coase

Despite the increase in social cost of gun violence that we anticipate may follow from *Heller* litigation, this new regime is not necessarily inferior to the status quo. The freedom to keep a handgun has value. In fact, this value might be greater if the premise of *Heller* is accepted—namely, that individuals have a legal entitlement to possess a handgun. Given *Heller*, that entitlement is not transferrable at a wholesale level through ordinary democratic politics, but it is interesting to speculate about the "bargain" that would result if exchange were allowed.

Imagine that the population consists of two groups, "gun lovers" and "safety lovers." The two groups bargain in a Coasian fashion, free of the usual impediments of scarce information and transactions costs. It is possible that the gun lovers would relinquish their *Heller* right—that is, that their willingness to accept payment would in total be less than the willingness of the safety lovers to pay for a handgun-free community. We have no basis for predicting without having detailed information about preferences. What we can say with confidence is that the gun-free bargain is less likely if there is a legal entitlement to keep a gun, than if the property rights are shifted to potential victims.

Indeed, one could imagine a quite different legal entitlement, awarded to those who wished to be free of the threat of gun violence—as suggested by the first right of the trilogy "life, liberty, and the pursuit of happiness." Under this alternative assignment of rights, the Coasian bargaining would be reversed, and a gun ban would prevail unless the gun lovers' willingness to pay for a gun exceeded other residents' willingness to accept payment for giving up a gun-free environment.

While the famous Coase "invariance" result suggests that the equilibrium allocation following costless bargaining will be unaffected by the initial assignment of property rights, that is not the case here (Hovenkamp 1990). The valuations are subjective and likely to vary with wealth. In particular, for a gun lover, the willingness to pay for the right to possess a gun is likely to be a good deal less than the willingness to accept payment for relinquishing a gun. The same can be said for the valuation of a gun-free community by the safety lovers. Thus the initial entitlement matters, and the safety-rights regime is more likely to produce a ban than a gun-rights regime.

There is some evidence available on the individual valuation of gun violence. Ludwig and Cook (2001) inserted referendum-type questions on gun violence into a national survey conducted by the National Opinion Research Center (NORC) finding that two-thirds of respondents were willing to pay at least $200 for a 30 percent reduction in gun violence in their community. Most interesting for the current purpose is that estimated willingness to pay increased with household income, despite the fact that those with higher incomes typically face a lower objective risk of victimization. Based on that and a vast array of related evidence (Viscusi and Aldy 2003), we believe that safety from gun violence is a normal commodity, implying that the willingness to accept compensation for a unit increase in risk will exceed willingness to pay for avoiding a unit increase (Cook and Graham 1977). We know of no direct evidence on the valuation of the right to possess a handgun, but casual observation suggests that there is an intense minority of the population that feel strongly about this right as evidenced by their political behavior—

Table 5.1   **Hypothetical cost-benefit calculations under two scenarios**

	Scenario I Gun rights	Scenario II Safety rights
Gun lovers ($n = 20$)	WTA = 1,000	WTP = 300
Safety lovers ($n = 80$)	WTP = 200	WTA = 400
Total surplus for ban over no ban	−4,000	+32,000

letter writing, attendance at meetings, financial contributions to candidates and advocacy organizations, and single-issue voting patterns (Schuman and Presser 1981; Spitzer 1998). It is plausible that this intensity of preference would be reflected in a very high willingness to accept payment for giving up gun rights—higher than their income-constrained willingness to pay.

A numerical example serves to illustrate the conceptual point. Suppose that the community consists of twenty gun lovers and eighty safety lovers. Under the "gun rights" scenario, gun lovers would voluntarily give up their guns only if their combined willingness to accept (WTA) were less than the combined willingness to pay (WTP) of the safety lovers for a gun-free community. Alternatively, under the "safety rights" scenario, gun lovers would voluntarily give up their guns unless their combined WTP for a gun exceeded the combined WTA by the safety lovers to tolerate guns in the community. As explained about, for gun lovers the WTA to give up the gun (under the gun rights scenario) is far higher than the WTP to acquire a gun (under the "safety rights" scenario). For safety lovers the situation is reversed. If under the gun rights scenario, for example, the twenty gun lovers' WTA to give up the gun is 1,000, while the eighty safety lovers' WTP is 200, the ban fails a cost-benefit test against free exercise of the right. But a ban prevails under the safety rights scenario if (again for the sake of illustration) the gun lovers WTP is 300 while the safety lovers' WTA is 400. (See table 5.1.)

In this analysis, then, the *Heller* ruling may be justified (though this is by no means how the majority *did* justify it) on the basis of two linked claims: (a) the Second Amendment provides a legal entitlement for individuals to keep a handgun in their home; and (b) given that entitlement, it is most likely the case that a ban would not pass a cost-benefit test—that is, it would not be possible to compensate the losers from the resulting gains. If we accept the first claim, then the second becomes plausible, and suggests that the *Heller* decision is not obviously inefficient.

The *Heller* decision overturns regulations put in place by the democratically elected City Council of the District of Columbia and kept in place for over three decades.[23] While antidemocratic, this decision places the Sec-

23. For a history of this legislation, see Rostron (2008).

ond Amendment on the same footing with other Constitutional rights that limit the scope for legislative and regulatory action, including the rights spelled out in the First Amendment. These rights are generally not subject to transfer through ordinary politics, which blocks potential bargains at the community-wide level. Indeed, many people believe that the freedom of speech must receive some insulation from government regulation in order for ordinary politics to function well. In the real world, where bargaining in the political or economic arena is vulnerable to various distortions, perhaps the Supreme Court may reasonably impose its judgment about the shape of the equilibrium allocation rather than open the door to a far-from-perfect bargaining process.

While this discussion is entirely speculative, it does suggest an interesting possibility: that the ban on bans in the *Heller* decision would be characteristic of the efficient allocation starting from the award of the entitlement to gun lovers—and quite at odds with the efficient allocation starting from the alternative entitlement to be free of gun violence.

Of course, one might believe that the Supreme Court's interpretation of the Second Amendment was flawed. One might also believe that other institutions are better situated to decide which competing group ought to receive legal entitlements regarding firearms. As we have emphasized, the balance of costs and benefits for gun control is different for different communities across the United States. But the politics of gun regulation today is hardly ideal. Many local governments are already unable to regulate as the majority sees fit given preemption by state law; and gun policy is often the product of legislative jousting and not careful analysis by experienced agency officials. Nor are handgun bans obviously efficacious in the large cities where useful data are available. And so the Court's rejection of the District of Columbia's handgun ban might turn out to be sound policy, depending, in part, on which side is entitled to the initial entitlement.

5.6   Conclusions

The much-discussed conundrum of gun control in America has been the evident disparity between majority opinion (which has had strong majorities in favor of an array of moderate gun control measures) and the actual enactments of Congress and state legislatures (Goss 2006; Teret et al. 1998). Much has been written about the ability of the minority in this arena to dominate policy choice, noting that there is a subset of those who oppose regulations who tend to be politically mobilized single-issue voters (Schuman and Presser 1981; Spitzer 1998). The mass tort litigation by the cities can then be interpreted as an effort to help redress this apparent failure of the political process to represent the public interest as defined by majority opinion (Lytton 2005b; Cook and Ludwig 2002).

In this essay we consider the reverse possibility, that the *Heller* decision serves to correct the failure of the democratic process to give appropriate weight to the *minority* interest of DC residents in keeping handguns.[24] Our argument rests on the reasonable possibility that the public interest is likely to be closely tied to the initial entitlement. If DC residents are entitled to keep a handgun in the home, then it is conceivable that even in the District of Columbia the "no ban" allocation would pass a cost-benefit test vis-à-vis the handgun ban adopted in 1976. The argument is simply that the majority of residents who favor this ban would not have been willing to pay enough to fully compensate all those residents who wish to keep a handgun legally. That is, we speculate that there is no potential bargain that makes the ban Pareto-preferred to no ban, if bargaining begins with an entitlement to possess. The same conclusion may apply to Chicago, New York City, and some other jurisdictions where stringent handgun regulations are being litigated.

Note that this conclusion hinges on a particular assignment of rights. An alternative regime, in which residents are entitled to live free of the threat of handgun violence, may lead to quite a different conclusion, since it seems unlikely that in the District of Columbia the gun lovers would be able to compensate those who favored a handgun-free environment. Of course neither of these entitlements characterizes the status quo ante-*Heller,* where the political process sorted things out for better or worse without an explicit cost-benefit test and with no entitlements either way.

Our other conclusion is that incorporation through the Fourteenth Amendment would lead to easing of gun restrictions in several jurisdictions in which gun ownership has been low, and the result is quite likely to be an expansion of gun ownership.[25] Based on our assessment of the literature, an intensification of violence with higher homicide and suicide rates will follow. The private decision to keep a handgun, however precious, comes at a cost.

References

Azrael, D., P. J. Cook, and M. Miller. 2004. State and local prevalence of firearms ownership: Measurement, structure, and trends. *Journal of Quantitative Criminology* 20 (1): 43–62.

24. Note that while a strong majority of the American public supports moderate gun control, that is not true for a handgun ban, which a majority opposes (Teret et al. 1998). It is only in particular urban jurisdictions that a ban receives majority support.

25. We offer this judgment with some uncertainty, simply because the jurisdictions that have stringent measures tend to have porous borders that make the existing measures hard to enforce. If the Supreme Court went further and broadened the Second Amendment right so as to ban the special federal excise tax, for example, that may make more of a difference.

Barnett, R. E., and D. B. Kates. 1996. Under fire: The new consensus on the Second Amendment. *Emory Law Journal* 45:1139.

Bonnie, R. J., C. E. Fulco, and C. T. Liverman, eds. 1999. *Reducing the burden of injury: Advancing prevention and treatment.* Washington, DC: National Academy Press.

Brief for Amici Curiae 55. Members of United States Senate, the President of the United States Senate, and 250 Members of United States House of Representatives in Support of Respondent, in District of Columbia v. Heller, 128 S.Ct. 2783. 2008. Available at: http://www.supreme.lp.findlaw.com/supreme_court/briefs/07-290/07-290.mer.ami.resp.cong.pdf.

Bureau of Alcohol, Tobacco, and Firearms (ATF). 2000a. *ATF regulatory actions: Report to the secretary on firearms initiatives.* Washington, DC: U.S. Department of the Treasury.

———. 2000b. *Commerce in firearms in the United States.* Washington, DC: U.S. Department of the Treasury.

Chemerinsky, E. 2006. *Constitutional law: Principles and premises,* 3rd ed. New York: Aspen Publishers.

Cohen, M. A., R. T. Rust, S. Steen, and S. T. Tidd. 2004. Willingness-to-pay for crime control programs. *Criminology* 42 (1): 89–109.

Cook, P. J. 1980. Reducing injury and death rates in robbery. *Policy Analysis* 6 (1): 21–45.

———. 1991. The technology of personal violence. In *Crime and justice: An annual review of research,* ed. M. Tonry, 1–71. Chicago: University of Chicago Press.

Cook, P. J., and A. A. Braga. 2001. Comprehensive firearms tracing: Strategic and investigative uses of new data on firearms markets. *Arizona Law Review* 43 (2): 277–309.

Cook, P. J., W. Cukier, and K. Krause. 2009. The illicit firearms trade in North America. *Criminology and Criminal Justice* 9 (3): 265–86.

Cook, P. J., and D. A. Graham. 1977. The demand for insurance and protection: The case of irreplaceable commodities. *The Quarterly Journal of Economics* 91 (1): 143–56.

Cook, P. J., and J. Laub. 1998. The unprecedented epidemic in youth violence. In *Youth violence,* ed. M. Tonry and M. H. Moore, 101–38. Chicago: University of Chicago Press.

Cook, P. J., and J. A. Leitzel. 1996. Perversity, futility, jeopardy: An economic analysis of the attack on gun control. *Law and Contemporary Problems* 59 (1): 91–118.

Cook, P. J., and J. Ludwig. 1996. *Guns in America: Results of a comprehensive survey of gun ownership and use.* Washington, DC: Police Foundation.

———. 2000. *Gun violence: The real costs.* New York: Oxford University Press.

———. 2002. Litigation as regulation: The case of firearms. In *Regulation through litigation,* ed. W. K. Viscusi, 67–90. Washington, DC: Brookings Institution.

———. 2003. Guns and burglary. In *Evaluating gun policy* ed. J. Ludwig and P. J. Cook, 74–120. Washington, DC: Brookings Institution Press.

———. 2006. The social costs of gun ownership. *Journal of Public Economics* 90 (1-2): 379–91.

Cook, P. J., J. Ludwig, and A. A. Braga. 2005. Criminal records of homicide offenders. *Journal of the American Medical Association* 294 (5): 598–601.

Cook, P. J., J. Ludwig, and D. Hemenway. 1997. The gun debate's new mythical number: How many defensive gun uses per year? *Journal of Policy Analysis and Management* 16:463–69.

Cook, P. J., J. Ludwig, and A. Samaha. 2009. Gun control after *Heller:* Threats and sideshows from a social welfare perspective. *UCLA Law Review* 56:1041–93.

Cook, P. J., J. Ludwig, S. A. Venkatesh, and A. A. Braga. 2007. Underground gun markets. *Economic Journal* 117 (524): F588–F618.

Cook, P. J., S. Molliconi, and T. Cole. 1995. Regulating gun markets. *Journal of Criminal Law and Criminology* 86:59–92.

Cottrol, R. J., and R. T. Diamond. 1991. The Second Amendment: Toward an Afro-Americanist reconsideration. *Georgetown Law Journal* 80:309.

Dahl, R. A. 1957. Decision-making in a Democracy: The Supreme Court as a national policy-maker. *Journal of Public Law* 6:279.

Denning, B. P. 2005. Gun litigation and the Constitution. In *Suing the gun industry,* ed. T. D. Lytton, 315–38. Ann Arbor: University of Michigan Press.

Donohue, J. J., III. 2003. The final bullet in the body of the more guns, less crime hypothesis. *Criminology and Public Policy* 2 (3): 397–410.

Duggan, M. 2001. More guns, more crime. *Journal of Political Economy* 109 (5): 1086–114.

Epstein, L., and J. Knight. 1998. *The choices justices make.* Washington, DC: Congressional Quarterly, Inc.

Friedman, B. 2005. The politics of judicial review. *Texas Law Review* 84: 257.

Goss, K. A. 2006. *Disarmed: The missing movement for gun control in America.* Princeton, NJ: Princeton University Press.

Graham, J. D., and J. B. Wiener, eds. 1995. *Risk vs. risk: Tradeoffs in protecting health and the environment.* Cambridge, MA: Harvard University Press.

Hemenway, D. 1997a. Survey research and self-defense gun use: An explanation of extreme overestimates. *Journal of Criminal Law and Criminology* 87:1430–45.

———. 1997b. The myth of millions of self-defense gun uses: An explanation of extreme overestimates. *Chance* 10:6–10.

———. 2004. *Private guns, public health.* Ann Arbor: University of Michigan Press.

Hepburn, L., M. Miller, D. Azrael, and D. Hemenway. 2007. The U.S. gun stock: Results from the 2004 National Firearms Survey. *Injury Prevention* 13:15–19.

Horan, D. 2008. Evanston latest suburb to repeal handgun ban in wake of high court ruling. *Chicago Tribune,* August 12. www.chicagotribune.com/news/local/chi-gun-ban_13aug13,0,1421061.story.

Hovenkamp, H. J. 1990. Marginal utility and the Coase theorem. *Cornell Law Review* 75:783.

Karlson, T. A., and S. W. Hargarten. 1997. *Reducing firearms injury and death: A public health sourcebook on guns.* New Brunswick, NJ: Rutgers University Press.

Kleck, G. 1991. *Point blank: Guns and violence in America.* New York: Aldine de Gruyter.

———. 1997. *Targeting guns: Firearms and their control.* New York: Aldine de Gruyter.

———. 2004. Measures of gun ownership levels for macrolevel crime and violence research. *Journal of Research in Crime and Delinquency* 41 (1): 3–36.

Kleck, G., and M. Gertz. 1995. Armed resistance to crime: The prevalence and nature of self-defense with a gun. *Journal of Criminal Law and Criminology* 86:150–87.

Kopel, D., and R. Gardiner. 1995. The Sullivan principles: Protecting the Second Amendment from civil abuse. *Seton Hall Legislative Journal* 19:737.

Legal Community Against Violence (LCAV). 2009. *Regulating guns in America: An evaluation and comparative analysis of federal, state and selected local gun laws.* Available at: http://www.lcav.org/library/reports_analyses/regulating_guns.asp.

Levinson, S. 1989. The embarrassing Second Amendment. *Yale Law Journal* 99:637.

Levitt, S. D. 2001. Deterrence. In *Crime: Public policies for crime control,* ed. J. Q. Wilson and J. Pertersilia, 435–50. Oakland: Institute for Contemporary Studies.

Lewis, H. S., Jr., and E. Norman. 2001. *Civil rights law and practice.* St. Paul, MN: West Group.

Lott, J. 2000. *More guns, less crime,* 2nd ed. Chicago: University of Chicago Press.

Ludwig, J., and P. J. Cook. 2001. The benefits of reducing gun violence: Evidence from Contingent-Valuation Survey data. *Journal of Risk and Uncertainty* 22 (3): 207–26.

Lytton, T. D. 2005a. Afterward: Federal gun industry immunity legislation. In *Suing the gun industry,* ed. T. D. Lytton, 339–54. Ann Arbor: University of Michigan Press.

———. 2005b. Introduction: An overview of lawsuits against the gun industry. In *Suing the gun industry,* ed. T. D. Lytton, 1–35. Ann Arbor: University of Michigan Press.

McDowall, D., C. Loftin, and S. Presser. 2000. Measuring civilian defensive firearm use: A methodological experiment. *Journal of Quantitative Criminology* 16:1–19.

Milne, J. S., S. W. Hargarten, A. L. Kellerman, and G. H. Wintemute. 2003. Effect of current regulations on handgun safety features. *Annals of Emergency Medicine* 41 (1): 1–9.

Nagin, D. S. 1998. Criminal deterrence research at the outset of the twenty-first century. In *Crime and justice: A review of research,* vol. 23, ed. M. Tonry, 1–42. Chicago: University of Chicago Press.

Rengert, G. J., and J. Wasilchick. 1985. *Suburban burglary: A time and a place for everything.* Springfield, IL: Charles Thomas.

Rostron, A. 2006. Book review (of *Lawyers, guns and money*). *Santa Clara Law Review* 46 (2): 481–511.

———. 2008. Incrementalism, comprehensive rationality, and the future of gun control. *Maryland Law Review* 67 (3): 511–69.

Roth, J. A., and C. S. Koper. 1999. *Impacts of the 1994 Assault Weapons Ban: 1994–1996.* Research-in-Brief. Washington, DC: U.S. Department of Justice.

Saad, L. 2007. Shrunken majority now favors stricter gun laws. *Gallup News Service,* October 11. http://www.gallup.com/poll/101731/Shrunken-Majority-Now-Favors -Stricter-Gun-Laws.aspx.

Schuman, H., and S. Presser. 1981. The attitude-action connection and the issue of gun control. *The Annals of the American Academy of Political and Social Science* 455 (May): 40–7.

Segal, J. A., and H. J. Spaeth. 2002. *The Supreme Court and the attitudinal model revisited.* Cambridge: Cambridge University Press.

Shavell, S. 1984. Liability for harm versus regulation of safety. *Journal of Legal Studies* 13:357–74.

———. 2004. *Foundations of economic analysis of law.* Cambridge, MA: Harvard University Press.

Sheley, J. F., and J. D. Wright. 1995. *In the line of fire: Youth, guns, and violence in urban America.* New York: Aldine de Gruyter.

Shover, N. 1991. Burglary. In *Crime and justice: A review of research,* vol. 14, ed. M. Tonry, 73–113. Chicago: University of Chicago Press.

Siebel, B. J. 1999. City lawsuits against the gun industry: A roadmap for reforming gun industry misconduct. *St. Louis University Public Law Review* 18 (1): 247–90.

Spitzer, R. J. 1998. *The politics of gun control,* 2nd ed. New York: Chatham House.

Stipulation Regarding Settlement and Dismissal of Defendants San Francisco Housing Authority and Henry Alvarez III Without Prejudice, *Guy Montaq Doe v. San Francisco Housing Authority,* No. CV-08-03112 TEH (N.D. Cal. Jan. 12, 2009). Available at: http://volokh.com/files/sfpublichousingguns.pdf.

Teret, S. P., D. W. Webster, J. S. Vernick, T. W. Smith, D. Leff, G. J. Wintemute, P. J.

Cook, et al. 1998. Support for new policies to regulate firearms: Results of two national surveys. *New England Journal of Medicine* 339 (12): 813–18.

Tushnet, M. V. 2007. *Out of range: Why the Constitution can't end the battle over guns.* New York: Oxford University Press.

Vernick, J. S., and S. P. Teret. 1999. New courtroom strategies regarding firearms: Tort litigation against firearm manufacturers and Constitutional challenges to gun laws. *Houston Law Review* 36 (5): 1713–54.

———. 2000. A public health approach to regulating firearms as consumer products. *University of Pennsylvania Law Review* 148 (4): 1193–2111.

Viscusi, W. K., and J. E. Aldy. 2003. The value of a statistical life: A critical review of market estimates throughout the world. *Journal of Risk and Uncertainty* 27 (1): 5–76.

Volokh, E. 1998. The commonplace Second Amendment. *New York University Law Review* 73:793.

Wellford, C. F., J. V. Pepper, and C. V. Petrie, 2005. *Firearms and violence: A critical review.* Washington, DC: National Academies Press.

Wells, W., and J. Horney. 2002. Weapon effects and individual intent to do harm: Influences on the escalation of violence. *Criminology* 40: 265–96.

Winkler, A. 2007. Scrutinizing the Second Amendment. *Michigan Law Review* 105:683.

———. 2009. *Heller*'s catch-22. *UCLA Law Review* 56:1551.

Wintemute, G. J. 1994. *Ring of fire: The handgun makers of southern California.* Sacramento: Violence Prevention Research Program, University of California, Davis.

Wise, D. 2008. Defense lawyers fire first shot in challenge to state gun law. *New York Law Journal,* July 16.

Wright, J. D., and P. H. Rossi. 1994. *Armed and considered dangerous: A survey of felons and their firearms* (expanded edition). New York: Aldine de Gruyter.

Wright, R., and S. Decker. 1994. *Burglars on the job: Streetlife and residential break-ins.* Boston: Northeastern University Press.

Zimring, F. E. 1968. Is gun control likely to reduce violent killings? *University of Chicago Law Review* 35: 21–37.

———. 1972. The medium is the message: Firearm calibre as a determinant of death from assault. *Journal of Legal Studies* 1: 97–124.

———. 1975. Firearms and federal law: The gun control Act of 1968. *The Journal of Legal Studies* 4 (1): 133–98.

Zimring, F. E., and G. Hawkins. 1997. *Crime is not the problem: Lethal violence in America.* New York: Oxford University Press.

6

The Effects of Product Liability Exemption in the Presence of the FDA

Tomas J. Philipson, Eric Sun, and Dana Goldman

6.1 Introduction

In the United States, the safety and efficacy of drugs and medical devices are primarily regulated by the United States Food and Drug Administration (FDA) through premarket activities, such as mandatory clinical testing, and post-market activities, such as the use of the Adverse Event Reporting System to monitor the incidence of adverse events. However, while the FDA is the primary and most visible regulator of drug safety, the presence of legal liability after a product has entered the market gives firms large incentives to provide safe drugs.

The overlap between the FDA and product liability in regulating drug safety has received substantial attention from policymakers, particularly in light of several high profile lawsuits against drug manufacturers, such as those involving the drug Vioxx (rofecoxib).[1] Of particular interest has

Tomas J. Philipson is the Daniel Levin Professor of Public Policy Studies in the Irving B. Harris Graduate School of Public Policy Studies and an associate member of the Department of Economics at the University of Chicago, and a research associate of the National Bureau of Economic Research. Eric Sun is an MD/PhD student in the Booth School of Business and the Pritzker School of Medicine at the University of Chicago, and a researcher and fellow at the Bing Center for Health Economics at RAND Corporation. Dana Goldman is the Norman Topping Chair in Medicine and Public Policy and a professor at the University of Southern California and a research associate of the National Bureau of Economic Research.

Prepared for the NBER conference "Regulation and Litigation," September 11–12, 2009, Arizona. We are indebted to Yang Lu for excellent research assistance, the conference participants at the NBER Law and Economics conference, and two anonymous referees for comments and suggestions. Sun gratefully acknowledges funding from the Medical Scientist Training Program at the University of Chicago (NIGMS Grant number 5 T32 GM07281).

1. Vioxx, a selective COX-2 inhibitor, was withdrawn from the U.S. market in 2004 after several high profile lawsuits alleging that the drug significantly increased patients' risk of adverse

been the issue of preemption, which states that FDA approval of a drug's label, which lists the indications that the drug is approved to treat as well as warnings about any side effects, gives the manufacturer immunity against lawsuits based on state law. In 2006, this doctrine was formally adopted by the FDA through a modification in the *Federal Register*. The FDA's adoption of the preemption doctrine has been controversial in legal circles, with lower federal courts offering conflicting views on the doctrine. Recently, in *Riegel v. Medtronic*, the Supreme Court of the United States upheld the preemption doctrine for medical devices, although in a 5-4 decision in *Wyeth v. Levine*, the Court ruled the doctrine did not apply to drugs.

Supporters of preemption argue that it frees pharmaceutical firms from the chaos of having fifty separate states regulate drug safety, thereby reducing the potential that pharmaceutical firms will "over-warn" patients about the risks of drugs (Calfee 2008; Calfee et al. 2008). Opponents argue that product liability is a useful complement to the FDA, and has resulted in safer drugs (Kessler and Vladeck 2008; Curfman, Morrisey, and Drazen 2008; Glantz and Annas 2008).

Despite the debate over the potential consequences of preemption, there has been little explicit economic analysis that has attempted to determine under what circumstances preemption, or limits on damages more generally, might improve economic efficiency. In this chapter we provide a formal analysis of the dual regulation of medical product safety and the potential efficiency effects induced by product liability in the presence of the FDA. Our main argument is that the standard efficiency implications of product liability are altered when there is dual regulation of safety through another government agency such as the FDA. In particular, lowering liability (through preemption or other means) in the presence of the FDA can raise welfare under conditions when it would otherwise lower welfare in the agency's absence. Two central aspects of the FDA's activities drive these opposite effects. First, the FDA generates information about product quality prior to marketing beyond what would be the case with liability alone. Second, the FDA requires a minimum level of product quality before marketing.

As is well known, when consumers are fully informed about product quality, product liability cannot improve on an already efficient outcome. Any efficiency gains from either product liability or the FDA must therefore come from lack of full information about product quality on the demand side. When the demand side is uninformed, particularly when it underestimates the potential harms of a drug, product liability accomplishes two socially desirable actions. First, it helps provide the efficient level of *quality*

---

cardiovascular events. On November 9, 2007, the manufacturer of Vioxx, Merck, agreed to establish a $4.85 billion settlement fund to compensate Vioxx patients who experienced a myocardial infarction or ischemic stroke while using the drug.

or safety by giving firms incentives to provide safe products. Second, it ensures the efficient level of product *quantity*. Since consumers will overconsume a drug when they underestimate its risk, product liability acts as a beneficial tax.

However, by imposing and verifying a minimal safety level, the FDA addresses both of these issues directly. On the quality side, to the degree that the FDA's safety standards are binding on firms, product liability may not induce them to provide additional safety. In terms of quantity, since the FDA verifies safety, consumers are more informed, mitigating the concern of overconsumption. In the agency's presence, product liability thereby merely acts as a tax. Even if this tax is paid back to patients in the form of damages, a dead-weight loss still exists due to reduced access. Thus, while product liability may raise efficiency in the absence of the FDA by inducing firms to provide safety and appropriately restrict access, in the agency's presence it can actually reduce welfare by inappropriately reducing access. We offer an empirical test of the conditions under which increased liability may reduce efficiency through the quantity-dimension that involves testing for changes in the price and safety effects of liability changes.

Clearly, our efficiency analysis for preemption should by no means be interpreted as abolishing product liability altogether (e.g., for fraud or activities for which FDA has no jurisdiction), but simply for those activities in which a public entity like the FDA is overseeing the same type of behavior as product liability—in these cases, the duplication of regulation and liability is inefficient. To reiterate, our arguments do not apply to all activities, just those for which there are dual government interventions.

We consider the National Vaccine Injury Compensation Program (NVICP) as a case study to illustrate how to test for the welfare effects of changes in liability. This program shielded vaccine makers from liability in exchange for a special compensation program funded by an excise tax on vaccines. This program therefore essentially mimicked preemption by lowering the cost of liability dramatically for manufacturers. Prior to the implementation of NVICP, there was a substantial increase in liability actions relating to vaccines, and this increase is associated with a rapid increase in prices. After the NVICP was implemented, prices fell. However, we find no evidence that the NVICP led to more unsafe vaccines. If the effects of this program are indicative of a more general pattern of no safety effects and reduced prices when reducing liability in the presence of FDA, then preemption may be efficiency enhancing.

The chapter is briefly organized as follows. Section 6.2 provides background on the dual regulation of drug safety. Section 6.3 presents and discusses our analysis of the efficiency effects of preemption. Section 6.4 discusses our case studies for vaccines covered by the NVICP. Lastly, section 6.5 concludes and discusses future research.

6.2 Background on U.S. Medical Product Safety Regulation

In the United States, the FDA is the federal agency charged with regulating drug safety and efficacy. The majority of the agency's efforts are devoted toward premarket activities, whereby the agency supervises and evaluates a series of clinical trials undertaken by drug manufacturers in order to establish drug safety and efficacy. The clinical trial process begins when a firm files an Investigational New Drug application, which requests permission from the FDA to conduct clinical trials on humans. Typically, this application contains the available preclinical information, as well as protocols for the drug's clinical trials, and any data on trials conducted overseas.

Once the FDA gives its approval, the firm may begin conducting clinical trials for the drug, which proceed in three phases. The goal of Phase I is to evaluate the drug's safety and to obtain data on its pharmacologic properties. Typically, Phase I trials enroll small numbers (twenty to eighty) of healthy volunteers. Phase II trials then enroll slightly larger (100 to 130) numbers of sick volunteers. The goal of these trials is to begin investigating a drug's efficacy and optimal dosage, and to monitor the drug's safety in diseased patients. Finally, Phase III testing typically involves larger numbers (more than 1,000) of sick patients and is the most costly stage of the approval process. Phase III testing seeks to establish more definitively the efficacy of a drug, as well as to discover any rare side effects. Upon the completion of Phase III testing, the firm submits a New Drug Application to the FDA, which is accompanied by the results of the clinical trials. The FDA may then reject the application, require further clinical testing, or approve the drug outright.

In addition to issuing approval of the drug, the FDA must approve the label that accompanies it. This label provides data on the drug's pharmacologic properties and side effects, as well as brief summaries of the clinical trials reported to the FDA. Perhaps most importantly, the label also lists the indications (or diseases) that the drug is approved to treat. Thus, approval by the FDA is not merely approval of the drug, it is approval of the drug for specific uses. If a firm wishes to obtain approval for additional indications, it typically must begin a new set of clinical trials for those indications. Use of a drug for an indication not listed on the label ("off-label use") is not illegal, and indeed occurs regularly in many areas, such as oncology. However, it is illegal for a manufacturer to advertise a drug for a nonapproved indication. In addition, insurers may not always pay for off-label use of a drug.

The FDA also oversees the safety and efficacy of medical devices. Here, the process is more complex, because the statutory definition of a medical device is extremely broad[2] and includes a wide variety of implements, such

---

2. According to the Food, Drug, and Cosmetic Act, a medical device is defined as "an instrument, apparatus, implement, machine, contrivance, implant, in vitro reagent, or other

as tongue depressors, home pregnancy tests, and drug eluting stents. All devices are categorized into one of three classes (I, II, and III), based on the degree of patient risk. Class I devices are the least risky, and typically require no premarket approval from the FDA, although the manufacturer must register with the FDA prior to marketing the device. Class II devices pose more risk to patients, and must receive prior approval via the 510(k) review process, which typically seeks to establish that the given device is substantially equivalent to another device that has received FDA approval. The most risky (class III) devices require approval via the premarket approval process (PMA), which, similar to the process for pharmaceuticals just described, involves the submission of a PMA application establishing the device's safety and efficacy, usually through the results of clinical trials. After receipt of a PMA or 510(k) application, the FDA reviews it and decides whether to allow the device to be marketed in the United States. For devices approved via PMAs, further changes require different types of supplemental applications (supplemental PMAs), depending on the nature of the modification. Large-scale changes to the device, such as changes in its indication or substantial changes in design, require a Panel Track Supplement, which is in effect equivalent to submitting a new PMA. More modest changes require a 180-day Supplement, and minor modifications require a Real-time Supplement. In addition, changes in the manufacturing process must be approved via a 30-day Supplement.

While the FDA is the primary and most visible player in drug and device safety regulation, product liability also plays a role in ensuring safety by allowing patients to sue manufacturers for unsafe drugs or devices and recover damages for any adverse events that they suffer. Patients can generally sue manufacturers under one of three theories of legal liability. The first, *defective design,* allows a patient to sue on the basis that the design of a drug or device was inherently unsafe. Second, patients can sue for *defective manufacturing* of an otherwise safe drug or device. Finally, under the theory of *defective warnings,* patients can sue by showing that the firm failed to provide sufficient warning of the possibility of an adverse event if it knew or shown that it knew about the risks. Given that the FDA approval encompasses a drug or device's safety and the sufficiency of the warnings in the drug label, firms have tried to use FDA approval as a shield against product liability

similar or related article, including any component, part, or accessory, which is (1) recognized in the official National Formulary, or the United States Pharmacopeia, or any supplement to them, (2) intended for use in the diagnosis of disease or other conditions, or in the cure, mitigation, treatment, or prevention of disease, in man or other animals, or (3) intended to affect the structure or any function of the body of man or other animals, and which does not achieve its primary intended purposes through chemical action within or on the body of man or other animals and which is not dependent upon being metabolized for the achievement of its primary intended purposes." (See http://www.fda.gov/RegulatoryInformation/Legislation/FederalFoodDrugandCosmeticActFDCAct/FDCActChaptersIandIIShortTitleandDefinitions/UCMO86297.htm.)

suits. For drugs, this argument has generally been accepted by the courts (Garber 1993), under a widely cited comment included in *Restatement (Second) of Torts,* which states that drugs are an example of an "unavoidably unsafe product"—in other words, drugs are not generally *unreasonably* dangerous, and the dangers associated with them are not evidence of defects in the drugs themselves. However, for medical devices, rather than drugs, design lawsuits are more common, since there is more ability to design a device with a better safety profile. Since courts have generally held that drug manufacturers cannot be sued for faulty design, the vast majority of drug lawsuits to date have been for failure to warn, and here, courts have in general held that FDA approval of the warnings on the label does not provide a shield against liability lawsuits. Courts have generally held that compliance with FDA regulations is a minimum standard. Thus, failure to comply with the FDA leaves a firm extremely vulnerable to lawsuits, but compliance does not shield a firm against lawsuits. However, it is important to note that the FDA maintains tight control over the information that a firm can release about a drug, including the release of warnings. For example, the FDA can prohibit the firm from adding a warning to the product label. Even if the FDA prohibits the firm from adding a warning, the firm can still be found liable for failing to warn consumers (Garber 1993; Calfee 2006). Lawsuits against firms proceed under state laws, and therefore, the determination of whether the firm knew, or should have known, about a particular risk is based on state-specific legal standards. If the patient prevails at the trial, he can recover compensatory damages for the adverse event, as well as punitive damages, if it is found that the firm intentionally hid evidence from the FDA.

While estimates of the costs of liability for pharmaceuticals and devices are few, there are indications that these costs are substantial, especially when viewed as a share of marginal costs. The latter is an important issue, as from an economic perspective, legal costs will have a larger effect on welfare when they comprise a large portion of marginal costs. Given that the marginal costs of drug production are low for drugs, even small legal costs may account for a significant proportion of marginal costs. A report prepared by the Council of Economic Advisers (2002) found that in 2000, liability costs across all U.S. industries were $180 billion, or roughly 1.8 percent of gross domestic product (GDP). The same report suggested that the inefficiencies from the liability system were equivalent to the inefficiencies that would occur from a 2 percent increase in consumption taxes, a 3 percent tax on wages, and a 5 percent tax on capital income.

There is research suggesting these relative liability costs are even higher for drugs. Manning (1994) identified liability costs for the diphtheria-pertussis-tetanus vaccine by comparing changes in the vaccine's price against changes in the price of the diphtheria-tetanus vaccine, as the only difference in the vaccines is the pertussis component, which adds a negligible cost to the production price of the vaccine and was the subject of numerous lawsuits.

Using this approach, Manning found that liability accounted for up to 90 percent of the price of the diphtheria-pertussis-tetanus vaccine's price. In addition, in related work (Manning 1997), Manning finds that differences in product liability regimes can explain much of the difference in the Canadian and U.S. prices of drugs.

6.3   An Efficiency Analysis of Regulation and Liability of Medical Products

In this section, we analyze the efficiency effects of preemption. Our analysis begins with a brief review of standard models of product liability (see Shavell 2007; Polinsky and Shavell 2007 for a review), which concern how post-market legal activities affect firms' safety and pricing decisions. It is well known that under perfect information, product liability has no effect on the level of safety firms provide or social welfare. Thus, the purpose of product liability is to give firms proper incentives to provide safety when consumers are uninformed. In addition, product liability helps achieve the optimal quantity in the face of consumer misinformation by affecting the prices that consumers pay.

We then add to this model the presence of premarket regulations governed by the FDA. We assume that FDA (a) mandates and verifies a minimum safety level, which may or may not be binding given the deterrence effect of product liability, and (b) that FDA generates information about product quality beyond what is generated under product liability alone. We show that these aspects of FDA may affect the sign of the efficiency effects of increased liability. Under perfect information about product quality, neither product liability nor any quality screening activities of the FDA will raise efficiency, so we focus on the case of an uninformed demand side.

6.3.1   The Framework

Consider when marginal are constant and for a given level of safety s are given by

(1) $$C(s) = c(s) + d(s),$$

where $c(s)$ is the marginal cost of production that rises in safety and $d(s)$ is the marginal cost of legal costs that falls in safety. Our notion of safety s is extremely flexible, and can accommodate a wide variety of specifications. For example, s could refer to a vector of drug characteristics, such as the safety of the drug itself, as well as the adequacy of warnings about the drug. For the informed consumer, the inverse demand curve $p(q,s)$ is given by a component of a perfectly safe drug, $p(q)$ less the expected harm he faces given the drug's safety $h(s)$, plus the damages he expects to receive:

$$p(q,s) = p(q) - h(s) + d(s).$$

The demand curve adopts the form

$$(3) \qquad q(p,s) = q(p + h(s) - d(s)),$$

showing that the informed consumer treats the expected harm as a tax and the expected damages received as a subsidy. Social welfare is therefore given by

$$(4) \qquad W(q,s) = \int_0^{q(p,s)} p(x,s) - c(s) - h(s)dx.$$

While damage payments $d(s)$ do not directly enter the equation for social welfare, as they simply represent a transfer payment from firms to consumers, they may indirectly affect social welfare through their effects on price p and therefore the quantity consumed $q(p,s)$.

6.3.2   The Neutrality of Product Liability under Perfect Information

With perfectly informed consumers, the firm chooses the level of safety that maximizes its profit function, given by

$$(5) \qquad \pi(q,s) = q(p,s)(p - c(s) - d(s)).$$

It is easy to show that with perfect information, damages do not affect the firm's safety provision. Although damages enter into the firm's cost function, they also increase the consumer's valuation for the good by an equivalent amount. Therefore, in choosing the optimal safety level, the firm ignores the effect of damages on marginal costs and demand and simply chooses the safety level that equates the marginal revenue of increased safety with the marginal cost. Moreover, while damages raise the firms' costs and therefore price, they have no effect on output since consumers are aware in advance of the damages they receive. Thus, under perfect information, liability has no effect on social welfare or the firm's provision of safety.

6.3.3   Product Liability with Uninformed Consumers

Given that product liability and the FDA cannot have any welfare-enhancing effects in the case of perfectly informed consumers, we consider the case where consumers are uninformed. We assume that consumers underestimate[3] the harm of the product and are uninformed of damages so that the inverse demand curve is simply $p(q)$. Under these assumptions, the firm's profit function is given by

$$(6) \qquad \pi(p,s) = q(p)(p - c - c(s) - d(s)).$$

The first-order condition for the optimal level of safety under product liability, denoted s^{PL}, is then given by

$$(7) \qquad c_s + d_s = 0.$$

---

3. Clearly, if consumers overestimate harm, this would strengthen our arguments, as in this case quantity is already undersupplied.

This simply states that the firm chooses the level of safety that minimizes costs through equating increased costs of production with reduced liabilities. Social welfare is now given by

$$(8) \qquad \int_0^{q(p)} p(x,s) - c(s) - h(s)dx,$$

which stands in contrast to social welfare under perfect information in that the total quantity consumed is now determined by the uninformed demand curve $q(p)$.

The effect of product liability on welfare is twofold. In terms of product quality, it gives firms incentive to provide safety by forcing them to internalize the costs of safety—clearly, they would have no such incentives in the absence of product liability with uninformed consumers. Second, for a given level of safety, product liability affects quantity as shown in figure 6.1. This figure plots the uninformed demand curve $q(p)$, the cost of production $c(s)$, the firm's marginal cost $c(s) + d(s)$, and the social cost of the good, which is the cost of production plus the expected harm, $c(s) + h(s)$. The socially optimal consumption level occurs when price equals social cost (point A). However, in the absence of product liability, consumption occurs where price equals the marginal cost of production (point B). As shown in the figure, product liability therefore acts as a Pigouvian tax that reduces overconsumption by having consumers internalize the expected harm (point C). Indeed, optimal consumption is attained by setting damages $d(s)$ equal to expected harm $h(s)$ so that points C and A converge.

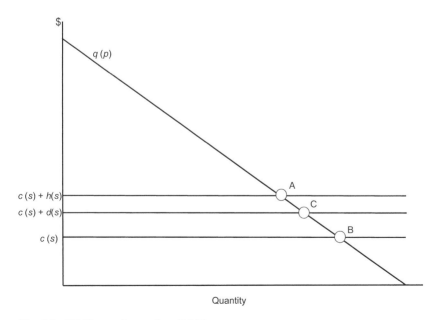

Fig. 6.1   **Welfare under product liability**

6.3.4   Product Liability with the FDA

The previous section discussed the traditional efficiency role of product liability to give firms incentives to provide levels of safety by facing firms with the social cost associated with unsafe products. To extend our analysis to incorporate the FDA, suppose that the agency mandates and monitors a minimal level of safety denoted s^{FDA}. For example, this minimum level of safety could refer to product design, manufacturing practices, or the adequacy and timeliness of warnings about adverse effects. With the addition of the FDA, there are now two possibilities. If the level of safety the firm chooses to provide under product liability is higher than the level mandated by the FDA, then the firm will continue to provide the safety level s^{PL} and in this case, the addition of the FDA has no safety effects. However, if s^{PL} is less than s^{FDA}, then the firm will provide the minimal level of safety enforced by the FDA. We refer to the latter case as a situation where the FDA-mandated level of safety is *binding* on firms. Thus, if product liability alone, perhaps through imperfect enforcement or underestimation of risks, does not give firms sufficient incentives to provide safety, the addition of the FDA can improve safety if the FDA mandates a level of safety higher than what firms would choose to provide under product liability alone.

In the face of a binding FDA, the effects of product liability on safety and output are now different. If the FDA's regulations are binding, then by definition product liability has no additional effect on the firm's provision of safety. The effects on output are shown in figure 6.2. We assume that the FDA verifies safety and provides information prior to marketing so that patients are informed about safety but not about the damages they receive.[4] In that case, the demand curve for the good $q(p,s)$ is the uninformed demand curve $q(p)$ shifted down by the expected harm $h(s)$, and the socially optimal level of consumption occurs where the informed demand curve meets the marginal cost of production (point E). As shown in figure 6.2, product liability in the face of the FDA now leads to an inefficiently low level of output (point D). When consumers are uninformed, product liability acts as a Pigouvian tax that serves a social benefit by pricing in the expected harm of the drug. However, when the FDA provides safety information prior to marketing product liability simply serves as an additional tax that reduces output with a dead-weight loss. The presence of the FDA therefore affects the sign of the impact on efficiency by increased liability.

6.3.5   The Welfare Effects of Preemption

The preemption doctrine, as described in the introduction, would allow FDA approval to shield firms from lawsuits based on state law. In effect, the

---

4. Note that even if consumers are informed about safety, if they are uninformed about damages, then the legal regime $d(s)$ will affect the firm's safety provision, since damages raise the firm's costs without affecting consumers' valuation of the good.

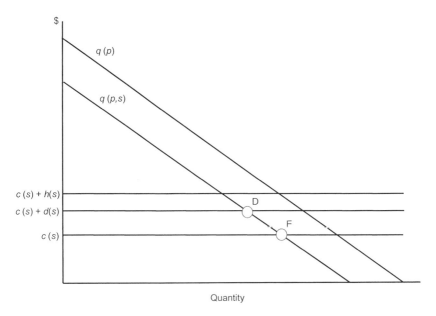

Fig. 6.2   Welfare under product liability and the FDA

doctrine would set legal costs $d(s)$ equal to zero if the firm provided safety at least as high as the FDA mandated level. To analyze the effect of a product liability exemption on welfare, consider figure 6.3, where the x-axis shows the level of safety s and the U-shaped curve $C(s)$ is the firm's costs. The optimal choice of safety chosen by the firm s^{PL} is the bottom of $C(s)$ (point A), where the marginal cost of producing safety equals the marginal benefits in terms of reduced liability costs. Under a regime that lowers product liability, the cost curve shifts to $C^0(s)$, which differs from the initial cost curve in two dimensions. First, costs are lower under $C^0(s)$, since firms pay lower liability costs. Second, with the reduced liability, the optimal level of safety is reduced to s^{PL0}. The firm's costs are therefore given by point B.

The level of safety mandated by the FDA, s^{FDA}, may lie to the left or to the right of the level of safety induced by liability s^{PL}, depending on whether FDA safety levels are binding. Consider the first case, as shown in figure 6.3. In this case the level of safety mandated by the FDA is not binding on firms, so they will provide safety s^{PL} in the absence of a product liability exemption and s^{PL0} with the exemption. In this case, the welfare effect of the exemption is ambiguous, as the exemption lowers marginal costs and price, but also safety.

On the other hand, suppose that the safety mandated by the FDA lies to the right of s^{PL}, as shown in figure 6.4. In this case, the level of safety mandated by the FDA is binding on firms; they will provide s^{FDA} with or without the reduced level of liability. In this case, the preemption raises

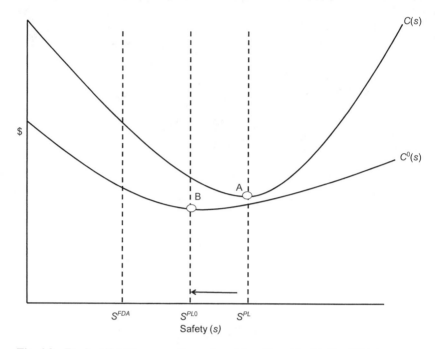

Fig. 6.3 Product liability exemption and social welfare: Nonbinding FDA

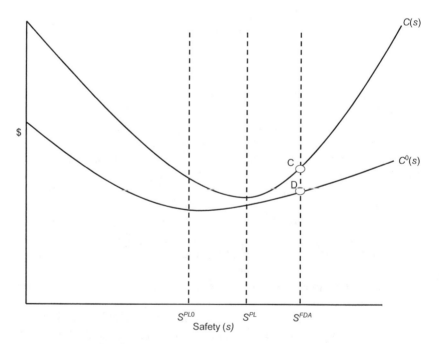

Fig. 6.4 Product liability exemption and social welfare: Binding FDA

welfare by lowering marginal costs from point C to point D, while having no effects on safety.

This analysis suggests that the preemption doctrine has the potential to increase welfare in the case where the presence of the FDA is binding on firms. Intuitively, product liability in general affects welfare by inducing firms to provide safe drugs and by raising prices, thereby reducing overconsumption by uninformed consumers. When the level of safety mandated by the FDA is binding, the agency mitigates the beneficial effects of product liability. Since the level of safety is binding, product liability has no additional effect on safety. And since consumers are informed, there is no need for a tax to reduce overconsumption. Since the agency's actions duplicate those of product liability, the latter simply acts as a tax that raises prices and inefficiently restricts access. It is worth reiterating that two components of FDA regulation drive this result. The first is that the FDA verifies and therefore informs consumers about safety. As previously discussed, with uninformed consumers, price increases due to product liability may actually be socially desirable, but with informed consumers these price increases reduce welfare. The second is that under the FDA, consumers are still uninformed or at least underestimate the damages they receive, so that price increases from product liability actually reduce output.

Several additional points are worth noting. First, since our discussion makes no assumptions on whether the level of safety chosen by the FDA is first- or second-best, our fundamental result holds: as long as the FDA-mandated level of safety is binding, liability reductions will increase welfare, regardless of whether the FDA's choice is socially optimal. Second, product liability serves as a form of forced product insurance by raising price for all patients and compensating those who suffer harm. The effect of removing product liability, therefore, is to eliminate this source of insurance for patients, which could reduce welfare if patients are risk averse. However, this loss could be averted if it is possible for patients to purchase insurance from third-party providers or the government, as in the case of the vaccines, which we discuss in the next section. Moreover, to the degree that the liability system inefficiently compensates patients—for example, because of high legal and administrative costs, patients may be better off self-insuring or obtaining insurance through third parties.

6.4   A Case Study of Recent Drug Liability Limitations

In this section, we consider a case study of the prices and safety effects of the National Vaccine Injury Compensation Program, which sharply reduced vaccine manufacturers' legal liability by creating a patient compensation fund supported by excise taxes on vaccine users. As discussed in the previous section, if FDA regulations are binding on vaccine makers, then a product liability exemption could reduce prices without affecting safety. Since the

National Vaccine Injury Compensation Program shielded vaccine makers from the larger liability risk before the program, it serves as a useful case study of whether a product liability exemption would impact price and safety. Section 6.4.1 provides background on the program, while section 6.4.2 details our analysis.

6.4.1   Background on the National Vaccine Injury Compensation Program

Vaccines are credited with sharply reducing morbidity from several diseases, such as pertussis, polio, and tetanus (CDC 1996). Currently, vaccinations for diphteria, pertussis, tetanus, measles, mumps, rubella, and polio are required for children attending kindergarten or middle school in all fifty states, and most states require vaccinations against hepatitis B and varicella zoster (chicken pox) virus as well. In addition to these required vaccines, several optional vaccines also exist for childhood and adult diseases, such as Hepatitis C and influenza.

Although vaccines are generally safe, as with all drugs, there is the potential for adverse side effects. For example, the pertussis vaccine (typically given in combination with vaccines for diptheria and tetanus) has long been associated with severe neurologic illnesses such as convulsions (Manning 1994; CDC 1996), while more recently, there has been controversy over the association between thiomersal, a preservative used in many vaccines, and autism.[5] Prior to the passage of the National Childhood Vaccine Injury Act in 1986, patients could sue vaccine manufacturers by alleging manufacturing defects, failures to provide proper warnings to the physician or patient, and/or failures to provide for safer alternatives (Ridgway 1999). These lawsuits appear to have been substantial in the amount of damages relative to sales. For example, between 1980 and 1986, vaccine lawsuits alleged a total of $3.6 billion in damages (Davis and Bowman 1991).

Concerns that lawsuits might lead vaccine manufacturers to exit the market or reduce the supply of vaccines led Congress to pass the National Childhood Vaccine Injury Act in 1986, which established the National Vaccine Injury Compensation Program (NVICP) on October 1, 1988. The NVICP requires payment of an excise tax for the vaccines covered, which funds a pool of money, the Vaccine Injury Trust Fund, used to compensate victims of adverse events. Prior to 1998, excise taxes were set at the estimated level of liability costs. For example, the excise tax for the diptheria-pertussis-tetanus vaccine, which contains the pertussis component associated with neurologic disease and lawsuits, was $4.56, compared to only $0.06 for the

---

5. While the Institute of Medicine (IOM), American Medical Association (AMA), Centers for Disease Control (CDC), and Food and Drug Administration (FDA) have stated there is no causal link between thiomersal and autism, to date, over 5,000 claims relating to autism have been filed with the National Vaccine Injury Compensation Program.

diptheria-tetanus vaccine. In 1998, the program was changed so that all vaccine recipients pay a common excise tax of $0.75 per dose[6] to fund the Vaccine Injury Trust Fund. If a patient suffers an adverse reaction after vaccination, he must first file a claim with the NVICP before proceeding to civil litigation against the vaccine manufacturer. In order to receive compensation, the patient's claim must establish that the vaccine caused the adverse event. Alternatively, the NVICP also maintains a table of vaccines, associated adverse effects, and time periods. If the patient's adverse effect is listed on the table and occurs within the specified time period, causality is presumed and the patient is entitled to compensation.

Claims with the NVICP are decided by Special Masters of the Court of Federal Claims. Patients who are found to have suffered an adverse event that was caused by a vaccine are entitled to recovery of damages for medical and other expenses, such as lost earnings. However, in the case of death, payments to the patient's estate are limited to $250,000; this cap also applies to pain and suffering damages. As long as the claim meets certain minimal standards, legal expenses up to $30,000 are reimbursed, regardless of the Special Master's decision. Acceptance of the Special Master's decision forecloses future legal claims against the vaccine manufacturer. If a patient disagrees with the decision, he can proceed to sue the manufacturer, but is barred from utilizing several approaches, such as lawsuits based on failures to warn.

The previous description of the NVICP applies to patients who received a vaccine from 1988 onwards, and generally applies to patients who received a vaccine prior to 1988, with a few differences. First, patients who received a vaccine prior to 1988 are allowed to bypass the NVICP and proceed directly to civil litigation. However, if they choose to file a claim with the NVICP, they must have done so by January 31, 1991. In addition, they face a limit of $30,000 for attorney's fees, pain and suffering, and lost income. Instead of an excise tax, payments to these patients are funded by general revenues.

Table 6.1 provides a brief summary of the economic costs of the program. For several vaccines, the table lists the CDC price per dose, which is the price available to organizations receiving CDC grant funds, such as state health departments, as well as the private sector price, which is the price mandatorily reported by the manufacturer to the CDC. Table 6.1 also reports the excise tax for each vaccine, which is fairly small relative to the private sector price for most of the vaccines.

Table 6.2 provides summary statistics on inflation adjusted payments made by the NVICP between Fiscal Year (FY) 1989 and FY 2009. The first column shows award amounts and attorney's payments for claims that were

---

6. A dose is defined *per disease,* so combination vaccines count as more than one dose. For example, the excise tax for the Measles-Mumps-Rubella (MMR) vaccine is $2.25, since it counts as having three doses.

Table 6.1   Prices and excise taxes for selected vaccines, 2010

Disease	Brand name	CDC price/dose (U.S. $)	Private sector price/dose (U.S. $)	Tax (U.S. $)
	Childhood			
Diptheria/Pertussis/Tetanus	Tipedia	13.25	23.05	2.25
Diptheria/Pertussis/Tetanus/ Polio/Hepatitis B	Pediarix	48.75	70.72	3.75
Hepatitis A	Havrix	12.75	28.74	0.75
Hepatitis B	ENGERIX B	9.75	21.37	0.75
Measles, Mumps, and Rubella	MMRII	18.30	48.31	2.25
	Adult			
Hepatitis A	Havrix	20.59	63.10	0.75
Hepatitis B	ENGERIX-B	26.70	52.50	0.75
Diptheria/Tetanus	None	13.25	18.23	1.50
Influenza	Fluzone	8.15	9.72	0.75

Source: CDC Vaccine Price List, accessed at http://www.cdc.gov/vaccines/programs/vfc/cdc-vac-price
-list-archives.htm on February 1, 2010.
Note: Prices shown are as of January 12, 2010.

Table 6.2   Summary statistics on payments made by the NVICP, FY 1989–FY 2009

	Compensable claims	Dismissed claims
Total number of payments	2,355	2,226
Total payments	$2,411,085,611	$51,794,790
Average payment per claim	$1,023,816	$23,268
Average award per claim	$988,019	n.a.
Average attorney's fee per claim	$35,795	$23,268

Source: January 20, 2010 statistics report from the National Vaccine Injury Compensation
Program, available at http://www.hrsa.gov/vaccinecompensation/statistics_report.htm.
Note: All dollar amounts are in 2008 dollars.

compensated by the NVICP, while the second column shows attorney's payments for claims dismissed by the NVICP. Between FY 1989 and 2009, the
NVICP paid out a total of nearly $2.4 billion for 4,581 claims. However,
as previously noted, the NVICP reimburses legal costs even for dismissed
claims, as long as minimal standards are met, so not all of these payments
were made for successful claims against the Program. For compensable
claims, the average award was roughly $1 million, of which roughly $36,000
was used for attorney's fees.[7] The program paid an average of roughly
$23,000 for attorney's fees associated with dismissed claims.

7. We previously stated that the NVICP caps attorney's fees at $30,000 in nominal terms; the
reason why this average is higher is due to discounting and adjusting for inflation.

Table 6.3　　　　**Vaccine excise taxes**

Vaccines	1988–1996 excise tax (U.S. $)	1988 price (U.S. $)	Excise tax (% of price)
Measles	4.44	13.79	32
Mumps	4.44	15.26	29
Rubella	4.44	14.24	31
MMR	4.44	23.23	19
DTP	4.56	11.03	41
DT	0.06	0.78	7.7
OPV	0.29	8.67	3.3

Source: CDC Vaccine Price List, accessed at http://www.cdc.gov/vaccines/programs/vfc/cdc-vac-price-list-archives.htm on February 1, 2010
Note: Prices shown are in nominal (1988) dollars.

6.4.2　The Price and Safety Effect of the National Vaccine Injury Compensation Program

Table 6.3 shows the nominal excise tax for each vaccine between 1988 and 1996 and the nominal price of the vaccine in 1988. Recall that between 1988 and 1996, the excise taxes for each vaccine were set to represent expected liability costs. Thus, table 6.3 suggests significant variation in vaccine liability. The DT (diptheria and tetanus toxoids) vaccine and OPV (oral polio vaccine) appear to have had low legal exposure, as excise taxes comprised between 3 to 8 percent of the 1988 prices. Conversely, the measles, mumps, rubella (MMR) and diptheria, tetanus, and pertussis (DTP) vaccines appear to have had higher legal exposure, as the excise taxes accounted for 19 to 41 percent of their 1988 prices.

Expanding on the work of Manning (1994), we begin by examining the prices of the DT and DTP vaccines before and after the NVICP. Comparing the prices of these two vaccines is particularly helpful, since they are essentially similar except for the pertussis component of the DTP vaccine, which was the subject of numerous lawsuits over neurological adverse events. As Manning (1994) discusses, the prices of the DT and DTP vaccines were quite similar prior to 1982, when lawsuits were rare. For example, in 1975 one dose of DTP cost 76 cents and one dose of DT cost 74 cents, a difference that remained largely unchanged up until 1982. However, after 1982, when the number of lawsuits for adverse events for the pertussis component began to rise sharply, the price of the DTP vaccine increased significantly compared to the price of the DT vaccine. Since the two vaccines are otherwise similar except for the presence of the pertussis component and had similar prices prior to 1983, Manning (1994) interprets the post-1982 difference in the prices of the two vaccines as the cost of liability for the pertussis component. At its peak in 1986, the difference in the price of the two vaccines

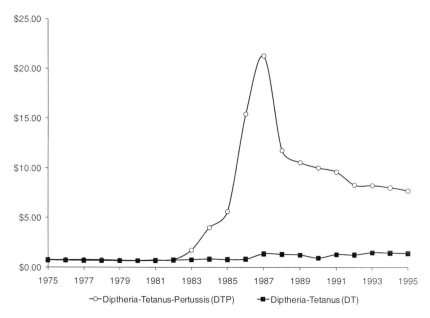

Fig. 6.5   Prices for the DTP and DT vaccines, 1975–1995

Notes: All values shown are in 2008 dollars. Sources described in text.

was $14.58, and liability costs accounted for nearly 96 percent of the DTP vaccine's price.

Figure 6.5 plots the prices, net of excise taxes, for the DT and DTP vaccines between 1975 and 1995.[8] Prices from 1975 through 1986 are Blue Book and Red Book wholesale prices collected by Manning (1994), who did not collect data after the NVICP program was implemented. To assess the time trend surrounding this program, from 1987 and beyond, we used private-sector vaccine prices reported by drug manufacturers and published by the Centers for Disease Control and Prevention (CDC). We chose 1995 as the end date because DTP prices were no longer available past this point, as the vaccine was replaced with the DTaP vaccine, a safer version of the DTP vaccine that uses an acellular form of the Pertussis pathogen. Figure 6.5 suggests that not only did prices of DTP rise with increased liability but they also fell after the introduction of the National Vaccine Injury Compensation Program in 1988, with the price (net of taxes) falling from $11.78 in 1988[9] to $7.73, a 34 percent decrease. Since price of the DT vaccine slightly rose during the same period, the fall in the price of the DTP vaccine is likely due

8. We performed similar analyses using prices inclusive of excise taxes; the results are similar to those shown here.
9. As stated in section 6.4.1, the NVICP took effect late in 1988, so we use the 1988 price as the last price prior to the program's introduction.

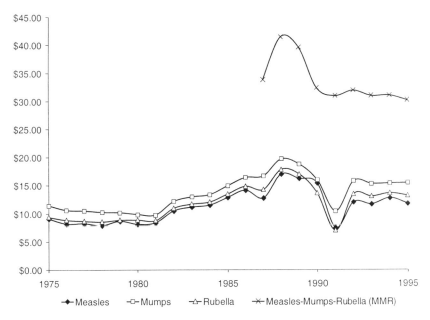

Fig. 6.6   Prices for the measles, mumps, rubella, and MMR Vaccines, 1975–1995
Notes: All values shown are in 2008 dollars. Sources described in text.

to changes in liability, as opposed to changes in the costs of production or increased competition.

As shown in figure 6.6, in addition to the DTP vaccine, the measles, mumps, rubella and MMR vaccines also appear to have faced high liability, given that that the excise tax accounted for a large percentage of each vaccine's price. Figure 6.6 plots the time series of the (net of tax) prices for each vaccine. As with the DTP vaccine, we find that the NVICP substantially lowered vaccine prices from their 1988 highs, with decreases ranging from 22 percent for the mumps vaccine to 31 percent for the measles vaccine. Taken together, figures 6.5 and 6.6 suggest that the prices for heavily litigated vaccines fell significantly following the NVICP. As controls, figure 6.7 plots the time series of prices (net of excise taxes) for two less heavily litigated vaccines, the DT and OPV vaccines. In contrast to the other more heavily litigated vaccines, we find that prices for these vaccines actually increased or stayed constant following passage of the NVICP, suggesting that the observed price decreases for heavily litigated vaccines were not due to other factors such as changes in market conditions.

With information about the demand for vaccines, standard methods can be used to estimate the welfare gains from these price reductions induced by reduced liability. Specifically, consider when demand function has a constant price elasticity, so that the inverse demand function is

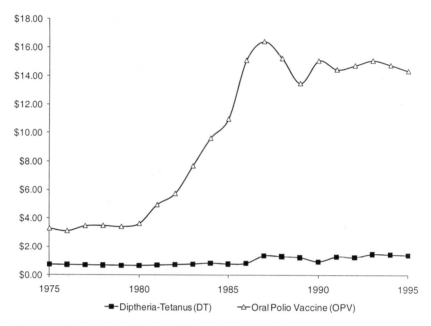

Fig. 6.7   Prices for the DT and OPV vaccines, 1975–1995
Notes: All values shown are in 2008 dollars. Sources described in text.

$$(9) \qquad p(x,s) = \left(\frac{x}{A(s)} \right)^{-1/\varepsilon},$$

where ε is the elasticity of demand and $A(s)$ is a shifter of demand based on safety s. With this demand specification can easily be shown that increase in welfare from a z percent reduction in price is given by

$$(10) \qquad \Delta W = (1 - z)^{1-\varepsilon} - 1.$$

We consider an elasticity of 1.25, based on Philipson and Sun (2008). They utilize patent expiration evidence (Grabowski and Vernon 1992; Berndt, Cockburn, and Griliches 1996; Caves, Whinston, and Hurwitz 1991), which implicitly estimates the demand elasticity for drugs by from supply-induced price-reductions from patent expiry. This elasticity of demand differs from the copay elasticity of demand estimated by others (Goldman, Joyce, and Karaca-Madic 2006; Goldman, Joyce, and Zheng 2007), because the latter is the elasticity of demand from patients who already have insurance, and only need to pay their insurance copay for the drug. Our elasticity of demand is the elasticity of demand facing the manufacturer, which takes into account the demand for health insurance itself and other factors as well.

Given an elasticity of 1.25, figure 6.8 shows the social surplus increases (ΔW from equation [10]) for the DTP vaccines, based on prices decreases

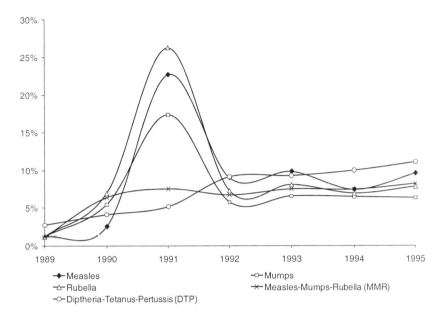

Fig. 6.8   Effect of NVICP on annual social surplus, 1989–1995
Notes: All values shown are in 2008 dollars. Source is author's calculations, as described in text.

from their peak values in each year of the NVICP. Overall, we find that the NVICP has substantial effects on consumer and producer surplus by lowering vaccine prices. For example, our results suggest that in 1995, the DTP vaccine was 34 percent lower than its pre-NVICP price, suggesting an increase in social surplus of 11 percent.

Although figure 6.8 shows that the NVICP likely had large effects on social welfare by reducing prices and increasing access, these gains must be balanced against any reductions in vaccine safety. There are two margins along which the NVICP may have affected safety. The first is on vaccines marketed before the program's implementation. Since the design of these vaccines did not change after the program, there was likely no change in safety for those vaccines.[10] Thus, the NVICP appears to have unambiguously raised welfare in the case of the vaccines discussed previously.

The second margin is on vaccines marketed after the program's implementation, as the NVICP may have given firms incentives to market less safe vaccines. As one approach for looking at this issue, we examined the incidence of reported adverse events to the vaccines listed in table 6.4. These vaccines were chosen because they comprise the recommended list of vaccinations

---

10. This concerns design effects. If there are safety issues in manufacturing that are affected by liability, they may be affected after the product has been invented.

for children, as given by the CDC. Table 6.4 also reports the recommended ages of administration for each vaccine, and the date each vaccine entered the market.

To estimate the incidence of adverse events, we used the Vaccine Adverse Event Reporting System (VAERS), which has collected reports on adverse events from immunizations since 1990. The VAERS consists of self-reported incidents of adverse events, from vaccine manufacturers (42 percent), health care providers (30 percent), state immunization programs (12 percent), patients (7 percent), and other sources (9 percent). It is important to reiterate that these events are self-reported, and that VAERS makes no effort to identify whether the vaccine actually caused the adverse event. Table 6.4 shows the total number of adverse events reported to VAERS for each vaccine between 1990 and 2006. To obtain the incidence, we divided the number of adverse events by the total number of children in the recommended ages during the periods for which the vaccine was available, using U.S. Census data on population estimates by single years of age between 1990 and 2006. Since the Census only reports population by single years of age, we rounded the recommended ages listed in table 6.4 up to the nearest whole year.

Overall, our results suggest that the newer vaccines are not less safe than vaccines introduced prior to the NVICP. For the five vaccines introduced prior to the NVICP, the mean number of adverse events per 100,000 doses is 15.4 (s.d. 10.8), while for the eight vaccines introduced after the NVICP, the mean probability of an adverse event is 9.28 (s.d. 9.03). Although the incidence of adverse events is slightly lower with the newer vaccines, the difference between the groups is not statistically significant ($p < 0.2$).

Overall, then, our analysis suggests that the NVICP has not resulted in more dangerous vaccines. However, it is useful to note several limitations to our analysis. First, as described before, the VAERS may not provide a completely accurate measure of the number of adverse events. On the one hand, VAERS may understate the true number of adverse events, since the data is self-reported; however, since VAERS makes no attempt to verify whether a vaccine did cause a reported adverse event, it may also overstate the true number of events. In addition, our measure of the total population at risk includes only the number of children who were at the recommended age for the vaccine. This value may understate the true number of patients receiving the vaccine to the degree that vaccinations are delayed and therefore received at later ages. Conversely, this approach may understate the number of patients taking the vaccine if compliance is not perfect. However, to the degree that these shortcomings equally affect the vaccines in our sample, they would not significantly affect our results. Overall, then, we find that the NVICP likely increased welfare by lowering prices, without affecting safety.

An additional benefit of the NVICP is that it may have compensated patients more efficiently than the product liability system. First, data from

Table 6.4   Incidence of adverse events for childhood vaccines, 1990–2006

Vaccine	Year of introduction	Recommended ages	Number of adverse events	Total population at risk (millions)	Number of adverse events per 100,000 doses
		Vaccines introduced prior to NVICP			
DTP	1950	≤ 6 yrs.	20,221	465	4.35
Poliovirus	1964	2–15 mos., 4–6 yrs.	23,574	332	7.10
Hepatitis B	1981	≤ 18 mos.	29,741	199	19.0
Haemophilus B	1985	≤ 15 mos.	37,822	199	14.9
MMR	1987	12–15 mos., 4–6 yrs.	41,866	133	31.6
		Vaccine introduced after NVICP			
Influenza	Annually	Children 6 mos.–18 yrs.	28,203	1,262	2.23
DTaP	1994	≤ 6 yrs.	34,760	412	8.43
Varicella	1995	12–15 mos., 4–6 yrs.	28,407	94	30.4
Pneumococcal (Conjugate)	2000	≤ 15 mos.	13,268	166	7.99
Meningococcal Vaccine	2001	11–12 yrs.	1,150	20	5.68
Hepatitis A	2005	12–24 mos.	6,699	98	6.85
Rotavirus	2006	6–14 wks.	710	36	1.98
Human Papillomavirus	2006	11–12 yrs.	429	4	10.78

Manning (1994) and the NVICP itself suggest that the program did not, on average, reduce compensation to persons suffering vaccine injury. According to Manning (1994), between 1980 and 1985, prior to the passage of the NVICP, the average amount paid for vaccine injury claims was $420,185 (in 2008 dollars). As shown in table 6.2, since the NVICP, the average amount paid per compensated claim is roughly $1 million. While we cannot exclude the possibility that the nature of injuries and the probability of receiving compensation may have changed over time, these findings provide some evidence that compensation to injured patients has not fallen as a result of the NVICP. Moreover, Manning (1994) estimates that prior to passage of the NVICP, the cost of compensating a patient $1 cost firms between $7 to $22 in legal/administrative costs. By contrast, between FY 1989 and FY 2009 the NVICP compensated patients a total of $2.3 billion while paying out roughly $140 million in attorney's costs. While not definitive, since this latter figure leaves out the administrative costs of running the NVICP as well the legal costs associated with any cases that did go to trial, these findings suggest that the NVICP compensated patients more efficiently than the product liability system.

6.5 Concluding Remarks

Our analysis examined the value of liability reductions in the presence of FDA regulations to ensure medical product safety. When one mechanism dominates the other in providing safety then there may be efficiency gains in eliminating the second. We argued that this may be the case in medical product safety when FDA safety levels are binding on firms so that reductions in liability do not affect safety but lowers prices and hence expand output and access to medicines. We discussed qualitative evidence for a case study of the National Vaccine Injury Compensation Program, which suggested that prices (but not safety) fell after the government reduced liability. Although preemption is an obvious example of liability reduction, and one which has been the subject of recent Supreme Court decisions, it is useful to point out that our theoretical results also extend to other forms of liability reduction, such as caps on punitive damages and damage caps.

The fact that the NVICP program displayed these safety and price patterns is consistent with other observations that the level of safety mandated by the FDA is binding on manufacturers. First, because firms seldom exceed the safety investments required by the FDA, such as performing more clinical trials than what the agency demands (Garber 1993). Second, trials in which a firm is alleged to have violated FDA standards or misled the FDA are rare (Garber 1993). Given the strong possibility that the FDA mandates a higher level of safety than firms would be willing to provide under product liability alone, our analysis suggests that the adoption of the preemption doctrine could significantly increase welfare by reducing prices.

Our analysis stresses the substitutability between FDA and liability and therefore suggests the lowest cost substitute to minimize costs. There are two other reasons why FDA may be the best substitute to minimize costs. The first is that the ex ante regulations of FDA may trade off the safety of a product with the adverse R&D effects it may have by lengthening the time and cost to bring a product to market. Ex post court decisions are unlikely to take into account this trade-off at all. This is particularly true with lay juries, who are spending other peoples' money to compensate victims of product failures ex post with any deliberation about the R&D effects involved. The second argument against government-provided product liability is that the market can, and often does, provide warranties by itself if welfare enhancing. Product liability is essentially a mandatory warranty that the market has chosen not to provide, and it is not clear what market failure this mandatory warranty solves.

Recent policies and court decision have tended toward reducing firms' legal liability. For example, the recent inclusion of the preemption doctrine in the *Federal Register,* as well as the Supreme Court's decision in *Riegel v. Medtronic,* which upheld the doctrine in the case of medical devices, represent recent legislative and executive branch policies that reduced firms' liability. However, in *Wyeth v. Levine,* the Court ruled 5-4 that preemption does not apply to pharmaceuticals. While there may or may not be good legal justification for applying preemption to medical devices and not to pharmaceuticals, our analysis suggests that the economic rationale for doing so is less clear.

There are several useful extensions to our analysis that we believe are of further interest. First, we examined the impact of safety regulation on static efficiency. Since regulation affects firms' profits and therefore their incentives to invest in R&D (Grabowski, Vernon, and Thomas 1978), further work should also try to determine what types of regulatory regimes maximize dynamic welfare taking into account innovation incentives. For example, in the case of the NVICP, firms may have had less incentive to invest in safety for a given vaccine, since the Program reduced their legal liability. However, by lowering costs and increasing profits, the Program may have increased R&D efforts more generally. It may also be the case that vaccine R&D may be less responsive to reductions in liability compared to other markets, such as drugs and devices, because vaccine manufacturers operate in a monopsony market and therefore face lower profits. Second, further work should attempt to further quantify the discussed welfare gains from preemption. The model we developed suggests that potential welfare gains are larger when liability accounts for a significant fraction of marginal costs. Given that drugs and vaccines are typically thought to have low marginal costs of production, it is likely that even small legal costs can account for a significant fraction of overall marginal costs. The larger are the price reductions from preemption, the larger gains in access and welfare. Third, it would be interesting to examine the interplay of the FDA and product liability in affecting off-label drug use, such as whether firms may be less likely to invest in off-label studies, if doing so leads to increased liability exposure. Lastly, we did not discuss the potential complimentary roles of FDA and product liability, in which different forms of product safety are enhanced by the two different public interventions. For example, liability may make up for poor enforcement of the FDA. When there are such complementarities, preemption will still lead to price reductions but may now also induce a reduction in safety.

Overall, we hope that future theoretical and empirical analysis will better address the rationales for the dual nature of safety regulation and enforcement by governments around the world, and increase our understanding of when it adds costs larger than the benefits compared to using one form alone or compared to using the market itself.

References

Berndt, E., I. Cockburn, and Z. Griliches. 1996. Pharmaceutical innovations and market dynamics: Tracking effects on price indexes for antidepressant drugs. *Brookings Papers on Economic Activity, Microeconomics:* 133–99.

Calfee, J. 2006. Striking a balance: Drug labeling and the FDA. *AEI Online.* Available at: http://www.aei.org/publications/pubID.23868/pub_detail.asp.

———. 2008. Written testimony before the United States House of Representatives Committee on Oversight and Government Reform, May 14.

Calfee, J., E. Berndt, R. Hahn, T. Philipson, P. Rubin, and W. K. Viscusi. 2008. Amicus Brief to the Supreme Court in *Wyeth v. Levine.* Reg-Markets Center Brief no. 08-01.

Caves, R., M. Whinston, and M. Hurwitz. 1991. Patent expiration, entry, and competition in the U.S. pharmaceutical industry. *Brookings Papers on Economic Activity, Microeconomics:* 1–61.

Curfman, G., S. Morrisey, and J. Drazen. 2008. Why doctors should worry about pre-emption. *New England Journal of Medicine* 359:1–2.

Davis, T., and C. Bowman. 1991. No-fault compensation for unavoidable injuries: Evaluating the national childhood vaccine injury compensation program. *University of Dayton Law Review* 16 (2): 277–321.

Garber, S. 1993. *Product liability and the economics of pharmaceuticals and medical devices.* RAND Report R-4285-ICJ. Santa Monica, CA: RAND.

Glantz, L., and G. Annas. 2008. The FDA, pre-emption, and the Supreme Court. *New England Journal of Medicine* 358 (18): 1883–85.

Goldman, D., G. Joyce, and P. Karaca-Mandic. 2006. Varying pharmacy benefits with clinical status: The case of cholesterol-lowering therapy. *American Journal of Managed Care* 12 (1): 21–38.

Goldman, D., G. Joyce, and Y. Zheng. 2007. Prescription drug cost-sharing: Associations with medication and medical utilization and spending, and health. *Journal of the American Medical Association* 29 (1): 61–9.

Grabowski, H. G., and J. M. Vernon. 1992. Brand loyalty, entry, and price competition in pharmaceuticals after the 1984 Drug Act. *Journal of Law and Economics* 32 (2): 331–50.

Grabowski, H., J. Vernon, and L. Thomas. 1978. Estimating the effects of regulation on innovation: An international comparative analysis of the pharmaceutical industry. *Journal of Law and Economics* 21 (1): 133–63.

Kessler, D., and D. Vladeck. 2008. A critical assessment of the FDA's efforts to preempt failure-to-warn claims. *Georgetown Law Journal* 96: 462–95.

Manning, R. 1994. Changing rules in tort law and the market for childhood vaccines. *Journal of Law and Economics* 37 (1): 247–75.

———. 1997. Product liability and prescription drug prices in Canada and the United States. *Journal of Law and Economics* 40 (1): 203–43.

Philipson, T. J., and E. Sun. 2008. Is the Food and Drug Administration safe and effective? *Journal of Economic Perspectives* 22 (1): 85–102.

Polinsky, A. M. and S. Shavell. 2007. Public enforcement of law. In *Handbook of law and economics,* ed. A. M. Polinsky and S. Shavell, 400–54. North Holland: Elsevier.

Ridgway, D. 1999. No-fault vaccine insurance: Lessons from the National Vaccine Injury Compensation Program. *Journal of Health Politics, Policy, and Law* 24 (1): 59–90.

Shavell, S. 2007. Liability for accidents. In *Handbook of law and economics,* ed. A. M. Polinsky and S. Shavell, 139–81. North Holland: Elsevier.

U.S. Centers for Disease Control (CDC). 1996. Update: Vaccine side effects, adverse reactions, contraindications, and precautions. *Morbidity and Mortality Weekly Report* 45: no. RR-12.

U.S. Council of Economic Advisors. 2002. *Who pays for tort liability claims? An economic analysis of the U.S. tort liability system.* Washington, DC: GPO.

7
The Impact of Employment Protection on Workers Disabled by Workplace Injuries

Adam H. Gailey and Seth A. Seabury

7.1   Introduction

Employment protection statutes are designed to shield individuals in protected classes from discrimination in the workforce by providing them with legal redress when they face prohibited employer practices. The disabled constitute one such class, and employment protection for disabled workers entitles them to "reasonable" accommodations that allow them to perform necessary job functions and bars discrimination in hiring, termination, or compensation. Presumably, a key goal of offering this protection to the disabled is to improve their earnings and employment opportunities. However, past studies have demonstrated that employment protection, specifically the Americans with Disabilities Act (ADA), has had a negligible or even harmful effect on the labor market outcomes of the disabled (Oi 1991; Rosen 1991; DeLaire 2000a, 2000b; Acemoglu and Angrist 2001; Hotchkiss 2003, 2004; Jolls and Prescott 2004). In this chapter we study how the impact of employment protection differs for a specific subset of the disabled population—those who become disabled as a result of a workplace injury.

One factor that separates the disabled as a class from other protected groups, such as racial or ethnic minorities, is that a nondisabled individual

Adam H. Gailey is a doctoral fellow at RAND Corporation. Seth A. Seabury is an economist at RAND Corporation.

The authors would like to thank Dan Kessler, Alison Morantz, Dick Butler, Nick Pace, Paul Heaton, John Romley, and conference participants at the 2009 NBER Regulation and Litigation Conference for helpful comments and suggestions. All errors and omissions are the responsibility of the authors. The RAND Institute for Civil Justice provided financial support for this research. The views and opinions in this chapter are solely those of the authors, and do not reflect those of RAND.

can become disabled after experiencing an adverse health shock.[1] In particular, a nontrivial fraction of disabilities occur as a result of someone experiencing a workplace injury or illness.[2] This is noteworthy because an extensive regulatory and compensation system already governs workplace injuries and illnesses, and there are a myriad of ways in which these policies might interact with employment protection laws. Due to these interactions, the impact of employment protection on someone disabled at work could differ substantially from that of someone with a prior disability or a nonwork disability. This provides a useful opportunity to investigate the impact of overlapping regulatory and litigation-based policies targeting the employment of disabled workers.

This chapter studies how overlap between workers' compensation coverage and employment protection affect the labor market outcomes of the disabled. Central to our analysis is the idea that the accommodations required by employment protection policies can reduce the expected costs associated with workers' compensation benefits that employers must pay to injured workers. This implies that some of the employer costs of complying with the employment protection laws will be offset by lower workers' compensation costs. Thus, policies that protect the disabled from discrimination will be more effective when applied to those workers who become disabled through a workplace injury or illness.

The complementarity of employment protection and workers' compensation is tested using data on employment, disability status, and workers' compensation benefit receipt from the Current Population Survey (CPS). While past studies have primarily studied the impact of the ADA, we focus on the California Fair Employment and Housing Act (FEHA). In many ways FEHA mirrors the ADA, but it actually predates the ADA and offers stronger protections to the disabled. Additionally, the FEHA was revised in 2001 to place stricter requirements on employers to provide accommodations. After this reform, the number of allegations under FEHA that an employer failed to accommodate a disability more than doubled. This provides a natural experiment in which to examine the employment impact of FEHA on the disabled and how the impact differs for those with and without a workplace injury.

Our empirical analysis employs a difference-in-differences strategy that compares the labor force participation of disabled workers' compensation recipients relative to disabled workers without workers' compensation benefits before and after the changes to FEHA. The findings generally support

1. In principle, demographic changes in the ethnic composition of the population can make someone a minority. However, such changes generally occur over relatively long periods of time and far less frequently than people experience health shocks that leave them disabled.

2. Reville and Schoeni (2005) estimate that for people age fifty-one to sixty-one reporting a work-limiting disability, 36 percent of them became disabled due to a workplace injury, illness, or accident.

the predictions of the model. Specifically, we find that the labor force participation of workers' compensation recipients rose relative to that of other disabled workers after the employment protection provisions of FEHA were strengthened. The results appear to be largely driven by male workers, who are more likely to be subject to accommodations. Robustness checks indicate that there was no comparable trend in the employment of disabled workers' compensation recipients relative to other disabled workers outside of California during this time period.

These findings indicate that employment protection can have a positive impact on the labor market outcomes of the disabled, something that the prior literature has failed to demonstrate empirically. However, the effects appear to be limited to certain subgroups of the disabled population, which may help explain why the existing literature finds little effect. From the perspective of social welfare, the enhanced effect of the employment protection laws for workers' compensation recipients could be good or bad. The welfare effects ultimately depend on whether or not the level of accommodation that occurs under the litigation system is socially optimal. If they are, then the additional accommodation for workers' compensation beneficiaries could lead to excess accommodations. On the other hand, if the equilibrium accommodation for workers with nonwork disabilities is suboptimal, then the increase in accommodations for workers' compensation recipients should be welfare enhancing.

In the context of the literature studying the interaction between regulatory regimes and the court system, this chapter provides an example where regulation and litigation appear to be complements.[3] Liability and safety regulation are often—though not always—considered substitutes, suggesting that combining the two could be redundant and lead to inefficiencies.[4] For example, Phillipson and Sun (2008) argue that having dual litigation and regulatory systems in the case of pharmaceuticals leads to significant welfare losses by increasing the cost of prescription drugs without the benefit of increasing safety. While the welfare consequences in our application are still unclear, this chapter provides an empirical example that the combination of regulation and litigation is not always redundant.

The chapter proceeds as follows. In the next section we provide some

3. We take employment protection to be the litigation system and workers' compensation to be the regulation system in our example, because the penalties in employment discrimination cases are often leveled in civil court whereas workers' compensation benefits are prescribed ex ante. In truth, however, there are aspects of employment protection that operate like a regulatory system, and aspects of workers' compensation that operate like a system of litigation. We clarify how our application differs from a traditional model of regulation and litigation (and how this affects the implications of our findings) later in the chapter.

4. Litigation and regulation are not always considered redundant, at least theoretically. Kolstad, Ulen, and Johnson (1990) and Schwartzstein and Shleifer (2009) show how the combination of regulation and litigation can correct inefficiencies in liability or regulation alone, and lead to improved outcomes.

background on employment protection litigation and workers' compensation. In particular, we describe the California FEHA and the changes that were enacted in 2001. In section 7.3 we develop a model that illustrates how the consequences of employment protection for disabled workers can differ depending on whether or not a worker was disabled due to workplace injury. Section 7.4 describes our empirical approach and the data, and section 7.5 presents and discusses our empirical results. The chapter concludes with a brief discussion of next steps and implications for future work.

7.2   Background

This chapter is concerned with the interaction between workers' compensation benefits and employment protection laws targeting the disabled. In each case there is a considerable amount of variation across the United States in the design and scope of both types of policies. In this section we offer a brief discussion of each, with a particular focus on California (which is the subject of our empirical analysis).

7.2.1   Workers' Compensation

In the United States, workers' compensation laws regulate the compensation offered to workers who experience work-related injuries or illnesses. Coverage by workers' compensation is nearly universal: all fifty states and the federal government have some form of workers' compensation system, although it is optional in Texas (and to a lesser extent New Jersey). There is significant variation in the design of state programs, but there are some similarities in the kinds of benefits available to workers. Typically, employers are required to compensate injured workers for all medical expenses, and replace some fraction of lost wages.

The wage loss benefits, also called indemnity benefits, vary depending on whether the injury is permanent or temporary. Generally there are four types of indemnity benefits: temporary total disability (TTD) benefits, permanent partial disability (PPD) benefits, permanent total disability (PTD) benefits and fatality benefits. Most attention is typically paid to TTD and PPD benefits because they are more common by far. The TTD benefits are paid weekly and usually provide approximately two-thirds replacement of the injured worker's preinjury average wage, subject to weekly benefit caps and floors. The structure of PPD benefits varies more substantially, but they are typically determined as some function of the nature and severity of a worker's disability. All workers' compensation benefits are exempt from income tax, so the after-tax replacement rate of lost income can be significantly higher than the before-tax rate.[5]

---

5. For example, Viscusi and Moore (1987) estimated that that the before-tax replacement rate was 55 percent, compared to 83 percent after taxes.

In California, the maximum TTD benefits have changed over time. This fact is relevant for our empirical analysis, as we discuss in detail later. From July 1, 1996 through December 31, 2002, the maximum benefit was fixed at $448 per week. In 2003, 2004, and 2005, the maximum weekly benefit increased by approximately $120 per year.[6] Beginning in 2007, weekly benefits have been adjusted annually according to a cost-of-living adjustment (COLA) based on the state average weekly wage. Minimum benefits were fixed at $126 per week over this time period, though beginning in 2007 they, too, are adjusted by the COLA.

In California, temporary benefits are paid until a worker goes back to work or until a physician determines that the worker is no longer improving (i.e., the doctor declares their condition to be "permanent and stationary"). If they suffer residual impairment as a result of their injury, they will generally be eligible for PPD benefits. California PPD benefits are determined according to a schedule that assigns a disability rating (from 1 to 100) to injured workers based on the body part that was injured, the severity of the resulting impairment to the function of the body part, as well as the age and occupation at the time of the injury. The maximum benefits for PPD are determined in part by the disability rating, but they are generally much smaller than TTD benefits (almost always less than $300 per week).

For our purposes, an important distinction between TTD and PPD benefits in California is that only TTD benefits are dependent on current labor force participation. The PPD benefits are the same regardless of whether or not an employee is currently employed.[7] Thus, from the standpoint of thinking about how accommodating an injured worker and bringing them back to work early might affect workers' compensation costs, only TTD benefits are truly relevant.

7.2.2   Employment Protection for the Disabled

Probably the best known policy that protects the disabled from discrimination in the U.S. is the ADA. The ADA was enacted in 1991, but Title I, which provided employment protection for workers at employers with twenty-five or more employees, did not become effective until July 1992. In addition to explicitly barring discrimination in hiring, firing, promotion, pay, or other employment practices, the ADA also requires employers to provide "reasonable" accommodations to the worksite for disabled workers or prospective workers. These may include but are not limited to:[8]

6. Specifically, the weekly benefits rose to $602 in 2003, $728 in 2004, and $840 in 2005.

7. Starting in 2006 the law was changed to implement a tiered benefit structure that reduced PPD benefits if employers make an offer of return to work, and increased them if they did not. However, this difference was contingent entirely on the offer of return to work, and the levels do not change regardless of whether the employee accepted the job or accepted employment somewhere else.

8. These examples were provided by the Equal Employment Opportunity Commission, at http://www.eeoc.gov/types/ada.html, accessed on August 31, 2008.

- Making existing facilities used by employees readily accessible to and usable by persons with disabilities.
- Job restructuring, modifying work schedules, reassignment to a vacant position.
- Acquiring or modifying equipment or devices; adjusting or modifying examinations, training materials, or policies; and providing qualified readers or interpreters.

More generally, the ADA requires employers to provide accommodations that do not constitute an "undue hardship" on their operation.

While the ADA is perhaps the most widely known policy, it is not the only or even the first. There are many state policies, some of which predate the ADA. One example of this is the California Fair Employment and Housing Act (FEHA). The FEHA protects individuals against harassment or discrimination in employment and housing because of a disability and numerous other characteristics, including age, gender, race, and religion.[9] The FEHA was first passed in 1959 and has changed many times over the years, but laws preventing discrimination against the disabled began to be incorporated in the 1970s.

Under FEHA, employers are required to provide reasonable accommodations to employees with disabilities in order to enable them to perform their essential job functions, just as under the ADA. As part of this requirement, employers are required to participate in an "interactive process" with their disabled employees to determine if reasonable accommodations can be made that would allow the employee to continue working. In 2001, California revised the FEHA through Assembly Bill 2222 (AB2222).[10] The AB2222 expanded FEHA's broad definition of disability and it clarified that mitigating measures (such as medications or devices such as glasses) are to be excluded from disability determination.

The FEHA in California also provides for a definition of disability more encompassing than does the ADA and most other states. The FEHA provides protections for individuals with a "limitation" on a major life activity while the ADA and many states only a "substantial limitation." Also, the FEHA does not allow mitigation measures to be considered in the definition of disability, and extends protections to smaller businesses than does the ADA. The FEHA provides for higher potential damage awards than does the ADA and most other states. In almost every dimension the FEHA provides greater protections to a broader range of disabled persons than does nearly every other state. Some of the differences in definition of disability were removed in the Americans with Disabilities Act Amendments Act of 2008. Among other things, the act no longer allows for mitigation measures

9. Fair Employment and Housing Act (Title 2, Division 3, Part 2.8).
10. AB 2222, Chapter 1049, Civil Code sections 51, 51.5, 54, and CA Government Codes 12926, 12940, 12955.3, and 19231.

other than glasses/contact lenses to be considered in the determination of disability status.

The most important aspect of FEHA for this chapter is the change brought about by AB2222 that enhanced employers' responsibilities for initiating an interactive process with disabled employees. Essentially, after AB2222, if an employer fails to engage in an interactive process this can serve as sufficient grounds for a cause of action against the employer. While the ADA requires a similar process, it is not sufficient to show liability on its own. Obviously a worker would still have to show harm in order to recover any damages, but making the failure to engage sufficient grounds for a lawsuit substantially increases the access of disabled workers to the court system (as we demonstrate later). To our knowledge, this provision of FEHA makes California one of the most, if not the most, aggressive states in terms of requiring employers to accommodate disabled workers.

7.2.3   When Do Employment Protection Laws and Workers' Compensation Overlap?

Ostensibly the two systems just described target completely different issues. However, both are intensely concerned with the employment outcomes of someone after they experience a workplace injury. A failure to return injured workers back to work in a timely fashion will lead to both higher workers' compensation benefits and could increase an employer's exposure to antidiscrimination litigation. This is the key relationship between the two programs for our purposes, because it suggests that accommodating disabled workers in accordance with employment protection laws can reduce the amount employers have to pay in workers' compensation benefits.

The intuition behind this prediction is that accommodations that make it easier for a disabled worker to perform their duties also make it easier for workers to return to work at an earlier date. Such accommodations might include modifying the set of tasks so as to avoid particularly physical work, or some kind of worksite or physical modification. We do not necessarily think that these accommodations affect the actual recovery time of disabled workers. Rather, we argue that workers have the ability to modify the date at which they return to work, and by taking extra steps to accommodate workers, employers can accelerate that date.

There is some empirical support for the idea that accommodations will reduce the employer costs of workplace injuries. It is clear that workers have some ability to choose when to return to work, as shown by numerous studies finding that the duration of work-injury absences is positively related to the benefit level (c.f., Meyer, Viscusi, and Durbin 1995; Neuhauser and Raphael 2004; Kruger 1990; Galizzi and Boden 1996; Butler and Worral 1985; Johnson and Ondrich 1990). The direct evidence on the effect of accommodations is limited, but there is some evidence from past studies that employer return to work programs reduce the time out of work (c.f., Butler,

Baldwin, and Johnson 1995; Loisel et al. 1997; Bernacki et al. 2000; Krause, Dasinger, and Neuhauser 1998). These programs typically involve modifications to work tasks, equipment, or scheduling, all of which are items that may be required by the employment protection policies.

Another, potentially more direct, way in which workers' compensation and employment protection statutes for the disabled might interact is through second injury funds (SIFs). These were created as a means to encourage the hiring of disabled workers by alleviating employer concerns that workers with preexisting conditions might exacerbate the likelihood or severity of a future injury. The SIFs operate by either reimbursing employers (or insurers) for payments made to eligible claims or by simply appropriating the claim and making the payments directly. In this sense, SIFs and employment protection have similar implications for the employment of the disabled: SIFs offer incentives to reduce discrimination against disabled workers, whereas employment protection policies offer legal protection if discrimination is thought to have occurred. However, it is possible that SIFs offer additional protection to disabled workers by reducing the incentives of employers to challenge claims on the basis of compensability.[11]

As discussed in Uehlein and Nevils (2008), since the adoption of the ADA many states have begun to close their SIFs, under the argument that the protections provided against discrimination make the funds redundant. This potentially could increase the degree of overlap between employment protection and workers' compensation cases, because employers will face greater workers' compensation costs associated with disabling injuries related to preexisting conditions. In California there is the Subsequent Injuries Fund, which covers approximately 500 claims a year at a cost of approximately $6.5 million.[12] However, the provisions of the fund did not change significantly around the time of the changes to FEHA that we use in our empirical test, so we do not think it affects our identification. Nonetheless, the elimination of SIFs could have important implications for the overlap between workers' compensation and employment protection for workers in affected states such as New York and Florida.

In a typical study of the relationship between regulation and litigation, the overlap between the functions of the two systems is more direct than is the case here. The regulatory system requires a certain type of behavior and imposes fines and penalties for deviation from that behavior (if the deviation is detected). Litigation provides a means for individuals to recover com-

11. Under a SIF, employers have no incentive (or reduced incentives) to contest a workers' compensation claim for a worker with a preexisting condition on the basis of causality. This is not the case with employment protection, in that employers have just as much (if not more) incentives to contest compensability. We thank Richard Butler for suggesting this implication of SIFs.

12. This information is available from the California Division of Workers' Compensation (DWC) at http://www.dir.ca.gov/DWC/basics.htm (accessed October 15, 2009).

pensation if they are harmed as a result of behavior that deviates from the "reasonable" level set by the courts. In our case, the workers' compensation system is not a true ex ante regulatory system. Rather, it indirectly regulates accommodations by imposing a penalty (disability benefits) on employers when they fail to accommodate injured workers. This will be important to note when we discuss the policy implications of our findings.

7.3   Conceptual Framework

Previous studies of the impact of employment protection on labor market outcomes for the disabled have tended to focus on the aggregate employment and wage effects. For instance, Acemoglu and Angrist (2001) develop a model of the labor market for disabled workers and use it to show that the theoretical impact of the ADA on employment is ambiguous. While the ADA subsidizes hiring costs that should promote the employment of the disabled, it simultaneously imposes ex ante expected costs to firms hiring disabled workers by raising the costs of firing them.

However, while the general equilibrium effect of their model is to reduce employment, Acemoglu and Angrist acknowledge that the partial equilibrium effects could be much different. In particular, by increasing firing costs and requiring accommodation, the ADA could increase retention of already employed workers who become disabled due to a health shock. This is important for our purposes, because we hypothesize that the primary impact of the overlap between employment protection and workers' compensation receipt should be on the retention of newly disabled workers.

In this chapter, we argue that the existence of the workers' compensation system reinforces this retention effect for those workers who become disabled due to a workplace injury. Suppose that individual i is employed and has marginal productivity equal to θ_{it}, where $\theta_{it} = \theta^D$ if she is disabled in time t and $\theta_{it} = \theta^H$ if she is not. The disabled are assumed to be less productive in most jobs, so $\theta^H \geq \theta^D$. In a fully competitive market, wages would equal marginal product. However, suppose there are equal pay provisions that prevent employers from offering different wages based on disability status, so $w_i = \overline{w}$ for all i regardless of marginal product.[13] If we assume that $\theta^H > \overline{w} > \theta^D$, we have the extreme case where a firm always wants to hire nondisabled workers but never wants to hire disabled workers.

The Acemoglu and Angrist (2001) model generated turnover by incorporating exogenous productivity shocks for all workers. In our model, the only shock we consider is a nondisabled worker becoming disabled. Suppose that each nondisabled worker in period t faces the chance of becoming disabled

13. In this model we ignore the possibility that employers could differentiate job title or description based on disability status, which might give them some ability to alter wages. However, such practices could similarly run afoul of provisions that prohibit discrimination in promotion or hiring.

in period $t + 1$. For simplicity, assume that disability is an absorbing state. Once a worker becomes disabled, the employer has two choices: they can pay accommodation cost c and retain the disabled worker, or they can fire the disabled worker and absorb the associated litigation costs, denoted f.[14] The firing cost is equal to the expected cost that comes from a lawsuit that the disabled worker files under the employment protection provisions. Firing cost is assumed to be nonzero and randomly distributed with a density function $g(f)$.

In our model, the value of accommodation changes depending on whether or not the worker became disabled due to a workplace injury. If the injury occurred at work, the worker is eligible for income replacement benefits during the recovery period. This cost, which we denote b, cannot be avoided by firing the worker. However, benefits are paid weekly, so the cost is increasing in the length of time that an injured worker remains out of work. For the reasons discussed earlier, we assume that the time out of work—and thus the cost associated with workers' compensation benefits—can be reduced by making the accommodations; that is, $b(c) < b(0)$.

Under these assumptions, an employer will retain the newly disabled worker if:

$$\theta^D - \overline{w} - c \geq -E(f) \qquad \text{for nonwork disabilities}$$

$$\theta^D - \overline{w} - c + (b(0) - b(c)) \geq -E(f) \quad \text{for work-related disabilities.}$$

If $\overline{w} > \theta^D$, then employers always fire disabled workers in the absence of employment protection. Similarly, if employment protection requires accommodations without an adequate enforcement mechanism, such as the ability to sue the employer, employers would still choose to fire workers and not accommodate. However, if the firing costs are high enough, employers will find it profitable to retain disabled workers even if their marginal product is below the required wage.

The ability of accommodation costs to offset workers' compensation costs, as represented by $(b(0) - b(c))$, makes it cheaper for employers to retain disabled workers.[15] Essentially, this acts as a subsidy to complying with the guidelines of employment accommodation. This implies that employment protection and workers' compensation recipiency are complements: the threat of a discrimination lawsuit should have a bigger effect among workers' compensation recipients than nonrecipients.

This hypothesis about the differential impact of employment protection on workers' compensation recipients and nonrecipients motivates our empirical work. In order to test the predicted relationship, the ideal experiment

---

14. Implicitly we are assuming that marginal productivity of disabled workers is θ^D if the employer accommodates and zero otherwise.

15. We rule out the case where $(b(0) - b(c)) > c$. In such a scenario, employers could choose to accommodate and still fire the disabled workers.

would be to observe the employment of workers' compensation recipient compared to nonrecipients with and without any employment protection. However, our empirical test is implemented somewhat differently.

We do not observe a state of the world with no employment protection; rather, we observe employment outcomes before and after a random shock to the strength of employment protection. This can be interpreted in our model as a change in the distribution function $g(f)$, one that leads to an increase in the expected costs of firing a disabled worker. This is an important distinction, because the change in the differential impact of employment protection is not generally equal to the overall difference; in fact, it need not even have the same sign.

Figure 7.1 illustrates the impact of a hypothetical change in the distribution of firing costs on the expected employment of disabled workers. The functions $g^1(f)$ and $g^2(f)$ represent the distribution of firing costs before and after the change, respectively. The probability a worker is retained for a given value of f is the integral of $g(f)$ above that value. The values f^* and f^{wc} represent the respective firing cost thresholds that induce employers to retain workers with nonoccupational and occupational disabilities.

The area B represents the differential impact of employment protection on workers' compensation recipients before the change. After the change the differential impact is the area $A + B$. However, the experiment implemented in the empirical work in this chapter can only identify area A, the difference-in-differences after the change. While A is positive in our example, it is easy

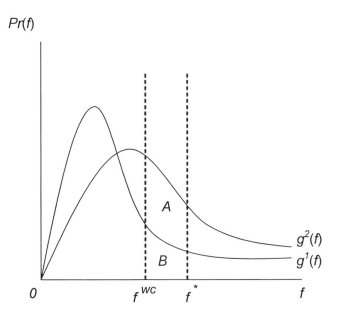

Fig. 7.1   **The impact of a change in the distribution of firing costs**

to see that this is not necessarily the case. Practically speaking, A will be positive as long as the change in the distribution of firing costs is large enough and as long as the threshold values are not too low. If firing costs are low enough before the change, so that area B is small, then the difference identified here will approach the full differential impact of the policy after the change.

7.3.1   Welfare Implications

A natural question that arises in our analysis is, does the result that workers' compensation and employment protection are complements lead to more socially desirable outcomes? The model suggests that workers who become disabled due to a workplace injury will receive greater accommodations and experience better employment outcomes. While this is clearly better for the workers' compensation recipients, it is not immediately clear whether or not it is socially optimal.

An ideally functioning system would have employers providing the optimal level of accommodations to both groups of workers. The complementary nature of employment protection and workers' compensation could improve social welfare in one of two ways. If we thought that employers were more likely to discriminate against workers' compensation recipients, then the implicit subsidy to accommodation could lead to more efficient outcomes.[16] Alternatively, suppose that inefficiencies inherent to the liability system (such as the high cost of filing a lawsuit) leads to inefficiently low levels of accommodation for all disabled workers. In this case, providing employers with additional incentives to accommodate workers' compensation recipients leads to better outcomes. Note that these two have significantly different policy implications. With the former, the optimal policy prescription would be to find some way to subsidize accommodations for all disabled workers. With the latter, no such intervention is (necessarily) called for.

From a social perspective, it is also possible that the complementarity between workers' compensation and employment protection actually worsens social welfare. As is the case with many applications of the tort system, the welfare implications of the analysis relies crucially on the ability of the courts to identify the socially optimal level of accommodation. If the true impact of employment protection is to impose an overly burdensome cost to employers, then anything that leads to higher accommodations could lead to a net decline in welfare. Such employer costs could also be exacerbated if the enhanced opportunity for discrimination litigation led to an increase in workers' compensation claims by injured workers.[17] Unfortunately, nothing in our empirical work allows us to identify the actual welfare conse-

16. This could happen if, for example, employers discriminated against workers' compensation recipients in order to retaliate against them for filing claims.

17. In our sample, we found no evidence that the rate of workers' compensation claims changed after the changes to FEHA were introduced.

quences of workers' compensation receipt and employment protection in our setting.

7.4 Empirical Approach and Data

In order to test the predictions of the aforementioned model, we need to be able to track workers over time, and observe whether they are disabled, employed, or receive workers' compensation. We also need to observe an exogenous shock to the costs associated with a failure to accommodate injured workers, and observe how this alters employment of the two groups. Because we are focusing on a policy change in California, we also need to be able to measure these things for workers by state.

The primary source of data that we use is the March Current Population Survey (CPS). The CPS includes information on employment outcomes, demographics, state, disability and health status, and workers' compensation benefit receipt. For a subsample of the population, it is possible to match observations across two years, allowing us to study changes in labor force participation. Additionally, the CPS is a relatively large database, allowing us to obtain reasonable sample size even though we focus on a single state.

Our main outcome of interest is the post-disability employment of workers. Because our model specifically considers changes in separation rates from employers, we need to know if the worker was employed in the initial period. Because the matched CPS sample has two periods of data, we limit our sample to people who are employed in the first period and then use employment in the second period as our primary outcome measure. Employment in both periods is defined as having reported working at least one week in the year.

The key policy change for us is the revision to the FEHA in 2001,[18] which we interpret as an exogenous increase in f. The empirical hypothesis that we are testing is that the impact on employment should differ according to whether or not a disabled worker receives workers' compensation benefits. This lends itself to a difference-in-differences specification. The differences we employ are: pre- and post-introduction to the reform, with and without workers' compensation benefits, and disabled versus not disabled. The estimating equation we employ is:

$$\text{Employed}_{it+1} = \beta^*x_{it} + \gamma_t + \alpha^*\text{disabled}_{it} + b^*wc_{it} + \omega^*\text{disabled}_{it}^*wc_{it}$$
$$+ \delta^*\text{disabled}_{it}^*\text{post}_{it} + \eta^*wc_{it}^*\text{post}_{it}$$
$$+ \boldsymbol{\theta}^*\textbf{disabled}_{it}^*\textbf{post}_{it}^*\boldsymbol{wc}_{it} + \rho^*\text{disabled}_{it+1} + \varepsilon_{it+1}.$$

In the model, x represents important demographic characteristics such as age, gender, and education; γ represents the impact of time trends (which

---

18. While the change was enacted in 2001, for reasons discussed in detail later, we actually do not think the change had much effect until 2002.

we implement as year fixed-effects); *wc* represents an indicator for workers' compensation receipt; *disabled* is an indicator for disability status; and *post* is an indicator for the time period corresponding to the post-reform period. The parameter θ identifies the effect of FEHA on people who were disabled and who received workers' compensation benefits. If the interaction of workers' compensation and employment protection increases the likelihood that a worker is retained then the expected sign of this coefficient is positive.

In order for θ to be identified in our model, we need to ensure that we capture the impact of the changes to FEHA and not some other factor that occurred around the same time, such as changes to the workers' compensation system. In fact, as discussed before, there were changes to the workers' compensation law in California that increased the level of TTD benefits paid to injured workers beginning in 2002. This is potentially a matter of concern, but we do not think that this confounds our results because: (a) we do not think that it should have had a different effect for disabled or non-disabled workers' compensation claimants (meaning, any effect should be picked up by the other terms in our difference-in-differences specification); (b) we have a separate control for the replacement rate of disability benefits, which should capture much of the relevant variation from the benefit change; and (c) the effect of a benefit increase actually works against our predicted effect—if benefits increase, the labor supply of workers' compensation claimants should fall—suggesting our results could be conservative.

There were other reforms that led to other changes in California, cutting PPD benefits and replacing vocational rehabilitation with a voucher program. These changes did not take effect until 2004 or later, however. To further verify that we are isolating the impact of changes to FEHA, we break our estimated effects down by year and replicate our analysis dropping years 2004 and later.

To implement this analysis, there are several key measurement issues that must be considered. First, we are basing our test off the assertion that the changes brought about by AB2222 significantly increased the expected costs associated with releasing a disabled worker. It is important to both (a) verify that AB2222 did increase firing costs associated with a failure to accommodate and (b) pinpoint when these increased costs started to arise. Second, we must settle on an appropriate definition of disability. Finally, there are some issues typically associated with matching the CPS data across years. We discuss each of these issues in turn.

7.4.1   Measuring the Timing and Effect of the Reforms

To investigate whether or not the changes to the FEHA increased incentives to firms to perform interactive processes, we acquired micro-level data from the California Department of Fair Employment and Housing (DFEH). The DFEH is the administrative body charged with overseeing the implementation of FEHA. In order to have a right to sue under FEHA, for disability or other types of discrimination, a complaint must first be filed with the DFEH. These data are collected for everyone alleging an act of discrimination, regardless of whether the DFEH is involved in the resolution, or if the claim is litigated.

We received data from DFEH on all claims alleging discrimination on the basis of disability, gender, or race or ethnicity from 1997 through 2007. These data contain both the basis for the claim (gender/race/disability) as well as the alleged acts for the claim (refusal to hire/refusal to accommodate, etc). We received data on 107,703 total claims, of which 32,923 (approximately 31 percent) involved alleged discrimination on the basis of disability. Of the disability claims, 11,790 (approximately 36 percent) alleged a failure to accommodate by the employer. In addition to the data from the DFEH, we retrieved data on the number of charges made at the federal level to the EEOC for employment discrimination from 1997 to 2007.[19] Of the 82,792 charges to the EEOC in 2007, 17,734 (21.4 percent) involved a claim of discrimination due to disability, substantially less than equivalent percentage in California.

Figure 7.2 illustrates the trends in the growth in the number of both California and Federal discrimination claims by basis of claim from 1997 to 2007. The vertical axis represents the percent change between the number of claims reported in the current year and in the baseline year (1997). As we can see, the number of claims in California alleging discrimination for nondisability bases displays a declining trend over time. In particular, there is a noticeable decline after 2003, with the total number of claims in 2007 declining approximately 25 percent from its 1997 level. This trend stands in sharp contrast to the growth in the number of disability discrimination claims in California over the same period. The number of disability claims displays a small amount of growth from 1997 to 2000, but there is a sharp increase in 2001 and then even more in 2002, until the trend levels off. By 2007, the total number of disability discrimination claims in California was approximately 62 percent higher than the number in 1997.

In Figure 7.3 we examine the growth in the number of Federal discrimination claims reported to the EEOC over the same period. The overall setup of the figure is identical to that of figure 7.2. It is clear from the figure that there is little or no comparable trend in Federal discrimination cases over the same period. Federal claims alleging discrimination for nondisability bases show a brief increase in 2002 with a slight decline thereafter. Federal disability claims actually drop steadily between 1997 and 2005, declining as much as 18 percent in 2005. There is an increase after that that brings the total number back very close to that in the baseline year (down approximately 2 percent in 2007).

19. See http://www.eeoc.gov/stats/charges.html, accessed August 12, 2009.

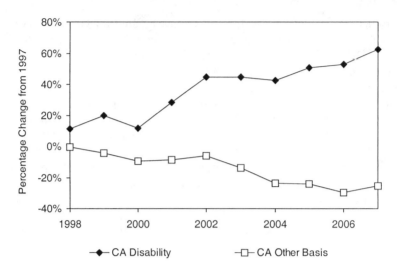

Fig. 7.2   Percentage change in discrimination claims in California by basis of claim, 1997–2007

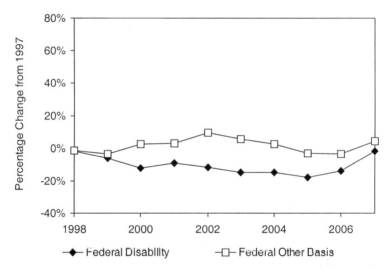

Fig. 7.3   Percentage change in federal discrimination claims by basis of claim, 1997–2007

Our analysis is predicated on the idea that the changes brought about by AB 2222 make it easier to allege that an employer failed to reasonably accommodate a disability. In figure 7.4 we compare the changes in the number of claims alleging a refusal to accommodate to changes in the number of other types of disability claims. As with figure 7.2 and figure 7.3, the values are measured as percent difference from the baseline year (1997). The series

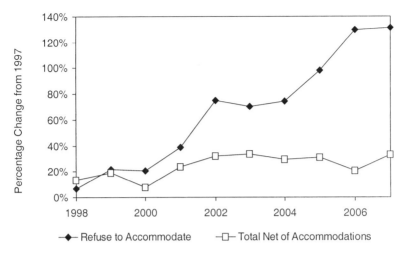

Fig. 7.4   Change in the number of disability claims in California by basis for claim, 1997–2007

"Total Net of Accommodations" represents changes in disability discrimination claims that did not allege any failure to accommodate.

The figure illustrates that a majority of the growth in disability discrimination claims after AB2222 was, indeed, driven by allegations of refusal to accommodate. The number of claims alleging a refusal to accommodate jumped from approximately 21 percent greater than the baseline value in 2000 to 39 percent greater in 2001 to 75 percent greater in 2002. Moreover, this change persists throughout subsequent years, with an additional spurt of growth in 2005 and 2006.[20] In 2007, the number of claims alleging a refusal to accommodate was 131 percent higher than in 1997. However, while there was growth in the number of other types of disability allegations over this time period, the growth is both less pronounced and less persistent.

These figures help support two points that are critical to our analysis. The first point is that AB2222 did lead to a significant increase in claims for disability discrimination. Not only do we see an increase in disability discrimination claims after AB2222 passes, but the trend appears to be mostly uncorrelated with any general trend in the filing for discrimination claims at the state or federal level. This suggests that employers likely did view the change as increasing the likelihood of being sued. Second, the changes were not immediate, and did not appear to take full effect until at least several

20. This latter period of growth may be due to changes in the workers' compensation, particularly the repeal of vocational rehabilitation benefits. A key part of the vocational rehabilitation system was the vocational rehabilitation counselor, the job of whom was generally seen to be consistent with engaging workers in an interactive process. The absence of a vocational rehabilitation counselor may have helped spur an additional increase in the number of refusals to accommodate claims.

months had passed. Therefore, in our empirical work, we focus on before 2001 and after 2001 in our analysis (essentially treating 2002 as the year of enactment).

7.4.2   Defining Disability Status

An important empirical challenge facing many studies that center on the labor market outcomes of the disabled is finding an appropriate measure of disability status to use. Many surveys include questions about the work limitations of individuals. The relevant question in the CPS is:

(Do you/Does anyone in this household) have a health problem or disability which prevents (you/them) from working or which limits the kind or amount of work (you/they) can do?

While economists are often required to rely on self-reported information, self-reported disability can be problematic in labor market studies because of the possibility that reported disability status is influenced by labor force participation. For example, if one is working, they may be less likely to report having a disability even if they have some form of functional limitation.

Reporting biases in disability status have been shown to have a significant impact on past work. Hotchkiss (2003, 2004) argues that the results of past studies suggesting that the ADA led to worse employment outcomes for the disabled in fact reflected changes in the propensity of individuals to report being disabled. Nonparticipants in the labor force became more likely to claim that they were disabled after the adoption in ADA, possibly in response to concurrent changes in welfare laws and more generous disability benefits. The potential for such bias is troubling for our purposes because we are focusing on individuals who are working (at least in the first period).

To avoid the possibility reporting biases, we use self-reported health status as an alternative definition of disability for our analysis.[21] We define someone as being disabled when they respond as having fair or poor health. While we are still relying on a self-reported measure of health limitations, because the question does not directly ask about employment the answer is more likely to be independent of current labor force participation. However, having fair or poor health is very highly correlated with self-reported disability status (approximately two-thirds of those reporting fair or poor health also report having a work limitation), so we think it captures the relevant variation in the ability to work.[22]

---

21. In this case, the relevant question we use is: "Would you say (name's/your) health in general is Excellent, Very good, Good, Fair, Poor?"

22. In the appendix we show that if we adopt the more standard definition of disability we obtain similar effects, in the sense that they have the predicted sign, though they are smaller in magnitude and not statistically significant.

7.4.3   Matching the CPS Data

While the CPS is not a true panel, portions of the sample can be linked across years. This approach has been used in past studies of workers' compensation (Krueger 1990) and employment protection (Acemoglu and Angrist 2001). About one-half of the CPS population for a particular year can be matched to the next year. A limitation to matching is that because it is a household survey, actual individuals are not identified. Rather, respondents are identified by their household and their place within the household. However, this can differ from year to year due to changes in the makeup of households (this can happen because of death, change in marital status, etc.).

The CPS contains a number of demographic characteristics that can be used to increase the accuracy of the match (such as age and gender). We initially match on household ID and line number. Next, we make sure that the potential match has not changed gender or race/ethnicity. Lastly, we make sure that the potential match is one year older in the second year than they were in the first year. This matching strategy results in a match rate of approximately 40 percent. While lower than the highest possible match rate of 50 percent, it leaves us confident that those people we have matched across years are very likely the same person.

Table 7.1 compares the matched sample to the entire CPS sample for California from 1996 to 2007. Note that we restrict the sample to the twenty-one to fifty-five age population, to focus on the prime labor market years. Overall, the matched sample appears quite close to the overall full sample. The percent of disabled workers is approximately 8.8 percent in the full sample and in the matched sample. The population with workers' compensation is

Table 7.1   **Comparison of matched and unmatched CPS samples**

Characteristic	Unmatched	Matched All workers	Disabled workers
Age	37.46	38.85	42.76
Male	49.95%	49.53%	46.17%
Employed	81.84%	83.06%	55.73%
High school	23.38%	22.41%	26.87%
Some college	21.50%	22.04%	19.76%
College degree	36.91%	38.99%	22.98%
White only	77.58%	79.80%	76.30%
Black only	6.90%	5.93%	9.94%
Other minority	15.52%	14.28%	13.76%
Disabled	8.75%	8.81%	
Workers' compensation	1.51%	1.63%	5.51%
Number of observations	98,959	38,417	3,413

Table 7.2   Changes in disability status from first to second year, matched
                   CPS sample

	Second year	
First year	Not disabled	Disabled
Not disabled	94.20%	5.80%
Disabled	54.08%	45.92%

1.51 percent in the entire sample and a slightly higher 1.63 percent in the
matched sample. All other demographic variables are within a percentage
point or two in the entire versus matched sample.

The final column of the table provides summary statistics for the disabled
population in the matched sample. As we expect, employment outcomes
for the disabled are substantially worse than for the general population. In
particular, the employment rate for the disabled population is 55.73 percent,
compared with 83.06 percent for the full sample. The rate of workers' compensation receipt is 5.51 percent among the disabled, significantly higher
than among the nondisabled population.

Before moving on to discuss the empirical results, we first consider the
transitions from health status between years. Table 7.2 illustrates the reported disability status in the second period for matched individuals based
on their reported disability status in the first period. Someone who is not
disabled in the first period becomes disabled in the second period about 5.8
percent of the time. On the other hand, someone who is disabled in the first
period reports a disability in the second period just 45.92 percent of the time.
This indicates that over half of reported disabilities are temporary.

This point is of interest partly because it confirms our earlier argument
that disability is far from static for most people, but it also has implications
for our analysis. Disabilities can vary in terms of their severity as well as
their persistence over time. Obviously the employment consequences of a
disability will be driven in part by disability severity. What could be problematic for our purposes is the possibility that disabilities associated with
workplace injuries are systematically different in terms of severity than other
disabilities. We control for this partly with our difference-in-differences specification, which should eliminate any systematic differences between workers' compensation and other disabling injuries that are constant over time.
However, we further control for differences in disability severity by including
the reported disability status in the second period as an independent variable
in all of our analyses.[23]

23. In principle, we could include the full set of self-reported health outcomes in the second
period. We have experimented with this and it did not significantly change our findings.

7.5   Results

Table 7.3 reports our central estimates for the differential employment effect of employment protection for workers' compensation recipients. The top panel reports results for all workers in our estimation sample, while the bottom panel reports results for men only.[24] We report results for three specifications: one with no fixed effects, one with fixed effects for county, and the other with fixed effects for the occupation of the job reported in the first period. We estimate a linear probability model, so the coefficients can be interpreted as percentage point differences. The other dependent variables in this model, and all other subsequent models, include controls for age, gender (in the model with both males and females), race, ethnicity, education, wage in the first year, the after-tax replacement rate of lost income from the workers' compensation system,[25] and year fixed effects.[26] Robust standard errors are reported, with clustering at the level used for the fixed effect.[27]

The results of table 7.3 indicate that the adoption of AB2222 significantly increased the likelihood of employment in the second period for disabled workers who received workers' compensation in the first period relative to those who were disabled and did not receive workers' compensation. Ignoring the models with fixed effects, the difference is 0.355 for the full sample and 0.542 for the sample that just includes men. The results are very consistent across the different fixed-effects specifications.

We suspect that the difference is higher for men because, on average, they are more likely to be employed in physical jobs that may be more likely to require accommodation. However, we do note that with this explanation we might expect some change when we include occupation fixed effects. The fact that we observe no such change in our analysis could indicate that some other explanation is more relevant.

In addition to the main interaction effect indicating the impact of the change to FEHA, table 7.3 also reports the coefficients for the direct effects of workers' compensation and disability. As expected, these direct effects are negative. However, it is perhaps somewhat surprising that the interaction between workers' compensation and disability status is also negative. The model in the previous section indicates that disabled workers' compensa-

---

24. The sample size for female workers' compensation recipients in California is too small to make it feasible to show results for females only.

25. The after-tax replacement rate is computed as a fraction of wages (two-thirds in California) of preinjury weekly wage subject to minimum and maximum amounts, and convert the benefits to after-tax status using the average tax rate in the state. Data on taxes come from the National Bureau of Economic Research (http://www.nber.org/~taxsim/), and the information on minimum and maximum benefit levels are taken from the Chamber of Commerce annual *Analysis of Workers' Compensation Laws.*

26. Here we only report the primary coefficients of interest, but in an appendix we include the full set of covariates for our preferred model.

27. The level of clustering appears to have no significant impact on the standard errors in our analysis.

Table 7.3   Estimated employment effects of the change to the FEHA by disability
                   status and workers' compensation benefit receipt

	Fixed effect		
	None	County	Occupation
All workers			
Workers' comp·Post2002·Disabled	.355***	.356***	.362***
	(.124)	(.081)	(.124)
Post2002·Disabled	−.021	−.021	−.022
	(.027)	(.027)	(.026)
Workers' comp	−.081**	−.082*	−.08**
	(.036)	(.041)	(.032)
Disabled	−.044**	−.044**	−.043**
	(.018)	(.02)	(.016)
Workers' comp·Disabled	−.156	−.155*	−.160*
	(.096)	(.086)	(.089)
Male only			
Workers' comp·Post2002·Disabled	.542***	.538***	.555***
	(.155)	(.184)	(.168)
Post2002·Disabled	−.037	−.038	−.041
	(.033)	(.033)	(.05)
Workers' comp	−.084*	−.088*	−.081**
	(.046)	(.046)	(.036)
Disabled	−.017	−.017	−.014
	(.02)	(.023)	(.024)
Workers' comp·Disabled	−.22*	−.218	−.23*
	(.126)	(.139)	(.13)

Notes: Table reports linear probability estimates of the differential employment likelihood of disabled workers' compensation recipients versus disabled nonrecipients in the post-reform (i.e., after 2002) period. The sample is based on the matched CPS in California from 1996–2007, and the dependent variable is an indicator for whether the individual was working (at least one week worked) in the second year of the match. The sample is restricted to individuals who worked at least one week in the first year of the match. All regressions include demographic characteristics, as well as wages in the first year, the replacement rate of lost income in the workers' compensation system, and year fixed-effects. Robust standard errors are included in parentheses. In the models including fixed-effects for county and occupation, the standard errors are adjusted to allow for clustering by county and occupation, respectively.
***Significant at the 1 percent level.
**Significant at the 5 percent level.
*Significant at the 10 percent level.

tion recipients subject to FEHA should have better employment outcomes. However, we expect that the negative effect could be attributed to a correlation with disability severity, as past work has shown that injury severity is highly correlated with filing for workers' compensation benefits (Biddle and Roberts 2003; Lakdawalla, Reville, and Seabury 2007).

The dependent variable in this specification focuses only on whether or not the individual worked at all in the year. While this specification fits our conceptual model it is somewhat restrictive, because a majority of workers employed in year 1 are also employed in year 2; approximately 95 percent of the nondisabled workers in our sample and 86 percent of the disabled workers are employed in year 2. As an alternative model, we use the actual number of weeks worked as the dependent variable, and report the results in table 7.4. The findings are consistent with the previous specification. Disabled workers' compensation recipients work about seventeen to eighteen

Table 7.4   **Estimated effects of the change to FEHA on the number of weeks worked by disability status and workers' compensation benefit receipt**

	Fixed effect		
	None	County	Occupation
All workers			
Workers' comp·Post2002·Disabled	17.732***	17.683***	17.553***
	(6.329)	(5.701)	(5.945)
Post2002·Disabled	–.997	–.953	–1.037
	(1.475)	(1.464)	(1.288)
Workers' comp	–3.933**	–3.792***	–3.723**
	(1.897)	(1.242)	(1.497)
Disabled	–3.85***	–3.839***	–3.751***
	(1.02)	(.876)	(.605)
Workers' comp·Disabled	–9.467**	–9.379**	–9.418**
	(4.565)	(3.766)	(3.978)
Male only			
Workers' comp·Post2002·Disabled	28.538***	27.884**	28.545***
	(8.06)	(10.699)	(8.028)
Post2002·Disabled	–1.679	–1.589	–1.808
	(1.92)	(1.975)	(2.585)
Workers' comp	–3.453	–3.541*	–3.086
	(2.407)	(1.753)	(2.134)
Disabled	–3.122**	–3.226**	–3.014**
	(1.266)	(1.419)	(1.277)
Workers' comp·Disabled	–14.372**	–13.833**	–14.389***
	(5.636)	(6.177)	(4.899)

Notes: Table reports ordinary least squares (OLS) estimates of the differential weeks worked of disabled workers' compensation recipients versus disabled nonrecipients in the post-reform (i.e., after 2002) period. The sample is based on the matched CPS in California from 1996–2007, and the dependent variable is the number of weeks the individual worked in the second year of the match. The sample is restricted to individuals who worked at least one week in the first year of the match. All regressions include demographic characteristics, as well as wages in the first year, the replacement rate of lost income in the workers' compensation system, and year fixed-effects. Robust standard errors are included in parentheses. In the models including fixed-effects for county and occupation, the standard errors are adjusted to allow for clustering by county and occupation, respectively.

***Significant at the 1 percent level.

**Significant at the 5 percent level.

*Significant at the 10 percent level.

more weeks relative to nonparticipants in the post-reform period. If we focus on men only, the effect is an increase of about twenty-eight to twenty-nine weeks worked.

Figure 7.2 and Figure 7.3 both indicate that the increase in disability discrimination claims was most pronounced in 2002 and was fairly persistent afterwards. We also know there were other changes to the workers' compensation system that took place in 2004 that might have affected employment for the disabled. Thus, if the effect that we find is really attributable to the adoption of AB2222 we would expect to see an effect in 2002 that persisted over time. In table 7.5 we report results from an alternative specification that allows the effect to vary over time. Specifically, we interact each year from 2001 through 2006 with the interaction term between workers' compensation benefit receipt and disability status. As before, we present separate results for all workers and for men, and report the results with and without county and occupation fixed effects.

From the table we see that there is no significant effect in 2001. If anything, the effect appears to be negative. Beginning in 2002, there appears to be a positive effect that is mostly consistent over time. For all workers, all five of the interaction terms from 2002 to 2006 are positive and four are positive and significant. For men as well, all five of the years 2002–2006 are posi-

Table 7.5   Estimated employment effects of the change to FEHA by disability status and workers' compensation benefit receipt, by year in the post-reform period

Coefficient	Interaction year					
	2001	2002	2003	2004	2005	2006
	All workers					
Workers' comp˙Year˙Disabled	−.368	.288***	.404***	.104	.316***	.414***
	(.222)	(.061)	(.061)	(.292)	(.075)	(.065)
	Male only					
Workers' comp˙Year˙Disabled	−.348	.344***	.439***	.469***	.328***	.387***
	(.275)	(.103)	(.084)	(.114)	(.111)	(.114)

Notes: Table reports linear probability estimates of the differential employment likelihood of disabled workers' compensation recipients versus disabled nonrecipients in the post-reform (i.e., after 2002) period, with the estimated effect broken down by year. The sample is based on the matched CPS in California from 1996–2007, and the dependent variable is an indicator for whether the individual was working (at least one week worked) in the second year of the match. The sample is restricted to individuals who worked at least one week in the first year of the match. All regressions include demographic characteristics, as well as wages in the first year, the replacement rate of lost income in the workers' compensation system, and year fixed-effects. Robust standard errors are included in parentheses. In the models including fixed-effects for county and occupation, the standard errors are adjusted to allow for clustering by county and occupation, respectively.

***Significant at the 1 percent level.
**Significant at the 5 percent level.
*Significant at the 10 percent level.

tive; furthermore, they are all positive and statistically significant at the 1 percent level.[28]

Taken together, the results of tables 7.3, 7.4, and 7.5 indicate that the employment outcomes of disabled workers who received workers' compensation benefits improved significantly after reforms increased the level of protection the disabled received against discrimination. The effect size appears quite large; given that approximately 86 percent of the disabled are employed in the second year, these effects indicate approximately a 40 percent increase in the likelihood of employment, even larger for men. However, given that the increase in allegations indicated in figures 7.2 and 7.4 was so large, perhaps it is not surprising that the estimated employment effect is also large. Although not reported here, we have examined the impact of the reform on wages, but the effect was insignificant. This is consistent with the setup of the model, which is based on the idea that the primary effect of workers' compensation is to offset the costs of accommodations that affect the likelihood that a worker is employed.

We cannot directly test for the impact of the changes to FEHA on employment, because we do not observe the expected costs associated with a claim for any particular worker. Therefore, it is important to verify that the effects we find are not driven by more general trends in the employment outcomes of the disabled. To do so, we duplicated our analysis using the matched CPS sample for workers outside of California, which should be unaffected by changes to FEHA. In addition, we restricted the non-California sample just to the western states (Washington, Oregon, Arizona, Nevada, and New Mexico—the western seaboard and states that border California), to capture the effects of any regional trends. The specification of all dependent and independent variables is the same as in table 7.3.

The results of this analysis are reported in table 7.6. The top panel reports results for the full United States, while the bottom reports results for the western states. As before, we present results using no fixed effects and fixed effects for county and occupation, though in table 7.6 we only report the primary coefficient of interest (the interaction term for workers' compensation receipt with disability status and the post period). As the table reports, we find no statistically significant changes in the employment of disabled workers' compensation recipients after 2002. This is true for the entire United States and for the western states. In all cases the coefficients are small, statistically insignificant, and have the wrong sign. All of these facts help suggest that the results we find are not part of a larger regional trend, and instead are associated with the change in the disability laws in California.

In table 7.7 we replicate the analysis allowing the effects to vary by year.

28. As an alternative approach, we simply estimated the model dropping years 2005 and later. This approach provided qualitatively identical results, in that we found a positive effect on employment of disabled workers' compensation recipients in the post-reform period.

Table 7.6   Test of employment trends of disabled workers and workers'
                   compensation recipients outside of California in the post-reform period

	Fixed effect		
	None	County	Occupation
Entire U.S. (excluding California)			
All workers			
Coefficient on workers' comp · Post2002 · Disabled	–.011	–.012	–.012
	(.059)	(.039)	(.044)
Male only			
Coefficient on workers' comp · Post2002 · Disabled	–.013	–.013	–.013
	(.079)	(.047)	(.064)
Western states (excluding California)			
All workers			
Coefficient on workers' comp · Post2002 · Disabled	–.112	–.106	–.116
	(.162)	(.136)	(.123)
Male only			
Coefficient on workers' comp · Post2002 · Disabled	–.155	–.135	–.159
	(.206)	(.18)	(.187)

Notes: Table reports linear probability estimates of the differential employment likelihood of disabled workers' compensation recipients versus disabled nonrecipients in the post-reform (i.e., after 2002) period. The sample is based on the matched CPS in from 1996–2007, excluding California, and the dependent variable is an indicator for whether the individual was working (at least one week worked) in the second year of the match. The western states include Washington, Oregon, Arizona, Nevada, and New Mexico. The sample is restricted to individuals who worked at least one week in the first year of the match. All regressions include demographic characteristics, as well as wages in the first year, the replacement rate of lost income in the workers' compensation system, and year fixed-effects. Robust standard errors are included in parentheses. In the models including fixed-effects for county and occupation, the standard errors are adjusted to allow for clustering by county and occupation, respectively.

The sample size for the western states only is comparatively small, so we restrict this analysis to the full U.S. population only. As before, the effect sizes are smaller, statistically insignificant, and generally have the wrong sign. This further supports the notion that the effects we find in our analysis are driven by a California-specific change to the labor market experience of disabled workers' compensation recipients and not reflective of some general trend. While we cannot completely rule out the possibility of another explanation, the timing of the effect and the general lack of an effect outside of California suggests that our findings are causally attributable to the changes in FEHA brought about by AB2222.

7.6   Conclusions

This chapter studies the interaction between policies that protect disabled workers from discrimination and policies that mandate compensation for workplace injuries, and how this influences the employment of disabled

Table 7.7   **Test of national employment trends of disabled workers and workers'
compensation recipients in the post-reform period, by year
(excluding California)**

Coefficient	Interaction year				
	2002	2003	2004	2005	2006
All workers					
Workers' comp · Year · Disabled	–0.065	–0.061	–0.008	–0.011	–0.016
	(0.056)	(0.068)	(0.077)	(0.090)	(0.066)
Male only					
Workers' comp · Year · Disabled	–0.080	–0.009	0.045	–0.091	–0.054
	(0.072)	(0.081)	(0.079)	(0.106)	(0.082)

Notes: Table reports linear probability estimates of the differential employment likelihood of disabled workers' compensation recipients versus disabled nonrecipients in the post-reform period with the effects broken down by year. The sample is based on the matched CPS in from 1996–2007, excluding California, and the dependent variable is an indicator for whether the individual was working (at least one week worked) in the second year of the match. The sample is restricted to individuals who worked at least one week in the first year of the match. All regressions include demographic characteristics, as well as wages in the first year, the replacement rate of lost income in the workers' compensation system, and year fixed-effects. Robust standard errors are included in parentheses. In the models including fixed-effects for county and occupation, the standard errors are adjusted to allow for clustering by county and occupation, respectively.

workers. We predict that workers' compensation claimants should be more sensitive to changes in employment protection policies, specifically an exogenous increase in the costs associated with firing a disabled worker. We test this hypothesis using changes to the California Fair Employment and Housing Act (FEHA), making it easier for disabled workers to sue their employers for a failure to accommodate. The findings suggest that, as we suspected, workers' compensation recipients appeared to benefit more than other disabled workers from this policy change.

Often when comparing a private policy enforced through litigation with a regulatory public policy we are concerned with redundancy, but in this particular instance the overlap between the two systems actually helps to make the private litigation system more effective. In the broader context of studying the interaction between regulation and litigation, one aspect of our application that is somewhat unusual is that we are not considering the canonical example of overlap between ex ante regulation and ex post litigation over the same behavior. Nevertheless, we feel our results provide some insight into cases where the overlap between a regulatory system and a litigation system could be beneficial.

More generally, the addition of ex post taxes or subsidies for a regulatory system can help attain better outcomes when the socially optimal activity level varies across different subsets of the population. Such could be the case in our example if, in an example discussed previously, employers are more likely to discriminate against workers' compensation claimants as a form of retaliation for filing a claim. There are other possible applications where this combination of ex post regulatory fines and litigation could generate socially optimal outcomes. Suppose, for example, that producers are subject to litigation if they pollute and impose external harm on private residents. Further suppose that the pollution has greater social harm in certain areas (e.g., a wetland) that will not be reflected in the private harm experienced by residents (and thus compensated by the litigation system). In such a case, social welfare could potentially be improved by allowing litigation and imposing a regulatory regime in the more sensitive area. That is not to say that this approach is the *only* way to achieve optimal outcomes in this example—an appropriately set Pigovian tax could achieve the same outcome—but it is an illustration of how a regulatory system and a litigation system can be used in a complementary fashion to improve social welfare.

There are numerous ways in which the work here can be expanded upon. The preliminary findings here do little to control for other important factors, such as firm size, that could affect the results. In addition, the CPS tracks individuals for such a short time that we have a very fixed window to track changes in labor force participation and separation. We will explore using panel data to consider a longer time horizon. Finally, while we focus on FEHA because of the specific changes in accommodation requirements, we might also expect the ADA to have different impact for workers who receive workers' compensation benefits.

Appendix

Estimation Results for the Full Set of Covariates

In table 7A.1 we provide the estimation results for the full set of covariates in our preferred specification. This is the model with the full sample of California workers (male and female), where employment is used as the dependent variable and no occupation or county fixed-effects are included. This corresponds to the results presented in the top row and first column of table 7.3.

The dependent variable is employment in the second period, so we expect that those factors that are generally predictive of better employment outcomes (e.g., higher levels of education) should have positive coefficients. We find that this is generally the case. Workers with a high school or college degree are significantly more likely to keep working, as are workers with higher wage rate. Our quadratic specification indicates that age has a positive but concave impact on the likelihood of working. Nonwhites are less likely to work in the second year. The temporary disability replacement rate in work-

Table 7A.1   **The full set of estimated coefficients for the employment model**

Explanatory variable	Coefficient	Standard error	t-stat	$P(t)$
Disabled and workers' comp in the post-period	0.355	0.124	2.870	0.004
Workers' compensation	−0.081	0.036	−2.250	0.025
Workers' comp in 2001	0.134	0.039	3.440	0.001
Workers' comp after 2002	−0.016	0.058	−0.270	0.785
Disabled	−0.044	0.018	−2.460	0.014
Disabled in 2001	0.058	0.037	1.590	0.113
Disabled in the post-period	−0.021	0.027	−0.800	0.426
Disabled and workers' comp	−0.156	0.096	−1.630	0.103
Disabled and workers' comp in 2001	−0.340	0.221	−1.540	0.124
Disabled in the post-period	−0.093	0.013	−7.170	0.000
Female	−0.042	0.004	−10.200	0.000
Age	0.014	0.002	6.580	0.000
Aged squared	−0.000	0.000	−6.000	0.000
Hispanic	−0.024	0.010	−2.430	0.015
African American	−0.011	0.006	−1.860	0.063
High school	0.042	0.008	5.330	0.000
Some college	0.042	0.008	5.300	0.000
College degree	0.054	0.007	7.480	0.000
Temporary disability rate · 1,000	−0.372	0.409	−0.910	0.364
Wage rate	0.000	0.000	−0.750	0.453
1997	−0.008	0.008	−0.940	0.348
1998	−0.005	0.008	−0.610	0.544
1999	−0.019	0.009	−2.170	0.030
2000	0.002	0.008	0.310	0.757
2001	−0.007	0.008	−0.780	0.435
2002	−0.017	0.009	−1.830	0.067
2003	−0.006	0.008	−0.720	0.469
2004	−0.022	0.010	−2.290	0.022
2005	−0.003	0.008	0.360	0.719
2006	−0.021	0.009	−2.390	0.017
Constant	0.672	0.040	16.650	0.000

Notes: Table reports linear probability estimates of the differential employment likelihood of disabled workers' compensation recipients versus disabled nonrecipients in the post-reform (i.e., after 2002) period. The sample is based on the matched CPS in California from 1996–2007, and the dependent variable is an indicator for whether the individual was working (at least one week worked) in the second year of the match. The sample is restricted to individuals who worked at least one week in the first year of the match. Robust standard errors are included in parentheses.

ers' compensation is negatively associated with the likelihood of working, though the impact is small and not statistically significant. The year fixed-effects display no clear trend in employment, though there appears to be some general decline in the likelihood of working relative to base year (1996).

While we present the results for only our preferred specification, the same overall pattern arises in other specifications as well. Those factors that predict employment in more general models also predict the likelihood of employment in the second year in our model.

Alternate Specification of Disability

In our main empirical work we use fair or poor self-reported health to indicate disability. We adopt this measure because (a) the definition of disability in FEHA is broad, and the self-reported health measure is more inclusive, and (b) we feel that there exists a greater potential for bias in the question that asks about work limitations. In table 7A.2 we present estimates of the model using a self-reported work limitation as our indicator of disability. The table presents results for the full sample (men and women) with our preferred model, using employment as the dependent variable (analogous to the model in the top panel of table 7.3).

In general, the results are consistent with our central findings, in terms of the signs of the estimated coefficients. The primary coefficient of interest, the interaction between disability and workers' compensation receipt in the post-reform period, is positive, though it is not statistically significant. The impact of this measure of disability on the likelihood of working, both on its own and interacted with workers' compensation receipt, is noticeably stronger than in the preferred model. This could be because this measure of

Table 7A.2	Model estimates using self-reported work limitations as the disability measure		
	All workers		
Workers' comp·Post2002·Disabled	.153	.153	.157
	(.138)	(.12)	(.132)
Post2002·Disabled	−.047	−.047	−.047
	(.051)	(.049)	(.041)
Workers' comp	−.000	−.000	−.000
	(.026)	(.023)	(.024)
Disabled	−.113***	−.115***	−.112***
	(.033)	(.027)	(.017)
Workers' comp·Disabled	−.308***	−.308***	−.310***
	(.093)	(.066)	(.061)
Fixed effect	None	County	Occupation

Notes: Table reports linear probability estimates of the differential employment likelihood of disabled workers' compensation recipients versus disabled nonrecipients in the post-reform (i.e., after 2002) period. The sample is based on the matched CPS in California from 1996–2007, and the dependent variable is an indicator for whether the individual was working (at least one week worked) in the second year of the match. The sample is restricted to individuals who worked at least one week in the first year of the match. All regressions include demographic characteristics, as well as wages in the first year, the replacement rate of lost income in the workers' compensation system, and year fixed-effects. Robust standard errors are included in parentheses. In the models including fixed-effects for county and occupation, the standard errors are adjusted to allow for clustering by county and occupation, respectively.
***Significant at the 1 percent level.

disability indicates worse overall health, but it is also consistent with a bias of unemployed workers being more likely to report a disability. Overall, we feel that self-reported health provides the most reliable measure of disability for this analysis. However, we do not that the statistical significance of our primary coefficient of interest is sensitive to the choice of specification.

References

Acemoglu, D., and J. D. Angrist. 2001. Consequences of employment protection? The case of the Americans with Disabilities Act. *Journal of Political Economy* 109 (5): 915–57.

Bernacki, E. J., J. A. Guidera, J. A. Schaefer, and S. Tsai. 2000. A facilitated early return to work program at a large urban medical center. *Journal of Occupational and Environmental Medicine* 42 (12): 1172.

Biddle, J., and K. Roberts. 2003. Claiming behavior in workers' compensation. *Journal of Risk and Insurance* 70 (4): 759–80.

Butler, R. J., W. G. Johnson, and M. L. Baldwin. 1995. Managing work disability: Why first return to work is not a measure of success. *Industrial and Labor Relations Review* 48:452–69.

Butler, R. J., and J. D. Worrall. 1985. Work injury compensation and the duration of nonwork spells. *The Economic Journal* 95 (379): 714–24.

DeLaire, T. 2000a. The unintended causes of the Americans with Disabilities Act. *Regulation* 23:194–97.

———. 2000b. The wage and employment effects of the Americans with Disabilities Act. *Journal of Human Resources* 35 (Fall): 693–715.

Galizzi, M., and L. Boden. 1996. *What are the most important factors shaping return to work? Evidence from Wisconsin.* Cambridge, MA: Workers' Compensation Research Institute.

Hotchkiss, J. L. 2003. *The labor market experience of workers with disabilities: The ADA and beyond.* Kalamazoo, MI: W. E. Upjohn Institute.

———. 2004. A closer look at the employment impact of the Americans with Disabilities Act. *Journal of Human Resources* 39 (4): 887–911.

Johnson, W. G., and J. Ondrich. 1990. The duration of post-injury absences from work. *The Review of Economics and Statistics* 72 (4): 578–86.

Jolls, C., and J. J. Prescott. 2004. Disaggregating employment protection: The case of disability discrimination. NBER Working Paper no. 10740. Cambridge, MA: National Bureau of Economic Research, September.

Kolstad, C. D., T. S. Ulen, and G. V. Johnson. 1990. Ex post liability for harm vs. ex ante safety regulation: Substitutes or complements? *American Economic Review* 80 (4): 888–901.

Krause, N., L. K. Dasinger, and F. Neuhauser. 1998. Modified work and return to work: A review of the literature. *Journal of Occupational Rehabilitation* 8 (2): 113–39.

Krueger, A. B. 1990. Workers' compensation insurance and the duration of workplace injuries. NBER Working Paper no. 3253. Cambridge, MA: National Bureau of Economic Research.

Lakdawalla, D. N., R. T. Reville, and S. A. Seabury. 2007. How does health insurance affect worker's compensation filing? *Economic Inquiry* 45 (2): 286–303.

Loisel, P., L. Abenhaim, P. Durand, J. M. Esdaile, S. Suissa, and L. Gosselin. 1997. A population-based, randomized clinical trial on back pain management. *Spine* 22 (24): 2911–18.

Meyer, B. D., W. K. Viscusi, and D. L. Durbin. 1995. Workers' compensation and injury duration: Evidence from a natural experiment. *American Economic Review* 85 (3): 322–40.

Neuhauser, F., and S. Raphael. 2004. The effect of an increase in worker's compensation benefits on the duration and frequency of benefit receipt. *Review of Economics and Statistics* 86 (1): 288–302.

Oi, W. Y. 1991. Disability and a workfare-welfare dilemma. In *Disability and work: Incentives, rights, and opportunities,* ed. C. L. Weaver, 45. Washington, DC: American Enterprise Institute Press.

Philipson, T. J., and E. Sun. 2008. Is the Food and Drug Administration safe and effective? *Journal of Economic Perspectives* 22 (1): 85–102.

Reville, R. T., and R. F. Schoeni. 2005. The fraction of disability caused at work. *Social Security Bulletin* 65 (4): 31–7.

Rosen, S. 1991. Disability accommodation and the labor market. In *Disability and work: Incentives, rights, and opportunities,* ed. C. L. Weaver, 18–30. Washington, DC: American Enterprise Institute Press.

Schwartzstein, J., and A. Shleifer. 2009. Litigation and regulation. NBER Working Paper no. w14752. Cambridge, MA: National Bureau of Economic Research, February.

Uehlein, W. F., and M. Nevils. 2008. Second injury funds in flux; opportunities, changes, and questions. *The Journal of Workers Compensation* 17 (3): 19–28.

Viscusi, W. K., and M. J. Moore. 1987. Workers' compensation: Wage effects, benefit inadequacies, and the value of health losses. *The Review of Economics and Statistics* 69 (2): 249–61.

Opting Out of Workers' Compensation in Texas
A Survey of Large, Multistate Nonsubscribers

Alison Morantz

8.1 Introduction

The "great compromise" of workers' compensation, whereby workers injured on the job relinquished the right to sue their employers in exchange for no-fault occupational-injury insurance, was one of the major tort reforms of the twentieth century. Every U.S. state adopted a workers' compensation law between 1910 and 1948.[1] To this day, the program remains the primary conduit of cash benefits, medical care, and rehabilitation services for workers disabled by work-related injuries and illnesses.[2] Although details such as the level and duration of benefits vary widely across states, the hallmark of the program is its near universality. In most U.S. states, every company is required to purchase workers' compensation insurance, whether through a private insurance carrier, a state insurance fund, or self-insurance.[3] It is an open question whether the transition from a negligence-based tort system to a no-fault strict liability system enhances workplace safety, let

Alison Morantz is associate professor of law and the John A. Wilson Distinguished Faculty Scholar at Stanford Law School.

This research was supported by National Science Foundation Grant No. 0850636. I would like to express my gratitude to Yo-Jud Cheng, Adam Greenberg, Brian Karfunkel, and especially Charlie Wysong for their help in administering the surveys and collecting the background information upon which this study was based.

1. See Fishback and Kantor (1998a).
2. See Krueger and Burton (1990).
3. A handful of states with compulsory laws provide exemptions for very small firms with fewer than five employees. See Shields and Campbell (2002) for a discussion. Railroad workers are also exempted from the workers' compensation system and are instead covered by a tort-based compensation system under the Federal Employers' Liability Act (FELA). See Transportation Research Board (1994) for a discussion.

alone allocative efficiency.[4] Yet given the virtual ubiquity of the workers' compensation system, it is not surprising that most empirical scholars have taken the program's existence for granted, and focused their inquiry on how different aspects of regulatory design (such as waiting periods, benefit levels, experience rating, and provider choice) affect employers' and employees' incentives, and in turn, the frequency, duration, and cost of claims.

This chapter explores an issue that has received almost no attention in prior literature: the consequences of converting workers' compensation from a compulsory system to a voluntary one. Until the early 1970s, many state laws *were* elective.[5] In 1972, the National Commission on State Workmen's Compensation Laws recommended that workers' compensation be compulsory rather than elective, and by the mid-1970s, nearly all states amended their laws to make participation mandatory.[6] After South Carolina passed such an amendment in 1997, Texas became the only state in the United States with a truly voluntary program.[7] To this day, a substantial number of so-called "nonsubscribing" firms decline to offer workers' compensation coverage in Texas.[8] In 2008, for example, about 33 percent of Texas firms—which jointly employed a quarter of Texas's workforce—were nonsubscribers.[9] Although very small firms (those with one to four employees) have always been the most likely to forgo participation in the traditional workers' compensation system, increasing numbers of "very large" employ-

---

4. Although a shift to workers' compensation systems apparently lowered the nonmotor vehicle machine death rate from 1900 to 1940, given the difficulty of measuring accident prevention costs, one cannot conclude from these findings alone that the latter system is more efficient. See Chelius (1976) for a more detailed discussion. Schwartz (1994) notes that from an economic perspective, it is unclear whether tort or workers' compensation systems provide better incentives for workplace safety. Fishback (1987) finds that in the coal mining industry, fatal accident rates *rose* with the shift to workers' compensation in the early twentieth century.

5. See Shields and Campbell (2002). The New York Court of Appeals' famous opinion in *Ives v. South Buffalo Railway Company,* 94 N.E. 431 (N.Y. 1911), which struck down a compulsory workers' compensation statute under the state constitution, encouraged many other states to pass elective laws, while "keeping benefits low and so restricting employers' legal defenses that most employers would 'freely' elect to join the new system" (Howard 2002, 33). The Supreme Court's ruling in *Mountain Timber Co. v. Washington,* 243 U.S. 219 (1917), upholding the constitutionality of a compulsory law, finally put such constitutional concerns to rest. Interestingly, however, it was not until nearly half a century later that some states made their workers' compensation statutes compulsory.

6. See Shields and Campbell (2002). See also National Commission on State Workmen's Compensation Laws (1972).

7. Although workers' compensation coverage is generally voluntary for *private* Texas employers, it is mandatory for employees of public employers (Texas Labor Code § 406.022), and for private-sector employees hired to perform work on public construction projects (Texas Labor Code § 406.096).

8. New Jersey is the only other state that technically does not require firms to carry workers' compensation coverage. However, given the restrictive nature of the statute, no firms in New Jersey have so far chosen to opt out. See Shields and Campbell (2002).

9. Workers' Compensation Research Group (2008, 5).

ers (those with 500 or more employees in Texas) have followed suit.[10] Indeed, since the mid-1990s, this is the only firm type for which nonsubscription has been steadily increasing. As of 2008, approximately 26 percent of all very large firms operating in Texas declined to provide workers' compensation coverage.[11]

The rise of the nonsubscription phenomenon in Texas raises important questions about the rationale for—and consequences of—the mandatory regime that governs the remainder of the country. Virtually all historians agree that the adoption of workers' compensation laws was endorsed not only by workers and insurers, but by employers as well.[12] Economic historians Fishback and Kantor, for example, have emphasized the gains to employers of reducing uncertainty in accident costs and demonstrated employers' capacity to offset much of the increased costs of the program through reduced wages.[13] If workers' compensation laws received broad-based employer support at the time of their passage, why have so many Texas employers chosen to forgo the benefits of the "great compromise" and expose themselves to tort liability? Surprisingly, this question has received almost no prior scholarly attention.

This chapter offers a first glimpse at the real-world consequences of nonsubscription from the perspective of large, multistate companies. The study design is straightforward. After identifying the population of large, multistate companies operating in Texas that have opted out of workers' compensation, I invited each to participate in a confidential phone survey. Most firms (89 percent) that were identified agreed to participate. The survey covered four major content areas: the characteristics of the company; the process of becoming a nonsubscriber; the characteristics of the benefit plan offered in lieu of workers' compensation; and the perceived consequences of nonsubscription.

The survey results contain a number of interesting findings. First, the typical risk management environment and panoply of employee benefits offered by participating firms differ markedly across industries. For example, although the majority of all firms offer employee wellness programs, manufacturing firms are considerably less likely than other firms to hire consultants and/or third-party administrators (TPA) to help administer their plans. The prevalence of unions, and the percentage of firms offering group health coverage, disability coverage, and/or life insurance to all workers also vary by industry.

Nevertheless, respondents were virtually unanimous in stating that their main motivation for becoming nonsubscribers was the desire to achieve

10. Ibid., 8.
11. Ibid.
12. See, for example, Fishback and Kantor (1998a, 1998b); and Howard (2002).
13. Fishback and Kantor (1998a).

cost savings. The majority of respondents (except for manufacturing firms) hired a consulting firm and/or consulted with other nonsubscribers during the nonsubscription process.

The occupational injury plans that firms offered in lieu of workers' compensation were also remarkably similar. In some respects—for example, the typical absence of any waiting period prior to the receipt of wage-replacement benefits, and the absence of any cap on weekly benefits—such plans were more generous than workers' compensation. Yet in other respects—for example, the commonplace twenty-four-hour reporting deadlines, absence of employee choice over medical providers, absence of any permanent partial or permanent total disability coverage, and prevalent caps on total benefits—such plans appeared less favorable to employees. Moreover, presumably in an effort to curb tort liability, a very high fraction (about 85 percent) of nonsubscriber plans channeled disputes to mandatory arbitration. Not only did virtually all companies deem their programs to be a success and report cost savings, but most were pleasantly surprised by the magnitude of these savings, which reportedly exceeded (on average) 50 percent across all industries.

Finally, although the majority of respondents reported little or no trouble with litigation, costly claims (exceeding $500,000) were the most common among manufacturing firms and companies that became nonsubscribers in the early 1990s. Retailers were the least likely to report having paid any costly claims. As one might expect, firms with mandatory arbitration were also much less likely to have paid out half-million-dollar claims. Although about a quarter of all respondents reported settling some claims outside of the nonsubscription plan, this practice was especially common among firms that required mandatory arbitration.

The remainder of the chapter proceeds as follows. Section 8.2 introduces the Texas workers' compensation system and nonsubscribing sector. Section 8.3 reviews prior literature on workers' compensation, highlighting several strands of scholarship that are especially pertinent to Texas nonsubscription. Section 8.4 describes the design and methodology of the survey. Section 8.5 presents the results. Section 8.6 reviews the main conclusions and suggests promising areas for future research. The detailed survey findings, as well as an appendix listing the survey questions, can be found at the end of the chapter.

8.2   Overview of Texas Workers' Compensation System and the Nonsubscription Alternative

In order to grasp the key features of nonsubscription, it is helpful first to understand the basic structure of the workers' compensation program in Texas. Except for its elective nature, Texas' workers' compensation statute is similar to those that govern other U.S. jurisdictions. To receive benefits, employees must report injuries within thirty days of the date that the injury occurred.[14] As in most states, the statute provides for full medical benefits (with no copays, time limits, or monetary caps), and wage replacement benefits are untaxed.[15] Texas also allows employees to select their treating physician, unless their employer has taken advantage of recent legislation enabling firms to join Certified Workers' Compensation Networks.[16] Employees suffering from temporary total, permanent total, or permanent partial disabilities receive 70 to 75 percent of their weekly wage, tax-free[17]—a relatively generous reimbursement rate by national standards.[18] Like about half of U.S. states, Texas's statute imposes a seven-day waiting period prior to the receipt of any wage replacement benefits, although the first week's benefits can be claimed retroactively if the absence persists for at least fourteen days.[19]

Although the basic statutory features of Texas's workers' compensation system resemble those of other states, trends in the frequency and cost of claims have been surprisingly variable in recent years. As recently as 2001, Texas had among the highest costs per claim (including medical payments per claim) among a group of fourteen states analyzed in a "benchmark-

14. Office of Injured Employee Counsel of the State of Texas. If an employee sustains an occupational disease, however, the "date of injury" is the date on which the employee knew or should have known that the disease was related to his/her employment (Texas Labor Code § 408.007). In practice, therefore, an occupational disease may be reported *more* than thirty days after the date on which it was contracted.

15. See International Association of Industrial Accident Boards and Commissions, and Workers Compensation Research Institute (2009, 21–27), which refers to laws in effect as of July 1, 2008.

16. Ibid., 25. For an overview of the network program, see Health and Workers' Compensation Division. If the employee is not in a Workers' Compensation Health Care Network, (s)he may choose any doctor willing to treat his/her injury. See Office of Injured Employee Counsel of the State of Texas.

17. Employees earning less than $8.50/hour receive 75 percent of lost wages during the first twenty-six weeks of disability, and 70 percent of lost wages thereafter. All other employees receive wage replacement benefits at a rate of 70 percent of lost wages (Texas Labor Code § 408.103).

18. See International Association of Industrial Accident Boards and Commissions, and Workers Compensation Research Institute (2009, 29–47). Until October 1, 2006, Texas' maximum benefit amounts were relatively low by national standards. Since that date, however, the maximum rates have been increased by about 15 percent (to $773 for temporary total and permanent total disability, and $541 for permanent partial disability). See Division of Workers' Compensation (2009). Although these maximum rates are close to the middle of the national distribution, the maximum periods applicable to most injury types (104 weeks for temporary total disability, 401 for unlisted permanent total disabilities, and 300 weeks for permanent partial disability) remain relatively short by national standards (as of July 1, 2008). See International Association of Industrial Accident Boards and Commissions, and Workers' Compensation Research Institute (2009, 29–47).

19. The Texas legislature reduced the length of the "retroactive period" on September 1, 2005 (Texas Labor Code § 408.082) from twenty-eight days to fourteen days. Prior to the change, Texas had one of the longest "retroactive periods" in the country, but now has a "retroactive period" in the middle of the national distribution. See International Association of Industrial Accident Boards and Commissions, and Workers' Compensation Research Institute (2009, 76–78).

ing" study conducted by the Workers' Compensation Research Institute (WCRI).[20] The percentages of claims involving over a week of lost time, permanent partial disabilities, and/or lump-sum payments were also usually high. Beginning in approximately 2002, however, these trends underwent a striking reversal. A confluence of systemic trends—such as falling rates of medical care utilization, fee schedule decreases that took effect in 2003, and shortening duration of temporary disabilities—led to a decline in both medical costs and indemnity payments per claim.[21] By the middle of the decade, average costs in Texas were far more typical of the group as a whole. For example, among *all* claims arising in 2004 (and evaluated as of 2007), average total cost per claim was only 6.3 percent above the fourteen-state median; and among those claims involving more than a week of lost time, average per-claim cost was 7.7 percent *below* the median.[22] Although WCRI's detailed analysis of more recent claims (such as those arising in 2006 and evaluated as of 2007) revealed somewhat different patterns, overall, the cost structure of Texas' workers' compensation system has remained fairly typical of the group as a whole.[23]

Given these recent trends, using Texas nonsubscribers' experiences to predict the likely effects of nonsubscription in other states is no simple matter. For example, if Texas' unusually high costs prior to 2002 were driven by the very peculiarities of its regulatory regime that later became targets for statutory reform, then the state may have provided a uniquely hospitable (and profitable) environment for nonsubscription during the pre-reform era.[24] Nevertheless, since Texas remains the only available "laboratory" in which nonsubscription can be examined, understanding large nonsubscribers' own views of the "nonsubscription experience" in a granular fashion— including *which* programmatic features they have chose to include in their "home-grown" plans, and which aspects they have viewed as particularly problematic or beneficial—is a useful first step toward understanding the consequences of an elective regime.

Although nonsubscribers have probably existed in Texas ever since the passage of the first workers' compensation statute in 1913, data on such firms was not collected in a systematic fashion for most of the twentieth century.[25] Not until the early 1990s, in fact, did the Texas Workers' Compen-

---

20. See Eccleston et al. (2009, 3).
21. Ibid.
22. Ibid., 77.
23. Ibid., 11, 15, 17.
24. Recent changes in the regulatory environment have also probably complicated the ability of participants to discern the underlying drivers of trends in costs per claim. For example, although firms that opted out prior to 2002 may have attributed any and all subsequent cost savings to the adoption of the nonsubscription plan, it is possible that they would have accrued at least some of these savings even if they had remained in the workers' compensation system. For this reason, estimates of cost savings reported by nonsubscribers that opted out just prior to or during the period of declining costs (i.e., from around 2000 to 2002) should be viewed with particular caution. (See table 8.5).
25. Shields and Campbell (2002).

sation Research Center and Texas Department of Insurance (TDI) begin commissioning periodic surveys to shed light on the prevalence and attributes of nonsubscribers. Administered to firms of all types (and in some cases, their employees) every one to three years, these surveys (the "TDI Surveys") were much more abbreviated than the survey used for the present study. However, since they were administered to a broad cross-section of firms, it is helpful to review their key findings.

First of all, the surveys reveal that by most measures, nonsubscription has become increasingly prevalent over the past fifteen years. The first TDI Survey, conducted in 1993, estimated that 44 percent of employers in Texas were nonsubscribers and 20 percent of workers were employed by nonsubscribing firms.[26] Although the 2008 survey found that the percentage of nonsubscribing firms had fallen to 33 percent, the percentage of workers employed by nonsubscribers had *risen* to 25 percent.[27] This puzzling trend is explained by the fact that rates of nonsubscription have increased dramatically (from 14 percent to 26 percent) among very large firms (those employing 500 or more employees), despite the general decline in nonsubscription rates among Texas employers since 1996.[28] Interestingly, once a firm chooses to become a nonsubscriber, it is likely to remain so: only 5 percent of subscribers surveyed in 2001 reported having been nonsubscribers at an earlier point in time.[29]

A second important finding is the frequency with which nonsubscribers—especially large ones—offer occupational injury benefit plans ("nonsubscription plans") to their employees, even though they are not legally obligated to do so. In 2008, for example, an estimated 83 percent of large firms offered occupational benefits plans to their workers.[30] Since large firms employ a disproportionate number of workers, the estimated proportion of injured employees employed by nonsubscribers who received occupational benefits was 86 percent.[31]

---

26. Ibid.
27. Workers' Compensation Research Group (2008, 6–7).
28. Ibid., 8.
29. Shields and Campbell (2002, 18).
30. Workers' Compensation Research Group (2008, 24). The fact that the prevalence of non-subscription plans in 2008 was reportedly *lower* among large firms than among medium-sized firms in 2008—a pattern that was reversed in 2006—is puzzling. See Workers' Compensation Research Group (2006). Although it is possible that the prevalence of such plans among large firms has declined in the last several years, this curious finding could also be explained by reporting error, sampling error, and/or changes in the way firms are categorized across survey years. In addition, a prominent stakeholder (who requested anonymity) suggested that the true figure is higher than 83 percent because many nonsubscribers that do not "officially" offer occupational-injury insurance nevertheless provide benefits to their injured workers on an informal basis (telephone interview, October 13, 2009). Using publicly available data, I could neither verify nor disprove this claim.
31. Workers' Compensation Research Group (2008, 24). Once again, it is puzzling that the prevalence figures reported for 2008—although still very high—are lower than for previous years. It is uncertain whether such trends are genuine or simply reflect reporting error, sampling error, and/or inconsistency of definitions across survey years.

Finally, nonsubscribing firms appear to be more satisfied with their risk-management programs than are firms that subscribe to workers' compensation. For example, nonsubscribers in 2008 reported higher satisfaction with the "adequacy/equity of occupational benefits paid to workers" (62 percent v. 53 percent); "overall satisfaction" (69 percent v. 61 percent); "whether the plan is a good value for the company" (69 percent v. 56 percent); and "ability to manage medical and wage replacement costs" (68 percent v. 50 percent). These disparities were even more pronounced among firms with at least 100 employees, with 84 percent of nonsubscribers describing themselves as "extremely" or "somewhat" satisfied with their risk-management programs, as opposed to just 59 percent of workers' compensation subscribers.[32]

The TDI's 1997 survey of nonsubscribers' injured employees—the most recent employee survey available—contains several important findings. First, most workers received substantial medical care and wage-replacement benefits.[33] For example, over 80 percent of respondents were reimbursed for full medical costs for as long as was medically necessary, as well as wage-replacement benefits for their time out of work.[34] Although 58 percent reportedly earned less than their full salaries (as would also have been the case under workers' compensation), 62 percent received wage-replacement benefits for the entire duration of their lost work time. Moreover, unlike the seven-day waiting period required under workers' compensation, injured employees typically begin receiving benefits on their first day of lost work.[35] Although 74 percent of respondents were sent to designated health-care providers or selected physicians from a preapproved list, almost two-thirds said that they could switch doctors if they were dissatisfied. A similar proportion (68 percent) said they "were treated fairly" by their employer after sustaining an injury, with more than half indicating that their employer in some way assisted their return to work.[36] Overall, when asked to rate their satisfaction with medical treatment on a scale of 1 to 5 (with 5 being "extremely satisfied" and 1 being "not satisfied"), 63 percent reported satisfaction levels of 4 or higher.[37]

Yet a significant minority did face considerable obstacles under nonsubscription. For example, among workers who lost more than one year of

---

32. Ibid., 16–18.

33. Since 91 percent of sampled employees worked for firms with fifty or more employees, the results of the survey should be construed as typical only for this employer size class. Workers' Compensation Research Group (1997, 6–7).

34. Ibid., 15.

35. Workers' Compensation Research Group (2004, 30) notes that 75 percent of nonsubscriber plans have no waiting period for receipt of wage replacement benefits. See Butler (1996).

36. Workers' Compensation Research Group (2008, 23). The 56 percent was calculated by summing the percentage who gave their employer's support a "4" or "5" rating on a 5-point scale.

37. Ibid.

work, only 42 percent received wage-replacement benefits for the full duration of their disability.[38] About one-seventh of respondents (14 percent and
16 percent, respectively) also reported difficulties in obtaining medical treatment or wage-replacement checks from their employer or insurance carrier.[39]
Finally, 46 percent of injured workers said they "suffered financial hardship"
as a result of their on-the-job injury, and this proportion rose slightly (to
52 percent) among workers who had been severely injured. Possibly for the
aforementioned reasons, almost one-fifth (18 percent) of respondents rated
their "satisfaction with medical treatment" as a 1 or 2 (the lowest ratings)
on a 5-point scale.[40]

Several other trends in the employee survey are worthy of note. First, only
35 percent of respondents said they knew about their employer's nonsubscriber status at the time of hiring, although 65 percent did learn of it before
their injury occurred. Secondly, although the Texas Labor Code requires
employers to post a notice indicating whether or not they carry workers'
compensation coverage, only 55 percent of respondents reported having
seen such a notice.[41] Finally, reported rates of attorney involvement were
remarkably low; only 13 percent of respondents hired an attorney and only
9 percent filed a lawsuit in the wake of an injury.[42]

Although the preceding findings are suggestive, the TDI Surveys must
be interpreted with caution. The employee satisfaction surveys, in particular, are more than a decade out of date and are based only on employees
of nonsubscribers. Without an appropriate "control group" of employees
whose injuries are treated under workers' compensation, there is no way to
determine whether workers are better or worse off under a nonsubscription
regime. Secondly, since most of the results are pooled, they rarely reveal
whether (and how) outcomes differ by company size.

Nevertheless, these surveys do bring several interesting patterns to light.
First and foremost, most nonsubscribers did *not* ask employees to shoulder
the costs of injuries that were noncompensable under a traditional (tort)
standard of employer negligence. Rather, most nonsubscribers offered some
form of "no-fault" insurance coverage for all occupational injuries. Second,
at least in their basic attributes, the nonsubscription plans offered by large
nonsubscribers resembled the benefits provided under workers' compensation, typically including both medical and wage-replacement components.
Finally, although most workers were unaware that they were ineligible for
workers' compensation when hired, the majority seemed fairly satisfied
with their coverage and treatment following an injury (although again, it

---

38. See table 8.4 for summary of maximum durations under Texas workers' compensation
regime.
39. Workers' Compensation Research Group (2008, 23).
40. Ibid.
41. Ibid. See Texas Labor Code § 406.005.
42. Ibid.

is unknown whether they would have fared better or worse under workers' compensation).

The survey used for the present study is both narrower and "deeper" than those administered by TDI. On one hand, the population from which the sample is drawn includes *only* large, multistate companies, and only risk management executives (not their injured employees) were interviewed. On the other hand, the survey contains more extensive and granular questions about each firm's motivation for opting out of workers' compensation, the characteristics of its occupational injury plan, and its experience with non-subscription.

8.3   Key Issues in Workers' Compensation Research

Richard Butler is the only prior scholar to have compared trends among subscribing and nonsubscribing firms in Texas. Using aggregate company-level data, Butler (1996) compared fatality rates, nonfatal claims rates, injury durations, and rates of chronic injuries (i.e., sprains and strains) across subscribing and nonsubscribing firms. The data did not allow him to control for cross-firm (let alone cross-claimant) disparities in risk, and the period analyzed (1992 to 1994) predated the influx of most large, multistate companies into the nonsubscribing sector.[43] Nevertheless, Butler's findings are suggestive. He reported that fatal injury rates were no higher among nonsubscribers than among other firms, which he interpreted as evidence that "real" safety levels were probably quite similar. Yet he did find differences in several other outcome variables, which he attributed to two different forms of moral hazard. The fact that nonsubscribers experienced slightly higher *nonfatal* injury rates, he suggested, was probably explained by the fact that most nonsubscriber plans provided first-day wage-replacement benefits, as opposed to the seven-day waiting period applicable under workers' compensation. Meanwhile, nonsubscribers' lower average claim duration, and lower average frequency of chronic conditions, likely stemmed from the fact that nonsubscriber plans (unlike statutory workers' compensation) did not compensate employees for permanent partial disabilities.[44] Although Butler attempted to compare per-claim cost differences across sectors, his projections were based on projected rather than actual cost data.[45] Notwithstanding the inherent limitations of the data available for analysis, Butler's study

---

43. Butler (1996, 405, 407).

44. Ibid., 412, 426.

45. Rather than using real cost data, Butler's "expected indemnity" cost index calculation of cost differences simply takes the industry-wide aggregate differences in frequencies calculated earlier as given, further assuming that benefits are comparable across sectors, and then makes projected cost calculations on that basis. Similarly, his calculations of legal expenses are not based on data for all claims, since TDI only records cost figures for claims that exceed $5,000. Although he also culls settlement award data from legal reporting services for 1993 and 1994, Butler notes that the available data are likely to be incomplete. See Butler (1996, 429).

underscored the disparate incentives faced by workers in the subscribing and nonsubscribing sectors, and suggested that such disparities could have detectable effects on the frequency, distribution, severity, and duration of claims.

With the exception of Butler's study, all other empirical research on workers' compensation has taken the program's existence for granted and focused on how different elements of statutory design affect key outcomes.[46] Consequently, most prior work does not speak directly to the issue examined here: the impact of forfeiting state regulation. Nevertheless, since many nonsubscribers do offer occupational benefit plans whose provisions resemble those of workers' compensation, several recurring themes addressed in prior scholarship merit a brief summary.

The first key issue with which prior scholarship has grappled is the pervasive and dizzyingly complex ways in which changes in systemic design encourage moral hazard. With "risk-bearing" moral hazard, generous occupational injury plans incentivize employees to take fewer precautions on the job, thereby lowering real (and reported) safety levels. Meanwhile, when benefits rise, "claims-reporting" moral hazard encourages employees to file claims even if they were injured off the job (or were not injured at all). By parallel logic, reducing the share of occupational-injury costs borne by an employer—for example, by lowering benefit levels or eliminating experience rating—weakens employers' incentives to invest in safety-enhancing work practices or technologies. Health care providers, in turn, may charge higher fees or order more procedures if treating workers' compensation patients is more remunerative than Medicare and/or group health insurance. In short, because changes in systemic design alter the behavior of industry stakeholders in myriad ways, discerning the true effects of any given policy intervention poses difficult challenges.

The empirical literature on moral hazard effects in the workers' compensation system is vast and multifaceted. Nearly all studies have found that increasing benefits and/or lowering waiting periods increases the frequency, cost, and/or duration of claims, apparently confirming the presence of risk-bearing and/or claims-reporting moral hazard.[47] The claims-reporting form

---

46. The only exceptions of which I am aware are two historical studies of the passage of workers' compensation laws in the early nineteenth century. See Chelius (1976) and Fishback (1987).

47. See Chelius (1982); Worrall and Appel (1982); Butler and Worrall (1983); Ruser (1985); Worrall and Butler (1985); Butler and Worrall (1985, 1988); Ehrenberg (1988); Kniesner and Leeth (1989); Krueger (1990b); Butler and Worrall (1991); Ruser (1991); Butler (1994); Meyer, Vicusi, and Durbin (1995); Kaestner and Carroll (1997); Bolduc et al. (2002); Waehrer and Miller (2003); Neuhauser and Raphael (2004). Krueger (1990a) finds that higher benefits are not associated with higher injury claims among female current population survey (CPS) respondents. Krueger and Burton (1990) find costs to be less responsive to benefit levels than previous estimates, and in some cases not significantly different from unit elastic. Lakdawalla, Reville, and Seabury (2007) find that the level of benefits offered by the employer did not affect respondents' likelihood of filing a claim in National Longitudinal Survey of Youth (NLSY)

of moral hazard, which one study suggested is larger in magnitude,[48] seems especially pronounced for injuries that are hard to diagnose, such as muscle strains and back injuries.[49] Empirical research has also lent credence to the hypothesis that firms bearing a greater proportion of the cost of injuries invest more in safety. For example, although increasing wage-replacement benefits seems to improve "real" safety levels,[50] the effect is attenuated in experience-rated firms, whose insurance premiums already (by definition) reward safe work practices.[51] Similarly, employees of self-insured firms return to work more quickly than other workers, presumably because a prolonged absence is more costly to their employers.[52] Although studies of medical care providers have found that medical costs for similar injuries are generally higher in workers' compensation than in group health, the underlying causal mechanism remains a fertile subject of debate.[53] Several authors have speculated that price-discriminating medical providers charge workers' compensation patients more than group health patients for the same care,[54] but one recent study found that the disparity is driven instead by higher utilization rates and the use of more costly providers.[55]

A second salient theme explored in prior scholarship is the impact of systemic design on the incidence of occupational injury costs. If labor markets are relatively well-functioning, the cost to employers of providing workers' compensation should be at least partially offset by lower wages (although the magnitude of such an offset will depend on the size of compensating wage differentials and the degree of workers' compensation experience rating). Although nearly all studies have confirmed the existence of a wage-benefit

---

data). In a related vein, Smith (1990) interprets the fact that a disproportionate number of workers' compensation claims for sprains and strains are filed on Mondays (a disparity that does not exist for harder-to-conceal injuries like cuts and lacerations) as evidence that workers are "post-dating" weekend back injuries and strains to obtain workers' compensation coverage. A more recent empirical study, however, has disputed the existence of this so-called "Monday effect." See Card and McCall (1996).

48. Butler and Worrall (1991).

49. See Smith (1990); Butler and Worrall (1985); Worrall and Butler (1985); Biddle (2001); Waehrer and Miller (2003); Johnson, Baldwin, and Butler (1998); and Bolduc et al. (2002).

50. See Chelius (1982); Moore and Viscusi (1992); Kniesner and Leeth (1989); and Kaestner and Carroll (1997). But Fishback (1987, 306) finds that the adoption of workers' compensation in the mining industry in the early 1900s increased rates of fatal injuries, presumably because of the rise in moral hazard associated with rising compensation.

51. The theory—which these studies seem to support—is that the firm's enhanced incentives to improve workplace safety lowers the frequency of injuries, thereby dampening the moral hazard effects triggered by higher benefits levels. See Ruser (1991); Worrall and Butler (1988); and Ruser (1985).

52. See Krueger (1990b).

53. See Fields and Venezian (1991); Baker and Krueger (1993); Roberts and Zonia (1994); and Durbin, Corro, and Helvacian (1996).

54. See Fields and Venezian (1991) and Baker and Krueger (1993). Roberts and Zonia (1994) find that health care providers successfully circumvented fee schedules by doing more in less time and exploiting textual ambiguities.

55. See Durbin, Corro, and Helvacian (1996).

trade-off, estimates of its magnitude vary by industry, region, and historical era. The implication seems to be that although workers are sufficiently
well-informed to exchange at least some proportion of their wages for the
insurance benefits that the system provides, variations in systemic design and
labor market conditions can affect the content of the implicit bargain.[56]

Finally, although many scholars have tackled the question of ultimate
policy interest—the effects of systemic design changes on occupational
safety and health—identification of "real" safety effects remains fraught
with methodological challenges. In part, this is because of the sheer complexity of incentives facing industry stakeholders, the scarcity of disaggre-
gated data on workers' compensation in the public domain, and the fact that
so many dimensions of workers' compensation regimes differ across state
lines. Probably the single most important obstacle, however, is the paucity
of truly exogenous safety metrics that are invulnerable to changes in over- or
underreporting. For example, an increase in benefit levels can be expected
to simultaneously increase claims-reporting moral hazard (which increases
reported claims but does not affect real safety); risk-taking moral hazard
(which increases reported claims and lowers real safety); and employer
investments in safety (which lower reported claims and increase real safety).
The net effect of such a change on occupational safety is therefore not only
theoretically indeterminate, but also typically unobservable, since the only
safety metric usually available to researchers is the frequency of reported
claims. Thus, although the literature on the effect of systemic design on occupational injury claims is immense, studies that purport to distinguish
"true" safety effects from over- (or under-) reporting are scarce.

Those few studies that have sought to discern the effects of systemic design
on "true" safety levels contain mixed findings. For example, two studies have
linked an increase in workers' compensation benefits to a decline in occupational fatalities and to a decline in injury severity, respectively.[57] Similarly,
a historical study found that the passage of workers' compensation laws in
the early nineteenth century reduced occupational fatalities.[58] However, a
historical analysis of the introduction of workers' compensation laws in
coal mining, relying on more granular and precise data, found that fatal
accidents *rose* with the introduction of workers' compensation.[59] Studies
on the effects of provider choice (permitting employees to choose their own
physician) were equally equivocal: although one found that state-enforced
limits on provider choice did not lower the frequency of nonfatal injuries,[60]
another found that limiting injured workers' control over their providers

56. See Kaestner and Carroll (1997); Moore and Viscusi (1989); Viscusi and Moore (1987);
Meng and Smith (1999); Ehrenberg (1988); Arnould and Nichols (1983).
57. See Moore and Viscusi (1989); See also Chelius (1982).
58. See Chelius (1976).
59. See Fishback (1987).
60. See Boden and Ruser (2003).

lowered costs and shortened the time spent out of work, although it also reduced employee satisfaction.[61]

By uncovering the characteristics, motivations, and experiences of an important group of large nonsubscribers, the present study builds on past literature by providing a more sustained glimpse inside the "black box" of nonsubscription in Texas. Identifying systemic design features that corporate risk managers have chosen to forgo in a free-market system suggests which characteristics of state regulation employers perceive as the most costly or inefficient. More broadly, understanding the consequences of nonsubscription from the perspective of participating firms is an important first step in understanding the costs and benefits of an elective statutory regime.

8.4   Survey Design and Methodology

Since nonsubscribers are an extremely heterogeneous group—ranging from "mom and pop" shops to multinational retail chains—I sought at the outset to limit the study criteria in a manner that would be advantageous from a research design perspective. First of all, I adopted a minimum size restriction. Large firms are the only group for which nonsubscription rates have increased (and dramatically so) in recent years, making them particularly interesting and important from a policy perspective.[62] Moreover, risk management executives at large companies are more likely to be full-time professionals with prior experience in the risk management field, whose responsibilities include the periodic review of occupational-injury insurance costs and trends in injury claims. In contrast, their counterparts at smaller companies are more likely to be "jacks-of-all-trades" with little background in risk management who devote much of their time to unrelated managerial tasks. Restricting the sample to large firms, therefore, maximized the chances that survey respondents would be well-informed about the costs and benefits of nonsubscription.

Secondly, I restricted the sample to firms that operate in a sizable number of U.S. states besides Texas. This "minimum dispersion" restriction was chosen because many of the survey questions, whether explicitly or implicitly, asked respondents to draw comparisons between their experience under statutory workers' compensation and their experience in Texas as nonsubscribers. Although it is fair to presume that all risk managers of large nonsubscribers have at least a rudimentary familiarity with the workers' compensation system, executives that oversee such programs in many other

---

61. See Neumark, Barth, and Victor (2007).
62. According to Texas Department of Insurance survey data, the participation rate among companies with 500+ employees nearly doubled from 1996 to 2008 (from 14 percent to 26 percent). In contrast, the percentage of nonsubscribers declined in all other employer size classes during the same time period. See Workers' Compensation Research Group (2008, 8).

states are in the best position to make credible and nuanced comparisons between the nonsubscription and workers' compensation regimes.

In order to include a diverse mix of companies, I did not impose uniform size and dispersion thresholds across the entire population of large, multi-state nonsubscribers. For example, while a retail chain or commercial bank with fewer than 100 locations would not generally be considered "large," even the largest manufacturing firms typically operate (at most) only a few dozen facilities. Therefore, imposing uniform thresholds would have meant either excluding all large manufacturing firms (by choosing a high threshold) or including many smaller retailers (by choosing a low threshold). I divided the population into six groupings—manufacturing firms; restaurant chains; other retail chains (such as department stores, gas stations, and "big-box" retailers); hotel chains; transportation companies; and other services companies (such as assisted living facilities, nursing homes, and banks)—and selected separate minimum thresholds for each group in such a way that only the largest and most geographically dispersed firms in each grouping were included. Table 8.1 presents the minimum size thresholds (as defined by number of employees and number of locations) and minimum dispersion thresholds (as defined by number of states of operation) for each grouping. Although all of the firms identified would generally be considered large, multistate corporations, the population as a whole was still reasonably het-

Table 8.1 Industry categorizations and thresholds

Industry	Minimum thresholds (Number of)			Number of firms identified	Number of firms surveyed
	Employees	Locations	States		
Manufacturing	4,000	30	13	8	7
Retail				31	28
Restaurants	7,500	100	12	(10)	(8)
Nonrestaurant retail[a]	11,000	325	9	(21)	(20)
Services				22	19
Hotels	10,000	40	10	(4)	—
Transportation	2,800	11	7	(4)	—
Other services[b]	5,000	100	20	(14)	—
Total				61	54

Notes: Total number of firms identified (based on the thresholds above): 61. Total number of firms surveyed: 54 (89% response rate). This table presents the minimum requirements for inclusion in this survey of large, multistate firms that nonsubscribed from the Texas workers' compensation system. Firms were identified through the assistance of industry stakeholders and through the analysis of a list of nonsubscribers maintained by the Division of Workers' Compensation at the Texas Department of Insurance. All industry subgroups reported above contain at least two firms that participated in the survey. Fields marked with "—" are intentionally left blank in order to preserve the anonymity of survey participants and their responses. Values in parentheses indicate number of firms belonging to subgroups of industries.

[a] Includes big-box retailers, department stores, gas stations, and supermarkets.
[b] Includes assisted living facilities, banks, health care providers, and property management firms.

erogeneous with regard to the minimum number of employees, number of facilities, geographic dispersion, and industrial attributes.

Since there is no comprehensive listing of Texas nonsubscribers in the public domain, identifying the population of nonsubscribers that met the study criteria was no simple task. I used a two-stage strategy. First, I identified key industry stakeholders and other well-informed individuals, and secured their assistance in identifying and recruiting potential participants.[63] By the end of this process, I had identified forty-seven firms meeting the study criteria. Next, I culled through the list of nonsubscribers maintained by the Texas Department of Insurance. Although the list is notoriously incomplete and outdated, listing only about 7,500 establishments (less than 5 percent of the estimated population), it nevertheless yielded an additional fourteen names.[64] Once the final list had been compiled, I contacted the risk manager of each company by e-mail and/or phone—sometimes independently, and sometimes after an introduction by another stakeholder—to personally introduce myself, describe the survey, and request his/her participation. Of the sixty-one companies that were identified as meeting the survey criteria, fifty-four (about 89 percent) agreed to participate under strict confidentiality provisions, although several declined to answer a few survey questions.[65]

Table 8.1 describes the distribution of the population identified. The retail sector comprised about half of the study population and includes restaurants, department stores, big-box retailers, gas stations, and supermarkets. (Special thresholds were imposed for restaurants because they tend to be slightly more geographically dispersed, yet have fewer total locations, than other retailers.) Comprising about a third of the population, the services group included a diverse admixture of hotels, transportation companies, assisted living facilities, banks, health care providers, and property management companies. (Once again, special thresholds were imposed for two sub-

---

63. The organizations with whom I spoke included the Texas Alliance of Nonsubscribers (generally known as the "Alliance"); another industry organization that requested anonymity; and a consulting firm, PartnerSource, that specializes in assisting firms to become nonsubscribers.

64. See Texas Non-Subscribers Download File. Although a query on to http://www.tracer2 .com/ indicates that there were 439,614 employers doing business in 2009, and the 2008 TDI survey found that about 33 percent of Texas employers were nonsubscribers (Workers' Compensation Research Group 2008, 6–7), the most recent Texas Non-Subscribers Download File contains only 7,549 entries. Therefore, it appears that only about 5 percent of nonsubscribers are included in the list.

65. As should be evident from the earlier description, the process of identifying firms was not foolproof. Therefore, the true number of qualifying firms may exceed sixty-one. For example, any firm that was not identified by any stakeholder, and did not comply with state reporting requirements, would probably not have come to light. Moreover, it is possible that even some nonsubscribers that *were* listed in the Texas Non-Subscribers Download File were not identified because they were listed through a subsidiary, holding company, or other related corporate entity whose identity was not readily apparent. For these reasons, it is possible that there are a few large, multistate nonsubscribers that met the study criteria but eluded detection.

groups, hotels and transportation firms, to account for their slightly different industrial characteristics.) Manufacturing, at about one-eighth of the study population, included relatively low thresholds for both employment and minimum number of locations.

The survey covered four general content areas: (a) corporate characteristics (including the respondent's employee benefit profile and risk management environment); (b) the nonsubscription process (including the motivations for and timing of the firm's opt-out decision); (c) the nonsubscription plan (reporting deadlines, benefit levels, time limits, and so forth); and (d) the non-subscription experience. Although following a loose script (see the appendix), the phone survey was administered in a flexible, responsive manner, and typically took between fifteen and thirty minutes to complete. All fifty-four participating firms were surveyed between March and July of 2009.

I chose not to emulate the TDI Surveys by presenting respondents with a "laundry list" of responses from which to choose, and/or asking them to rate their experience along a fixed numeric scale. Rather, questions that were not purely factual in nature—for example, questions that asked respondents to describe the nonsubscription process, or to opine on the benefits and drawbacks of nonsubscription—were posed in an open-ended and somewhat individualized fashion, and ambiguous responses were clarified through follow-up questions. This approach has its drawbacks. For example, some respondents may have forgotten to mention aspects of their experience that more specific prompting could have elicited, and minor variations in the way that questions were phrased and/or ordered conceivably could have affected the quality or quantity of responses. However, I felt that a more rigidly structured survey design—for example, adhering carefully to a script and/or asking respondents to weight or rank the relative importance of a predetermined list of factors—could inadvertently "frame" the manner in which respondents viewed their own experiences, and make them hesitant to editorialize on issues that fell outside the technical confines of the survey. Given the importance of eliciting information about aspects of nonsubscribers' experiences that I did *not* anticipate, I decided that on balance, the benefits of a more open-ended, unstructured survey design outweighed its drawbacks.

Because I did not administer a similar survey to firms that *did* subscribe to workers' compensation in Texas, I could not rule out the possibility that large, multistate firms that opted out of Texas' workers' compensation differed systematically, yet unobservably, from those that did not. For example, as compared to large Texas firms included in an online database maintained by the Texas Workforce Commission (TWC), the study participants seemed to employ more workers, operate more facilities, and report higher total sales within Texas. The magnitude of such disparities varied by industry and ranged anywhere from 10 percent to 200 percent. The survey respondents also appeared to be more heavily concentrated in the retail sector—and less concentrated in services—than the firms in the TWC sample. However, because of the poor quality of the TWC data and the difficulty of making credible apples-to-apples comparisons, such apparent differences could be statistical artifacts.[66] In short, self-selection by large, multistate firms into the nonsubscription sector remained a theoretical possibility whose real-world importance I could not reliably determine.

However, even if such selection bias did exist, it would not negate the import of the study. To the extent that Texas resembles a "natural experiment," the form of treatment that it represents is *not* the abolishment of the workers' compensation system, or the random assignment of firms across the workers' compensation and nonsubscription sectors. Rather, the "treatment" at issue is the replacement of a mandatory (universal) system with an elective one. Thus, even if the sole effect of an elective statute were to permit a group of "well-positioned" companies (i.e., the subset for which it is advantageous) to self-select into the nonsubscribing sector, the decision-making processes and experiences of this group would remain a subject of scholarly interest.

8.5   Results

The survey results, presented in tables 8.2 through 8.6, address five different areas: the basic characteristics of the firm and its employee benefit

66. Comparing the study participants to a credibly "similar" group of subscribers was fraught with empirical difficulties. Since the Texas Department of Insurance does not maintain data on companies that subscribe to workers' compensation in Texas, the only publicly-available source of such data appeared to be the TWC database. The TWC database lists the name, industry, number of employees (in ranges), and approximate annual sales figures (reported in ranges) of companies operating in Texas. (See the "Employer Search" on the Standardized Occupational Components for Research and Analysis of Trends in Employment System for the Texas Workforce Commission, at http://socrates.cdr.state.tx.us/.) However, the database was limited in several critical respects. First, it did not distinguish multistate companies from companies that operate exclusively within Texas. Since all of the survey participants operated in multiple states, one might expect them to be larger, on average, than a comparison group including many single-state firms. (In this sense, they are not truly comparable to the firms contained in the TWC sample.) Secondly, although all information in the TWC database was recorded at the individual facility level, careful scrutiny revealed many facilities of large companies to be missing from the database. (Indeed, some large companies were missing entirely.) Therefore, the company-wide figures calculated from the TWC database—derived by summing across all facilities—underestimated the true values for many workers' compensation subscribers. Finally, the TWC database reported only *ranges* of numerical values, including a top category comprising all firms above a certain cutoff (e.g., "1,000 or more employees"). Since I did not know the distribution of firms above the top size cutoff, I had little choice but to use this cutoff for purposes of the estimates. (In other words, if a facility was recorded as having "1,000 or more employees," I simply coded that facility as employing 1,000 workers.) In short, because of the poor quality and insufficient granularity of the TWC data, it was not possible to make reliable apples-to-apples comparisons between large, multistate nonsubscribers and large, multistate firms that subscribed to workers' compensation. All of the problems observed in the TWC data would be expected to *downwardly* bias the estimates of workforce, sales, and number of locations, and could—at least in theory—have fully explained the observed disparities.

program, the process of becoming a nonsubscriber, the provisions of the nonsubscription plan, the firm's overall experience with nonsubscription, and legal issues and concerns. In addition to aggregate figures, I present separate results for each of the three major industry groupings (manufacturing, retail, and services), and for each of the two time periods in which firms first opted out of workers' compensation (1990 to 1994 and 1997 to 2009). Although each major industry (and subindustry) grouping contains at least two firms that participated in the survey, I do not report how the participants are distributed within the subgroups that comprised the services sector in order to preserve the anonymity of all respondents and the confidentiality of their survey responses.

As table 8.2 reveals, the sample exhibits significant heterogeneity across industries and cohorts. For example, the mean numbers of employees and claims were more than twice as large in the retail sector as in the other two industries. Manufacturing firms also tended to be less geographically dispersed and higher in union density than other firms. Although union density and geographic dispersion varied only modestly by date of nonsubscription, mean employment (and claims) levels were about twice as large among the early (1990 to 1994) cohort, suggesting that some of the very largest companies were the first to opt out.

Risk management characteristics were fairly similar across groups: at least half of respondents in all sectors and across both cohorts employed PartnerSource (a Dallas-based consulting firm and insurance agency that caters to Texas nonsubscribers); used a third-party administrator (TPA) to process claims; and self-insured and/or purchased high-deductible insurance plans in other (i.e., workers' compensation) jurisdictions. Since these forms of outsourcing and self-insurance are common among large companies, their predominance among the study participants is not surprising. Interestingly, however, both trends were markedly less common among manufacturing firms and among the earlier cohort.

Information on employee benefits also revealed interesting disparities. One half of manufacturing firms offered in-house first-aid clinics, as compared to only about a third of retail and services companies. Although almost three-quarters of all companies offered employee wellness programs, their prevalence was once again the highest (83 percent) among manufacturing firms. There was also considerable cross-industry variation in the provision of group health insurance, disability coverage, and life insurance. Whereas most manufacturing firms (86 percent) provided such benefits to their entire workforce, a significantly smaller majority (68 to 74 percent) of services firms, and only a minority (29 to 43 percent) of retail firms did so. Members of the later cohort were more likely to offer all types of benefits.

Table 8.3 sheds light on the *process* of nonsubscription by examining companies' reported motivations for nonsubscribing, the timing of their decisions, and the form(s) of outside assistance, if any, that they received.

Table 8.2   Sample description

	Across all firms	By industry			By date of nonsubscription[a]		Response rate
		Manuf.	Retail	Services	1990–1994	1997–2009	
% Firms identified[b]	61	13%	51%	36%	[unknown]	[unknown]	54/61
% Firms surveyed[c]	54	—	—	—	19%	81%	
Basic firm characteristics							
Average number of employees							
Nationwide	65,585	28,686	92,929	38,884	110,800	55,309	54/54
In Texas	6,742	4,634	9,359	3,662	12,565	5,419	54/54
Average number of claims per year	3,866	1,640	5,210	2,545	5,989	3,495	47/54
% Covering at least 40 states	52%	14%	57%	58%	50%	52%	54/54
% with any union facilities	39%	83%	25%	47%	44%	38%	51/54
% With union facilities in Texas	16%	50%	7%	18%	11%	17%	51/54
Risk management profile							
Uses third-party administrator for nonsubscription claims	81%	50%	79%	94%	67%	84%	51/54
Uses PartnerSource[d]	78%	50%	85%	78%	50%	85%	51/54
Workers' comp. plan characteristics outside Texas (in at least one state)							
High-deductible plan	90%	100%	90%	88%	100%	89%	42/54
Self-insured	74%	67%	79%	68%	89%	70%	53/54
Conventional workers' compensation plan	4%	0%	0%	11%	0%	5%	49/54
Employee benefits profile							
Offers wellness program	74%	83%	74%	71%	67%	76%	50/54
Uses in-house first-aid clinics	35%	50%	29%	35%	33%	35%	52/54

							Response Rate
Offers group health insurance							54/54
Yes—to all employees	59%	86%	43%	74%	50%	61%	
Yes—to full-time/salaried employees	35%	0%	54%	21%	30%	36%	
No	2%	0%	4%	0%	10%	0%	
Don't know	4%	14%	0%	5%	10%	2%	
Offers short-term/long-term disability coverage							54/54
Yes—to all employees	56%	86%	39%	68%	50%	57%	
Yes—to full-time/salaried employees	33%	0%	57%	11%	30%	34%	
No	7%	0%	4%	16%	10%	7%	
Don't know	4%	14%	0%	5%	10%	2%	
Offers life insurance							54/54
Yes—to all employees	52%	86%	29%	74%	40%	55%	
Yes—to full-time/salaried employees	26%	0%	43%	11%	20%	27%	
No	11%	0%	14%	11%	10%	11%	
Don't know	11%	14%	14%	5%	30%	7%	

Notes: This table presents results from a survey of fifty-four large, multistate firms that opted out of workers' compensation in Texas. Unless otherwise specified, percentages represent the fraction of all firms within the applicable column that answered the question and met the specified criterion. (In other words, firms that declined to respond and/or did not know the answer are excluded.) The "Response Rate" column indicates the number of firms that responded to each question.

[a]Survey respondents opted out of workers' compensation during the following years: 1990 (1 firm); 1991 (3 firms); 1992 (3 firms); 1993 (1 firm); 1994 (2 firms); 1997 (1 firm); 1998 (1 firm); 1999 (3 firms); 2001 (2 firms); 2002 (3 firms); 2003 (5 firms); 2004 (6 firms); 2005 (8 firms); 2006 (5 firms); 2007 (5 firms); 2008 (4 firms); and various years between 2001 and 2009 (1 firm). Fifteen firms opted out during the three-year period (20C2–2004) when average cost per claim decreased significantly, and another fifteen firms opted out during the seven-year period (2000–2006) that includes the two years just prior to, and just subsequent to, this decline.

[b]Percentages are calculated as a proportion of all firms identified. The Date of Nonsubscription is not reported for Identified Firms because this information is not known for firms that declined to participate in the survey.

[c]Percentages are calculated as a proportion of all firms surveyed. Fields marked " —" have been left blank to preserve the anonymity of survey participants.

[d]PartnerSource is a consulting firm and insurance agency that designs programs and provides ongoing support for nonsubscribers in Texas.

Table 8.3   Process of nonsubscription

	Across all firms (%)	By industry			By date of nonsubscription		Response rate
		Manuf. (%)	Retail (%)	Services (%)	1990–1994 (%)	1997–2009 (%)	
Reasons for nonsubscription (all that apply)							53/54
Cost savings	89	86	89	89	100	86	
Better care for employees	47	43	52	42	56	45	
Control medical providers	25	14	22	20	44	20	
Control program benefits	25	29	30	16	33	23	
Faster return to work	9	0	4	21	0	11	
Reduce litigation	6	0	7	5	33	0	
Faster closing of claims	2	0	4	0	0	2	
Types of assistance received (all that apply)							[variable]
Consulted with PartnerSource	65	25	67	73	0	72	43/54
Consulted informally with other nonsubscriber(s)	62	50	78	40	50	63	42/54
Consulted with third-party administrator(s)	33	0	39	33	0	37	42/54
Consulted with outside attorney(s)	14	0	8	27	40	11	43/54
Consulted with other(s)[a]	17	25	22	7	25	16	42/54
Timing of nonsubscription (all that apply)							42/54
As soon as preparations complete	36	60	35	29	25	37	
Convenient date/no particular reason	21	20	17	29	50	18	
Renewal date with workers' compensation insurance or third-party administrator	19	0	17	29	0	21	
At start of fiscal year	12	0	17	7	0	13	
At start of firm-specific business cycle	12	0	17	7	25	11	
As soon as firm learned about it	5	0	4	5	0	5	
Following firm acquisition	5	40	0	0	0	5	
Changed other policies or practices at the time of nonsubscription	32	57	27	29	22	34	50/54

Notes: This table presents results from a survey of fifty-four large, multistate firms that opted out of workers' compensation in Texas. Unless otherwise specified, percentages represent the fraction of all firms within the applicable column that answered the question and met the specified criterion. (In other words, percentages represent the fraction of all firms within the applicable column that answered the question and met the specified criterion. (In other words, firms that declined to respond and/or did not know the answer are excluded.) The "Response Rate" column indicates the number of firms that responded to each question.

[a] Other entities with whom respondents reportedly consulted included independent consultants (3 respondents), the Texas Association of Responsible Nonsubscribers (TXANS) (2 respondents), the state of Texas (1 respondent), a risk management services firm (1 respondent), and a professor from a Texas university (1 respondent).

By far the single most common reason for becoming a nonsubscriber, cited by 89 percent of the entire sample (and at least 85 percent of each industry and cohort), was the desire to achieve cost savings. About half of respondents (47 percent of the entire group and 42 to 56 percent of each industry and cohort) also mentioned the desire to take better care of injured workers, and about a quarter (with some variation by industry and cohort) cited the desire for greater control over medical providers and program benefits. Although about a fifth of services companies described expediting employees' return to work as an important goal, and a third of the earlier cohort saw nonsubscription as a means to reduce litigation, few of the other respondents expressed these views.

The types of outside assistance received during the nonsubscription process varied significantly by both industry and cohort. Overall, manufacturing firms received relatively little outside assistance. One-half of respondents in this sector consulted with other companies; a quarter consulted with PartnerSource and/or "other" entities; and none consulted with TPAs or outside attorneys.[67] On the other hand, the majority of retail firms consulted with PartnerSource (67 percent) and other nonsubscribers (78 percent), and significant minorities (39 percent and 22 percent, respectively) consulted with TPAs and/or "other" entities. Services firms displayed an intermediate pattern: while 74 percent consulted with PartnerSource, significant minorities (40 percent, 33 percent, and 27 percent, respectively) consulted with other nonsubscribers, TPAs, and/or outside attorneys. These patterns also varied markedly by cohort. Whereas a majority of late-cohort members consulted with PartnerSource and/or other nonsubscribers, early-cohort members sought less assistance overall, and usually confined their consultations to other nonsubscribers (50 percent) and/or outside attorneys (40 percent).[68]

The timing of nonsubscription shows a fair degree of uniformity across industries and cohorts. Across all groups, a majority of respondents suggested that the start date was relatively arbitrary—for example, the program began "as soon as preparations were complete," "as soon as they learned about it," at a "convenient" date, or on a date chosen for "no particular reason." Only a third of the respondents changed other policies or practices at the time that they adopted their nonsubscription plans. However, several interesting cross-group disparities did come to light. For example, manufacturing firms—as well as retail firms and members of the later cohort—were more likely to harmonize the start date of nonsubscription with a significant corporate milestone (such as the renewal date of an insurance policy or TPA

67. The "other" entities with whom the survey respondents reportedly consulted included independent consultants, the Texas Association of Responsible Nonsubscribers (TXANS), the state of Texas, a risk management services firm, and a professor from a Texas university.

68. The absence of any early-cohort firms that consulted with PartnerSource during the initial nonsubscription process is at least partly explained by the fact that the firm was not founded until 1994.

contract), or with the start of the fiscal year or business cycle. Manufacturing was also the only industry in which a majority of firms (57 percent) changed other policies coincident with nonsubscription, and in which a substantial proportion (40 percent) adopted nonsubscription plans in the wake of a corporate acquisition.

Table 8.4, summarizing the attributes of the respondents' nonsubscription plans, reveals that the benefits typically offered were in some respects more generous, and in other respects less generous, than the workers' compensation regime. On one hand, across all industries and cohorts, the majority of nonsubscribers imposed no maximum dollar amount on weekly wage-replacement benefits, as opposed to the statutory maximum of $712 under workers' compensation. (Although wage-replacement rates were also nominally higher in most nonsubscription plans, because such benefits are taxable income—unlike under workers' compensation—rates of wage replacement were similar in after-tax dollars.) Also in marked contrast to workers' compensation, most nonsubscribers offered first-day wage-replacement coverage. Even among those nonsubscribers that did impose waiting periods, they were significantly shorter in duration (three to five days) than under workers' compensation (seven days). Finally, although most nonsubscription plans limited the duration of wage-replacement benefits for temporary total disability, the average time limit (except for manufacturing) exceeded the 104-week limit applicable under workers' compensation.

On the other hand, several common features of nonsubscription plans appeared less advantageous to employees than workers' compensation. Regardless of industry or cohort, most firms imposed an end-of-shift or twenty-four-hour reporting deadline, unlike the thirty-day deadline for reporting workers' compensation claims.[69] Most companies also declined to provide permanent partial and/or permanent total disability benefits (although manufacturing and early-cohort firms were slightly more likely to do so than other respondents)[70]; and the majority limited the receipt of medical benefits to about two years (although the average time limit varied across industries and a significant minority of manufacturing and early-cohort firms imposed no time limits at all). Although most nonsubscription plans

69. One prominent stakeholder (who requested anonymity) indicated that some nonsubscribers make exceptions, on a case-by-case basis, to their twenty-four-hour (or end-of-shift) reporting policies (Telephone interview, October 13, 2009). However, since survey participants were not specifically asked whether (and if so, how often) they granted such exceptions, it was not possible to verify this claim.

70. One prominent stakeholder (who requested anonymity) claimed that nonsubscribers occasionally provide injured workers with lump-sum settlements—including payments made outside the plan—that are, in effect, intended to compensate them for permanent disabilities, notwithstanding the fact that such injuries are technically outside the plan's scope of coverage (telephone interview, October 13, 2009). If this is correct, then the apparent absence of permanent-disability coverage in nonsubscription plans could be misleading, at least for some firms. However, since this question was not posed to the survey participants, this hypothesis could not be verified.

Table 8.4 Nonsubscription plan characteristics

	Across all firms	By industry			By date of nonsubscription		Response rate	Texas WC statute
		Manuf.	Retail	Services	1990–1994	1997–2009		
Reporting deadline for injuries								
24 hours/next day	48%	14%	57%	47%	70%	43%	54/54	30 days
End of shift	39%	57%	32%	42%	20%	43%		
2–3 days	4%	0%	4%	5%	0%	5%		
1 year	2%	0%	4%	0%	0%	2%		
Don't know	7%	29%	4%	5%	10%	7%		
Time limit on medical care								
% with limit	90%	60%	95%	93%	78%	94%	40/54	No limit
Limit in weeks (if applicable)	107	80	107	113	111	106	35/54	
Wage-replacement benefits								
% with waiting period	21%	17%	21%	21%	33%	18%	53/54	7 days
Avg. waiting period in days (if applicable)	4	3	5	3	4	4	11/54	
Wage-replacement rate	88%	84%	89%	87%	38%	88%	52/54	70–75%[b]
% with maximum weekly dollar amount	18%	40%	19%	11%	33%	15%	49/54	
Maximum weekly $ amount (if applicable)[a]	$778	$700	$860	$650	$933	$700	9/54	$773[c]
% with time limit on wage benefits	94%	100%	100%	84%	39%	95%	51/54	
Time limit in weeks (if applicable)	115	96	120	115	143	110	47/54	104 (temp.) 401 (perm.)
Covers permanent partial/total disabilities	4%	17%	0%	6%	11%	3%	48/54	Yes
Offers capped dismemberment benefit	92%	100%	92%	89%	78%	95%	51/54	70% of wage[d]
Mean $ cap in thousands (if cap is known)	$231	$100	$200	$302	$350	$214	39/54	
Offers capped death benefit	92%	100%	92%	89%	78%	95%	51/54	75% of wage
Mean $ cap in thousands (if cap is known)	$231	$100	$200	$302	$350	$214	39/54	
Directs medical care	98%	100%	100%	94%	100%	98%	52/54	No[e]
Method(s) of claim dispute resolution (all that apply)								Benefits review conference, arbitration[f]
Mandatory arbitration	85%	50%	89%	89%	50%	91%	52/54	
Internal committee	70%	50%	68%	79%	71%	70%	50/54	
Mediation	10%	17%	0%	21%	0%	11%	52/54	

(continued)

Table 8.4 (continued)

	Across all firms	By industry			By date of nonsubscription		Response rate	Texas WC statute
		Manuf.	Retail	Services	1990–1994	1997–2009		
Limit on total benefits (in thousands, where applicable)								
% with no limit	13%	0%	11%	21%	44%	7%	52/54	No limit
% with per-person limit only	60%	100%	59%	47%	44%	63%	52/54	
Average per-person limit (for this group)	$283	$367	$231	$303	$375	$268	28/54	
% with per-person and per-event limits	27%	0%	30%	32%	11%	30%	52/54	
Average per-person limit (for this group)	$393	n.a.	$256	$575	$250	$404	14/54	
Average per-event limit (for this group)	$2,007	n.a.	$625	$404	$500	$2,123	14/54	
Excess liability deductible under nonsubscription plan in thousands	$2,381	$625	$3,288	$1,612	$3,700	$2,084	49/54	
Firm response when benefit time limit is reached (all that apply)								
Would settle	59%	40%	60%	63%	67%	57%	46/54	
Never happened	40%	40%	35%	50%	11%	47%		
Alternate policy picks-up	30%	80%	24%	25%	44%	27%		
Benefits end	30%	20%	20%	50%	11%	35%	[47/54]	

Notes: This table presents results from a survey of fifty-four large, multistate firms that opted out of workers' compensation in Texas. Unless otherwise specified, percentages represent the fraction of all firms within the column that answered the question and met the specified criterion. (In other words, firms that declined to respond and/or did not know the answer are excluded.) The "Response Rate" column indicates the number of firms that responded to each question. Response rates vary due to some respondents' unfamiliarity with detailed attributes of their nonsubscription plans. Characteristics of Texas' workers' compensation statute are reported in the right column. Excess Liability Deductible under Nonsubscription Plan refers to the amount at which excess liability coverage begins to cover a claim. n.a. = not applicable.

[a] May be restricted by time limits and/or maximum medical improvement (MMI).

[b] Employees that earn less than $8.50/hour receive wage replacement benefits at a rate of 75 percent of his/her lost wages for the first twenty-six weeks of disability and 70 percent of lost wages thereafter. All other employees receive wage replacement at 70 percent of his/her lost wages (Texas Labor Code § 408.103).

[c] Although in theory the wage replacement rate is 70 to 75 percent, the proportion may be much lower for higher-income workers, because the wage level is capped at the State Average Weekly Wage (SAWW) (Texas Labor Code § 408.061). In 2006, the method for calculating the SAWW was revised, resulting in a significant increase in the maximum weekly benefit, so that fewer workers have been limited by the statutory cap. See Eccleston et al. (2009, 19).

[d] Subject to a maximum of 70 percent of the state average weekly wage, for up to 401 weeks.

[e] The employee can choose his/her own medical provider unless the employer belongs to a workers' compensation medical network.

[f] The employee can opt for a contested case hearing in lieu of arbitration. If desired, appeals and requests for judicial review can be filed with the Appeals Panel and the State County Court, respectively (Texas Labor Code § 410).

mimicked the statutory regime in offering both death and dismemberment benefits, such benefits were capped at anywhere from $100,000 (the average for manufacturing firms) to $302,000 (the average for services firms). In contrast to the choice of provider permitted (with rare exceptions[71]) under Texas workers' compensation, most firms also directed injured employees' medical care.

Interestingly, although most respondents described control over providers as a key benefit of nonsubscription, they did not all offer the same rationale for this view. Some firms stressed the benefits that (allegedly) accrued to employees in the form of higher-quality care. For example, one retail company emphasized that the capacity to direct an employee to a nonworkers' compensation specialist meant that the worker could be treated "as a person, not a claim." On the other hand, other respondents viewed limitations on provider choice as a way to reduce fraudulent claims and/or moral hazard among health care providers. For example, one restaurant claimed that under nonsubscription employees learned that "they couldn't game the system" as they allegedly did under workers' compensation, and one services firm observed that under nonsubscription, the company could avoid the "knife-happy physicians" to which workers' compensation attorneys reportedly steered employees.

Presumably in an effort to limit their exposure to tort liability, the overwhelming majority of all firms (85 percent) used mandatory arbitration provisions, although half of manufacturing firms and of early-cohort firms did not. Finally, most respondents imposed per-person and/or per-event caps on the total amount of benefits that any employee could receive (although 21 percent of services firms and 44 percent of early-cohort firms did not).

Table 8.4 reveals another interesting cross-industry disparity. Average excess liability deductibles (the amount at which excess liability coverage begins to cover a claim) were much lower in manufacturing than in other industries. Moreover, manufacturing firms were much more likely than others to report that when a benefit time limit was reached for a given claim, an alternate policy (such as group health care and long-term disability coverage) would kick in. It could be that manufacturing workers are at higher risk of experiencing catastrophic injuries, in which case one would expect firms in this sector both to purchase more excess liability coverage and to offer their workers greater insurance against long-term disability. Available data seems to lend credence to this hypothesis.[72] In contrast, the majority of

71. Employers that belong to a Workers' Compensation medical network can direct medical care under the auspices of that network (Texas Insurance Code § 1305).

72. Based on national data from the Bureau of Labor Statistics, manufacturing companies do in fact exhibit higher rates of serious injuries than companies in the retail and services sectors. For injuries requiring days away from work—the most severe category of nonfatal occupational injuries and illnesses—manufacturing companies in 2007 reported an injury and illness rate of 1.3 per 100 full-time workers, as compared to 1.2 for retail companies and 1.1 for companies

retail and services firms reported that they would try to reach a settlement if a plan-imposed time limit on benefits was reached.

Table 8.5 summarizes respondents' reported experiences with nonsubscription. For this section of the survey, each risk manager was initially asked whether (s)he deemed the program to be a success. Regardless of industry or cohort, virtually all respondents (94 percent) said yes. Of the remaining three companies—all of which belonged to the late cohort—one transportation company said that its experience with nonsubscription had been "hit or miss," depending on the quality of the TPA; one retail company said it was "too soon to tell" because it had opted out so recently; and the third, a services company, said that it could not make informed comparisons because the TPA handled most aspects of its program. With minor variations across industries, most respondents claimed to be tracking the success of their nonsubscription programs using data, although only about three-quarters reportedly calculated and compared costs per claim.

Respondents' opinions regarding the benefits, drawbacks, and surprises of nonsubscription displayed a remarkable degree of uniformity across industries and cohorts. Across all groups, benefits and positive surprises were cited much more frequently than drawbacks and negative surprises. Virtually all respondents (98 percent) cited cost savings as a benefit of nonsubscription, and most (86 percent) cited the magnitude of cost savings as a positive surprise. The average reported cost savings for all groups exceeded 50 percent. This was the case not only for the sample as a whole, but also for the subgroup of respondents that opted out before 2000 or after 2006, well before (or after) the three-year period (2002 to 2004) in which per-claim costs fell substantially within the Texas workers' compensation system.[73] A substantial majority of respondents also cited greater control over medical providers and/or benefits, and higher-quality medical care for injured employees, as advantages. The most commonly-cited drawback—tort liability—was mentioned by half of all respondents (albeit somewhat less frequently by retail firms and early-cohort members).

Notwithstanding such commonalities, the data did reveal interesting cross-group disparities in the perceived benefits, drawbacks, and surprises of nonsubscription. For example, a disproportionate fraction of retail companies cited greater control over program benefits (61 percent) and less litigation (36 percent) as advantages, whereas manufacturing firms were more likely to emphasize faster return to work (86 percent), access to better doctors (71 percent), better safety outcomes (57 percent), and faster medical care (43 percent). (The services sector fell in between in these two extremes.)

---

in the services industry (as industries are defined in this chapter). See "Table 1. Incidence rates of nonfatal occupational injuries and illnesses by selected industries and case types, 2007," available at http://www.bls.gov/news.release/osh.t01.htm.

73. See discussion of Eccleston et al. (2009, 7–8).

Table 8.5   Experience with nonsubscription (relative to workers' compensation)

	Across all firms (%)	By industry Manuf. (%)	Retail (%)	Services (%)	By date of nonsubscription 1990–1994 (%)	1997–2009 (%)	Response rate
Considers nonsubscription to be successful							54/54
Yes	94	100	96	89	100	93	
Uncertain (too soon to tell and/or don't track outcomes)	4	0	4	5	0	5	
Hit-or-miss, depending on third-party administrator	2	0	0	5	0	2	
Tracks success of nonsubscription with data	91	86	100	79	90	91	54/54
Tracks cost per claim (among firms that track data)	76	83	72	79	75	76	45/54
Benefits							54/54
Cost savings	98	100	96	100	100	98	
Estimated % cost savings (only if exists and % was given)	58	62	60	54	63	58	[38/54]
Estimated % Savings if opted out before 2000 or after 2006[a]	53	57	56	43	63	45	[15/24]
More control over medical providers/benefits	74	71	82	63	80	73	
Employees receive better care	64	86	64	56	70	63	
More control over program benefits	50	14	61	47	50	50	
Employees return to work faster	46	86	32	53	60	43	
Access to better doctors	46	71	32	58	30	50	
Better safety outcomes	35	57	32	32	30	36	
Fewer injury claims filed	28	43	29	21	20	30	
Less litigation	22	14	36	5	20	23	
Faster medical care	19	43	7	26	20	18	
Faster claim closing	17	14	21	11	10	18	
Less ambiguity in processing of claims	15	0	18	16	10	16	
Faster injury reporting	13	33	7	16	10	14	
Access better doctors through higher doctor pay	9	14	11	5	10	9	
Can keep closer tabs on each claim	2	0	0	5	0	2	
Reported any positive surprises	39	29	46	32	40	39	53/54
Among firms citing positive surprises:							
Magnitude of cost savings	86	100	77	100	100	82	
Infrequent internal appeals/lawsuits	24	0	38	0	25	24	
Lack of employee backlash	14	50	15	0	0	18	
Ease of administration	5	0	8	0	0	6	
Ability to recover from third parties	5	0	8	0	25	0	

(continued)

Table 8.5 (continued)

Drawbacks	Across all firms (%)	By industry			By date of nonsubscription		Response rate
		Manuf. (%)	Retail (%)	Services (%)	1990–1994 (%)	1997–2009 (%)	
Tort liability	50	57	43	58	30	55	54/54
Burden of educating workforce	30	0	36	32	40	27	
General administrative time and hassle	19	14	25	11	20	18	
Burden of educating management	15	14	18	11	10	16	
Resistance from management	4	14	0	5	0	5	
Burden of finding suitable medical providers	4	14	4	0	0	5	
Employees lose benefits for late reporting	2	0	4	0	10	0	
Arbitration can be unfair to employees	2	14	0	0	0	2	
Employee doubts about quality of care	2	0	4	0	0	2	
Burden of directly supervising medical care	2	0	4	0	0	2	
More claims are shifted to group health	2	0	4	0	10	0	
Reported any negative surprises	11	0	11	16	0	14	53/54
Among firms citing negative surprises:							
Large arbitration awards	50	n.a.	33	67	n.a.	50	
High frequency of frivolous lawsuits	33	n.a.	33	33	n.a.	33	
Too few third-party administrators from which to choose	17	n.a.	33	0	n.a.	17	
High frequency of internal appeals/lawsuits	17	n.a.	0	33	n.a.	17	
Nonsubscription affected safety practices outside Texas	21	29	25	12	20	21	52/54
Expressed desire to opt out in other states	26	29	29	21	10	30	54/54
Knows of a former large, multistate nonsubscriber that returned to the workers' compensation system	0	0	0	0	0	0	54/54

Notes: This table presents results from a survey of fifty-four large, multistate firms that opted out of workers' compensation in Texas. Unless otherwise specified, percentages represent the fraction of all firms within the applicable column that answered the question and met the specified criterion. (In other words, firms that declined to respond and/or did not know the answer are excluded.) The "Response Rate" column indicates the number of firms that responded to each question. n.a. = not applicable.

[a]Because average costs per claim under Texas workers' compensation fell markedly from 2002 to 2004, this line reports estimated cost savings *only* among firms that answered this question and did *not* opt out between 2002 and 2006. When only firms that opted out between 2002 and 2004 were excluded, the percentages were even closer to those for the entire sample. (The "across all firms" percentages were identical, and those for individual industries and cohorts differed by no more than 6 percentage points.)

Manufacturing was also the only sector in which a substantial fraction (50 percent) of firms cited the lack of employee backlash as a positive surprise (which could reflect the industry's much higher rates of unionization). Manufacturing firms also held somewhat idiosyncratic views of the *negative* aspects of nonsubscription. For example, unlike about a third of retail and services companies, no manufacturing firm described educating its workforce as a burden of nonsubscription, a disparity that once again could be explained by the sector's high rates of unionization. Moreover, although at least a third of retail and services firms mentioned bad arbitrationr awards and/or the frequency of frivolous lawsuits as negative surprises, no manufacturing firms shared this view. In fact, rather surprisingly, manufacturing firms (and members of the early cohort) reported no negative surprises at all.

Table 8.5 contains three other noteworthy findings. First of all, a sizable minority of respondents (ranging from 12 percent in services to 29 percent in manufacturing) reported that the company's experiences with nonsubscription caused them to change their safety practices in other states. (For example, the online injury reporting system developed by one services company under nonsubscription was rolled out nationwide to streamline reporting procedures. Similarly, another services company designed new documentation for claims reporting that was later adopted outside of Texas.) Secondly, at some point during the interview, about a quarter of respondents volunteered their opinion (unprompted) that other states should allow the non-subscription option. Finally, although every risk manager was asked whether (s)he knew of any large, multistate firms that had been nonsubscribers but subsequently rejoined the workers' compensation system, all said no.

Finally, table 8.6 examines various legal dimensions of nonsubscription. The majority of respondents in all groups reported little or no trouble with litigation, and complaints about related issues (such as bad arbitration awards, frivolous lawsuits, and/or the frequency of internal appeals or lawsuits) were relatively rare. However, manufacturing firms and early-cohort firms were considerably more likely than others to report at least "some" litigation troubles. Similarly, whereas only about a quarter of retail, services, and late-cohort firms paid out any claims above $500,000, most manufacturing firms (83 percent) and two-thirds of early-cohort firms reported having done so. Meanwhile, retail companies' experiences with litigation seemed to be unusually favorable: not only did few report "trouble" with litigation and/or paying out expensive claims, but a sizable minority also described less litigation and the infrequency of internal appeals and lawsuits as benefits and/or positive surprises.[74]

Another striking trend was the pervasive use of mandatory arbitration

74. Several firms mentioned that they carried high-deductible insurance policies to help cover the cost of expensive tort judgments or settlements. However, since respondents were not routinely asked whether they carried such policies, it is uncertain how many of the costly claims to which respondents alluded (i.e., those exceeding $500,000) were paid for out-of-pocket.

Table 8.6   Legal issues under nonsubscription

	Across all firms (%)	By industry			By date of nonsubscription		Response rate
		Manuf. (%)	Retail (%)	Services (%)	1990–1994 (%)	1997–2009 (%)	
Overview of legal issues							
Uses mandatory arbitration in the event of a claim dispute[a]	85	50	89	89	50	91	52/54
Mentioned reducing litigation as a reason for nonsubscription[a]	6	0	7	5	33	0	53/54
Any trouble with litigation?							53/54
No	45	29	43	56	30	49	
Hardly any (no)	36	29	43	28	30	37	
Some (yes)	15	43	14	6	40	9	
Yes	4	0	0	11	0	5	
Has paid nonsubscription claims over $500k	31	83	22	28	67	24	51/54
Has paid more than one claim over $500k	14	50	4	17	22	12	50/54
Has settled outside the plan	27	40	22	31	33	25	41/54
Drawbacks and negative surprises							
Mentioned tort liability as a drawback[a]	50	57	43	58	30	55	54/54
Mentioned large arbitration awards as a negative surprise[a]	6	0	4	11	0	7	53/54
Mentioned frequency of frivolous lawsuits as a negative surprise[a]	4	0	4	5	0	5	53/54
Mentioned high frequency of internal appeals/lawsuits as a negative surprise[a]	2	0	0	5	0	2	53/54
Advantages and positive surprises							
Mentioned less litigation as a benefit[a]	22	14	36	5	20	23	54/54
Mentioned infrequency of internal appeals/lawsuits as a positive surprise[a]	9	0	19	0	11	9	53/54

Overview of legal issues, by use of mandatory arbitration

	Across all firms	Among firms that use mandatory arbitration	Among firms that do not use mandatory arbitration	Response rate
Mentioned reducing litigation as a reason for nonsubscription[a]	6	0	25	51/54
Mentioned tort liability as a drawback of nonsubscription[a]	50	52	38	54/54
Any trouble with litigation?				52/54
No	45	52	0	
Hardly any (no)	36	34	57	
Some (yes)	15	9	43	
Yes	4	5	0	
Has paid nonsubscription claims over $500k	31	24	63	52/54
Has paid *more than one* claim over $500k	14	10	38	52/54
Has settled outside the plan	27	31	13	52/54

Notes: This table presents results from a survey of fifty-four large, multistate firms that opted out of workers' compensation in Texas. Unless otherwise specified, percentages represent the fraction of all firms within the applicable column that answered the question and met the specified criterion. (In other words, firms that declined to respond and/or did not know the answer are excluded.) The "Response Rate" column indicates the number of firms that responded to each question.

[a]Similar information is presented in earlier tables. In this table, however, figures are uniformly calculated as a percentage of all firms that answered the question. (In some previous tables, figures are calculated as a percentage of the subgroup of firms that answered "yes" to a previous question.)

among nonsubscribers. The overwhelming majority (85 percent) of respondents used such provisions, although they were much more common among retail, services, and late-cohort firms. The bottom panel, which breaks down respondents by the use of mandatory arbitration, displays several salient patterns. Although firms that use mandatory arbitration provisions did not mention reducing litigation as a reason for opting out of workers' compensation, they were far more likely to describe tort liability as a drawback of nonsubscription—indeed, this concern may be what led them to adopt such provisions in the first place. This theory is seemingly borne out by the fact that "trouble with litigation" and claims above $500,000 were much less common among firms that used mandatory arbitration.

Finally, it is interesting to note that about a quarter of all firms reported having settled claims outside of the nonsubscription plan. The prevalence of this practice was particularly high among manufacturing firms (40 percent) and among early-cohort members (33 percent). Moreover, as is revealed in the bottom panel, settlements outside of the plan were considerably more common among firms that used mandatory arbitration (31 percent) than among firms that did not (13 percent). It is possible that such settlements had been offered to compensate workers for permanent disabilities that were technically outside the scope of the plan—a practice that one stakeholder claimed was not uncommon among large nonsubscribers.[75] However, since this follow-up question was not posed to the survey participants, this hypothesis could not be confirmed.

8.6   Conclusions and Suggestions for Future Research

Although participation in the workers' compensation system is compulsory for virtually all private-sector employers, Texas' unique law—the only truly elective statute in the United States[76]—presents researchers with a valuable opportunity to explore the "path not taken." Unlike in every other U.S. state, about one-third of Texas firms have elected to become "nonsubscribers" and opted out of the workers' compensation system. Remarkably, the prevalence of nonsubscription has been on the rise among very large firms, whose "deep pockets" might make them particularly averse to lawsuits by employees injured on the job. Why are large employers choosing to forgo the benefits of tort immunity? What are the real-world consequences for those firms that choose to become nonsubscribers? Such questions have received almost no prior scholarly attention.

This chapter is the first to comprehensively examine Texas nonsubscription from the perspective of companies that have opted out of workers'

75. See note 70.
76. For a list of the minor exceptions to this rule, see notes 3 and 7.

compensation. I focus on an important group of Texas firms—large companies that span many U.S. states. This group is of particular interest not only because large companies usually employ full-time, professional risk managers who are well-informed about workers' compensation and its alternatives, but also because large firms are the *only* group for which nonsubscription has been rising (and markedly so) in recent years. Instead of letting injured workers without viable tort claims bear the costs of their own occupational injuries, these employers typically offer "home-grown" benefits plans to their Texas employees that approximate the benefits available through workers' compensation. After identifying those firms that met the study criteria, I administered a confidential phone survey to 89 percent of this group to learn more about their attributes, motivations, behavior, and experiences.

The survey responses revealed many important trends. Large, multistate firms that nonsubscribed in recent years were likely to rely on consultants and/or third-party administrators to help guide them through the nonsubscription process and to administer their plan in subsequent years. They were also likely to self-insure and/or use high-deductible plans in states that mandated workers' compensation coverage. Although a majority operated employee wellness programs, less than half used in-house first-aid clinics. There were considerable disparities in the provision of other employee benefits such as group health plans, disability coverage, and life insurance; whereas most manufacturing firms and a majority of services firms offered such benefits to all workers, only a minority of retail firms did so.

For nearly all large, multistate firms, the main reason for opting out of workers' compensation was to achieve cost savings, although a sizable minority of respondents were also motivated by the desire to provide better care for employees, control medical providers, and/or control program benefits. Firms did not seem to perceive the timing of the nonsubscription process as a strategically important decision, although some coordinated the start date with the beginning of the fiscal year or the renewal of contracts with insurers or third-party administrators. A sizable minority of firms did change other policies or practices at the same time that they phased in a nonsubscription plan.

Overall, the occupational injury plans that nonsubscribers offered in lieu of workers' compensation were remarkably homogenous. Unlike workers' compensation, most plans did not impose any maximum weekly dollar amount or waiting period on the receipt of wage-replacement benefits. Moreover, the maximum duration of wage-replacement benefits for temporary total disabilities typically exceeded the statutory cap. On the other hand, most nonsubscription plans imposed end-of-shift or twenty-four-hour reporting deadlines, did not cover permanent partial or permanent total disabilities, limited medical benefits to about two years, capped death and dismemberment benefits, and imposed per-person and/or per-event caps on total benefits. The vast majority of respondents also directed employees' medical care.

There were also striking similarities in respondents' reported experiences with nonsubscription. Virtually all (94 percent) of firms judged these programs to be a success. Not only did virtually all (98 percent) of companies report cost savings, but most were pleasantly surprised by the magnitude of these savings, which reportedly exceeded 50 percent (on average) across all industries. Other commonly-cited benefits of nonsubscription were greater control over medical providers, greater control over program benefits, improved quality of medical care, faster return to work, and access to better doctors. The only drawback or negative surprise cited by an appreciable number of respondents was tort liability, which half of all firms viewed as a drawback. However, presumably in an effort to curb such liability, a very high fraction (about 85 percent) of nonsubscriber plans channeled disputes to mandatory arbitration. About a fifth of respondents reported that nonsubscription had affected safety practices outside of Texas, and a quarter spontaneously expressed a desire to spread nonsubscription to other states.

Although the majority of all survey respondents reported little or no trouble with litigation, follow-up questions revealed intriguing patterns across groups. Manufacturing firms and companies that opted out in the early 1990s were the most likely to report "some" trouble with litigation. At least two-thirds of respondents in all of these groups, for example, had paid out at least one claim exceeding $500,000. At the other extreme, retail companies rarely reported any trouble with litigation, and less than a quarter had paid out any claims above $500,000. The services sector fell somewhere between these two extremes. Litigation trends also varied by the presence (or absence) of mandatory arbitration. Firms that required mandatory arbitration were much less likely to report "trouble" with litigation, such as having paid out at least one half-million-dollar claim. Finally, about a quarter of respondents in all industries reported having settled claims outside the plan, and this practice was especially common among firms that used mandatory arbitration.

Although the study findings help to illuminate the real-world consequences of nonsubscription for an important and growing segment of Texas employers, many critical questions merit further investigation. First and foremost, the data consisted entirely of company self-reports, and as such were inherently prone to imprecision and subjectivity. Lacking detailed claim records, I could not test in a rigorous manner whether—and if so, to what extent—nonsubscription truly affected the frequency, distribution, cost, or duration of occupational injury claims. Secondly, my data did not allow me to test for the possibility of cost shifting. For example, some occupational injuries that apparently "disappeared" with nonsubscription may have been covered by group health care plans and/or by private disability insurance, unbeknownst to the survey respondents. If nonsubscription caused many workers' compensation claims to "migrate" to nonoccupational benefit programs in this manner, it could have decreased costs far less than the survey results suggested (or not at all). Third, the experiences of small- and medium-sized nonsubscribers may have differed substantially from the experiences of the large multistate firms examined here. Finally, my findings shed little light on the consequences of nonsubscription for affected employees. Probing whether nonsubscription is a Pareto improvement—or simply redistributes economic surplus from employees to employers—is an especially critical and timely subject for future inquiry.

Appendix

Telephone Survey Questions[77]

Process of Nonsubscription

a. When did you nonsubscribe?

b. How and when did you first learn of nonsubscription as an option in Texas?

c. Did you consult with outside parties, such as other companies or your Third Party Administrator (TPA), in choosing to become a nonsubscriber?

d. Why did you nonsubscribe?

e. After you decided to become a nonsubscriber, how did you choose when to switch to nonsubscription?

f. Did you change any other company safety policies or practices at the same time you became a nonsubscriber?

Experience with Nonsubscription (Relative to Workers' Compensation)

a. Do you think nonsubscription has been successful? If so, why and how?

b. What are the benefits and drawbacks of nonsubscription for your company?

c. What are the challenges, logistical or otherwise, with nonsubscription for your company?

d. Have you had much trouble with litigation under nonsubscription?

e. Have you had any large litigated nonsubscription claims, over $500,000?

---

77. This script was followed loosely, and questions inviting more than a straightforward factual answer were posed in a flexible, open-ended, and individualized manner.

f. Do you use data to systematically measure the success of nonsubscription? If so, what types of benchmarks do you use (such as cost per claim or other measures)?

g. Have there been any surprises with nonsubscription, either positive or negative?

h. Has nonsubscription affected company safety practices outside of Texas? If so, how?

Nonsubscription Plan Characteristics

a. What is the deadline for notifying the company of an injury?
b. Is there a time limit on medical benefits?
c. What is the waiting period for receiving wage-replacement benefits?
d. What is the wage-replacement rate?
e. Is there a maximum weekly wage benefit? If so, what is it?
f. Is there a limit to the number of weeks of disability? If so, what is it?
g. Can employees choose their own doctor?
h. Do you provide a benefit for permanent partial disabilities?
i. Do you provide a death benefit? If so, what is it?
j. What is the limit on dismemberment benefits?
k. What is the method for resolving claim disputes?
l. What is the total cap on benefits, if there is one?
m. What happens if there are still ongoing medical costs or lost time when a nonsubscription claim reaches the time limit of the nonsubscription plan (do you settle the claims, could another insurance policy cover some of the ongoing costs)?
n. Have you ever provided benefits outside the plan?
o. Do you have excess liability coverage? If so, when does it kick in?

Basic Company Information

a. *Roughly* how many employees does your company have nationwide? In Texas?
b. How many locations do you have nationwide?
c. In about how many states do you operate?
d. *About* how many workers' compensation claims do you handle per year?
e. Do you self-insure in workers' compensation states where you have the option? If you do not self-insure, do you have a high deductible workers' compensation plan?
f. Do you have in-house clinics that handle first aid claims?
g. Do you have employee wellness programs? If so, when did they start?
h. Do you have any union locations? In Texas?
i. Do you handle nonsubscription claims in-house, or use a third-party administrator (TPA)?

j. Are your employees eligible for:
   i. Group health insurance
   ii. Long-term disability insurance
   iii. Short-term disability insurance
   iv. Life insurance
k. What other benefits does your company offer?
l. Do these benefits vary across states, particularly in and out of Texas?
m. Have you ever worked with PartnerSource?

Other[78]

a. Do you know of any company that was a nonsubscriber, but then returned to the workers' compensation system in Texas?

References

Arnould, R. J., and L. M. Nichols. 1983. Wage-risk premiums and workers' compensation: A refinement of estimates of compensating wage differential. *Journal of Political Economy* 91 (2): 332–40.

Baker, L. C., and A. B. Krueger. 1993. Twenty-four-hour coverage and workers' compensation insurance. *Health Affairs* 12 (supp. 1): 271–81.

Biddle, J. 2001. Do high claim-denial rates discourage claiming? Evidence from workers compensation insurance. *Journal of Risk and Insurance* 68 (4): 631–58.

Boden, L. I., and J. W. Ruser. 2003. Workers' compensation "reforms," choice of medical care provider, and reported workplace injuries. *Review of Economics and Statistics* 85 (4): 923–29.

Bolduc, D., B. Fortin, F. Labrecque, and P. Lanoie. 2002. Workers' compensation, moral hazard and the composition of workplace injuries. *Journal of Human Resources* 37 (3): 623–52.

Bureau of Labor Statistics. 2007. Table 1: Incidence rates of nonfatal occupational injuries and illnesses by selected industries and case types, 2007. U.S. Department of Labor. Available at: http://www.bls.gov/news.release/osh.t01.htm.

Butler, R. J. 1994. Economic determinants of workers' compensation trends. *Journal of Risk and Insurance* 61 (3): 383–401.

———. 1996. Lost injury days: Moral hazard differences between tort and workers' compensation. *Journal of Risk and Insurance* 63 (3): 405–33.

Butler, R. J., and J. D. Worrall. 1983. Workers' compensation: Benefit and injury claims rates in the seventies. *Review of Economics and Statistics* 65 (4): 580–89.

---

78. The survey also included four questions regarding a planned future study of detailed claim-level data provided by a subset of the survey respondents. These questions were the following: "Did you know this study was being conducted?"; "How did you learn about it?"; "Did you consider participating in the data portion of the study?"; and "Why did you decline to participate in the data portion of Prof. Morantz's study of nonsubscription?". Because these four questions did not pertain to the current study, the responses to them are not reported in tables 8.2 through 8.6.

————. 1985. Work injury compensation and the duration of nonwork spells. *The Economic Journal* 95 (379): 714–24.

————. 1991. Claims reporting and risk bearing moral hazard in workers' compensation. *Journal of Risk and Insurance* 58 (2): 191–204.

Card, D., and B. McCall. 1996. Is workers' compensation covering uninsured medical costs? Evidence from the Monday effect. *Industrial and Labor Relations Review* 49 (4): 690–706.

Chelius, J. R. 1976. Liability for industrial accidents: A comparison of negligence and strict liability systems. *Journal of Legal Studies* 5 (2): 293–309.

————. 1982. The influence of workers' compensation on safety incentives. *Industrial and Labor Relations Review* 35 (2): 235–42.

Division of Workers' Compensation. 2009. Maximum and minimum weekly benefits. Texas Department of Insurance. Available at: http://www.tdi.state.tx.us/wc/employee/documents/maxminbens.pdf.

Durbin, D. L., D. Corro, and N. Helvacian. 1996. Workers' compensation medical expenditures: Price vs. quantity. *Journal of Risk and Insurance* 63 (1): 13–33.

Eccleston, S. M., E. Radeva, C. A. Telles, R. Yang, and R. P. Tanabe. 2009. *Monitoring the impact of reforms in Texas: CompScope benchmarks,* 9th ed. Cambridge, MA: Workers Compensation Research Institute.

Ehrenberg, R. 1988. Workers' compensation, wages, and the risk of injury. In *New perspectives in workers' compensation,* ed. J. F. Burton, 71–96. Ithaca: ILR Press.

Fields, J. A., and E. C. Venezian. 1991. Medical cost development in workers' compensation. *Journal of Risk and Insurance* 58 (3): 497–504.

Fishback, P. V. 1987. Liability rules and accident prevention in the workplace: Empirical evidence from the early twentieth century. *Journal of Legal Studies* 16 (2): 305–28.

Fishback, P. V., and S. E. Kantor. 1998a. The adoption of workers' compensation in the United States. *Journal of Law and Economics* 41 (2): 305–41.

————. 1998b. The political economy of workers' compensation benefit levels, 1910–1930. *Explorations in Economic History* 35 (2): 109–39.

Health and Workers' Compensation Networks Division. Texas Department of Insurance. Available at: http://www.tdi.state.tx.us/wc/wcnet/index.html#certified.

Howard, C. 2002. Workers' compensation, federalism, and the heavy hand of history. *Studies in American Political Development* 16 (1): 28–47.

International Association of Industrial Accident Boards and Commissions, and Workers Compensation Research Institute. 2009. *Workers' compensation laws,* 2nd ed. Cambridge, MA: Workers Compensation Research Institute.

Johnson, W. G., M. L. Baldwin, and R. J. Butler. 1998. Back pain and work disability: The need for a new paradigm. *Industrial Relations* 37 (1): 9–34.

Kaestner, R., and A. Carroll. 1997. New estimates of the labor market effects of workers' compensation insurance. *Southern Economic Journal* 63 (3): 635–51.

Kniesner, T. J., and J. D. Leeth. 1989. Separating the reporting effects from the injury rate effects of workers' compensation insurance: A hedonic simulation. *Industrial and Labor Relations Review* 42 (2): 280–93.

Krueger, A. B. 1990a. Incentive effects of workers' compensation insurance. *Journal of Public Economics* 41 (1): 73–99.

————. 1990b. Workers' compensation insurance and the duration of workplace injuries. NBER Working Paper no. 3253. Cambridge, MA: National Bureau of Economic Research.

Krueger, A. B., and J. F. Burton Jr. 1990. The employers' costs of workers' compensation insurance: Magnitudes, determinants, and public policy. *Review of Economics and Statistics* 72 (2): 228–40.

Lakdawalla, D. N., R. T. Reville, and S. A. Seabury. 2007. How does health insurance affect workers compensation filing? *Economic Inquiry* 45 (2): 286–303.

Meng, R., and D. A. Smith. 1999. The impact of workers' compensation on wage premiums for job hazards. *Applied Economics* 31 (9): 1101–8.

Meyer, B. D., W. K. Viscusi, and D. L. Durbin. 1995. Workers' compensation and injury duration: Evidence from a natural experiment. *American Economic Review* 85 (3): 322–40.

Moore, M. J., and W. K. Viscusi. 1989. Promoting safety through workers' compensation: The efficacy and net wage costs of injury insurance. *RAND Journal of Economics* 20 (4): 499–515.

———. 1992. Social insurance in market contexts: Implications of the structure of workers' compensation for job safety and wages. In *Contributions to insurance economics,* ed. G. Dionne, 399–422. Boston: Kluwer Academic Publishers.

National Commission on State Workmen's Compensation Laws. 1972. The report of the National Commission on State Workmen's Compensation Laws. John Burton's Workers' Compensation Resources. Available at: http://www.workerscomp resources.com/National_Commission_Report/national_commission_report .htm.

Neuhauser, F., and S. Raphael. 2004. The effect of an increase in workers' compensation benefits on the duration and frequency of benefit receipt. *Review of Economics and Statistics* 86 (1): 288–302.

Neumark, D., P. S. Barth, and R. A. Victor. 2007. The impact of provider choice on workers' compensation costs and outcomes. *Industrial and Labor Relations Review* 61 (1): 121–42.

Office of Injured Employee Counsel of the State of Texas. Notice of injured employee rights and responsibilities in the Texas workers' compensation system. Texas Department of Insurance. Available at: http://www.tdi.state.tx.us/pubs/factsheets/ ierrenglish.pdf.

Roberts, K., and S. Zonia. 1994. Workers' compensation cost containment and health care provider income maintenance strategies. *Journal of Risk and Insurance* 61 (1): 117–31.

Ruser, J. W. 1985. Workers' compensation insurance, experience-rating, and occupational injuries. *RAND Journal of Economics* 16 (4): 487–503.

———. 1991. Workers' compensation and occupational injuries and illnesses. *Journal of Labor Economics* 9 (4): 325–50.

Schwartz, G. T. 1994. Reality in the economic analysis of tort law: Does tort law really deter? *UCLA Law Review* 42:377–444.

Shields, J., and D.C. Campbell. 2002. A study of nonsubscription to the Texas workers' compensation system: 2001 estimates. Texas Department of Insurance. Available at: http://www.tdi.state.tx.us/reports/wcreg/documents/nonsub.pdf.

Smith, R. S. 1990. Mostly on Monday: Is workers' compensation covering off-the-job injuries? In *Benefits, costs, and cycles in workers' compensation,* ed. P. S. Borba and D. Appel, 115–27. Boston: Kluwer Academic Publishers.

Standardized Occupational Components for Research and Analysis of Trends in Employment System. Texas Workforce Commission. Available at: http://socrates. cdr.state.tx.us/.

Texas Non-Subscribers download file. Texas Department of Insurance. Available at: http://www.tdi.state.tx.us/general/download/nonsubscribe.csv.

Transportation Research Board. 1994. *TRB special report 241: Compensating injured railroad workers under the Federal Employers' Liability Act.* Washington, DC: National Academy Press.

Viscusi, W. K., and M. J. Moore. 1987. Workers' compensation: Wage effects, benefit inadequacies, and the value of health losses. *Review of Economics and Statistics* 69 (2): 249–61.

Waehrer, G. M., and T. R. Miller. 2003. Restricted work, workers' compensation, and days away from work. *Journal of Human Resources* 38 (4): 964–91.

Workers' Compensation Research Group. 1997. Experiences of injured workers employed by nonsubscribing employers. Texas Department of Insurance. Available at: http://www.tdi.state.tx.us/reports/wcreg/inj_ees.html.

———. 2004. Employer participation in the Texas workers' compensation system: 2004 estimates. Texas Department of Insurance. Available at: http://www.tdi.state .tx.us/wc/regulation/roc/documents/wc0904est.pdf.

———. 2006. Employer participation in the Texas workers' compensation system: 2006 estimates. Texas Department of Insurance. Available at: http://www.tdi.state .tx.us/reports/wcreg/documents/Employer_Participati.ppt.

———. 2008. Employer participation in the Texas workers' compensation system: 2008 estimates. Texas Department of Insurance. Available at: http://www.tdi.state .tx.us/reports/wcreg/documents/2008_Employer_Partic.ppt#8.

Worrall, J. D., and D. Appel. 1982. The wage replacement rate and benefit utilization in workers' compensation insurance. *Journal of Risk and Insurance* 49 (3): 361–71.

Worrall, J. D., and R. J. Butler. 1985. Benefits and claim duration. In *Workers' compensation benefits: Adequacy, equity, and efficiency,* ed. J. D. Worrall and R. J. Butler, 57–70. Ithaca: ILR Press.

———. 1988. Experience rating matters. In *Workers' compensation insurance pricing: Current programs and proposed reforms,* ed. P. S. Borba and D. Appel, 81–94. Boston: Kluwer-Nijhoff.

9

M&A Break Fees
U.S. Litigation versus
UK Regulation

John C. Coates IV

The United States and the United Kingdom have well-developed economies and capital markets. They also share a legal tradition, including a liberal approach to economic activity. In some key areas of capital market governance, however, their legal systems formally diverge. One example—salient to merger and acquisition (M&A) academics—is the treatment of hostile bids (e.g., Armour and Skeel 2007). This chapter analyzes another difference, one more routinely of importance to M&A practitioners: the treatment of "deal protection"—that is, contracts that reduce the risk to a bidder of a competing bid, such as "break fees" paid by a target if acquired by a competing bidder. The United Kingdom caps such fees with a bright-line rule set by a regulatory body. In the United States, courts review break fees in ex post litigation, applying a standard developed over time in the common law tradition. This chapter explores the effects of this formal contrast between regulation and litigation on the same behavior by two similar countries, using data on bids, fees, bid outcomes, and bid litigation to explore whether the formal difference matters in practice, and whether and how the two approaches to governance change and diverge over time.

Any comparison of law in two countries faces a serious omitted variable problem, and one can only generalize so far about trade-offs between litigation and regulation from one law. Still, a comparison of deal protection in the United Kingdom and the United States should yield some information.

John C. Coates IV is the John F. Cogan Jr. Professor of Law and Economics at Harvard Law School.

I extend thanks for comments and discussions to Dan Kessler, Andrei Shleifer, Luigi Zingales, Fred Schauer, Anup Malani, John Donohue, and other participants in the NBER Regulation and Litigation Conference, the Harvard Law School Law and Economics Workshop, Guhan Subramanian, Jennifer Arlen, Paul Davies, and John Armour. All rights reserved.

The two nations have similarly active M&A markets, with a large number of bids for public companies comprising 75 percent of worldwide bid volume (Rossi and Volpin 2004). They have similar corporate governance systems (e.g., Kraakman et al. 2009), with large companies and dispersed ownership (e.g., La Porta, Lopez-de-Silanes, and Shleifer 1999), which (as discussed later) generates the need for deal protection. And they have shared political, legal, and cultural traditions (U.S. State Department 2009), including M&A practitioners that work in both nations. The topic should also be of independent value to those who study or work in the M&A markets: deal protection is used regularly in friendly M&A, which is far more prevalent and may be more economically important than hostile bids.

Section 9.1 briefly reviews relevant literatures on (a) regulation and litigation, (b) the evolution of laws over time, and (c) deal protection, including the reasons deal protection contracts are used. Section 9.1 also briefly describes the legal treatment of break fees in the United Kingdom and the United States, and conjectures why the nations have diverged in this aspect of capital markets governance. Section 9.2 summarizes data, including break fees, on large friendly control bids for nonfinancial targets drawn from Thomson, representing approximately 50 percent of total bid volume in the United States and United Kingdom over the past twenty years. Trends in the size of break fees in the United States and the United Kingdom are depicted against the backdrop of changes in regulation of break fees. Section 9.3 then relates break fee size to rates of deal competition and deal completion, two deal outcome variables that break fees are intended to affect. Univariate and multivariate results are presented, and the robustness of the findings is tested with alternative specifications. Section 9.4 concludes with observations on trade-offs between litigation and regulation and the evolution of law more generally.

9.1 Prior Literature

9.1.1 Regulation and Litigation

A growing literature in economics and law recognizes and explores trade-offs in different modes of political governance of economic activity.[1] One mode, associated with classical liberalism, is for the state to assign clear property rights ex ante, permit private parties to write their own legal rules through contracts, enforce those contracts through privately initiated lawsuits heard by independent courts, and otherwise refrain from interfering with production or trade. Because this mode of governance relies on court

---

1. One can also contrast socialism, with state ownership of the means of production and/or trade, as with the U.S. Postal Service; and anarchy, with no clear specification of property rights, as with secondhand cigarette smoke, or no effective state enforcement of regulations or contract rights, as with trade in sex or drugs.

enforcement of property and contract rights, it is often identified as "*litiga-tion.*" A second mode, associated with political reactions to industrialization in the late nineteenth and twentieth centuries, is for the state to establish expert regulatory agencies, subject to political control, which "regulate" economic activity through explicit ex ante controls, enforce those controls directly with criminal or civil penalties imposed by state-controlled enforcement agencies, subject to judicial oversight and override, and forbid or control private contracts. This mode is often identified as "*regulation.*"

Ex ante Rules versus Ex Post Standards

The contrasts between litigation and regulation are various, including general content, the method by which law is created and enforced, and features of the institutions charged with lawmaking and enforcement. A common focus of contrast, however, is the timing of lawmaking and enforcement (e.g., Shavell 1984a, 1984b; Schwartzstein and Shleifer 2009). Regulation specifies and enforces entitlements in detail ex ante before activities occur, so (if perfect) violations are avoided. Litigation relies on private parties to sue for money in court ex post, after activities and potential legal violations have occurred. If parties are judgment proof, for example, ex ante specification and enforcement may be beneficial (Shavell 1984a, 1984b, 1993; Summers 1983). But courts can grant injunctions as well as award damages, and many economic harms are not so large as to cause insolvency. If economic activities have positive externalities and both ex ante regulations and ex post court decisions are prone to error, then regulation can improve welfare by eliminating or reducing the risk of mistaken ex post liability and so inducing socially beneficial activities, such as drug research (e.g., Schwartzstein and Shleifer 2009). But much regulation has been developed to address negative externalities, rather than positive ones, and spans domains of activity where the risk and potential harm of error in law enforcement varies significantly.

Given rational expectations, the timing of lawmaking matters because agents can better estimate their entitlements under regulation than under litigation. If they could perfectly foresee how courts would apply law to given facts, or if their ability to predict application of law to their behavior was invariant as between regulation and litigation, there would be no difference between litigation and regulation as a result of the timing of lawmaking and enforcement.[2] Research on litigation and regulation conceived

2. Other differences between the two general modes of lawmaking, such as expertise or political control of lawmakers or law enforcers, might still matter. If judges are generalists, and regulatory agencies specialists, for example, the latter may have expertise that may be beneficial (Landis 1938; Glaeser, Johnson, and Shleifer 2001). But courts can be (and often are) specialized (e.g., Revesz [1990], who discusses twelve specialized Federal courts in the United States, and Dreyfuss [1995], who discusses the Delaware Chancery Court, which specializes in business litigation). If regulatory agencies are subject to more and courts less political control, the latter could more optimally address harms imposed by politically powerful agents on politically

this way is related to a separate line of legal research that also describes trade-offs between ex ante specification of law ("rules") and ex post application of general laws to specific facts ("standards") (von Jhering 1883; Ehrlich and Posner 1974). That literature recognizes that courts sometimes develop "rules" that function much as do regulations (e.g., contracts cannot be enforced against persons under the age of eighteen), and emphasizes that such rules specified ex ante—whether by courts *or* regulatory agencies— increase certainty and reduce the costs of legal advice and adjudication ex post, but are more costly to enact (Kaplow 1992) and more frequently lead to specific case outcomes that reduce welfare, by being both over- and under-inclusive (Kennedy 1976), particularly when they will apply over a broad range of behaviors over a long period of time, or where lawmakers' information is limited (Sunstein 1995).

Regulation of M&A: Mandatory versus Default Law

Another use of "regulation" is relevant in the context of corporate and securities laws governing M&A. Legal scholars have long argued over whether those bodies of law are or should be mandatory ("regulatory") or optional ("default" rules) (e.g., Bebchuk 1989). Should use of the corporate form—or the raising of capital from dispersed investors—trigger laws that can be freely tailored through the corporate charter or bylaws or contract, or should they be binding? And if binding, should they be binding with respect to issues other than fraud? Laws that are "regulatory" in this sense are not necessarily clear ex ante rules, and they may require ex post litigation to clarify their meaning as well as for enforcement; in effect, the content of key M&A contracts, including the risk of litigation, may be imposed by regulation.

Legal scholars tend to classify laws as mandatory or default formally, based on whether they expressly permit companies to "opt out" of their provisions. But many laws relevant to M&A that are, on their face, "regulatory" in this sense can, with some ingenuity and effort, be "contracted around."[3] But "opt outs" of such core elements of corporate law are rare in the United

---

weak agents (Pace et al. 2007; Cook and Ludwig 2002). But in the United States, at least, many regulatory agencies (e.g., the Federal Reserve Board) are arguably subject to weaker political control than judges, who are elected in most states Rottman (2000), and precisely the opposite argument has been made in favor of regulation on the ground that judges or law enforcers required to impose large ex post fines may be more vulnerable to persuasion or bribery (Becker and Stigler 1974; Glaeser and Shleifer 2003).

3. For example, every U.S. state provides that, with board approval, a majority of shareholders may approve a merger with another corporation, and in the merger dissenting shareholders will have a choice of accepting the merger consideration or cash at a "fair value" set ex post by a court. In effect, shareholders can have their shares converted into cash by majority vote through merger. Coates (1999) shows that the risk of such ex post litigation can be eliminated by contract. Further, the ability of a majority of shareholders to force through a merger could be eliminated by contract—a corporate charter could, for example, require unanimous shareholder approval of a merger.

States, possibly because of transaction costs exacerbated by network effects (Coates 1999). In practice, laws that are formally mandatory may not bind, and laws that are formally default rules may bind. Key aspects of M&A law are, in practice, "regulatory" in the sense specified earlier—there are clear ex ante rules that typically structure the deal process. They are not "regulatory" in a formal sense, in that they can be contracted around. But in practice, they rarely are.

An important set of examples for U.S. M&A practice arises from the "fiduciary duties" applicable to corporate directors and officers. Fiduciary duty law is widely thought to represent an attempt to supplement private contract—not for any of the reasons just summarized for regulation, but because detailed specification of contracts ex ante is too expensive or in some cases impossible, whether because of imperfect information, collective action problems, or both. Fiduciary duty law is "regulatory" in the sense that, in general terms, private parties cannot opt out of it—it is binding on them whether they include it in their contracts or not, and often has a moral flavor similar to criminal laws. But it is enforced through private litigation ex post in courts; it remains relatively unspecified in detailed content until applied to specific facts (is a set of "standards"); and, in some particulars, it may be contracted around (e.g., Coates 1999). An overly strong distinction between litigation and regulation as modes of lawmaking may obscure the fact that many laws partake of both.

9.1.2   Evolution of Laws Over Time

Overlapping with the literature contrasting litigation and regulation is research exploring the degree to which particular kinds of laws change of time. Here, the contrast is made between "civil law"—codes and statutes that remain relatively unchanged over time—and "common law"—bodies of judicial decisions accompanied by some explanation of the principles used to reach specific outcomes that provide a degree (but only a degree) of guidance about future cases. The general relationship to the bodies of research summarized before should be apparent. Civil law is (the output of) regulation, it consists of many rules, and it changes rarely. Common law is (the output of) litigation; it consists of many standards, made into rules only for purposes of each case as it happens; and it adapts routinely, as every case presents at least some relevant facts that may distinguish it from prior cases.

One line of research explores whether and how a common law system would tend toward efficiency over time and, implicitly, whether and how the common law would evolve "rules" out of "standards" (as is commonly asserted or assumed in much legal scholarship; e.g., Kaplow [1992]). Posner (1973) claimed appellate judges have personal or career incentives to maximize efficiency. Rubin (1977) proposed that inefficient outcomes are more likely to be challenged in court, resulting in litigation that over time produces efficient laws, even if judges are unaware they are doing so. Llewellyn (1951) and Posner (2005) reasoned that even with biased judges the common law would evolve toward efficiency because it involves sequential decision-making of judges with diverse preferences, which would cancel out over time, although this assumes judges respect precedent, to some extent, else there would be no trend over time. Gennaioli and Shleifer (2007) suggest that appellate courts in a common law system tend toward efficiency because they preserve information by distinguishing current cases from prior decisions.

Other conjectures about the evolution of law can be found in the aforementioned literatures. Sunstein (1995) claims that a system of rules entails "no rapid changes in the content of law," consistent with a common view that civil law is less flexible or adaptable than common law, and that regulation tends toward sclerosis. Rajan and Zingales (2003) argue that civil law countries (i.e., countries that rely on regulatory agencies subject to political controls as their primary means of lawmaking) can undergo more rapid and transformative legal changes in response to changes in private interests, than can the common law. This claim could be consistent with claims about regulatory sclerosis if, over periods of time, private interests remain stable, producing little change in a regulatory system, but occasionally, in response to factor, technological, or unrelated political shocks, private interests shift suddenly, leading to regulatory change that is more rapid and significant than could occur through litigation in a common law system. Kennedy (1986) suggests reasons (and offers some qualitative evidence) that rules and standards may cycle, evolving into the other over time: rules evolve into standards as the welfare loss commanded by a rule in a given case will induce a court to invent an exception, with the exceptions eventually swallowing the rule; conversely, standards induce rules, as private parties lobby for (or persuade courts to adopt) rules to assist them in planning.

Niblett, Posner, and Shleifer 2009 provide one of the few empirical tests of some of these claims by tracking the evolution of one aspect of U.S. tort law (the economic loss rule) from 1970 to 2005 and find that while the law did appear to converge toward one version of the rule in the first twenty-five years of their sample period, courts have begun to deviate and splinter in their approach to the rule—that is, the law did not converge to any stable resting point. This chapter attempts to provide another empirical test of theories of how common law evolves over time, in a different domain.

9.1.3   Deal Protection and Break Fees

In both the United Kingdom and the United States, M&A involving public company targets face a law-derived risk of noncompletion: (a) the law requires target shareholders to approve or accept a bid, either by tendering or voting; (b) compliance with disclosure and other laws governing the process of obtaining target shareholder tenders or votes entails delay, ranging from a minimum of thirty days up to six months in some situations;

and (c) target shareholders may decide not to accept or approve a bid for any reason, including a third-party bid that emerges after agreements for an initial bid are signed. In effect, an M&A agreement or bid gives shareholders of a public target an option to accept the bid, and does not effectively bind the target or its shareholders to the bid, even if approved by the target's ordinary agents (i.e., its board or officers).

Deal protection contracts, including break fees, have emerged as a second-best way for bidders to protect their reliance interests in pursuing a bid for a public target. Even if they are unable to acquire the target, they can at least get paid a fee, if their bid is rejected and (typically) if the target is acquired by a competing bidder. Unlike the underlying bid, the target's promise to pay a break fee (often included in the deal agreement) is not generally subject to shareholder approval, in either the United States or the United Kingdom. Targets, in turn, agree to break fees—even though they may reduce competitive bids—because they encourage bidder participation in the face of valuation uncertainty and bidding costs, including significant and difficulty-to-quantify opportunity costs, and compensate a bidder for the inevitable release of valuable information to third parties (including potential competitors) upon the announcement of a bid for the target. Targets may also use break fees to control a sales process where the failure of that process to produce a completed deal can harm the target. Alternatively, target managers may agree to break fees to favor a bidder out of personal interests—better jobs after the deal, higher severance pay, or other private benefits.

Prior literature focused on break fees and other forms of deal protection can be found in both legal academic writing and in finance scholarship. In the United States, legal scholars have long debated whether and when break fees can represent a breach of the duty of loyalty of a target's board of directors. Prominent theoretical articles in the legal literature include: Schwartz (1986), who suggested a ban on break fees, to encourage bid competition; Ayres (1990), who noted that break fees reduce an initial bidders' valuation of a target as well as competing bidders, and would reduce welfare only if they deterred competing bids and not if a competing bidder in fact emerged; Fraidin and Hanson (1994), who applied the Coase theorem to argue for a permissive attitude toward break fees; and Kahan and Klausner (1996), who argued that courts should be more permissive toward break fees that induce an initial bid, and more skeptical of those granted to subsequent bidders, particularly when solicited by target managers, whose choice of bidder may be biased by agency costs.

Empirical research on break fees was initiated by Coates and Subramanian (2000), who studied break fees and other forms of deal protection granted by U.S. targets in friendly bids for control greater than $50 million in value in the period 1988 to 1999. They found that break fee size was dispersed and grew nonmonotonically throughout that period, ranging from 1 percent (twenty-fifth percentile) to 3 percent (seventy-fifth percentile) in 1988 and from 2 percent (twenty-fifth) to 4 percent (seventy-fifth) in 1999, consistent with a potential "Lake Woebegone effect," in which bidders sought a fee that was slightly larger than the average fee in a recent period sample, producing ever-increasing fees.[4] They also found that fee size correlated with court decisions, including 1994 and 1997 Delaware Supreme Court decisions in *Paramount* and *Brazen,* and with other bid characteristics, including larger bid size and the use of a tender offer by the bidder. They found, finally, in both univariate and multivariate tests, that the fact and size of break fees correlated with completion rates, both in general and conditional on publicly reported bid competition.

Subsequent research, using U.S. data from 1988 to 2000, confirmed their findings, and also found that break fees reduce the incidence of subsequent publicly reported competing bids, and (using a simultaneous equations system) that deal premiums were higher where targets agreed to pay break fees, consistent with the hypothesis that—at least at the fee levels observed in the sample period, and conditional on judicial scrutiny, discussed later— break fees were on average effective both at reducing bid competition and beneficial for target shareholders (Officer [2003]; Bates and Lemmon [2003]; see also Burch [2001], who examines deal protection in the form of stock options). Empirical research on break fees has also been reported for Canada (André, Khalil, and Magnan 2007), which reaches similar general conclusions, and for Australia (Chapple, Christensen, and Clarkson 2007), which finds that break fees in Australia—which must comply with a bright-line rule similar to the one imposed in the United Kingdom—appear actually to correlate *inversely* with bid completion, and with bid premiums. No studies appear to have been done of break fees in the United Kingdom, and none compares break fee size or the effects of break fees between the United Kingdom and the United States.

9.1.4   Legal Treatment of Break Fees

Why is deal protection regulated (or the subject of a special type of litigation)? There are three justifications for having special laws for break fees, one from antitrust theory, one from agency theory, and one from contract theory. First, they can deter bids, reduce competition, and reduce welfare

---

4. Boone and Mulherin (2007) find (and André, Khalil, and Magnan [2007] confirm) that Thomson's data on break fee *incidence* is biased in several respects: first, there is a general underreporting of fees and other forms of deal protection, relative to what is revealed by a careful review of SEC filings; second, there is a greater underreporting earlier in time, creating the spurious impression of time trends in fee incidence; and third, there is greater underreporting for smaller bids, creating the spurious impression of a relationship between toeholds and break fees. Since these biases emerge from underreporting by Thomson, they should not affect data on fee *size,* since such data is only available where Thomson reports fee data. They also confirm the finding, reported in Coates and Subramanian (2000), that fee incidence increased significantly after the 1994 Delaware Supreme Court decision in *Paramount.*

by allowing the target to be transferred to a lower-valuing bidder. In the presence of market power, contracts between a bidder and target (such as break fees) can impose externalities on other bidders and reduce social welfare because they both deter breach and reduce the benefits of search (see Diamond and Maskin 1979; Aghion and Bolton 1987). Second, for public targets, the "owners" of the target are dispersed shareholders, who cannot effectively represent themselves in the sales process. Target managers effectively choose among bidders in the first instance, subject to shareholder approval. Target manager preferences over bidders, moreover, can be expected to systematically differ from those of target shareholders. Traditional fiduciary duty law would thus constrain, to some extent, target managers' ability to use break fees to favor one bidder over another, absent a justification, particularly if the target managers had some evident tangible interest in the choice, such as a better job or severance package. Third and finally, there is a broader justification rooted in the basic structure of corporate law common to the United Kingdom and its former colonies, which is that a fee cannot be so large as to essentially eliminate the option target shareholders have to accept or reject the bid. Put differently, even if there is no specific concern about target managers in the context of a particular bid, a law permitting any and all break fees to be enforced would crucially undermine more generally laws requiring shareholder consent for sale of the company. One can view limits on break fees as reflecting an implicit term in the underlying contract between a target and its investors. Those more general laws can be justified on contract grounds—they were part of the bargain by virtue of being part of corporate law at the time investors purchased stock in a company—and on efficiency grounds—shareholder approval or consent requirements constrain agency costs in general, even if they are unnecessary or even inefficiently costly for a given company with given managers in the context of a given bid. For any or all of these reasons, the law in both the United States and the United Kingdom constrains break fees. But it does so differently in each nation.

UK Regulation of Break Fees

In the UK, break fees are constrained in theory by three sets of laws, but in practice only two are binding, and both have identical effects (Davies and Palmer 2004; Montgomery, Davies, and Palmer 2005). The Takeover Code limits break fees to 1 percent of the value of the bid.[5] That Code was originally a set of rules self-imposed by major institutional participants in the city, including representatives of the Bank of England, the London Stock Exchange (LSE), leading merchant banks, and organizations representing institutional investors, and is now statutorily binding on all tender offers

5. The Panel on Takeovers and Mergers, the Takeover Code § 21.2.

for public companies in the United Kingdom, by virtue of the UK's implementation of the EU-wide Takeover Directive.[6] Prior to 2006, the Takeover Code did not formally have the force of law, but was practically binding (Armour and Skeel 2007; Tarbert 2003), in part because UK courts deferred to its judgments because they recognized that the United Kingdom's formal regulatory bodies (the Department of Trade and Industry and the Bank of England) had sponsored its formation.[7] The direct sanction for flouting its requirements was expulsion from the LSE and trade organizations representing institutional investors, disinvestment by the British institutional investor community (who were required by the terms of the Code to divest from anyone breaking the Code), and an inability to obtain services or other assistance from others subject to the Code. In essence, Code enforcement piggy-backed on private organizations and relationships that would be considered essential for ongoing business activities in the United Kingdom.

Currently, the Takeover Panel, responsible for interpreting and resolving disputes under the Takeover Code, includes members nominated by trade organizations of insurance companies, investment companies, investment managers and brokers, commercial and investment bankers, industrial companies, accountants, and pension funds, and those members also constitute a majority of the members of the Hearing Committee, which hears disputes and imposes sanctions under the Code.[8] It is thus an "expert" regulatory body. But as long as it retains its public, bright-line character and is backed by the threat of significant sanctions, UK law on break fees functions as a self-enforcing bright-line rule that requires no ongoing expertise. In principle, the Takeover Panel could raise or lower the cap over time, in response to changing market conditions or evidence regarding the welfare or other effects of break fees, but they have not done so in the ten years since the rule was first formally adopted.[9] Few if any disputes concerning the rule's

6. European Parliament and Council Directive 2004/05, 2004 O.J. (L142) 12 (EC), art. 4 (supervisory authorities may include private bodies recognized by national law, such as the Takeover Panel), 9 (target board obligations include not taking frustrating actions, including limits on break fees); the Takeovers Directive (Interim Implementation) Regulations 2006, 2006 S.I. 2006/1183 (Eng.), available at www.opsi.gov.uk/SI/si2006/20061183.htm (transitional provisions); Companies Act, 2006, c. 46, §§942-65 (Eng.), statute giving Takeover Panel authority to write Takeover Code, and its Hearing Committee authority to give binding rulings on its application.

7. Regina v. Panel on Take-overs and Mergers, Ex parte Datafin Plc., 1987 Q.B. 815, 838-39 (C.A.). (The Panel's "source of power is only partly based upon moral persuasion and the assent of institutions and their members, the bottom line being the statutory powers exercised by the Department of Trade and Industry and the Bank of England. In this context I should be very disappointed if the courts could not recognize the realities of executive power and allowed their vision to be clouded by the subtlety and sometimes complexity of the way in which it can be exerted.")

8. See http://www.thetakeoverpanel.org.uk/structure/panel-membership.

9. Takeover Panel, Inducement Fees, Panel Statement 1999/10 (7/16/1999), available at http://www.thetakeoverpanel.org.uk/wp-content/uploads/2008/12/1999-10.pdf. See also Takeover Panel, Practice Statement No. 23, Rule 21.2—Inducement Fee Agreements and Other Agreements Between an Offeror and the Offerree Company (7/10/2008).

application to conventional break fees, and the rule can only be deviated from with advance permission of that same body, which reportedly they rarely grant. (These statements are consistent with the data discussed in Section 9.2.)

A second law—the Companies Act—has long forbidden public companies in the United Kingdom from providing "financial assistance" to anyone purchasing their shares, including in the context of a takeover bid.[10] "Financial assistance" for this purpose includes any contingent payment to the bidder by the target, with certain exceptions. Break fees are covered, unless they are less than 1 percent of the bid value. Violations of the law could result in civil and even criminal penalties for any officer or director of the target that approved the violation. Thus, even if a bidder would be prepared to endure expulsion from the UK financial community in order to obtain a break fee larger than 1 percent, targets risk significant sanctions if they agree. Agreements for such fees would also be unenforceable in UK courts, making it risky for a bidder to rely on an agreement for such a fee, even if a target were willing to risk sanctions. Unlike the Takeover Code, the Companies Act was adopted as a general statute by Parliament, and to that degree differs from the modal form of regulation described earlier. But as with the Takeover Code, the Companies Act provisions as applied to break fees appear to function in practice as a set of rules, with the ex ante character of regulation, and generate few disputes and little litigation (Davies and Palmer 2004).

Third, and unimportantly in the United Kingdom, there are general fiduciary duty obligations, enforced in a common law fashion by the UK courts. Because the aforementioned Takeover Code and Companies Act provisions effectively rule out legally controversial break fees, no competing bidders have sought an injunction or other judicial remedy as a result of a break fee on fiduciary duty grounds. In short, ex ante bright-line UK regulation of break fees by an expert body, supplemented by a statute establishing the legal authority of that body, has crowded out break fee litigation and the use of ex post standards in practice, even if they remain formally available.

U.S. Law on Break Fees

In the United States, there is no equivalent to the UK Takeover Code or the statutory UK ban on "financial assistance." Nor are break fees constrained by Federal law. Instead, the only legal constraints are the general fiduciary duties imposed on target directors and officers by state corporate law enforced through litigation (Coates and Subramanian 2000). Target shareholders—including a competing bidder that purchases a single share of the target—have standing to sue in court on the ground that the agreement to pay a break fee was disloyal, grossly negligent, or both. While courts

10. Companies Act 2006 (c. 46), Part 18, Chapter 2; Companies Act 1985 §§ 151–158.

typically defer to the "business judgment" of a company's board in such cases, if the bidder can plausibly argue that the fee was designed to favor incumbent managers, it will often be able to get a court to scrutinize the facts surrounding the fee agreement. The standard directly applicable to "deal protection" in the leading U.S. jurisdiction (Delaware)—a break fee is permissible if it induces a bid and impermissible if it forecloses bidding[11]—but nearly all fees have the potential to do both, that formal standard provides little guidance to practitioners, and courts review many other facts in reviewing fees. One relevant consideration, but only one, will be the size of the fee. Other factors, such as the target board's plausible interests in favoring a particular bidder, the information they had at the time they granted the fee, the process that preceded the grant of the fee provision, and the size of comparable fees in comparable transactions, will all generally be considered by the reviewing court, in a typically fact-intensive fiduciary duty case.[12]

Because there is no bright-line rule setting a maximum amount for break fees in the United States, bidders or target shareholders unhappy with a given fee must seek to attack it ex post, in court, without any assurance as to the outcome. Bidders that want break fees must negotiate for them without knowing precisely how large the fee can be without risking a court finding that it represents a breach of the target's fiduciary's duties. (Courts view a bidder as participating in any violation represented by an agreed-upon fee, so a bidder may not claim an entitlement arising from a breach by the target's directors.[13])

The courts reviewing the claims can be state (judges typically elected for terms) or federal (appointed judges with life tenure), and typically have "general jurisdiction"—they do not specialize in M&A. In the leading U.S. jurisdiction for M&A law (Delaware), however, the reviewing court will be the Court of Chancery, which specializes to a large extent in corporate law cases, including M&A and deal protection. While there is no requirement that plaintiffs sue in Delaware when a Delaware target's directors are alleged to have breached their fiduciary duties, the data presented in figure 9.2 show that specialized Delaware courts retains a "market share" roughly in line with Delaware's share of public companies generally. On mode of regulation, then, the United States thus uses a part-hybrid model: ex post review through litigation in courts which, more than half of the time, have specialized knowledge.

11. QVC Network, Inc. v. Paramount Communications, Inc., *Del. Ch., 635 A.2d 1245 (1993),* aff'd, *Del. Supr., 637 A.2d 34, 50 (1994)* (citing Revlon, Inc. v. MacAndrews & Forbes Holdings, Inc., *Del. Supr. 506 A.2d 173, 179 (1986)* and Mills Acquisition Co. v. Macmillan, Inc., *559 A.2d 1261 (1988)).*

12. For example, Louisiana Municipal Police Employees' Retirement System v. Crawford, 918 A.2d 1172, Del. Ch. (Chandler, C.), February 23, 2007 (No. Civ. A. 2635-N, Civ. A. 2663-N) (listing a number of factors to be considered in evaluating break fees).

13. For example, Paramount Communications, Inc. v. QVC Network, Inc., 637 A.2d 34, 55 (Del. 1994).

Why the Divergence?

Why have the United States and the United Kingdom diverged in their treatment of break fees? In both countries, law on break fees emerges from the law on hostile takeovers, despite the relatively minor role that hostile takeovers now play in the United States. In the United Kingdom, break fees were attacked in the mid-1980s as a type of "frustrating action" by a target that was prohibited in general terms by the Takeover Code in force then and now. In the United States, break fees were attacked as violations of the target's fiduciary duties, which are given heightened scrutiny by courts in the takeover context. Both countries adapted their preexisting systems for governing hostile takeovers and target responses to the growth in the use of break fees, despite the fact that most break fees are not used primarily in the context of hostile takeovers.

That explanation, of course, only begs the question: why do the United Kingdom and the United States approach hostile takeovers differently? Part of that history has been told by Armour and Skeel (2007), drawing on interviews and newspaper accounts. Here is a summary: when hostile bids emerged in the 1950s, they received negative press, but opinion was insufficient to result in legislation or regulation, leaving them to the courts. Targets began to use defenses that were controversial for interfering with what were perceived as shareholder rights, but not so extreme as to lead courts to set aside their traditional reluctance to interfere with the business judgment of corporate boards. In the United Kingdom, institutional shareholders were more significant than in the United States, and more organized, facing lower costs for collective political action (Olson 1965). Legislative intervention posed political risks extending beyond M&A to economic regulation generally, so institutions and the financial community preempted Parliament by developing a self-regulatory body, with the implicit backing of the UK government. In the United States, by contrast, corporate managers were more politically powerful than shareholders, and the only Federal legislation to be proposed (the Williams Act) was intended to restrict takeovers, not takeover defenses. Although a preexisting regulatory agency (the Securities and Exchange Commission [SEC]) was able to lobby for a more neutral, disclosure-oriented takeover statute, defenses were largely left to the states to govern with ex post litigation.

This capsule comparative history of takeover governance suggests that the contrast between the United Kingdom's regulatory approach and the United States litigation approach is less stark than in the narrow case of break fees. That is because the UK Code, while bright-line with respect to break fees, is full of standards as applied to takeovers generally, and has generated a substantial body of litigation. But most of this "litigation" is of a different character than is true in U.S. courts, in three respects. First, it does not involve lawyers. Second, partly due to not involving lawyers, it is faster. Third, partly due to being faster, it takes place ex ante, before a given action that might create a conflict occurs—bidders and targets go to the Panel to ask permission for a given action, and the Panel decides whether they can. In essence, the United Kingdom has in general formalized a means to combine the benefits of certainty that come from ex ante regulation with the benefits of tailoring that come from ex post standards. But as applied to break fees, they have chosen a much starker form of ex ante regulation.

9.2   Hypotheses and Data on Break Fees in the United States and the United Kingdom

9.2.1   Hypotheses

The following hypotheses, drawn from the literatures just reviewed, can be tested against the subsequent samples. First, if break fee law binds in the United States and the United Kingdom, then one would expect:

HYPOTHESIS 1 *UK break fees will not exceed 1 percent of bid value.*

HYPOTHESIS 2 *U.S. break fees will vary more than UK break fees.*

HYPOTHESIS 3 *UK bids will encounter little if any break fee litigation.*

HYPOTHESIS 4 *U.S. bids will encounter more break fee litigation.*

Further, if break fee law binds, if the demand for break fees varies from bid to bid, if the modal demand for a break fee would result (but for law) in a fee greater than 1 percent being agreed between a bidder and target, then one would expect:

HYPOTHESIS 5 *UK break fees will cluster at 1 percent.*

HYPOTHESIS 6 *U.S. break fees will typically exceed 1 percent.*

Turning to time trends, if "common law" courts in the United States develop rules out of standards over time, and improve law with repeated disputes, then one would expect:

HYPOTHESIS 7 *U.S. break fee litigation would diminish over time.*

HYPOTHESIS 8 *U.S. break fees themselves would exhibit less variation over time, as applicable law became more certain and practitioners conformed to legal norms.*

Finally, if U.S. fees exceed 1 percent on average, as predicted by hypothesis 6, then one would also expect:

HYPOTHESIS 9 *Post-bid competition will be higher in the United Kingdom than in the United States.*

HYPOTHESIS 10 *Bid completion rates will be lower in the United Kingdom than in the United States.*

HYPOTHESIS 11 *Bid incidence will be lower in the United Kingdom than in the United States.*

9.2.2   Descriptions of Samples

The foregoing hypotheses are tested using four samples. The first sample—on break fees and bid activity—is drawn from Thomson Financial's M&A Database. All bids for UK or U.S. targets in the time period 1989 through 2008 are initially sampled ($n = 17,977$). Because bid techniques (including deal protection) vary by deal size (see Coates and Subramanian 2000), because deal size may vary between the United Kingdom and the United States, and because bid size has varied over time, the sample is then constrained to consist of bids over $1 billion, which is roughly the ninetieth percentile of bid size in 1989—this chapter refers to these bids as "large bids" for convenience. (None of the qualitative findings reported following depend on the precise size cut-off.) This produces a total of 5,171 bids.

Bids that are reported by Thomson as still pending—that is, bids with no effective date or withdrawal date—are dropped, leaving 4,404 bids. Of those, Thomson classifies 865 as "hostile," meaning the target publicly resisted the bid. Because a target's consent is required to obtain standard deal protection, deal protection is less likely to be found in hostile bids, and they are dropped.[14] Of the remaining bids, 194 bids sought less than a controlling interest, and are accordingly dropped. Because banks and other financial institutions are generally cash- and capital-constrained, making conventional cash break fees difficult or impossible to pay (see Coates and Subramanian [2000] for a discussion and evidence in the U.S. context), while economic substitutes are available (e.g., stock or asset options), they are regulated differently than break fees, at least in the United States. Bids for targets with Standard Industrial Classification (SIC) codes 6000-6999 ($n = 766$) are dropped. These procedures leave a total of 2,579 bids. Of those, Thomson reports stock price and premium data for only 1,346, consisting of 209 bids for UK companies and 1,136 bids for U.S. companies. This subsample is the focus of the remaining analysis,[15] and represents approxi-

14. There are, in fact, more hostile bids as a share of large bids in the United Kingdom (7 percent of the broader sample of large bids) than in the United States (3 percent, p-value $< .01$). But as noted at the outset, there are many more friendly deals in each country. Break fees are also much less common in the dropped hostile bids (13 percent) than in the retained friendly bids (37 percent). Rossi and Volpin (2004) report fewer hostile bids in the United Kingdom (4.4 percent of listed firms versus 6.4 percent in the United States) for a sample that includes smaller bids.

15. More UK bids lack premium data (58 percent) than U.S. bids (51 percent), but the basic results discussed later regarding incidence and size of break fees, and their relationships with bid completion and bid competition, are not qualitatively affected by retaining all large nonpending friendly control bids for nonbank targets.

mately 50 percent of the total friendly control bid volume for nonfinancial targets in the United States and United Kingdom over the past twenty years.

A second "placebo" sample used to test the robustness of the findings from the main M&A sample consists of resolved bids dropped from Thomson because they sought less than a control interest (including noncontrol bids for financial institutions). This sample is by construction not likely to be affected by break fee law, since the reason for break fees is to constrain competition in control bids.

The third sample consists of all control bids (i.e., all bids for more than 50 percent of the target) for companies listed on the main stock exchanges in the United States (Amex, NYSE, and Nasdaq) and the United Kingdom (London). This sample is used to estimate annual bid incidence in each nation, normalized by the annual numbers of firms listed on each nation's stock exchanges, which are taken from the World Federation of Exchanges, which reports that data for the years 1990 to 2008.

The fourth sample, on break fee litigation, is drawn from a search of the Westlaw "all cases" database for reported judicial opinions on fiduciary duty disputes involving break fees in the period 1989 to 2009. The search returned 225 reported case decisions that mention both mergers or tender offers and "break fee" or synonymous phrases.[16] A review of those decisions shows that a third—the sixty-one cases listed in the appendix—were in cases concerned with the legitimacy of M&A break fees, either on their own or in combination with other claimed facts supporting a claim for breach of the target fiduciaries' duties.[17] Grossed up to account for cases not generating reported decisions, a rough estimate of break fee litigation in the United States in that period would be approximately ninety-five cases.[18]

---

16. A search of Westlaw's all cases database (including both Federal and state courts), using the search phrase "(merger or 'tender offer')" and "('break fee' or 'bust-up fee' or 'break-up fee' or 'termination fee') and 'fiduciary duty'" returned 224 cases.

17. The sixty-one cases concerned with break fees are listed in the appendix. The rest consist of cases in bankruptcy courts, which govern break fees differently than in normal bids; reverse termination fee cases, which involve fees payable by bidders rather than targets; disclosure cases; cases involving "termination fees" in unrelated contexts that happen to mention "merger" or "tender offer"; cases in which break fees are mentioned in passing; and cases not involving fiduciary duty claims. Of those cases, thirty-four were reported by Delaware courts, roughly 67 percent of the sample over the whole period, in line with Delaware's market share of U.S. public companies (Coates 2001). However, as illustrated in figure 9.1, Delaware's "market share" of break fee cases has declined in recent years, from an average of 95 percent from 1989 through 1998, to 57 percent from 1999 to 2008.

18. While reported decisions do not represent all cases filed, the multiple of complaints-to-reported-decisions is not as large as one might think: Thomas and Thompson (2004) report 348 fiduciary duty cases were filed in Delaware Chancery Court in 1999 and 2000; a search for "fiduciary duty" in the Westlaw Delaware cases database returns 224 reported decisions for the same time period.

Table 9.1   **Summary statistics, all bids and United States vs. United Kingdom bids over $1 billion, 1989–2008**

	Mean (standard deviation) for all bids ($n = 1,346$)	Mean (standard deviation) for UK bids ($n = 209$)	Mean (standard deviation) for U.S. bids ($n = 1,137$)	*p*-value of *t*-test of means (U.S. vs. UK)
% sought in bid	98.5 (6.4)	97.3 (7.6)	98.7 (6.2)	0.01
Bid value ($mm)	4.9 (9.9)	4.7 (8.6)	5.0 (10.2)	0.72
% bid premium over 1-day prior market price	29.8 (28.0)	30.0 (29.2)	29.8 (27.8)	0.91
% with break fees[a]	70.4 (45.7)	18.7 (38.7)	70.3 (40.1)	0.00
Break fee as % of bid value	2.6 (1.0)	0.9 (0.3)	2.6 (1.0)	0.00
% using tender offer	26.9 (44.4)	72.2 (44.7)	18.6 (38.9)	0.00
% cash bids	56.7 (49.6)	65.1 (47.8)	55.1 (49.8)	0.01
% stock bids	28.0 (44.9)	5.3 (22.4)	32.1 (46.7)	0.00
% cross-border	19.9 (39.9)	36.8 (48.3)	16.9 (37.4)	0.00
% bidder and target in same industry (one-digit SIC)	63.4 (48.1)	52.4 (50.1)	65.4 (47.6)	0.00
Duration of completed bids, in days	145 (107)	128 (82)	148 (111)	0.02

[a]But see Boone and Mulherin (2007) on underreporting of break fees in Thomson's database.

9.2.3   Summary Data and Simple Comparisons of Large Bids in the United States and the United Kingdom

As shown in table 9.1, 88 percent of large U.S. and UK bids were completed, the rest withdrawn. Average (median) bid size was $4.9 billion ($2.1 billion). Mean (median) duration of a completed bid was 145 (114) days. Bids were at an average (median) premium over the prior day's target stock price of 30 percent (26 percent). Break fees—again, including U.S. and UK bids—were used in 70 percent of bids,[19] and were an average (median) of 2.6 percent (2.7 percent) of deal value.[20] In nominal dollars, the average break fee was $124 million; the largest was $3.9 billion. While these fees may seem small relative to bid size, it should be remembered that the best evidence

19. But see Boone and Mulherin (2007) on underreporting of break fees in Thomson's database.
20. Thomson reports "deal value," defined to include the "total consideration paid," including liabilities assumed if disclosed, excluding fees and expenses. Thomson also reports "enterprise value" and "rank value," which attempt to reflect debt and other claims against the target or the acquiror after the bid differently, as well as "equity value," which is simply the prebid equity market capitalization of the target. The qualitative findings presented following persist regardless of whether break fees are calculated as a percentage of deal value, equity value, enterprise value, or rank value. The remainder of this chapter uses "deal value" as the basis for the calculation of break fees, but uses the term "bid value" to reflect the fact that not all bids in the data set are completed.

about the expected effect of M&A bids on bidder share prices is that they are close to zero, often negative, and at most increase bidder share prices by 0 to 2 percent (Andrade, Mitchell, and Stafford 2001). While buyers are typically larger than targets, moving from a 1 percent to a 3 percent fee could substantially erode or even wipe out the expected net benefit of a bid for a typical prospective competing bidder.

Bid size between the two nations was similar: $4.7 billion in the United Kingdom, on average, versus $5.0 billion in the United States. Bids using stock consideration were larger than cash bids, but this was true in both nations. Yet, as reflected in table 9.1, break fees were significantly smaller and vary less in the United Kingdom than in the United States. In the United States, 95 percent of break fees were greater than 1 percent, the maximum for the United Kingdom. Over 60 percent of the UK fees fall between 0.9 percent and 1.1 percent; less than 2 percent of fees in the United States fall in that range. The standard deviation of UK break fee size is less than a third of that in the United States. Consistent with hypothesis 5, UK break fees are left skewed (−1.7), and less peaked (kurtosis = 5.0), whereas U.S. break fees are much less skewed (0.6), and are more peaked (kurtosis = 8.9). In short, at all moments of the distribution, UK and U.S. break fees differ as predicted, as reflected on figure 9.1.

In nominal dollars, the average agreed-upon UK fee was $41 million, a third the size of the average U.S. break fee, at $128 million; the largest agreed-upon fee in the United Kingdom was $212 million, in the 2007 buy-

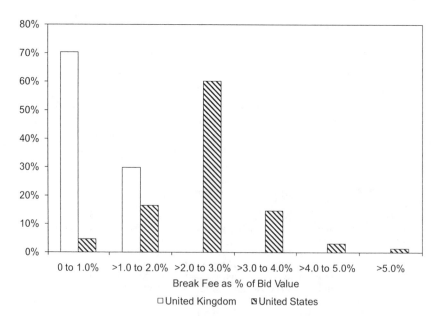

Fig. 9.1   **Break fees distribution, United States versus United Kingdom**

out of Alliance Boots, compared to the largest U.S. fee, the $3.9 billion fee agreed to in the 2000 stock merger of Time-Warner and AOL. Among withdrawn bids, where the fee would typically have been required to be paid, the average fee in the United Kingdom was $25 million, 15 percent of the size of the average triggered in the United States ($184 million). The largest paid triggered in the United Kingdom was a mere $35 million, in the 2000 acquisition of Lasmo by Amerada Hess, compared to the largest fee triggered in the United States, the $1.8 billion paid in the 2000 acquisition of Warner-Lambert by Pfizer.

The U.S. bids took longer to complete than UK bids. The reason for the timing difference has to do with the interaction of law—stock deals require a more lengthy regulatory process in both nations, due to disclosure and registration requirements   and bid financing, which is weighted more toward cash in the United Kingdom than in the United States. Specifically, UK bids are most frequently for all cash (65 percent) than for all stock (5 percent) or for other securities or a blend of deal currencies (30 percent). While large U.S. bids are also most commonly for all cash (55 percent), they are more frequently for stock (32 percent) than in the United Kingdom, with the rest for other securities or a blend of deal currencies (13 percent). Each pairwise difference is statistically significant at a p-value of $< .01$. As shown in table 9.2, cash bids take roughly the same amount of time in both countries. The UK bids were also more likely to involve an overlap between a bidder's and a target's one-digit SIC code, even in cash bids.

9.2.4   Trends in Break Fee Size

Trends in the size of break fees in the United States and the United Kingdom are presented in table 9.3. As previously reported in Coates and Subramanian (2000) (for a sample including smaller deals than reported on in this chapter), break fees increased over the course of the 1990s in the United States. However, any trend in U.S. break fees in large deals appears to have moderated in the 2000s. As a more formal test, break fee size as a percent of bid value is regressed against the bid announcement date; and against bid announcement date; a dummy indicating that the year of announcement is after 1999, and the interaction of announcement date and the year 1999. In both regressions (unreported), bid announcement date correlates strongly with break fee size, but the signs on post-1999 and date*1999 interaction are negative and statistically insignificant.

By comparison, there is no marked time trend in break fees in the United Kingdom—other than the initial jump from no fees to 1 percent fees in 1999, the same year that the Takeover Panel approved 1 percent fees through rule-making. While break fees were used on occasion in the United Kingdom prior to the 2000s, they were sufficiently suspect—viewed as potentially a type of "frustrating action" barred by the UK Takeover Code— that they did not occur frequently in the 1990s, and only began to appear

Table 9.2   **Summary statistics, cash bids in United States vs. cash bids in United Kingdom, 1989–2008**

	Mean for UK cash bids (n = 209)	Mean for U.S. cash bids (n = 1,137)	p-value of t-test of means (U.S. vs. UK cash bids)
% sought in bid	96.4	98.4	0.00
Bid value ($mm)	4.1	4.2	0.93
% bid premium over 1-day prior market price	29.8	29.9	0.93
% with break fees[a]	26.4	80.3	0.00
Break fee as % of bid value	0.9	2.7	0.00
% using tender offer	72.1	28.6	0.00
% cross-border	35.3	21.3	0.00
% bidder and target in same industry (one-digit SIC)	44.4	56.4	0.01
Duration of completed bids, in days	126	133	0.44

[a]But see Boone and Mulherin (2007) on underreporting of break fees in Thomson's database.

Table 9.3   **Trends in break fee size, United States vs. United Kingdom, 1989–2008**

	UK		U.S.	
	Mean (%)	Median (%)	Mean (%)	Median (%)
1989	—	—	1.5	1.0
1990	—	—	2.6	2.6
1991	—	—	3.0	3.0
1992	—	—	1.6	1.2
1993	—	—	2.1	2.1
1994	—	—	2.3	2.2
1995	—	—	2.2	2.4
1996	—	—	2.5	2.5
1997	—	—	2.5	2.5
1998	—	—	2.4	2.5
1999	0.7	0.7	2.4	2.6
2000	0.9	0.9	3.0	2.8
2001	—	—	2.7	2.7
2002	0.4	0.4	2.8	2.8
2003	—	—	3.0	3.2
2004	1.0	1.0	2.8	3.0
2005	1.5 (0.8)	1.0 (0.8)	2.6	2.8
2006	0.7	0.8	2.8	2.9
2007	1.0	1.0	2.7	2.9
2008	1.0	1.0	2.9	2.8

Notes: Dashed cells indicate no observed break fees; for 2005, the UK fee statistics are listed as derived directly from Thomson, and in parentheses as corrected after dropping a misclassified target (see text).

regularly after they were implicitly legitimized by the adoption of the 1 percent cap in 1999.[21] Thus, the idea that the United Kingdom experienced a regulatory "shock" à la Rajan and Zingales (2003)—the 1 percent rule not only capped fees but made them legitimate, increasing their use—is consistent with practitioner reports and the fact that already in 2000, break fees already are clustering in the United Kingdom near the legal cap of 1 percent, and remain there throughout the sample period. In only one year— 2005—are there any reported break fees in excess of 1.0 percent, and that one outlier is an erroneous datum in Thomson, which lists PetroKhazakhstan as a UK target, when it fact it was Canadian. In unreported regressions, there is no relationship of break fee size on bid announcement date over any part of the sample period.

Table 9.4 depicts trends in variation of break fee size in the United Kingdom and in the United States in available years, showing the interquartile difference (i.e., the seventy-fifth percentile-sized fee for the year less the twenty-fifth percentile-sized fee) and the annual standard deviation in break fee size, as a percentage of bid value. In all years but 2005, both measures of variation of fee size are more than double for the United States than for the United Kingdom, and sometimes much larger, than its counterpart in the United Kingdom. After dropping the misclassified deal discussed earlier, the same is true for 2005. There do not seem to be any trends in the variation in the U.S. data: despite years of experience, thousands of deals, and hundreds of lawsuits (discussed later), there remains as much variation in observed break fee size in the early 1990s as there is in the late 2000s.

As an alternative measure, break fee size was regressed separately against industry controls (one-digit SIC codes) and the observed deal characteristics used in the multivariate regressions described following (use of cash consideration, tender offer, cross-border deals, and bid value). Given the paucity of reported break fees in the United Kingdom prior to 2000, this regression was run for the subsample consisting of years after 1999, although the qualitative result is the same without this restriction. For the United Kingdom, this (unreported) regression has an R-squared of 26 percent; for the United States, it is only 6 percent.

In litigation, this variation in the U.S. fees means that defendant fiduciaries will truthfully be able to list a number of billion-dollar bids with fees well above the average—eight over 5 percent since 2000 in this sample, for

21. This statement is based less on the data in Thomson, which is unreliable on break fee incidence, and more on statements in practitioner commentary on break fees (Davies and Palmer 2004; Montgomery, Davies, and Palmer 2005; Tarbert 2003), and the general absence of such commentary prior to 2000. Technically, break fees in deals structured not as tender offers but amalgamations or restructurings would not be subject to the Takeover Code, but the Code's approval of 1 percent fees seems to have increased used of such fees in those types of deals as well, as reflected in the general norm of 1 percent of firm value followed by M&A practitioners under the Companies Act's exception for immaterial financial assistance. See Davies and Palmer 2004.

Table 9.4   **Trends in variation in break fee size, United States vs. United Kingdom, 1989–2008**

	Interquartile range of break fee size		Standard deviation of break fee size	
	UK	U.S.	UK	U.S.
1989	—	0.01066	—	0.00752
1990	—	0.02620	—	—
1991	—	0.00000	—	0.01525
1992	—	0.01965	—	0.01563
1993	—	0.01536	—	0.00820
1994	—	0.00980	—	0.00895
1995	—	0.00738	—	0.00736
1996	—	0.01055	—	0.00846
1997	—	0.00916	—	0.00938
1998	—	0.00995	—	0.00877
1999	0.00000	0.01063	—	0.00932
2000	0.00000	0.00878	—	0.01194
2001	0.00000	0.01258	—	0.00931
2002	0.00000	0.01151	—	0.00756
2003	0.00000	0.01163	—	0.01179
2004	0.00069	0.01314	0.00048	0.00809
2005	0.02523 (0.00556)	0.01062	0.01325 (0.00393)	0.00766
2006	0.00435	0.00815	0.00314	0.00699
2007	0.00060	0.00940	0.00247	0.00812
2008	0.00158	0.00951	0.00087	0.00850

Notes: Dashed cells indicate insufficient observations; for 2005, the UK fee statistics are listed as derived directly from Thomson, and in parentheses as corrected after dropping a misclassified target (see text).

example. Since break fees decrease as a percentage of bid size as bid size increases in this and other samples, a larger set of examples of 5+ percent break fees can be assembled by defendants in smaller, more typical U.S. bids than those in this sample. The U.S. case law—reviewed briefly in section 9.3—suggests it may suffice to defend a fee to show simply that it is not an outlier, and not satisfy the more difficult test that it is in line with overall averages. If so, then this variation will make it easier for defendants to prevail in U.S. court challenges to fees, even if they have to incur costs to do so.

In sum, the data show that M&A break fees in practice vary significantly more in the United States than in the United Kingdom, consistent with the litigation-driven U.S. law in practice providing less clear guidance than UK regulation on the appropriate size of break fees relative to bid value. Given the clarity of the UK rule (the 1 percent cap), and the varied messages U.S. courts have stated regarding the appropriate size of break fees, U.S. deal-makers have considerably more flexibility in choosing the amount of deal protection than their UK counterparts.

9.3   Evidence of Effects of Break Fees

9.3.1   Outcomes: Bid Competition, Bid Completion, and Bid Litigation

If break fees had no impact on bid outcomes, the differences between law and break fee size described before might be of practical importance to bid participants, but little overall significance. However, prior research has found that large break fees can have an impact on whether a given bid will attract competition, and on whether that bid will be completed. The difference in legal approaches to break fees—with the UK fees being kept below 1 percent and those in the United States typically exceeding double that level or more—has a potential effect on allocational efficiency, as higher-valuing bidders in the United Kingdom are more likely to acquire a target than in the United States, while bidders overall in the United Kingdom must take into account the risk that they will lose reliance interests (net of break fees) if they are outbid by competitors. In the United States that risk is substantially lower. The choice between regulation and litigation, in other words, may have an effect on bid incidence and the efficiency of the bid process. In addition, the ex ante and ex post approaches to governance can be expected to have another set of consequences: higher litigation costs for the latter. This section explores whether these effects can be observed in the large bid break fee data.

9.3.2   Univariate Results: Bid Competition and Bid Completion

As shown in table 9.5 (part A), UK bids are more than twice as likely to encounter competing bids than bids for U.S. targets. The UK bids are less likely to be completed than U.S. bids. This difference is attributable to the presence of competing bids, as the completion rate is statistically the same

Table 9.5   **Outcomes for large bids in the United States and United Kingdom, 1989–2008**

	UK bids	U.S. bids	*p*-value
	A. All bids		
% with public bid competition	19.6 (*n* = 209)	8.0 (*n* = 1,137)	0.00
% with litigation	0.0 (*n* = 209)	5.0 (*n* = 1,137)	0.00
% completed	82.8 (*n* = 209)	88.8 (*n* = 1,137)	0.01
Without competition	88.6 (*n* = 168)	91.7 (*n* = 1,046)	0.20
With competition	58.5 (*n* = 41)	56.0 (*n* = 91)	0.79
	B. Cash bids		
% with public bid competition	22.8 (*n* = 209)	10.0 (*n* = 1,137)	0.00
% with litigation	0.0 (*n* = 209)	3.9 (*n* = 1,137)	0.02
% completed	79.4 (*n* = 209)	88.5 (*n* = 1,137)	0.00
Without competition	84.7 (*n* = 105)	91.8 (*n* = 564)	0.02
With competition	61.3 (*n* = 31)	58.7 (*n* = 63)	0.81

for both countries for bids with competition, or for bids without competition, with bids being completed less than 60 percent of the time in the presence of competition, and roughly 90 percent of the time without competition. For bids overall, it is the competition rate that is different, rather than the way that bidders compete conditional on competition. Similarly, bids are much less likely to encounter post-announcement competition if protected by a fee greater than 1 percent than by a fee of less than 1 percent (20.6 percent vs. 7.9 percent, p-value < 0.001), and much more likely to be completed if protected by such a fee (91.4 percent vs. 82.5 percent, p-value < 0.01).

One might wonder, based on the differences in bid consideration and bid duration presented earlier, whether it is those differences that are affecting competition rates. On reflection, however, those differences only make the contrast between bid completion rates in the United States and the United Kingdom even more striking. The longer a bid takes to be completed, the longer third parties have to make a competing bid. Yet in the United Kingdom—where bids take less time because they are more commonly for cash—bids are completed less frequently than in the United States, where they take more time, because they are more frequently for stock. In fact, as reflected in table 9.5 (part B), the difference in completion rates spans choice of consideration: all-cash bids in the United States remain more likely to be completed (89 percent) than all-cash bids in the United Kingdom (79 percent, p-value < .01). As with bids generally, cash bids are much less likely to be completed in the presence of competition—roughly 60 percent of the time, versus 90 percent without competition—and as before the differences in completion rates in the presence of competition are not statistically different. There is a statistically significant difference in completion rates of cash bids even without competition—92 percent in the United States versus 85 percent in the United Kingdom, possibly reflecting greater power of institutional shareholders in the United Kingdom to refuse to tender to low-ball bids that may be attempted in the absence of competition—but the magnitude of that difference is much smaller than the difference in competition rates.

9.3.3   Bid Incidence

The data reviewed so far are consistent with the hypotheses that UK regulation constrains break fees, increases bid competition, and lowers bid completion rates, relative to U.S. litigation. If break fees are an importance inducement for bidding, the findings thus far suggest that we should also expect to see fewer bids in the United Kingdom. Of course, the United States is a larger economy, so the absolute number of bids would be expected to be higher in the United States. To normalize the bid data in the sample just analyzed, one would ideally want the number of listed firms that could generate $1 billion bids, but since bid premia themselves vary, and market capitalizations fluctuate frequently, generating the right stock of target firms for the aforementioned bid sample is not easy. A more direct approach is possible: gather a new sample from Thomson of all control bids for distinct listed companies and compare them to the total number of listed companies in each nation. Thomson includes competing bids—that is, bids pending at the same time for the same target—as separate records in its M&A database. Overlapping competing bids, which do not increase overall bid incidence, are removed (although doing this does not much affect the bottom line). This exercise produces the data set out in table 9.6.

The data are consistent with those presented in Andrade, Mitchell, and Stafford 2001, who use data from the Center for Research in Security Prices (CRSP) to construct estimates for total U.S. M&A activity in the years 1962 to 1998. Although they present activity rates ranging from 2 percent to 5 percent in the years 1990 to 1998, the rates presented here are *bid* rates, rather than *merger* rates, as presented there—recall from table 9.6 that 10 to 20 percent of bids are never completed. This time series also includes all *control* bids, and not just bids that result in delistings, as presented in Andrade and collegues. In the sample of large bids analyzed earlier, in both the United States and the United Kingdom, approximately 5 percent of completed control bids do not result in 100 percent of ownership, and an average of 15 to 20 percent of the target's shares remain outstanding after the bid, so that some would continue to be listed after the bid, and not appear in the CRSP M&A delisting sample.

Consistent with hypothesis 9, as reflected in the bottom right cell of the table, the overall control bid incidence rate in the United Kingdom from 1990 through 2008 was 77 percent of that in the United States, and in fourteen of the eighteen years in the sample, the U.S. rate exceeds that of the United Kingdom, usually by a significant margin. These findings are consistent with Rossi and Volpin (2004), who report that 66 percent of U.S. listed firms were acquired in their cross-country analysis of Thomson's M&A database from an earlier but overlapping period, versus only 54 percent of UK listed firms—a ratio of 82 percent. While many other factors may contribute to this difference, a lower bid incidence rate in the United Kingdom is consistent with the findings presented before—that break fee law inhibits some bids that might otherwise occur if the target were free to provide an initial bidder with insurance against the risk of competition.

9.3.4 Break Fee Litigation

What about litigation? Does U.S. reliance on court-enforced fiduciary duties to control the bidding process have an observable effect on the number of disputes generated by bids? The data in table 9.7 suggest the answer to that question is yes: bids in the United Kingdom simply do not generate reported litigation,[22] whereas 5 percent do in the United States. But that difference does not appear to be attributable to break fee disputes. Litigation

---

22. Prior to the adoption of the bright-line rule in the Takeover Code, there was occasional litigation concerning break fees. See Tarbert (2003); Takeover Panel (UK), Decision 1986/2 (Jan. 29, 1986) (approving break fee adopted in fight between Guiness PLC and Argyll Group PLC for Distillers PLC).

Table 9.6   Bid incidence, United States vs. United Kingdom, 1990–2008

| | UK | | | | U.S. | | | (i) |
	(a) No. of domestic listed firms	(b) No. of control bids for listed firms	(c) No. of competing control bids for listed firms	(d) Control bids per distinct listed firm [(b) − (c)] / (a) (%)	(e) No. of domestic listed firms	(f) No. of control bids for listed firms	(g) No. of competing control bids for listed firms	(h) Control bids per distinct listed firm [(f) − (g)] / (e) (%)	UK vs. U.S. control bid incidence (d) / (h) (%)
1990	2,047	163	10	7	6,134	395	22	6	123
1991	2,058	152	17	7	6,295	327	37	5	142
1992	1,952	90	6	4	6,080	286	23	4	99
1993	1,930	91	4	5	6,750	312	8	5	100
1994	1,933	76	12	3	7,121	422	32	5	60
1995	1,977	92	5	4	7,507	512	59	6	73
1996	2,098	79	9	3	7,993	537	43	6	54
1997	2,036	107	14	5	7,852	615	50	7	63
1998	1,963	167	20	7	7,520	725	36	9	82
1999	1,819	242	37	11	7,569	768	49	9	119
2000	1,923	197	13	10	6,830	666	58	9	107
2001	1,912	119	2	6	6,362	515	36	8	81
2002	2,400	92	4	4	5,664	359	26	6	62
2003	2,315	126	23	4	5,297	382	30	7	67
2004	2,497	82	11	3	5,243	310	27	5	53
2005	2,751	115	15	4	5,125	344	41	6	61
2006	2,898	159	19	5	5,104	441	46	8	62
2007	2,579	109	20	3	5,130	448	45	8	44
2008	2,415	108	14	4	5,611	324	21	5	72
Total	41,502	2,366	255	5	121,186	8,688	689	7	77

Sources: Worldwide Federation of Exchanges (listings and domestic listings) and Thomson Financial (control bids).

Notes: Control bids are bids for 50.1+ percent of a listed target, excluding self-tenders. For United States, listings include Amex, NYSE, and Nasdaq; for United Kingdom, listings are on the LSE. Bids need not be completed. Domestic listings are as reported for the years 1995–2008; for 1990–1994, the three-year average for 1995–1998 is used.

Table 9.7   Litigation reported by Thomson in large bids in the United States and United Kingdom, 1989–2008

	UK bids	U.S. bids	p-value
	A. All bids		
% with litigation	0.0 $(n = 209)$	5.0 $(n = 1,137)$	0.00
Break fee reported	0.0 $(n = 170)$	3.7 $(n = 908)$	0.22
No break fee reported	0.0 $(n = 39)$	10.0 $(n = 229)$	0.00
	B. Cash bids		
% with litigation	0.0 $(n = 136)$	3.9 $(n = 627)$	0.02
Break fee reported	0.0 $(n = 36)$	2.8 $(n = 504)$	0.31
No break fee reported	0.0 $(n = 100)$	8.9 $(n = 123)$	0.00

is actually less frequent in U.S. bids with break fees than in those without break fees (4 percent vs. 10 percent, p-value $< .0001$), and it is only in bids without reported break fees that bid-related litigation reported in Thomson is statistically higher in the United States than in the United Kingdom. Presumably this is because break fees deter bid competition, which is correlated with deal litigation in the United States (8.7 percent of bids facing competition generate litigation reported in Thomson, versus 4.7 percent of bids without competition, p-value $< .10$).

These conclusions should be treated carefully, however, as Thomson's data on litigation appears even more suspect than its data on break fee incidence. Thomson, for example, reports *zero* litigation in $1+ billion bids from 2000 onwards. This may surprise M&A litigators, who fought lawsuits over many of the $1+ billion bids in the Thomson database, including (for example) reported disputes (listed in the appendix) over the 2008 bid for William Wrigley Jr. Co.; the 2007 bids for Lear Corp. and Lyondell Chemical Co.; and the 2006 bid for Stone Energy Co.

To further investigate the extent of U.S. litigation specifically concerning break fees, the break fee cases listed in the appendix were reviewed. Few articulate any "law" that would guide break fee practice. Many concern procedural issues (e.g., whether a complaint, which includes allegations that target fiduciaries breached their fiduciary duties by, among other things, agreeing to a break fee, states a claim; whether plaintiffs' attorneys who sued in part based on break fees are entitled to fees for their efforts). Of those that directly address the substantive question of when and what break fees are legitimate, several Delaware decisions explicitly refuse to provide clear general guidance on the proper size of a break fee, or specific facts that could justify or attack a larger-than-typical break fee, or approve a fee on the primary ground that the same size fee had been approved in prior cases.[23]

---

23. For example, Louisiana Municipal Police Employees' Retirement System v. Crawford, 918 A.2d 1172, Del. Ch. (Chandler, C.) (2007) (stating in dicta: "Though a '3% rule' for termina-

Still, there are decisions[24] that explicitly allow custom and practice to guide case outcomes by dismissing complaints where the break fee in question was within norms, and it is hard to believe that courts would not be more inclined to approve a break fee within customary size ranges than one that is not.

What effects has the general reluctance of U.S. courts to articulate break fee rules had? One could characterize the overall level of break fee litigation as large or small. On the one hand, benchmarked against the United Kingdom, with zero litigation, it is significantly higher, and as reflected in figure 9.2, it has been increasing in absolute terms since the early 1990s. On the other hand, benchmarked against the approximately 8,000 bids for public targets in the United States in the same time period, however, it is less than the 5 percent litigation rate reported by Thomson for the large bid sample, and much smaller than the 34 percent of hostile bids reported by Thomson to encounter litigation in the United States (Armour and Skeel 2007). Also, the number of break fee cases divided by total bids has not increased significantly over the recent past.

More importantly, many of those litigated cases would likely have existed even if break fees were explicitly authorized up to some set percentage and forbidden beyond that percentage, as nearly all of the cases reviewed in the appendix involved claims that the target's boards breached their fiduciary duties in a number of respects, over and above the size of the break fee granted. Typical, for example, are allegations that target boards had insufficient information, overly rushed the sales process, or favored one bidder over another without a reasonable justification. Thus, the marginal effect on litigation incidence of the U.S. courts' reluctance to announce a rule regarding break fee size is likely to be nearly zero. Only if the entirety of the M&A process were to be governed by a set of bright-line rules would the incidence of M&A litigation diminish to UK levels, and even the United Kingdom (as noted before) does not do without M&A litigation—it merely speeds it up and excludes lawyers from participating in it.

In sum, the data are consistent with the general practitioner view that

---

tion fees might be convenient for transaction planners, it is simply too blunt an instrument, too subject to abuse, for this Court to bless as a blanket rule."); In re Netsmart Technologies, Inc. Shareholders Litigation, 924 A.2d 171, 32 Del. J. Corp. L. 941, Del. Ch. (Strine, V.C.) (2007) (stating, in reviewing a deal that included a break fee the court characterized as "modest" in size, "The mere fact that a technique was used in different market circumstances by another board and approved by the court does not mean that it is reasonable in other circumstances that involve very different market dynamics"). Cf. Coates and Subramanian (2000) (recommending courts give bids with fees over 3 percent a "particularly hard look"), quoted in In re Toys-R-Us Shareholder Litigation, 877 A.2d 975, Del. Ch. (Strine, V.C.) (2005) (rejecting any bright-line rules; citing fact that a 3.75 percent fee was not "unprecedented" as part of basis for upholding fee).

24. For example, *Gut v. MacDonough,* Not Reported in N.E.2d, 23 Mass.L.Rptr. 110, 2007 WL 2410131, Mass.Super., August 14, 2007 (NO. CIV.A. 2007-1083-C) (break fees "are customarily included in agreements of this nature . . . the independent financial consulting firm hired by Westborough, RBC, concluded that . . . the amount of the termination fee [i.e., 5 percent, was] reasonable . . .").

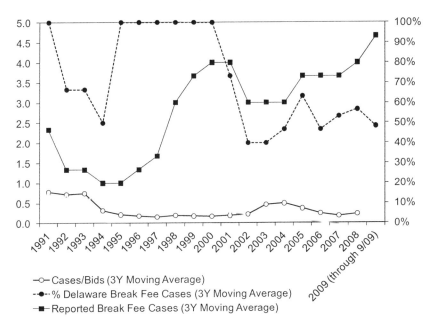

Fig. 9.2 Trends in break fee litigation

UK reliance on a regulatory approach to bid governance essentially eliminates bid-related litigation and its attendant costs, which is common in the United States. At the same time, the more permissive stance toward break fees that has developed in the U.S. litigation-based governance system may actually moderate the amount of bid-related litigation that occurs in the United States, because break fees deter competition and competition generates disputes.

9.3.5 Multivariate Results

The basic univariate results presented before, showing lower break fees, higher competition rates, and lower completion rates in the United Kingdom, may be caused by other factors. Table 9.8 presents multivariate regressions that test this possibility to the extent feasible with available data.

Regressions

In each case, a simple model is reported, with a single explanatory variable (UK = 1 if the target is a UK firm); a second model is reported, with available controls other than year or industry fixed effects; and then a third model is reported, with both year and industry (one-digit SIC code) fixed effects. In parentheses are robust standard errors; coefficients or odds ratios that are statistically significant at the 95 percent level are in bold. In unreported regressions, the limited data on toeholds in Thomson's database was

Table 9.8   Multivariate regressions

	Break fee size (% of bid value) coefficients		Competition rate Odds ratios			Completion rate Odds ratios		
UK	-1.728 **(0.07)**	-1.955 **(0.080)**	2.805 **(0.577)**	2.701 **(0.682)**	2.836 **(0.790)**	0.604 **(0.124)**	0.246 **(0.061)**	0.191 **(0.055)**
CASH	0.012 (0.064)	-0.128 (0.078)		2.048 (0.438)	1.825 **(0.456)**		0.619 (0.115)	0.527 **(0.120)**
TENDER	0.056 (0.079)	0.142 (0.079)		1.264 (0.299)	1.064 (0.279)		5.712 (1.578)	9.023 **(2.910)**
XBORDER	0.003 (0.079)	-0.022 (0.077)		0.740 (0.181)	0.760 (0.188)		1.557 (0.374)	1.653 (0.423)
BIDVALUE ($ billion)	-0.009 (0.003)	-0.008 **(0.002)**		1.026 (0.009)	1.024 **(0.008)**		0.992 **(0.007)**	0.989 **(0.007)**
SICIMATCH	0.002 (0.007)	0.005 (0.007)		0.901 (0.178)	0.858 (0.187)		1.617 (0.288)	1.660 **(0.318)**
LITIGATION							-0.387 (0.288)	0.877 **(0.381)**
Year FE	No	Yes	No	No	Yes	No	No	Yes
Industry FE	No	Yes	No	No	Yes	No	No	Yes
N	946	945	1,346	1,346	1,296	1,346	1,346	1,344
R^2/Pseudo-R^2	0.009	0.132	0.026	0.058	0.094	0.005	0.071	0.132
	OLS	OLS	Logistic		Logistic	Logistic		Logistic

Note: OLS = ordinary least squares; FE = fixed effects.

also included as a regressor, without affecting the reported results. Litigation is included in the models for completion rate, but omitted from the models for break fee size and competition rates, because of the likelihood of reverse causation.

As can be seen, after controlling for other observed factors, compared to the United States, UK break fees are estimated to be even lower, competition rates to be even higher, and completion rates to be even lower than univariate tests would suggest. For break fees, the only significant control (other than time and industry dummies) is bid size: break fees increase at a decreasing rate in bid size. Other factors held constant, UK break fees are nearly 2 percentage points lower than U.S. fees. For competition, cash bids encounter twice as much competition as other bids, other factors held constant; and for each ten billion dollars a bid is larger, the competition rate increases by a multiple of 10.3. Industry and time controls only sharpen the effects on bid competition, which is nearly three times as likely in the United Kingdom than in the United States. The UK bids, which appear to be completed about 60 percent as often as U.S. bids in a univariate regression, become even less likely to be completed after taking into account the combined effects of the higher incidence of cash consideration (which reduces the odds of bid completion), the higher incidence of tender offers (which dramatically increases the odds of bid completion), cross-border bids (which are more likely to close), and same-industry bids (which are also more likely to close). Litigation, present only in the United States, appears to reduce the odds of deal completion, but this effect does not persist after inclusion of time and industry controls.

If we replace the UK dummy with break fee size in the models of bid competition or bid completion, we get similar results. In unreported results, break fee size is statistically significant correlated ($p < .01$) with bid competition (inversely) and bid completion (positively), with and without the same controls show in table 9.8. The point estimates are reasonable and economically significant. In models with year and industry fixed effects, for every point higher a break fee is as a percentage of bid value, the odds of a competitive bid are reduced by 28 percent—for example, from a sample average of 10 percent to 7.2 percent. Likewise, the odds of bid completion are increased by 128 percent—for example, moving from a typical UK break fee of 1 percent to a typical U.S. break fee of 3 percent would increase the completion rate from 90 percent to about 93 percent.

Placebo Tests on Block Purchases

The results just presented are consistent with the hypothesis that the UK approach to break fees has important effects not only on break fee size but also on bid competition and bid completion rates. A skeptic might wonder about unobserved, omitted factors that might correlate with differences between the UK and U.S. M&A markets, on the one hand, and break fee size and bid outcomes, on the other hand. One way to test for this possibility is to run the same regressions using a different data set that consists of UK and U.S. bids that are much less susceptible (or not susceptible at all) to bid competition; namely, block purchases.

For this purpose, we examine bids that were drawn from the initial sample described earlier but were dropped because the bidders sought less than 50 percent of the target's stock in the bid. Such block purchases are either invulnerable to bid competition because the bidder already owns a control block of the target, because (as with a negotiated buyback from a existing blockholder) the bid would not be subject to shareholder approval, or because the block being sought would not plausibly provide control to a competing bidder, who would typically be better off seeking to purchase a similarly-sized block on the open market after the initial bid is completed. In effect, the subcontrol block bids dropped from the initial sample can be used as a "placebo test" of hypotheses 5 through 8.

The placebo sample consists of 626 bids. Of those, 65 percent ($n = 406$) are buybacks—bids by a company for its own stock. The rest ($n = 220$) are third-party bids, but the median bid is for 22 percent of the target, and over a third of the bids are for less than 10 percent. Of those where the bid seeks more than 22 percent, the bidder already owns more than 50 percent of the target in more than 75 percent of the bids, and more than 40 percent in more than 90 percent of the bids. Consistent with the basic idea that break fees are designed to deter competition, or provide insurance against the possibility competition emerges, only six of the nonbuyback placebo bids included a break fee, and only one of the buyback placebo bids included a break fee (the unusual buyback of John Malone's 16 percent toehold in News Corp., which helped preserve 30 percent blockowner's Rupert Murdoch's control and was subject to News Corp. shareholder approval. All were for U.S. targets.

In the placebo sample, unlike the main sample, UK bids encountered no competition, whereas U.S. nonbuyback bids did (although the difference is not statistically significant), and UK bids were more (not less) likely to be completed than U.S. bids, and were completed more often in the United Kingdom than were the aforementioned control bids (95 percent vs. 85 percent, p-value < 0.03). The fact of higher completion rates in the United Kingdom than in the United States—which, recall, is the opposite of what holds in the main sample, where competition is a threat—is not statistically significant when the sample is broken down into buybacks and nonbuybacks (for either subsample), but regains statistical significance for buybacks only after inclusion of the controls used in the main regressions. In sum, the placebo sample shows that in block purchases, where competition is not a serious threat, break fees are uncommon in either nation, UK bids encounter no more competition, and UK bids are, if anything, more likely to be completed than U.S. bids (for buybacks). If something other than break fees is driving the higher levels of competition and lower levels of completion in control bids in the United Kingdom, the omitted factor does not have the same affect on noncontrol block purchases.

9.4   Summary of Findings, Limits, and Lessons

9.4.1   Summary of Findings

The data reviewed in the previous section provide evidence consistent with a number of the hypotheses stated in section 9.2. Break fee law appears to bind in both the United Kingdom and the United States: (1) UK break fees do not exceed 1 percent; (2) U.S. break fees vary more than UK break fees; and (3) the United States experiences break fee litigation, whereas (4) the United Kingdom does not. Break fee demand appears to vary, and the modal demand appears to exceed 1 percent of bid value, so that (5) UK break fees cluster just below or at 1 percent, but (6) U.S. break fees typically exceed 1 percent by two to three times. On the other hand, the data appear inconsistent with common conjectures about the functioning of "common law" courts: (7) U.S. fee litigation appears to be increasing, not diminishing, over time; and (8) U.S. fee variation has not fallen. Finally, the effects of break fee law appears to matter more than to just break fee design: (9) bid competition is higher in the United Kingdom than in the United States; (10) bid completion rates are lower in the United Kingdom than in the United States; and (11) bid incidence for listed target firms is generally lower in the United Kingdom than in the United States.

9.4.2   Limits

A number of factors may limit the extendability of this chapter. First, M&A contests typically promise large benefits to well-funded participants. The parties affected can, in a general sense, afford to lobby and litigate, and are, in general terms, evenly matched. This is not a context in which disputes arise between large, organized, well-funded producers and dispersed resource constrained individuals. One exception—discussed briefly before—was the absence of organized institutional shareholders in the United States when hostile bids first emerged in the 1950s, but even that absence has dissipated over time. Second, M&A contests have few large externalities identifiable ex ante (other than on bidders and shareholders). While the choice of bidder may in fact have important third-party effects (through layoffs, increases in creditor risk, changes in taxes), these effects and their precise incidence are rarely known in advance. Third, M&A break fees are not generally salient—in either political or moral terms—to the public. No politician directly elected by the general population is ever likely to get elected because of his or her position on break fees.

9.4.3   Lessons

With those limits in mind, what are potential lessons from the contrast between the UK and U.S. approaches to M&A break fees?

Observed Advantages of Regulation

The United Kingdom's regulatory approach exhibits clear benefits. It generates little or no litigation, provides clear guidance for market participants, keeps fees low, and increases bid competition. More generally, it may make it harder for target fiduciaries to favor bidders for private benefits, but such a conjecture presumes target fiduciaries are not otherwise constrained or incentivized properly, and that ex post litigation would do a worse job of constraining target agency costs than regulation.

Observed Advantages of Litigation

On the other hand, by capping fees at what is a low amount, relative to that chosen in the less regulated U.S. M&A environment, UK regulation likely results in the underprovision of insurance for bidders for transaction and opportunity costs if they bid and another bidder ultimately prevails, and for the noncontractible certification benefit a bid gives a target. Given that 95 percent of U.S. break fees exceed the 1 percent cap applicable in the United Kingdom, it seems unlikely that all of these fees represent target agency costs. The U.S. litigation approach likely permits more value-adding fees to be used. The result is likely to be more bidding in the United States than in the United Kingdom. If targets are otherwise forced or pressured to sell themselves, the social loss may not be significant. But if targets can and do refuse to put themselves "in play" with a bid they consider too low, and if bidders hold back because they cannot insure against competition risk, there may be welfare losses from too little M&A in the United Kingdom.

To be sure, factors (legal or nonlegal) other than break fees may explain this difference: the U.S. economy may be more dynamic to achieve economies of scale or scope or other benefits of deal activity, and other rules or practices (e.g., inhibitions against high levels of executive compensation and severance in the United Kingdom) may drive the difference. Even if it could be established that the United Kingdom has less M&A than the United States as a result of break fee governance, some would argue that is a good thing, as many deals may be driven by misvaluations or other market imperfections (e.g., Shleifer and Vishny 2003). Net benefits of UK regulation of fees are difficult to gauge, at best.[25]

---

25. An interesting question, not taken up here, would be to compare the performance of firms acquired and not acquired in the United States and the United Kingdom, to see if the difference in bid rates may contribute to differences in observable corporate performance over time.

Missing Advantage of Regulation

While the UK approach seems to provide some of the conventionally identified benefits of regulation, it does not seem to reflect one: expertise. While the UK Takeover Panel does have greater expertise than generalist courts, it does not seem to have used that expertise in devising its rule on break fees. Nothing in the brief statement accompanying the adoption of the 1 percent rule suggests that any careful study or analysis went into the rule, and the Panel has left it unchanged for the past ten years. Indeed, given the character of the rule, it is hard to see how the Takeover Panel could develop expertise; with variation essentially eliminated, they have lost the ability to look for differential effects of different fees.

Missing Advantage of Litigation

Likewise, the U.S. approach, while preserving greater flexibility and variation in break fee use, does not seem to reflect one of the conventionally identified benefits of litigation: evolution toward clearer and better standards over time. The U.S. courts, particularly in Delaware, seem to go out of their way to refuse to provide guidance on what is or is not an acceptable fee, retaining discretion to find the same fee acceptable in one case and unacceptable in another, based on factors that they never identify clearly. As noted before, the general standard used in Delaware—fees that induce bids are acceptable, fees that preclude bids are not—is useless in practice, since nearly all fees may do both. This standard is the same standard used twenty years ago, after dozens of cases have presented Delaware's chancery with the opportunity to refine or clarify the standard. As a result, litigation over break fees in the United States continues at a high pace, showing no signs of diminishing over time.

Nor can Delaware's reluctance to clarify its fee standard be attributed to the general desire of courts to retain some discretion to prevent private parties from evading or working around a clear rule. It would be possible, for example, for the court to establish a presumption that a 2 to 3 percent fee would be presumed to be legitimate absent clear evidence suggesting that it was produced by a violation of the target board's duties in some other respect, or a presumption that a fee over 4 percent would be presumed to be excessive absent clear evidence that the bidder had incurred greater than normal bidding costs. Such presumptions could provide parties with guidance, increasing bidding certainty and lowering legal costs, without committing the court to strike down (or uphold) fees contrary to the presumptions. Delaware courts have not been willing to go even this far.

Stasis in Both Regimes

Neither the United Kingdom nor the United States seem to exhibit meaningful legal change over time, as applied to break fees. Legal inertia can be a benefit: it allows for greater awareness of the legal rule to spread and shape behavior, and it encourages private parties to make investments that depend on the law not changing. On the other hand, if laws are imperfect but can be improved over time, with experience, the fact of inertia in both regimes may be troubling. It is consistent with a public choice explanation of law in both nations.

Interaction of Lawmaker Incentives and Private Interests

In the United Kingdom, the Takeover Code is still dominated by institutional shareholders, who reap the immediate benefits of greater competition conditional on a bid, and whose power to choose among bids would be diminished by a looser regime governing break fees. A looser regime might benefit shareholders by encouraging more bidding, but the incidence of increased M&A would be hard to predict, and would be shared with bidders and other market participants, who face collective action problems already overcome in the United Kingdom by institutions represented on the Takeover Panel. By reflecting institutional shareholder dominance in the membership rules governing the Takeover Panel, the United Kingdom has institutionalized a political victory dating back to the 1950s, which seems highly unlikely to be open to legal changes that would hurt its dominant constituency, even if doing so would benefit the economy or society. In addition, the structure and incentives of the Takeover Panel may explain the initial choice of a bright-line rule. Although the Panel has a full-time staff, Panel members themselves (who decide Panel policy and resolve disputes) have other full-time jobs, and are not compensated for their work on the Panel, which at least blunts—and probably reverses—any incentive they might have to maintain vague standards to preserve disputes. When break fees began to be used more widely in the 1990s in the United Kingdom, the rule adopted by the Panel minimizes the need for Panel guidance or dispute resolution on break fees, reducing the time demanded of Panel members.

In the United States, break fee law remains an opaque preserve of professional lawyers and courts. The loose standards used to evaluate fees generate widely varying business norms and expensive litigation, and prevents others from easily knowing what is and what is not legal, in a key aspect of M&A practice. This state of affairs generates rents for litigators and transactional lawyers, who can honestly claim an ever-so-slightly greater ability to read the legal tea-leaves in a particular context, and leverage that advisory role into boardroom networks and repeat business. It also makes life more interesting for judges, who serve full-time multiyear terms, until they retire and join the ranks of well-compensated lawyers. Delaware's Chancellor Chandler, who wrote one of the recent Delaware decisions firmly rejecting bright-line rule-like approaches to fee review,[26] was a lawyer at one of the

---

26. Louisiana, supra note 12; see also *Orman v. Cullman,* 794 A.2d 5, 45 (2002) (declining to adopt bright-line test for whether a consulting fee was material for purposes of determining a

leading Delaware corporate litigation law firms before becoming a judge.[27] One need not imagine—and I do not suggest—that the Chancellor had any intent to benefit his future self, or his fellow jurists, in writing that decision. All that is required was a judiciary socialized in a culture of standards-based justice (Kamar 1998; Rock 1997). The other Vice Chancellors have exhibited similar concerns for "justice" as expressed in a resistance to rules in favor of standards.[28] In the United States, the cadre of deal lawyers are at the forefront of defending Delaware, and its judiciary, against the slightest risk of intrusion by Congress or the SEC and its tendency toward bright-line rules.[29]

At the same time, a simple dichotomy of UK regulation protected by institutions and U.S. litigation protected by lawyers is overly simple. The UK approach to break fees is in the context of a legal system that still relies to a significant extent on litigation. Even the subject of M&A is governed by a system that is at most a hybrid—a specialized regulatory body applying general standards—but using a bright-line rule for break fees. And the U.S. approach is in the context of a legal system that is replete with bright-line rules, including rules adopted by the SEC,[30] statutes adopted by the Delaware legislature,[31] and rules articulated by the Delaware courts.[32] In the United States, too, institutional shareholders have become increasingly

director's independence in reviewing a conflict transaction) (Chandler, C.). There is a certain irony in the Chancellor's refusal to provide better guidance to practitioners, given his criticism of the failure of practitioners to provide sufficient guidance to courts in drafting M&A contracts. Cf. *United Rentals, Inc. v. RAM Holdings, Inc.,* et al. Civil Action No. 3360-CC (Del. Ch. Dec. 13, 2007) (Chandler, C.), slip op. at 2 (characterizing use of hierarchical phrases such as "subject to" in lieu of harmonizing disparate contract language as "inartful drafting") with *United Rentals, Inc. v. RAM Holdings, Inc. and RAM Acquisition Corp.,* case: 937 A.2d 810 (Del. 2007) (Chandler, C.) (characterizing agreement as the product of "a deeply flawed negotiation in which both sides failed to clearly and consistently communicate their client's positions" but holding that an "interpretation of the Agreement that relies on the parties' addition of hierarchical phrases, instead of the deletion of particular language altogether, is not unreasonable as a matter of law" and acknowledging that "the law of contracts . . . does not require parties to choose optimally clear language; in fact, parties often riddle their agreements with a certain amount of ambiguity in order to reach a compromise").

27. See www.courts.delaware.gov/courts/court%20of%20chancery/?jud_off.htm (describing careers of current Delaware court); see also www.paulweiss.com/resources/news/detail .aspx?news=1947 (announcing move of recently retired vice-chancellor to start major New York law firm's Delaware office).

28. For example, Netsmart, supra note 25 (Strine, V.C.).

29. Comments from major law firms on the recently proposed SEC rule providing shareholders access to company proxy statements illustrates the point. See www.sec.gov/comments/ s7-10-09/s71009.shtml, and particularly the comment from seven law firms, available at www .sec.gov/comments/s7-10-09/s71009-212.pdf at 3 (suggesting the SEC not adopt its proposed rule 14a-11 "in the interests of federalism" in order to allow state law initiatives in Delaware and elsewhere "to flourish").

30. For example, companies with more than $10 million in assets and 500 shareholders must register with the SEC. Securities Exchange Act of 1934 § 12(g)(1); SEC Rule 12g-1.

31. A majority of directors and a majority of shareholders may approve a merger of a company with another and, if desired, cash out other shareholders, by following formal steps specified in D.G.C.L. § 251.

32. For example, Delaware shareholders may not seek to enjoin a merger simply on the ground that it will convert their stock into cash or stock of another company (Weiss 1983).

active in politics over the past twenty years, but have exhibited no general preference for regulation over litigation, and no interest in lobbying to law relevant to break fees. At a minimum, this suggests that a plausible theory of the incidence of regulation and litigation will require finer explanatory variables than those that apply to nations as a whole, such as their legal origin, and will need to include some allowance for historical contingencies. A theory that points to differential collective action costs will need to attend to the fact that the same set of trade organizations and institutions can produce a system that includes bright-line rules and vague standards simultaneously. The vices and virtues of each method are likely to have different values at different levels of legal specificity. Exploring law with that much precision will no doubt complicate the theory, and perhaps make it difficult to articulate any plausible regularities spanning laws within a nation, much less across multiple nations, and make it harder for an institution like the World Bank to use the analysis to create simple rule-like schemes to reward or punish growth-oriented legal reform. Resulting theories may lack the merit of simplicity, but have the virtue of truth.

9.5 Conclusion

This chapter has contrasted UK and U.S. governance of M&A break fees with a view to what the contrast can teach us about the trade-offs between litigation and regulation, including how laws change under each regime over time. The United Kingdom caps fees at a low level with a simple ex ante rule based not on regulatory expertise but on an arbitrarily chosen percentage of bid value, which nonetheless has the virtues of clarity and lower litigation costs, and enhances competition conditional on an initial bid. The U.S. courts evaluate fees ex post with a complex standard, allowing for greater variation and higher average fees, reducing the risk of bidding and possibly increasing M&A overall, at the cost of significant amounts of ongoing litigation, in part because courts resist articulating clear rules. Laws in each nation exhibit inertia; are protected by entrenched interest groups (institutions in the United Kingdom, lawyers in the United States); and coexist with the opposite approach (litigation in the United Kingdom, regulation in the United States), even within the domain of M&A law. Subject to strong limits on external validity, the case study suggests that interest groups may be the most important factors shaping the initial choice between regulation and litigation, even for otherwise similar nations in a similar context, and that a combination of interest groups formed in response to a given choice, as well as lawmaker incentives, may preserve those choices even after the conditions giving rise to the initial choice have passed away.

Appendix

List of U.S. Cases Concerning M&A Break Fees 1989 to 2009 Reported in Westlaw "Allcases"

Initial Search Terms: "(merger "tender offer")" and "("break fee" "termination fee" "bust-up fee" "break-up fee)" and "fiduciary duty". Search returned 225 opinions as of September 9, 2009. Each opinion was reviewed to verify that it concerned an M&A break fee, and an allegation that such a fee violated the target board's fiduciary duties, or was unenforceable as a matter of public policy. Opinions were excluded if they were in bankruptcy court (where bankruptcy law applies), only involved disclosure claims regarding break fees, or involved disputes between the bidder and the target as to whether the fee was payable (other than on grounds that it violated the target board's fiduciary duties or public policy).

2009

1. *Pennsylvania Avenue Funds v. Borey,* Slip Copy, 2009 WL 902070, W.D.Wash., March 30, 2009 (NO. C06-1737RAJ)

2. *Somers ex rel. EGL, Inc. v. Crane,*—S.W.3d—, 2009 WL 793751, Tex.App.-Hous. (1 Dist.), March 26, 2009 (NO. 01-07-00754-CV, 01-08-00119-CV)

3. *Indiana State Dist. Council of Laborers v. Brukardt,* Slip Copy, 2009 WL 426237, Tenn.Ct.App., February 19, 2009 (NO. M200702271COAR3CV)

4. *In re Wm. Wrigley Jr. Co. Shareholders Litigation,* Not Reported in A.2d, 2009 WL 154380. Del.Ch., January 22, 2009 (NO. CIV.A. 3750-VCL)

2008

5. *In re Bear Stearns Litigation,* 23 Misc.3d 447, 870 N.Y.S.2d 709, 2008 N.Y. Slip Op. 28500, N.Y.Sup., December 04, 2008 (NO. 600780/08)

6. *Greenspan v. Intermix Media, Inc,* Not Reported in Cal.Rptr.3d, 2008 WL 4837565, Nonpublished/Noncitable (Cal. Rules of Court, Rules 8.1105 and 8.1110, 8.1115), Cal.App. 2 Dist., November 10, 2008 (NO. B196434)

7. *County of York Employees Retirement Plan v. Merrill Lynch & Co., Inc.,* Not Reported in A.2d, 2008 WL 4824053, Del.Ch., October 28, 2008 (NO. CIV.A. 4066-VCN)

8. *In re Lear Corp. Shareholder Litigation,* 967 A.2d 640, Del.Ch., September 02, 2008 (NO. CIV.A. 2728-VCS)

9. *Ryan v. Lyondell Chemical Co.,* Not Reported in A.2d, 2008 WL 2923427, 34 Del. J. Corp. L. 333, Del.Ch., July 29, 2008 (NO. CIV.A. 3176-VCN)

2007

10. *Gut v. MacDonough,* Not Reported in N.E.2d, 23 Mass.L.Rptr. 110, 2007 WL 2410131, Mass.Super., August 14, 2007 (NO. CIV.A. 2007-1083-C)

11. *In re Topps Co. Shareholders Litigation,* 926 A.2d 58, Del.Ch., June 14, 2007 (NO. CIV.A 2786-VCS, CIV.A. 2998-VCS)

12. *In re Netsmart Technologies, Inc. Shareholders Litigation,* 924 A.2d 171, 32 Del. J. Corp. L. 941, Del.Ch., March 14, 2007 (NO. CIV.A. 2563-VCS)

13. *Shaper v. Bryan,* 371 Ill.App.3d 1079, 864 N.E.2d 876, 309 Ill.Dec. 635, Ill.App. 1 Dist., March 08, 2007 (NO. 1-05-3849)

14. *Louisiana Municipal Police Employees' Retirement System v. Crawford,* 918 A.2d 1172, Del.Ch., February 23, 2007 (NO. CIV.A. 2635-N, CIV.A. 2663-N)

2006

15. *Energy Partners, Ltd. v. Stone Energy Corp.,* Not Reported in A.2d, 2006 WL 4782287, Del.Ch., October 11, 2006 (NO. 2402-N, 2374-N)

16. *In re Guidant Corp. Shareholders Derivative Litigation,* Not Reported in F.Supp.2d, 2006 WL 290524, S.D.Ind., February 06, 2006 (NO. 1:03 CV 955 SEB WTL)

2005

17. *Romero v. U.S. Unwired,* Not Reported in F.Supp.2d, 2005 WL 2050280, E.D.La., August 11, 2005 (NO. CIV.A.04-2312, CIV.A.04-2436)

18. *In re Toys "R" Us, Inc. Shareholder Litigation,* 877 A.2d 975, Del.Ch., June 22, 2005 (NO. CIV.A. 1212-N)

19. *In re Prime Hospitality, Inc.,* Not Reported in A.2d, 2005 WL 1138738, Del.Ch., May 04, 2005 (NO. CIV.A. 652-N)

20. *In re Wachovia Shareholders Litigation,* 168 N.C.App. 135, 607 S.E.2d 48, N.C.App., January 18, 2005 (NO. COA04-402)

2004

21. *Jasinover v. Rouse Co.,* Not Reported in A.2d, 2004 WL 3135516, 2004 MDBT 12, Md.Cir.Ct., November 04, 2004 (NO. 13-C-04-59594)

22. *Orman v. Cullman,* Not Reported in A.2d, 2004 WL 2348395, 30 Del. J. Corp. L. 635, Del.Ch., October 20, 2004 (NO. CIV.A. 18039)

23. *Consolidated Edison, Inc. v. Northeast Utilities,* 332 F.Supp.2d 639, S.D.N.Y., August 24, 2004 (NO. 01 CIV. 1893 (JGK))

24. *Marcoux v. Prim,* Not Reported in S.E.2d, 2004 WL 830393, 2004 NCBC 5, N.C.Super., April 16, 2004 (NO. 04 CVS 920)

25. *In re MONY Group Inc. Shareholder Litigation,* 852 A.2d 9, 29 Del. J. Corp. L. 956, Del.Ch., February 17, 2004 (NO. CIV.A. 20554)

2003

26. *In re Cysive, Inc. Shareholders Litigation,* 836 A.2d 531, Del.Ch., August 15, 2003 (NO. CIV.A. 20341)

27. *Omnicare, Inc. v. NCS Healthcare, Inc.,* 818 A.2d 914, Del.Supr., April 04, 2003 (NO. 605, 2002, 649, 2002)

2002

28. *Shepard v. Humke,* Not Reported in F.Supp.2d, 2002 WL 1800311, S.D.Ind., July 09, 2002 (NO. IP 01-1103-C H/G)

29. *McMurray v. De Vink,* 27 Fed.Appx. 88, 2002 WL 13793, (Not Selected for publication in the Federal Reporter), C.A.3 (N.J.), January 03, 2002 (NO. 01-1346)

2001

30. *In re: POLICY MANAGEMENT SYSTEMS CORPORATION SHAREHOLDER LITIGATION,* Not Reported in S.E.2d, 2001 WL 34131445, S.C.Com.Pl., December 10, 2001 (NO. 00-40-CP-1289)

31. *First Union Corp. v. Sun Trust Banks, Inc.,* Not Reported in S.E.2d, 2001 WL 1885686, 2001 NCBC 09, N.C.Super., August 10, 2001 (NO. 01-CVS-10075, 01-CVS-8036, CIV.A. 01-CVS-4486)

32. *Shepard v. Meridian Ins. Group, Inc.,* 137 F.Supp.2d 1096, S.D.Ind., April 10, 2001 (NO. IP 00-1360-C H/G)

33. *McMichael v. U.S. Filter Corp.,* Not Reported in F.Supp.2d, 2001 WL 418981, Fed. Sec. L. Rep. P 91,406, C.D.Cal., February 23, 2001 (NO. DECV 00-340VAP(MCX), EDCV 00-196VAP(MCX), EDCV 00-341VAP(MCX), EDCV 00-528VAP(MCX), EDCV 99-182VAP(MCX), EDCV00-223VAP(MCX))

34. *In re Pennaco Energy, Inc.,* 787 A.2d 691, Del.Ch., February 05, 2001 (NO. CIV.A. 18606)

2000

35. *McMillan v. Intercargo Corp.,* 768 A.2d 492, Del.Ch., April 20, 2000 (NO. CIV. A. 16963)

36. *State of Wisconsin Inv. Bd. v. Bartlett,* Not Reported in A.2d, 2000 WL 238026, 26 Del. J. Corp. L. 469, Del.Ch., February 24, 2000 (NO. C.A. 17727)

1999

37. *In re IXC Communications, Inc. v. Cincinnati Bell, Inc.,* Not Reported in A.2d, 1999 WL 1009174, Del.Ch., October 27, 1999 (NO. C.A. 17334, C.A. 17324)

38. *ACE Ltd. v. Capital Re Corp.,* 747 A.2d 95, Del.Ch., October 25, 1999 (NO. CIV.A. 17488)

39. *Phelps Dodge Corp. v. Cyprus Amax Minerals Co.,* 1999 WL 1054255 (Del.Ch. Sept.27, 1999)

40. *Chaffin v. GNI Group, Inc.,* Not Reported in A.2d, 1999 WL 721569, Del.Ch., September 03, 1999 (NO. CIV. A. 16211-NC)

41. *Goodwin v. Live Entertainment, Inc.,* Not Reported in A.2d, 1999 WL 64265, Del.Ch., January 25, 1999 (NO. CIV. A. 15765)

1998

42. *Golden Cycle, LLC v. Allan,* Not Reported in A.2d, 1998 WL 892631, 24 Del. J. Corp. L. 688, Del.Ch., December 10, 1998 (NO. CIV.A. 16301)

43. *Matador Capital Management Corp. v. BRC Holdings, Inc.,* 729 A.2d 280, Del.Ch., November 25, 1998 (NO. C. A. 16758)

44. *In re First Interstate Bancorp Consol. Shareholder Litigation,* 729 A.2d 851, Del.Ch., October 07, 1998 (NO. 14623)

45. *In re Chips and Technologies, Inc. Shareholders Litigation,* Not Reported in A.2d, 1998 WL 409155, Del.Ch., June 24, 1998 (NO. C.A. 15832)

46. *United Vanguard Fund, Inc. v. TakeCare, Inc.,* 727 A.2d 844, 24 Del. J. Corp. L. 358, Del.Ch., June 08, 1998 (NO. CIV.A. 13343)

1997

47. *Brazen v. Bell Atlantic Corp.,* 695 A.2d 43, 65 USLW 2802, Del.Supr., May 27, 1997 (NO. 1997, 130)

1996

48. *Kahn v. Dairy Mart Convenience Stores, Inc.,* Not Reported in A.2d, 1996 WL 159628, 21 Del. J. Corp. L. 1143, Del.Ch., March 29, 1996 (NO. CIV. A. 12489)

49. *Kysor Indus. Corp. v. Margaux, Inc.,* 674 A.2d 889, Del.Super., January 31, 1996 (NO. CIV.A.94C-12-196-JOH)

50. *Wells Fargo & Co. v. First Interstate Bancorp.,* Not Reported in A.2d, 1996 WL 32169, 21 Del. J. Corp. L. 818, Del.Ch., January 18, 1996 (NO. CIV. A. 14696, CIV. A. 14623)

1995

51. *In re Santa Fe Pacific Corp. Shareholder Litigation,* 669 A.2d 59, Del. Supr., November 22, 1995 (NO. 224, 1995)

1993

52. *Paramount Communications Inc. v. QVC Network Inc.,* 637 A.2d 828, 1993 WL 544314, Fed. Sec. L. Rep. P 98,000, (Table, Text in WESTLAW), Unpublished Disposition, Del.Supr., December 09, 1993 (NO. 427,1993, 428,1993)

53. *In re Corporate Software Inc. Shareholders Litigation,* Not Reported in A.2d, 1993 WL 1501008, Del.Ch., November 23, 1993 (NO. CIV.A. 13209)

1992

54. *Seinfeld v. Bays,* 230 Ill.App.3d 412, 595 N.E.2d 69, 172 Ill.Dec. 6, Fed. Sec. L. Rep. P 97,024, Ill.App. 1 Dist., May 22, 1992 (NO. 1-90-3414, 1-90-3415, 1-90-3416)

1991

55. *In re Vitalink Communications Corp. Shareholders Litigation,* Not Reported in A.2d, 1991 WL 238816, Fed. Sec. L. Rep. P 96,585, 17 Del. J. Corp. L. 1311, Del.Ch., November 08, 1991 (NO. CIV.A. 12085)

1990

56. *Roberts v. General Instrument Corp.,* Not Reported in A.2d, 1990 WL 118356, Fed. Sec. L. Rep. P 95,465, 16 Del. J. Corp. L. 1540, Del.Ch., August 13, 1990 (NO. CIV.A. 11639)

57. *Lewis v. Leaseway Transp. Corp.,* Not Reported in A.2d, 1990 WL 67383, Fed. Sec. L. Rep. P 95,275, 16 Del. J. Corp. L. 815, Del.Ch., May 16, 1990 (NO. CIV. A. 8720)

1989

58. *Braunschweiger v. American Home Shield Corp.,* Not Reported in A.2d, 1989 WL 128571, Fed. Sec. L. Rep. P 94,779, 15 Del. J. Corp. L. 997, Del.Ch., October 26, 1989 (NO. CIV.A. 10755)

59. *In re Holly Farms Corp. Shareholders Litigation,* 564 A.2d 342, 58 USLW 2011, Fed. Sec. L. Rep. P 94,486, Del.Ch., June 14, 1989 (NO. CIV. A. 10350)

60. *Mills Acquisition Co. v. Macmillan, Inc.,* 559 A.2d 1261, 57 USLW 2674, Fed. Sec. L. Rep. P 94,401, Del.Supr., May 03, 1989 (NO. 415,1988, 416,1988)

61. *In re Formica Corp. Shareholders Litigation,* Not Reported in A.2d, 1989 WL 25812, Fed. Sec. L. Rep. P 94,362, Del.Ch., March 22, 1989 (NO. CIV.A. 10598)

References

Aghion, P., and P. Bolton. 1987. Contracts as a barrier to entry. *American Economic Review* 77 (3): 388–401.

Andrade, G., M. Mitchell, and E. Stafford. 2001. New evidence and perspectives on mergers. *Journal of Economic Perspectives* 15 (2): 103–20.

André, P., S. Khalil, and M. Magnan. 2007. Termination fees in mergers and acquisitions: Protecting investors or managers? *Journal of Business Finance and Accounting* 34 (3–4): 541–66.

Armour, J., and D. Skeel. 2007. Who writes the rules for hostile takeovers, and why?—The peculiar divergence of U.S. and U.K. takeover regulation. *Georgetown Law Journal* 95:1727.

Ayers, I. 1990. Analyzing stock lock-ups: Do target treasury sales foreclose or facilitate takeover auctions? *Columbia Law Review* 90 (3): 682–718.

Bates, T. W., and M. L. Lemmon. 2003. Breaking up is hard to do? An analysis of termination fee provisions and merger outcomes. *Journal of Financial Economics* 69 (3): 469–504.

Bebchuk, L. 1989. The debate on contractual freedom in corporate law. *Columbia Law Review* 89:1395–415.

Becker, G. S., and G. J. Stigler. 1974. Law enforcement, malfeasance and compensation of enforcers. *The Journal of Legal Studies* 3 (1): 1–18.

Boone, A. L., and J. H. Mulherin. 2007. Do termination provisions truncate the takeover bidding process? *Review of Financial Studies* 20 (2): 461–89.

Burch, T. R. 2001. Locking out rival bidders: The use of lockup options in corporate mergers. *Journal of Financial Economics* 60 (1): 103–41.

Chapple, L., B. Christensen, and P. M. Clarkson. 2007. Termination fees in a "bright line" jurisdiction. *Accounting and Finance* 47 (4): 643–65.

Coates, J. 1999. "Fair value" as a default rule of corporate law: Minority discounts in conflict transactions. *University of Pennsylvania Law Review* 147:1251.

———. 2001. Explaining variation in takeover defenses: Blame the lawyers. *California Law Review* 89 (5): 1301–421.

Coates, J., and G. Subramanian. 2000. A buy-side model of M&A lockups: Theory and evidence. *Stanford Law Review* 53 (2): 307.

Cook, P. J., and J. Ludwig. 2002. Litigation as regulation: Firearms. In *Regulation through litigation,* ed. W. K. Viscusi, 67–93. Washington, DC: AEI-Brookings Joint Center for Regulatory Studies.

Davies, G., and J. Palmer. 2004. Break fees common but not always legal. *International Financial Law Review* (April 2004 Supplement): 179–82.

Diamond, P. A., and E. S. Maskin. 1979. An equilibrium analysis of search and breach of contract, I: Steady states. *Bell Journal of Economics* 10 (1): 282–316.

Dreyfuss, R. C. 1995. Forums of the future: The role of specialized courts in resolving business disputes. *Brooklyn Law Review* 61:1–44.

Ehrlich, I., and R. Posner. 1974. An economic analysis of legal rulemaking. *Journal of Legal Studies* 3 (1): 257–86.

Gennaioli, N., and A. Shleifer. 2007. The evolution of common law. *Journal of Political Economy* 115 (1): 43–68.

Glaeser, E., S. Johnson, and A. Shleifer. 2001. Coase versus the Coasians. *Quarterly Journal of Economics* 116 (3): 853–99.

Glaeser, E. L., and A. Shleifer. 2003. The rise of the regulatory state. *Journal of Economic Literature* 41 (2): 401–25.

Hanson, J., and S. Fraidin. 1994. Toward unlocking lockups. *Yale Law Journal* 103 (6): 1739–834.

Kahan, M., and M. Klausner. 1996. Lockups and the market for corporate control. *Stanford Law Review* 48 (6): 1539–71.

Kamar, E. 1998. A regulatory competition theory of indeterminacy in corporate law. *Columbia Law Review* 98 (8): 1908–59.

Kaplow, L. 1992. Rules versus standards: An economic analysis. *Duke Law Journal* 42 (3): 557–629.

Kennedy, D. 1976. Form and substance in private law adjudication. *Harvard Law Review* 89 (8): 1685–778.

Kraakman, R. R., J. Armour, P. Davies, L. Enriques, H. B. Hansmann, G. Hertia,

K. Hopt, and H. Kanda. 2009. *The anatomy of corporate law: A comparative and functional approach,* 2nd ed. New York: Oxford University Press.

La Porta, R., F. Lopez-de-Silanes, and A. Shleifer. 1999. Corporate ownership around the world. *The Journal of Finance* 54 (2): 471–517.

Landis, J. 1938. *The administrative process.* Westport, CT: Greenwood Press.

Llewellyn, K. 1951. *The bramble bush: On our law and its study.* New York: Oceana.

Montgomery, A., G. Davies, and J. Palmer. 2005. Deal protection measures in the UK. *International Financial Law Review* 24:156–59.

Niblett, A., R. A. Posner, and A. Shleifer. 2008. The evolution of a legal rule. NBER Working Paper no. 13856. Cambridge, MA: National Bureau of Economic Research, March.

Officer, M. S. 2003. Termination fees in mergers and acquisitions. *Journal of Financial Economics* 69 (3): 431–67.

Olson, M. 1965. *The logic of collective action: Public goods and the theory of groups.* Cambridge, MA: Harvard University Press.

Pace, N. M., S. J. Carroll, I. Vogelsang, and L. Zakaras. 2007. *Insurance class actions in the United States.* Santa Monica, CA: Rand Corporation.

Posner, R. A. 1973. *Economic analysis of law,* 1st ed. Boston: Little Brown.

———. 2005. Foreward: A political court (the Supreme Court 2004 term). *Harvard Law Review* 119 (1): 31–102.

Rajan, R., and G. L. Zingales. 2003. The great reversals: The politics of financial development in the twentieth century. *Journal of Financial Economics* 69 (1): 5–50.

Revesz, R. 1990. Specialized courts and the administrative lawmaking system. *University of Pennsylvania Law Review* 138 (4): 1111–74.

Rock, E. 1997. Saints and sinners: How does Delaware corporate law work? *UCLA Law Review* 44:1009.

Rossi, S., and P. F. Volpin. 2004. Cross-country determinants of mergers and acquisitions. *Journal of Financial Economics* 74 (2): 277–304.

Rottman, D., M. T. Cantrell, C. R. Flango, R. Hansen, N. LaFountain, and D. B. Rottman. 2000. State Court Organization 1998. Available at: http://bjs.ojp.usdoj.gov/index.cfm?ty=pbdetail&iid=1203.

Schwartz, A. 1986. Search theory and the tender offer auction. *Journal of Law, Economics, and Organization* 2 (2): 229–53.

Schwartzstein, J., and A. Shleifer. 2009. Litigation and regulation. NBER Working Paper no. w14752. Cambridge, MA: National Bureau of Economic Research, February.

Shavell, S. 1984a. A model of the optimal use of liability and safety regulation. *The Rand Journal of Economics* 15 (2): 271–80.

———. 1984b. Liability for harm versus regulation of safety. *Journal of Legal Studies* 13:357.

———. 1993. The optimal structure of law enforcement. *The Journal of Law and Economics* 36 (S1): 255–87.

Shleifer, A., and R. W. Vishny. 2003. Stock market driven acquisitions. *Journal of Financial Economics* 70 (3): 295–311.

Summers, J. 1983. The case of the disappearing defendant: An economic analysis. *University of Pennsylvania Law Review* 132:145.

Sunstein, C. 1995. Problems with rules. *California Law Review* 83:953.

Tarbert, H. 2003. Merger breakup fees: A critical challenge to Anglo-American law. *Law and Policy in International Business* 34:627.

Thomas, R., and R. Thompson. 2004. The public and private faces of derivative lawsuits. *Vanderbilt Law Review* 57:1747.

U.S. State Department. 2009. Background note: United Kingdom (March). Available at: www.state.gov/r/pa/ei/bgn/3846.htm (visited 8/19/09).

von Jhering, R. 1883. *Der Geist des Romischen Recht.* Leipzig: Breitkopf und Härtel.

Weiss, E. 1983. Balancing interests in cash-out mergers: The promise of Weinberger v. UOP, Inc. *Delaware Journal of Corporate Law* 8 (Fall): 1–58.

Exploring Ex Ante Regulatory Mechanisms for Detecting Prescription Drug Misuse

Stephen T. Parente

10.1 Introduction

The misuse of prescription drugs in the United States is a growing problem. Rates of prescription drug misuse in the United States have risen significantly during recent years, with one study reporting an increase of 2.5 million prescription drug misusers between 2002 and 2007 (SAMHSA 2007; McCabe, West, and Wechsler 2007). The issue is not contained to the United States. A recent report from the UK's National Institute for Clinical Effectiveness (NICE) estimates that 280,000 Britons are abusing prescription opioids.[1] This represents just under half of 1 percent of the UK's general population under the age of sixty-five. The issue is complex because of the many agents engaged in the provision of prescription medications, as well as the regulations placed on the prescribing agents. Beyond the first-party patient and the supplier of the prescription, there is the second-party physician who prescribed the medication, followed by the third-party public or private insurance company who financed the drug, and the fourth-party prescription benefit management firm setting the price for the drug. Complicating matters further, insurance claims data provide an electronic trace of the entire set of transactions that could demonstrate misuse ex post. The complication stems from the fact that ex post measurement using electronic point-of-sale transaction data suggests that an ex ante regulatory approach

Stephen T. Parente is the Minnesota Insurance Industry Professor of Health Finance in the department of finance in the Carlson School of Management at the University of Minnesota.

This project was supported by the Office of the National Coordinator for Health Information Technology, U.S. Department of Health and Human Services. Contract Number: HHSP23320054100EC.

1. See: http://www.nice.org./uk/CG51.

might have limited the scope of the problem, had agents two, three, and four used the available technology.

This chapter presents an exploratory analysis of the extent to which prescription drug abuse for pain medication could be identified prospectively for intervention by health insurers, and supported by law enforcement and the medical community. The chapter proceeds first with a general distinction between misuse and abuse, and how its remedy would be considered in the insurance contract. The second part of the chapter describes the current ex post process for detection after it has occurred by police and law enforcement. The third part presents an ex ante alternative to the ex post "litigation" approach. This alternative approach applies expert systems designed by doctors/pharmacists/statisticians/law enforcement/economists to insurance claims data in order to screen high probability misuse for intervention and education. The fourth section demonstrates how this "regulation" approach might work using the application of a published algorithm. The chapter concludes with a discussion of how this might work as a regulatory approach, either in the hands of law enforcement or private health plans.

10.2   Misuse versus Abuse

When considering the prospect of drug misuse, the question of whether or not drug abuse has occurred is confusing and warrants attention. One of the clearest distinctions between abuse and misuse comes from the American Medical Association's Committee on Alcoholism and Addiction's 1966 definition where abuse of stimulants (amphetamines, primarily) was defined in terms of "medical supervision." Specifically, the Committee stated:[2]

> "Use" refers to the proper place of stimulants in medical practice; "misuse" applies to the physician's role in initiating a potentially dangerous course of therapy; and "abuse" refers to self-administration of these drugs without medical supervision and particularly in large doses that may lead to psychological dependency, tolerance and abnormal behavior.

In this chapter, we will measure both the misuse and abuse of prescribed controlled substances with an understanding that both terms can apply. Misuse will be used as the principal concern, since the medications considered are, at least in the United States, only obtainable through a physician prescription. This process automatically involves the physician, whether willfully giving a potential abuser a stimulant or being deceived by a patient who presents a false medical need (e.g., severe pain from a sprain with no easy way to verify physical evidence that indicates damage to the patient). National Institute for Clinical Effectiveness (NICE) posits a more contemporary definition of misuse defined as:[3]

2. See: http://jama.ama-assn.org/cgi/content/abstract/268/8/1012.
3. See: http://www.nice.org.uk/CG51.

Intoxication by—or regular excessive consumption of and/or dependence on—psychoactive substances, leading to social, psychological, physical or legal problems. It includes problematic use of both legal and illegal drugs (including alcohol when used in combination with other substances).

This definition of misuse suggests that the physician must be playing a role in the prescribing of controlled substances. Furthermore, it emphasizes the societal costs of misuse of controlled substances and why law enforcement agencies seek to mitigate and prevent the inappropriate use of these pre-scribed medications.

10.3 The Problem of Controlled Substance Misuse

The diversion, abuse, and inappropriate use of controlled substances are subjects of continuing concern to law enforcement, the medical community, insurers, and policymakers alike. These parties seek a balance between pre-venting diversion/abuse and encouraging the use of controlled substances for legitimate medical need, particularly for pain management. A number of clinical practice guidelines, consensus statements from professional asso-ciations, and state laws and policies emphasize that it is essential for opioid analgesics to be available for the treatment of moderate to severe pain, and that prescribing should be individualized to the patient. Although some progress has been made in treating pain, under-treatment of pain is still prevalent.

Media coverage of diversion and abuse of controlled substances, as well as uncertainty regarding potential disciplinary action, may cause physicians to hesitate when considering treatment for a patient who could require long-term or high doses of opioids. This is exacerbated when physicians have trouble discerning between a patient with a legitimate pain problem and one who is feigning pain to obtain drugs for abuse or diversion. Because pain is subjective and cannot be measured or ruled out by laboratory tests or physical examination, physicians rely largely on their interpretation of patient interviews and histories to determine a patient's need for analgesics. However, they often find themselves in the predicament of wanting to treat seemingly legitimate patient needs without having information about their patients' prescription drug and medical histories, which would help identify and address any problems. A 1999 report from the Institute of Medicine stressed that most medical errors do not result from individual practitioners' recklessness. Instead, they can be attributed to faulty processes and systems that lead people to make mistakes or fail to prevent them through lack of in-formation and support in a complex working environment. Solving problems within the health care industry requires the design of systems and processes to help avoid errors, to minimize the damage caused by errors that do occur, and to analyze the pattern of errors to discover ways to prevent them.

Despite technological advances and the wealth of strategic knowledge within administrative health care claims databases, currently only seventeen states operate electronic prescription monitoring programs, which vary in their goals, structure, and oversight by the health profession. Presently, few health plans analyze the data to identify potential misuse of controlled substances. Access to this aggregate information on patients is not readily provided to physicians, restricting their ability to provide quality care. In response to this need, my colleagues and I developed a software program that identifies patients with potential prescription mismanagement or abuse/diversion issues.

10.4   Comparing Ex Post Litigation versus Ex Ante Regulation of Drug Misuse

In the last two decades, many public policy initiatives have been started to mitigate the misuse of controlled substances through education programs in schools and communities. Despite this emphasis on prevention, the most likely public policy interaction occurs through ex post litigation, where law enforcement officials seek to detect and prosecute systematic misuse and diversion schemes. In these cases, evidence of misuse and diversion is used to prosecute the drug users as well as the physician prescribers. This ex post litigation approach is expensive, and it is difficult to show its impact beyond media coverage of exceptional cases.

In contrast, an ex ante regulatory approach to drug misuse would take a more comprehensive approach. It would combine the law enforcement activity with surveillance of electronic prescribing systems and interventions to stop or delay prescriptions in order to make sure diversion or patient-initiated abuse does not occur. The intervention analysis uses the same data available to pharmacists (and some physicians) and could succeed in creating an ex ante regulatory system. Such a system would go beyond the current ex post use of electronic data to identify an adverse practice pattern for intervention as well as litigation. To be a truly ex ante system, the electronic data would be used in real time to prevent the prescription from being received by the abusing or diverting recipient. This ex ante approach would be more regulatory in nature and would have to carefully examine mechanisms to minimize false positives in misuse identification. Failure to do so would create an access-to-care problem for severe pain patients with legitimate need for prescribed medication.

A regulatory approach could also be viewed as a fraud mitigation device. For example, the ex ante risk scoring of credit card transactions at the point of sale to reduce fraudulent purchases is quite analogous to the issue of preventing prescribed medication misuse. Health care fraud is a serious and expensive issue in the United States. The National Health Care Anti-Fraud Association (NHCAA) estimates that in calendar year 2003, at least $51 billion, or 3 percent of the nation's annual health care outlay, was lost to outright fraud. Other estimates by government and law enforcement agencies place the loss as high as 10 percent of our annual expenditure or, in 2009 dollars, $250 billion.[4] In a conceptual model of fraud, a fraudulent consumer/potential patient derives no benefit from medical care through an improvement in health status. Fraud activities diminish consumer welfare by providing an additional cost (directly or indirectly) to patient care to cover the expense to the consumer or the consumer's insurer of an unneeded and possibly fictitious good or service. Thus, a regulatory mechanism that detects prescribed medication misuse can be defined as an activity that uncovers fraud and thereby restores societal resources lost to that crime.

10.5   Methods

The methods for this analysis have three components. First, metrics for identifying drug misuse are introduced based on a set of existing algorithms. Second, the study population for this analysis is introduced. Finally, the empirical specification for a multivariate analysis to identify the patient level attributes associated with most common metrics of abuse is presented.

10.5.1   Identifying Metrics for Drug Misuse

For this analysis, we will use a drug misuse algorithm developed in consultation with key experts in the field including a multidisciplinary expert panel consisting of addictionists, pain physicians, psychologists, psychiatrists, law enforcement officials, and pain management nurses. This algorithm, called CS-PURE, published in 2004 (see Parente et al. 2004), represents the most comprehensive nonproprietary tool available at present to measure drug misuse. The CS-PURE can be applied to claims databases in order to identify possible abuse or diversion of controlled substances by patients, or mismanagement by prescribers. The CS-PUREs are not conclusive on inappropriate use; rather they aim at improving patient safety and outcomes by alerting prescribers and insurers of potential problems so that further evaluation can be conducted. The expert panel reached consensus on a thirty-eight prototype CS-PURE for evaluation. Some of the CS-PUREs were based on similar patterns, but reflected variations in specific medications used and changes in the duration of consecutive or overlapping days of medication use; for example, continuous overlap of two or more benzodiazepines for at least thirty, sixty, or ninety days.

Computer programs based on the expert panel's originally suggested thirty-eight CS-PURE patterns were developed using SAS (statistical

---

4. *Healthcare Fraud: A Serious and Costly Reality for All Americans,* National Health Care Anti-fraud Association, http://www.nhcaa.org/pdf/all_about_hcf.pdf site visited on 8/14/2005.

analysis software), to apply the CS-PURE to the health care claims data. Detailed utilization profiles were produced for the patients identified by each of the prototype CS-PUREs. An interdisciplinary project team, comprised of pharmacists, computer programmers, and health services researchers, reviewed and assessed these profiles for the accuracy of the computer coding. At the conclusion of this process, the original thirty-eight CS-PUREs were reduced to thirty-four CS-PUREs. This change reflected the deletion of four of the original CS-PUREs because they identified an extremely low number of patients and, thus, determined to be of comparably limited use.

Table 10.1 presents the top ten metrics of prescribed opioid misuse based on the final thirty-four published CS-PUREs. The top ten metrics' distinction was based on an optimal mix of period prevalence of the pattern found in the population. In addition, the percent of expert agreement in patient profile review of whether the algorithm truly found a misuse case was also considered. The largest two metrics, measured at the patient level, defined as ≥ 6 pharmacies dispensing scripts to a patient for opioids and ≥ 4 physicians prescribing controlled substances in a year, constitute .21 percent and .13 percent of the health plan's population, respectively. Law enforcement officials agreed with roughly half of the cases. For two of the other eight remaining metrics, law enforcement agreed with 100 percent of the cases, presented through claims data alone, that intervention was required.

In figure 10.1 a national representation of drug-misuse from the ≥ 4 prescriber algorithm shows significant regional heterogeneity with no clear pattern by large regional census areas of the Northeast, South, Midwest, or West, or urban and rural state comparisons. At the very least, a national representation can help to prioritize resources for possible ex ante intervention. The data presented in figure 10.1 are from 2002. As a verification of the algorithm's potential, the state of Kentucky stands out as a high potential drug misuse and diversion state. This is supported by the July 2002 National Drug Intelligence Center report, which stated that from 1998 through 2000, treatment for the abuse of prescription drugs accounted for 20 percent of all treatment admissions in the state, and the number of patients seeking treatment for Oxycodone addiction increased 163 percent.[5] Since that time, Kentucky has installed an electronic prescriber early warning system, the Kentucky All Schedule Prescription Electronic Reporting (KASPER), to allow law enforcement officials to monitor controlled substance prescriptions dispensed in Kentucky.

For this analysis, we focused on the four substance abuse misuse algorithms. The criteria used for selection were the most prevalent patterns and those where law enforcement officials have the greatest agreement for intervention and, thus, support an ex ante regulatory mechanism. These algorithms are used in the following empirical analysis:

5. See: http://www.medicalnewstoday.com/articles/135591.php.

Table 10.1 Top 10 metrics for prescribed opioid misuse

CS-PURE	Pattern of controlled substance misuse	Period prevalence (%)	Experts agree misuse			Experts agree evaluation (%)	Experts agree intervention (%)
			Overall (%)	Clinical (%)	Legal (%)		
1	**Multiple prescribers (≥ 6 prescribers for same drug)**	0.21	55	59	48	60	59
2	**Multiple pharmacies (≥ 4 different pharmacies for same drug)**	0.13	59	64	51	64	64
3	Chronic use of (≥ 4 prescriptions in 6 months) carisoprodol	0.13	64	68	58	68	71
4	Continuous overlap of ≥ 2 different benzodiazepines for ≥ 30 days, when 1 is for alprazolam	0.06	56	58	50	56	55
5	**Estimated ≥ 4 g of acetaminophen/day**	0.03	100	100	100	100	100
6	**≥ 2 prescriptions for meperidine with > 2 days supply**	0.02	100	100	100	100	100
7	Chronic use of (≥ 4 prescriptions in 6 months) butorphanol	0.02	56	50	67	100	100
8	Continuous overlap of ≥ 2 different benzodiazepines for ≥ 90 days, when 1 is for clonazepam	0.01	63	67	54	65	63
9	Continuous overlap of ≥ 2 different benzodiazepines for ≥ 90 days, when 1 is for diazepam	0.00	63	65	60	60	60
10	Overlap of ≥ 2 different sustained-release or long-acting opioids for ≥ 90 consecutive days	0.00	63	67	50	69	69

Note: Bold = Used for Study.

Prevalence Range

High:>2+ SD   Medium: −2 <=Mean<=2SD   Low: <-2 SD

Fig. 10.1   National variationin pain medication misuse, multiple prescribers, ≥ 4, 2002

- Multiple Prescribers (six or more prescribing physicians) for controlled substance in one year.
- Multiple Pharmacies (four or more) where controlled substances were received in one year.
- Chronic Use (180+ days four or more grams), Stadol.
- 2+ concurrent scripts for Demerol w/day supply greater than two.

10.5.2   Data Sources

The data source for the analysis is a large national employer with over 300,000 covered lives in multiple states. Both medical and pharmacy claims data for two years were available for analysis. Enrollment data were available as well to ensure that the employee or their dependents were enrolled in a health plan for two years to avoid omitted variable bias. The employer's human resource data also included salary information of the contract holder. The data used in the analysis have a common structure, similar to that used by any employer, insurer, or government health insurance program such as Medicaid.

10.5.3   Empirical Approach

The empirical approach for this analysis was completed in three steps. First, the CS-PURE algorithms were run for the employer data previously described; this provided analytic files to generate descriptive statistics and run a bivariate analysis where the personal attributes of the population are compared between a group with any CS-PURE identification and those without any CS-PURE association. In the second step, a logistic regression analysis was completed to identify the factors most associated with the two most prevalent CS-PURE algorithms. The independent variables used in the regression model include:

- Age (and age-squared) and gender
- Primary contract holder (i.e., subscriber)
- Medicare/retiree contract
- Out-of-pocket premium for insurance contract
- Wage salary
- Prior year incidence of exceeding consumer cost of insurance (premium and pharmacy copayments)

Beyond the age, gender, and income variables, additional information was included to provide a proxy for health risk, as well as prior consumption based on the previous year's claims data. Specifically, the dollar amount of a person's excess expenditure beyond their own cost-sharing contribution to the health plan was computed for the prior year (2004). The cost-sharing contribution included premium price, copayments, deductibles, and coinsurance paid by the employee. In terms of insurance, a positive excess amount would be regarded as a medical loss greater than the insured contribution to the health plan. The expectation was that a patient with a history of health problems and a higher level of medical loss in the previous year would be likely to have high consumption in a second year. Also included in the model was whether or not the contract was for a Medicare recipient who would have prescription drug coverage provided by their employer as well as retiree designation, which could occur before the age of sixty-five. The concurrent out-of-pocket premium was also included to provide a control for the generosity of the health plan benefit, which could influence the likelihood someone would get a less costly (in terms of reduced cost sharing) prescription, intended for misuse or diversion, from their physician.

The last part of the empirical modeling was a generalized linear model (GLM) regression model on the overall CS-PURE count. This approach accounts for the fact that a patient may use multiple methods for drug misuse. Thus, a positive and significant coefficient would be associated with attributes of an individual likely to escalate drug misuse and diversion.

10.6   Results

Table 10.2 presents the period prevalence of the misuse metrics selected for analysis. One thing to note is the significant increase in the prevalence of multiple prescriber and multiple pharmacy algorithms compared to the 2004 article where they were first reported with a national sample of claims data. For example, in table 10.1, the period prevalence for multiple prescribers was 0.21 percent. In table 10.2, the prevalence has increased dramatically to 0.90 percent. Just over 2 percent (2.19 percent) of the population would be flagged for any CS-PURE. This is also a substantial increase since 2004, when the prevalence of any CS-PURE was 0.5 percent. With respect to the misuse metrics most identified by law enforcement as needing intervention, the prevalence ranged from 0.04 percent to 0.0089 percent. Of this employer's population, 0.04 percent would be eighty-one individuals a year who could face criminal charges for misuse or diversion.

Table 10.3 shows the results of the bivariate analysis. Of 202,791 continuously enrolled members, over 2 percent, or 4,431, have any indication of misuse indicated by CS-PURE metrics chosen for this analysis. Those who have a misuse flag are younger, are associated with a higher earning employee, and are less likely to be the contract holder. If not the contract holder, the insured would be the spouse or dependent of the contract holder. Those with less out-of-pocket payments are more likely to have a misuse flag. However, if the insured members have expenses greater than the amount paid for the insurance contract (including premium and copayments), they were more likely to have been flagged. This may be a cause for concern, as it suggests a serial pattern of fraud and misuse. It also could indicate someone in great pain from a chronic condition who relies on multiple pharmacies and prescribers. Even in the most generous cases, law enforcement officials found half of these flagged cases required intervention.

Tables 10.4 and 10.5 display the logistic regression results of the attributes

Table 10.2   **Misuse pattern period prevalence in sample ($N = 202,791$)**

Variable description	Sample mean
CS-PURE	
Multiple Prescribers (6 or more prescribing physicians) for controlled substance in one year.	0.9024%
Multiple Pharmacies (4 or more) where controlled substances were received in one year.	1.6115%
Chronic Use (180+ days 4 or more grams), Stadol	0.0464%
Chronic Use (180 days), Demerol, Brand+generic	0.0207%
2+ concurrent scripts for Demerol w/day supply greater 2	0.0089%
Any CS-PURE	2.19%
CS_PURE count	0.03

Table 10.3   **Attributes of individuals with any CS-PURE**

Variable description	Any CS-PURE flag		No CS-PURE flag	
	Sample mean	Standard deviation	Sample mean	Standard deviation
Insured characteristics	$N = 4,431$	$N = 198,360$		
Insured age in 2005	52.08	19.28	56.30	21.01***
Age squared in 2005	3,084.30	1,897.92	3,611.34	2,132.14***
Insured is female = 1, male = 0	62.5%	48.4%	62.0%	48.5%
Wage salary (in thousands)	$42.57	$32.78	$40.54	$34.56***
Insured is a primary contract holder = 1, else 0	58.6%	49.3%	68.8%	46.3%***
Medicare/retiree contract = 1, else 0	26.0%	43.8%	37.5%	48.4%***
Out-of-pocket insurance premium 2005 (in thousands)	$0.69	$1.54	$0.74	$1.47*
Amount over loss ratio in 2004 (in thousands)	$5.62	$7.27	$2.24	$4.01***

***$p \leq .001$
**$p \leq .01$
*$p \leq .05$

Table 10.4   **Logistic regression results: ≥ 6 prescribers**

Variable description	Coefficient	Standard deviation	P-value	Odds ratio
Intercept	−4.858	0.1219	<.0001	
Insured age in 2005	0.064	0.0059	<.0001	1.066
Age squared in 2005	−0.001	0.0001	<.0001	0.999
Insured is female = 1, male = 0	−0.026	0.0493	0.60	0.975
Wage salary (in thousands)	−0.00203	0.000877	0.02	0.998
Insured is a primary contract = 1, else 0	−0.5577	0.0516	<.0001	0.572
Medicare/retiree contract = 1, else 0	0.1395	0.101	0.17	1.15
Out of pocket insurance premium 2005 (in thousands)	−0.0307	0.0175	0.08	0.97
Amount over loss ratio in 2004 (in thousands)	0.057	0.003	<.0001	1.059
Observations	202,791			

of a person associated with the two most prevalent misuse metrics. In both tables, the attributes' statistical significance and direction of effect on the probability of misuse are nearly identical. While age is positively associated with misuse, older members have a more negative relationship as indicated by age squared term. Gender and retiree status are not significant factors. Income is negatively associated with misuse for both metrics. Out-of-pocket premiums have a negative but statistically insignificant association with misuse. However, the dollar amount paid in the previous year for insured

Table 10.5   **Logistic regression results: ≥ 4 pharmacies**

Variable description	Coefficient	Standard deviation	P-value	Odds ratio
Intercept	−4.430	0.0997	<.0001	
Insured age in 2005	0.033	0.0042	<.0001	1.034
Age squared in 2005	0.000	0.0001	<.0001	1.000
Insured is female = 1, male = 0	0.111	0.0376	0.00	1.117
Wage salary (in thousands)	−0.0035	0.000678	<.0001	0.997
Insured is a primary contract = 1, else 0	−0.3133	0.0397	<.0001	0.731
Medicare/retiree contract = 1, else 0	−0.0829	0.071	0.24	0.92
Out of pocket insurance premium 2005 (in thousands)	0.00159	0.0124	0.90	1.002
Amount over loss ratio in 2004 (in thousands)	0.087	0.003	<.0001	1.091
Observations	202,791			

care beyond the consumer's purchase of the insurance contract that year is positively and significantly associated with misuse. If the insured person is genuinely misusing a controlled substance, this suggests a serial behavior and significant opportunity for intervention, given that they would have been caught by law enforcement if ex post methods were successful. If ex post methods are used successfully, this person would have been caught.

Table 10.6 reports the results of a GLM regression to show the attributes most associated with multiple instances of misuse. This model shows more significant relationships with potential fraud/misuse than the metric-focused logistic regressions. Age remains a significant factor where older, but not too much older, insured individuals are more likely to misuse. There is now a significant and positive relationship associated with a female contract holder. One of the strongest negative relationships is associated with nonprimary contract holders. This makes sense because the consequence of being discovered misusing drugs would mean more to an employee; they could face job termination if caught. The consequences for a spouse or dependent are less direct and explain the negative relationship with primary contract holders. Income remains a negative factor. The loss ratio metric, however, is quite significant and positive.

10.7 Discussion

There are several original findings from this analysis. With respect to identifying patterns that could be used for ex ante regulation of controlled substance misuse, the analysis suggests that those likely to misuse are older (but not very much older), low wage earners, women, not the primary insurance contract holder, and are expending more than the actuarial fair value of an insurance contract. The analysis also indicates that the overall period

Table 10.6   GLM regression—CS-PURE count

Variable description	Coefficient	Standard deviation	T-stat
Intercept	0.021448	0.002114	10.15
Insured age in 2005	0.000533	0.000085	6.30
Age squared in 2005	−0.000009	0.000001	−9.04
Insured is female = 1, male = 0	0.003191	0.000837	3.81
Wage salary (in thousands)	−0.000039	0.000014	−2.71
Insured is a primary contract = 1, else 0	−0.008197	0.000975	−8.40
Medicare/retiree contract = 1, else 0	−0.004078	0.001581	−2.58
Out-of-pocket insurance premium 2005 in thousands)	0.000277	0.000279	0.99
Amount over loss ratio in 2004 (in thousands)	0.005333	0.000099	53.71
Observations	202,791		

prevalence for abuse may have increased from 2002 to 2005. Although it is only a first step in developing a predictive model for an ex ante screening algorithm, the results show there are some person-level attributes that could be strong factors for consideration in designing and implementing a regulatory mechanism.

From a litigation and regulatory perspective, this analysis demonstrates the potential of an ex ante approach that could go beyond programs like Kentucky's KASPER. This analysis suggests that to achieve its full potential, the ex ante approach needs to do more than simply monitor prescriptions out the door. It could assemble person-level profiles of drug utilization and update them in real time. While this would appear to be an aggressive step, it does have precedent in retail sector fraud detection and prevention systems used by the banking and credit card industries. In those systems, multiple data sources at the consumer level are combined and analyzed at the point of sale to suggest an apparent pattern, and to restrict a retail transaction such as the purchase of a flat panel TV at a discount electronics store. Many consumers experience this system when they travel out-of-state, use their credit cards to buy gas more than 500 miles away from home, and receive challenge questions for their zip code. Likewise, a consumer may be denied until completing a phone call with the credit card company when buying an extraordinary retail purchase. The technology exists, and this sort of ex ante regulatory mechanism could be used for controlled substances misuse prevention. A likely obstacle will be privacy advocates. However, a small pilot using credit and debit card purchases of controlled substances could be undertaken using the existing fraud and abuse infrastructure as a regulatory precedent.

The analysis has four limitations. First, the sample used—while large and located in several U.S. states—is not sufficiently large enough for a comprehensive analysis. This could be addressed with a larger sample from an insurer. However, the insurer will not necessarily have the wage information or the contract information that was helpful in identifying a patient level attribute of potential misuse. A second limitation is that the false positive misuse-flagging rate for the two most common metrics is 50 percent. While better than nothing, it suggests that a completely automated ex ante system would require refinement. Our more specific metrics with 100 percent law enforcement agreement had relatively low prevalence, but would need to be retested to make sure the accuracy of the metric has not degraded since 2004. A third limitation is that the algorithms could potentially be out of date, since they are based on older national drug codes. However, the therapeutic class-based algorithms should be accurate for the more specific metrics. Also, not expanding the algorithms to include new prescribed medications/controlled substances on sale since 2004 could constitute a more conservative metric of misuse.

The final limitation of this analysis is that we cannot verify the accuracy of the algorithms. Thus, our results are not conclusive in a fashion similar to ex post case where the accused drug misuser or diverter was found guilty. Instead, we use an expert opinion approach to gather the opinions of clinical and law enforcement that validated a set of cases with respect to their probability of misuse. While this approach is generally accepted in clinical research, it would be best to know, through random police investigations and ultimately criminal trials, whether a particular series of claims actually constituted illegal drug abuse or not.[6] Unfortunately, this research design is outside the scope of this analysis. It should be noted that the law enforcement officials who reviewed the results of the analysis commented several times for egregious cases that they wanted the names of those we profiled (we were not at liberty to share) and that they wanted to use the results as evidence in a court of law.

New electronic health records systems could offer even more opportunities for ex ante regulatory mechanisms. Electronic health record interoperability has tremendous potential to coordinate data systems, create more robust misuse surveillance systems, and could substantially lower detection costs (Brushwood 2003). The current CS-PUREs have substantially lower costs to identify cases with otherwise labor intensive police detective work through the ex post and litigation mechanisms. Interoperability allows for corroborating the validity of online and automated transactions from multiple data sources for any given patient in real or near real time. Interoper-

---

6. Delphi approaches are recently gaining acceptance for ex ante law enforcement planning. For example, in a 2009 working paper Zaloom and Subhedar from Lamar University and using Delphi methods to prioritize events impacting operations from a possible terrorist attack, disasters, or failures in the maritime domain. See: http://dept.lamar.edu/industrial/Ports/Subhedar_041609_MDP_041709-R4-MDP_060609-R1.pdf.

ability and a demand for cross-entity standardization of codes, data structures, and terminologies may be the key to creating the necessary incentive for better care practices, including controlled substance mitigation.

A critical issue to consider is the cost for identification and lack of intervention. Following the publication of the CS-PUREs in 2004, the manufacturer of an oxycodone product encouraged the use of the algorithms to mitigate misuse. The response from health plans was initially positive in 2005 and 2006. Subsequently, the health plans' implementation of the metrics have been challenged by some of the health plans' legal counsel about the consequences of identifying, but not intervening, and possibly being found negligent if an adverse event tied to misuse occurred. If this is indeed a threat to the use of these algorithms, then regulatory protection for public and private insurers might help health plans to detect, monitor, and develop (but not yet deploy) cost-effective strategies, possibly in consultation and open communication with law enforcement. If such a compact was developed, the best of the litigation and regulatory approaches could be combined to address this societal problem.

10.8   Conclusion

This chapter demonstrates the potential of a regulatory mechanism that could be used on an ex ante basis to detect drug misuse for future intervention by law enforcement officials. An analysis from a large employer shows the scope of the problem as well as the opportunity. The cost of insurance claims and e-prescribing surveillance is modest compared to the human capital expense of detection. Effective intervention continues to carry a substantial cost for controlled substance misuse. Using electronic data with a potentially more efficient but effective ex ante approach to tackle the problem of misuse warrants further investigation.

References

Brushwood, D. B. 2003. Maximizing the value of electronic prescription monitoring programs. *Journal of Law, Medicine, and Ethics* 31:41–54.

McCabe, S. E., B. T. West, and H. Wechsler. 2007. Trends and college-level characteristics associated with the nonmedical use of prescription drugs among U.S. college students from 1993 to 2001. *Addiction* 102 (3): 455–65.

Parente, S. T., S. Kim, M. Finch, L. Schloff, T. Rector, R. Seifeldin, and J. D. Haddox. 2004. Using claims data to identify controlled substance patterns of utilization requiring evaluation. *American Journal of Managed Care* 10 (11): 783–90.

Substance Abuse and Mental Health Services Administration (SAMHSA). 2007.

Results from the 2006 National Survey on Drug Use and Health. Rockville, MD: Office of Applied Studies.

Zaloom, V., and V. Subhedar. 2009. Use of the Delphi Method to prioritize events impacting operations in the maritime domain. Lamar University. Working Paper. http://dept.lamar.edu/industrial/Ports/Subhedar_041609_MDP_041709-R4 _MDP_060609-R1.pdf (accessed January 5, 2010).

Natural Disaster Management
Earthquake Risk and Hospitals' Provision of Essential Services in California

Tom Chang and Mireille Jacobson

11.1 Introduction

Regulation and litigation are two different, although often complementary approaches, to dealing with externalities. Where regulation takes an ex ante approach, establishing rules that force parties to internalize externalities, litigation relies on ex post deterrence. Litigation can be thought of as a form of ex post regulation administered by the courts. However, as discussed by Posner in this volume, if ex post damages are large, "the injurer may not have sufficient resources to pay the penalty." In such cases, the presence of an "ex post enforcement problem"[1] suggests courts are likely to fail, and ex ante regulation is the more effective policy tool.

In this work, we study a particular policy problem—California's efforts to ensure the earthquake safety of its hospital infrastructure that is subject to an ex post enforcement problem. The state first established hospital seismic safety requirements in 1973, following the 1971 Sylmar earthquake, which killed forty-eight people at a Veterans Administration hospital. These requirements applied only to the construction of new hospital buildings; existing hospital buildings were indefinitely exempt. As suggested by a wrongful death case after the 2003 San Simeon earthquake (discussed in more detail later), older hospital buildings were, at least in principle, subject to the threat of ex post litigation. The ineffectiveness of ex post litigation in this context is highlighted, however, by the fact that many hospitals responded to the

Tom Chang is assistant professor of finance and business economics at the Marshall School of Business, University of Southern California. Mireille Jacobson is a senior economist at RAND and a faculty research fellow of the National Bureau of Economic Research.

1. Shleifer used this term at the 2009 NBER Regulation and Litigation Conference proceedings.

legislation by deferring new construction in favor of extending the life span of their existing buildings. As such, the 1973 law had the perverse effect of increasing the susceptibility of California's hospitals to seismic damage. This failure had real consequences in 1994 when twenty-three hospitals had to suspend some or all services due to structural damage sustained during the Northridge earthquake.[2]

In many respects reliance on ex post litigation to ensure disaster preparedness seems foolhardy. The potential losses and liabilities from a major earthquake are so large as to strain the limited solvency of hospitals. The limited liability of hospitals creates significant problems for ex post regulation since the expected private costs for any given hospital are likely to be far below the expected social cost. As a result, California responded to the 1994 Northridge earthquake by enacting an extensive regulatory scheme to ensure hospital seismic safety.

While ex ante regulation may be an obvious choice for disaster preparedness efforts, the specific form of regulation adopted is critically important. Traditional regulatory approaches can be both needlessly costly, and generate significant unintended negative consequences. In the context of California's recent earthquake safety mandate for hospitals, the state adopted a traditional command and control type regulatory approach, mandating a timeline by which all general acute care (GAC) hospitals must retrofit or rebuild to remain (a) standing and (b) operational following a major seismic event. The latter goal—ensuring that all hospitals can maintain operations—was tantamount, as the Northridge earthquake caused disruption in services at twenty-three hospitals but little hospital-related injury or death. While hospitals can apply for low-interest loans and bonds from several state and federal sources, they are given no direct financial assistance.[3] Estimates of the direct costs of compliance with the mandate vary, but all put the price tag in the tens of billions of dollars.[4]

The sheer magnitude of these direct compliance costs has lead to significant, unintended distortions on whether and how hospitals provide care. By requiring all hospitals to reach the same earthquake standard, many of those in the highest risk areas are closing or merging, effectively eroding access in the very areas the state seeks to protect. We argue that "market-based" regulatory approaches, specifically the cap-and-trade type mechanisms that have grown in popularity in the context of environmental policy, hold specific promise for disaster management.

We proceed by first describing the evolution of California's approach to

2. See § 130000.8 of the Alfred E. Alquist Hospital Facilities Seismic Safety Act, available at: http://www.oshpd.ca.gov/FDD/seismic_compliance/SB1953/SeismicRegs/hssa.pdf.
3. These sources, which are general in nature, include the CalMortgage and HUD 242 insurance programs.
4. Mead and Hillestand (2007) provide the most recent and most comprehensive estimate—$45 to $110 billion.

ensuring the seismic safety of its hospital infrastructure, from an implicit reliance on ex post litigation to the current very detailed regulatory approach. We trace out some unintended consequences of the current regulation for the availability of hospital services. We provide a back-of-the-envelope estimate of the trade-off the state has made to ensure hospital operations after a seismic event. Finally, we discuss a market-based trading system for earthquake-safe bed obligations that could achieve the same functional goal as the mandate—to ensure that hospitals can sustain and, most importantly, remain operational following a major seismic event—but at a lower cost in terms of money, time, and the long-term availability of services. This approach could be adapted to other mandates that take a one-size-fits-all approach to compliance such as the uniform energy efficiency requirements for new building construction included as part of the American Clean Energy and Security Act of 2009.[5]

11.2   Background: California's Seismic Retrofit Requirements

Until quite recently, the state of California relied heavily on the threat of ex post lawsuits to ensure the safety of private buildings and spaces. Regulation, where passed, has often been weak. For example, a law requiring unreinforced masonry buildings to post "earthquake warning" signs stating a building may be unsafe in the event of an earthquake had no penalty for noncompliance. This law was so lax that full compliace did not ensure protection from liability. For example, in a wrongful death lawsuit brought by the families of two women who died in the 2003 San Simeon earthquake, the building's owners, despite being in compliance with all state and local seismic safety requirements, and being on track to comply with a 2018 deadline for scismic reinforcement, were required to pay $2 million in damages because they knew about "the danger and ignored it for years."[6]

California's original hospital earthquake code, the Alquist Hospital Facilities Seismic Safety Act, dates back to 1973. Prompted by the 1971 San Fernando Valley earthquake, it required all *newly* constructed hospital buildings to follow stringent codes. Consequently, according to experts, the pace of new hospital construction was relatively slow in California and in 1990 over 83 percent of hospital beds were in buildings that did not comply with the act (Meade and Hillestand 2007).

After the 1994 Northridge earthquake—a 6.7M earthquake that hit twenty miles northwest of Los Angeles, caused billions of dollars in damage, and left several area hospitals unusable—California amended the Alquist

---

5. Ironically the heart of the American Clean Energy and Security Act, a.k.a. the "Carbon Cap-and-Trade Bill," is to reduce carbon emissions through a strategy of cap-and-trade.

6. Press release from Friedman | Rubin Trial Lawyers (http://www.frwlaw.us/news.htm).

Act to establish deadlines by which all GAC hospitals had to meet certain seismic safety requirements.[7] The goal of the amendment, SB 1953, was to ensure not only the structural survival of the State's hospitals but also their continued operation after an earthquake (Meade, Kulick, and Hillestand 2002). Table 11.1 describes some of the key provisions of the mandate, which were finalized in March of 1998.[8] By January 2001, all hospitals were to submit a survey of the seismic vulnerability of its building and a compliance plan. Over 90 percent met this requirement (Alesch and Petak 2004). About 70 percent of hospital buildings were deemed to have major nonstructural elements that were not adequately braced to withstand a large earthquake.[9] Hospitals faced a January 1, 2002 deadline for bracing these systems. While we know of no estimates of compliance, this requirement was viewed as a relatively minor aspect of the law. Nonetheless, some (though relatively few) hospitals have requested extensions to comply with this aspect of the mandate.

The first major deadline was January 2008 (or January 2013 with an extension).[10] By this date, all hospitals were to have retrofitted collapse-hazard buildings or taken them out of operation. About 40 percent of hospital buildings were deemed collapse hazards; only 99 or about 20 percent of all hospitals had no such buildings and were thereby in compliance with the 2008 requirements (Meade, Kulick, and Hillestand 2002; Meade and Hillestand 2007). By January 1, 2030, the final SB 1953 deadline, all GAC buildings must be usable following a strong quake. While the legislature thought that hospitals would retrofit collapse-hazard buildings by 2008/2013 and then replace them completely by 2030, most hospitals have chosen to rebuild from the outset due to the high cost of retrofitting. This has effectively moved the final deadline up from 2030 to 2008/2013 and caused an unprecedented growth in hospital construction.

Recognizing that most hospitals would not meet the 2008/2013 deadlines and that initial building assessments were crude, the Office of Statewide Health Planning and Development (OSHPD) authorized on November 14, 2007 a voluntary program allowing hospitals with collapse-hazard buildings to use a "state-of-the-art" technology called HAZUS (Hazards U.S. Multi-Hazard) to reevaluate their seismic risk. Interested hospitals must submit a written request, their seismic evaluation report, and a supplemental report identifying how the original assessment was inaccurate. As of August 2008,

7. Six facilities had to evacuate within hours of the earthquake and twenty-three had to suspend some or all services. See Schultz, Koenig, and Lewis (2003) and http://www.oshpd.ca.gov/FDD/seismic_compliance/SB1953/SeismicRegs/hssa.pdf for details.

8. See http://www.oshpd.state.ca.us/FDD/SB1953/index.htm.

9. For details of how buildings were categorized, see Office of Statewide Health Planning and Development, *Summary of Hospital Seismic Performance Ratings,* April 2001. Available at: http://www.oshpd.ca.gov/FDD/SB1953/sb1953rating.pdf.

10. About 88 percent of hospitals in operation in 2005 applied for an extension to the 2008 deadline and 85 percent (or 96 percent of applicants) received them.

Table 11.1	Key provisions of SB 1953
Date	Requirement
Jan. 2001	Submit risk assessment with NPC and SPC ratings for all buildings and a compliance report plan.
Jan. 2002	Retrofit nonstructural elements (e.g., power generators) and submit a plan for complying with structural safety requirements.
Jan. 2008–Jan. 2013	Collapse hazard buildings should be retrofitted or closed. Extensions available through 2013.
Jan. 2030	Retrofit to remain operational following a major seismic event.

Notes: SPC stands for "Structural Performance Category"; NPC stands for "Nonstructural Performance Category." See http://www.oshpd.ca.gov/fdd/sb1953/FinalJan2008Bul.PDF for extension information.

over 37 percent of GAC hospitals had submitted a HAZUS request.[11] Participation moves the compliance deadline to 2013, if any buildings are still deemed collapse-hazards, or to 2030, if all buildings are reclassified as able to withstand a major earthquake.

Despite the extensions and reclassifications, many hospitals are already engaging in major capital investment projects. Figure 11.1 shows the mean and median value of hospital construction in progress since 1996. After 2001, the year hospitals submitted their building surveys, the mean value of construction in progress rose sharply, from $5.5 to almost $14 million (in 2006 terms). Construction costs increases drive some of this (Davis Langdon, LLP, 2006). While median construction increased as well, this trend started as early as 1996, two years before the details of SB 1953 were finalized. That the median is well below the mean value of construction in progress implies that a few hospitals are spending a lot on construction while the typical hospital is spending much less. Thus, the increase in construction is likely driven by hospitals disproportionately affected by the seismic retrofit mandate and is not simply a general trend.

11.3   Data and Methods

To estimate the effect of SB 1953 on hospital operations, we need to measure exposure to the mandate. Exposure is determined by two factors: (a) a hospital's location, specifically the inherent seismic risk associated with it; and (b) the quality of its buildings. Because building quality may be correlated with hospital operations even absent SB 1953 (e.g., hospitals with more decrepit buildings may be in worse financial condition), we rely on underlying seismic risk to measure exposure. Seismic risk is measured by the

11. Based on author's calculations from data available here: http://www.oshpd.ca.gov/FDD/Regulations/Triennial_Code_Adoption_Cycle/HAZUS_Summary_Report.pdf.

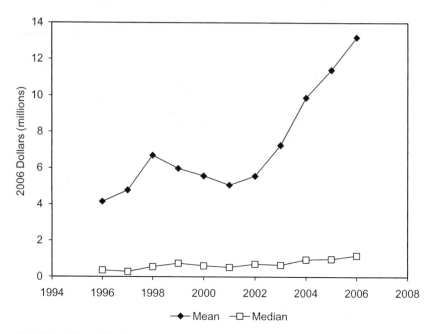

Fig. 11.1   Trends in the mean and median value of construction in progress by California hospitals: Fiscal Years 1996–2006
Source: OSHPD's Annual Hospital Disclosure Reports, 1996–2006.

peak ground acceleration factor (pga), or the maximum expected ground acceleration that will occur with a 10 percent probability within the next fifty years normalized to Earth's gravity.[12] This measure is from the California Geological Survey (CGS) and is matched to every GAC hospital in the state based on exact location.

We assess the relationship between a hospital's seismic risk and several measures of hospital operations—closures, consolidations, and changes in the provision of uncompensated care. Closures are based on OSHPD's Annual Utilization Reports and the California Hospital Association's records for 1996 to 2006.[13] Consolidation data was obtained through a request to OSHPD. Uncompensated care is identified from the 2002 and 2005 Annual Hospital Disclosure Reports (AHDR) as indigent care GAC days, emergency department visits, and clinic visits and is distinct from days/visits reimbursed by county indigent programs. We do not use earlier ADHR data because of changes in the reporting of service provision.[14]

12. This is a standard measure of seismic risk. See http://www.consrv.ca.gov/cgs/rghm/psha/ofr9608/Pages/index.aspx.
13. See http://www.calhealth.org/public/press/Article%5C107%5CClosedHospitals-10-30-08.pdf.
14. Based on discussions with OSHPD, we were advised to not use the data prior to 2001. Results using 2002 to 2006 are quite similar but somewhat less precisely estimated.

Our basic regression specification is:

(1) $$Y_h = \text{pga}_h + \beta X_h + \gamma_c + \varepsilon_{h,c},$$

where Y_h is our outcome of interest—separate indicators for whether hospital (h) shutdown or merged during the study period or the change in the number of days of care provided to indigent patients; pga_h is a hospital's inherent seismic risk, as measured by its predicted peak ground acceleration factor; X_h is a hospital's observable characteristics, and c is a county fixed effect.

County fixed effects allow us to control for persistent differences in outcomes that are correlated with broad geographic seismic risk patterns. This is important because coastal areas in California are generally wealthier and higher seismic risk than inland areas. In all regressions, we also control for the following basic set of hospital characteristics as of 1992—indicators for whether the hospital was public, for-profit, or not-for-profit (the omitted category); the total number of licensed beds; the license age as of 1992 and its square; and whether the hospital is in a rural area. We also control for the hospital's teaching status—whether it had an accredited residency program—and whether it is part of a multisystem chain. Due to data limitations, teaching and multisystem status are measured as of 1996, two years before the details of SB1953 were finalized.

We analyze closures and mergers, which are both dichotomous outcomes, using both linear probability and probit models. We assess changes in uncompensated care using linear regressions. To allow for spatial correlation in seismic risk and hospital operations, we cluster all standard errors by city.

Our identification strategy, which isolates the mandate's effect on hospital operations so long as underlying seismic risk is as good as randomly assigned within counties, is plausible for several reasons. First, most hospitals in the state were built between 1940 and 1970, at a very early stage in our understanding of seismic risk and well before the development of modern seismic safety standards. Second, new construction has been slow relative to estimates of a reasonable building life span (Meade, Kulick, and Hillestand 2002). And, although many hospitals have built new additions, most are in their original location (Jones 2004). And, many of the new additions have been so well-integrated into the original hospital structure that they will need to be replaced along with the older buildings (Jones 2004). Combined with high seismic variability at relatively small distances (e.g., see appendix figure 11A.1), the result is that well-performing hospitals are unlikely to have selected into "better" locations (along seismic risk dimensions), at least within a locality. Finally, this assumption is consistent with discussions between the authors and seismologists, who lament the fact that seismic risk is factored into building construction on only a very gross, highly-aggregated level (e.g., by county), and is further corroborated by empirical tests (shown following) of the distribution of observables.

11.4   Results

11.4.1   Descriptive Statistics

Table 11.2 provides basic descriptive statistics for nonfederal general acute care hospitals in California during our study period, 1996 to 2006. We show the summary statistics for the full sample and then separately for hospitals that are above and those that are at or below median seismic risk. The first row describes mean seismic risk, as measured by the maximum ground acceleration that is expected with a 10 percent probability over the next fifty years, normalized to Earth's gravity. Overall, the mean seismic risk is just below 0.5 g. It varies from a minimum of 0.05 and maximum of 1.15 g's and follows a rather bell-shaped distribution (see appendix figure 11A.2). The next set of rows show the means of the outcomes studied here. About 13 percent of hospitals closed between 1996 and 2006; closure rates do not vary across high and low seismic risk areas. About 12 percent of hospitals consolidated their licenses (i.e., merged their license with another hospital). Although consolidation rates are higher in high pga areas—13.7 versus 10.7 percent— these differences are not statistically significant. Similarly, hospitals in high g areas provide more total days of indigent care but the difference is not statistically distinguishable from zero.

The next set of rows provides means for the control variables included

Table 11.2   **Summary statistics by seismic risk status**

	Full sample	Above median pga	At or below median pga
Seismic risk, pga	0.480	0.659	0.326
	(0.207)	(0.130)	(0.118)
Closed after 1996	0.134	0.133	0.134
Consolidated after 1996	0.121	0.137	0.107
Indigent care days, 2002	271	296	249
	(901)	(994)	(816)
Public, 1992	0.186	0.171	0.200
For-profit, 1992	0.283	0.294	0.273
Not-for-profit, 1992	0.531	0.535	0.527
Multisystem, 1996	0.364	0.370	0.359
License age, 1992	61.3	60.4	62.0
	(13.7)	(14.2)	(13.2)
Licensed beds, 1992	203	234	177
	(188)	(223)	(147)
Residency program, 1996	0.261	0.309	0.221
Rural	0.090	0.005	0.163
Observations	456	211	245

Notes: Seismic risk is measured by the peak ground acceleration (pga) expected with a 10 percent probability over the next fifty years normalized to the Earth's gravity.

in our main regressions. About 19 percent of hospitals in our sample are government-owned; 28 percent are investor-owned, for-profit institutions. Although investor-owned are slightly more common (29.4 versus 27.3 percent) and government-owned slightly less common (17.5 versus 20.5 percent) in above-median pga areas, these differences are both small in magnitude and statistically insignificant. About 36 percent of hospitals were part of a multisystem chain in 1996, the first year we have such data. This characteristic is relatively invariant across low and high pga areas. Although we do not have building age, we can proxy for this by looking at the age of a hospital's license. We measure age as of 1992, the first year of our annual utilization report data. Consistent with Meade and Hillestand (2007), we find that the average GAC hospital is over sixty years old. Hospitals in above seismic risk areas are slightly newer—60.4 versus 62—although this difference is small and statistically insignificant. Starker differences emerge when we look at bed size and teaching status. The average GAC hospital had 203 beds in 1992. But, in high pga areas the mean is 234 beds and in low pga areas it is only 177. Overall, 26 percent of hospitals have a residency program in place in 1996. In high pga areas, over 30 percent have a program, whereas only 22 percent of hospitals in low pga areas have one. These differences in bed size and teaching status partly reflect the fact that low pga areas are disproportionately rural. About 16 percent of hospitals in low pga areas are rural, in contrast to less than 1 percent in high pga areas. Importantly, our analysis uses within-county comparisons in seismic risk, which eliminates much of the urban-rural differences. As we will show next, most of our baseline characteristics do not differ systematically with seismic risk once we control for county.

In table 11.3, we look at the within-county correlation between characteristics of the hospital itself as well as its neighborhood, defined as the hospital's zip code of operation and all zip codes within a five-mile radius of it. We run regressions, similar to equation (1), of a hospital's 1992 or 1996 characteristics, depending on availability, as well as the 1989 level and the 1989 to 1999 change in a hospital's neighborhood characteristics on seismic risk. In all cases we include an indicator for rural status, based on an OSHPD designation, and county fixed effects, because of systematic differences in seismic risk across larger areas within the state.[15] Except where used as a dependent variable for the purposes of this randomization check, our models control for a hospital's license age and its square, the number of licensed beds in 1992 and dummies for 1992 ownership status. In all models, standard errors are clustered at the city level to allow for spatial correlation in seismic risk.

15. For example, San Francisco County is both high seismic risk and high income relative to Sacramento County. As a result, our identification uses only within-county variation in seismic risk. Within-city variation would be even cleaner but many small to medium cities have only one hospital.

Table 11.3 **Seismic risk and the distribution of hospital observables**

A. 1992 hospital characteristics

	Share public	Share NFP	License age	Share with ER	Log (Avg. GAC Los)
pga	0.018	0.007	−8.61	−0.034	0.200
	(0.233)	(0.268)	(7.25)	(0.177)	(0.202)
R^2	0.352	0.108	0.100	0.268	0.089
Mean dep. var.	0.213	0.500	61.0	0.703	1.61
Observations	370	370	370	370	370

B. 1996 hospital characteristics

	Share with detox prog.	Share with NICU	Share with MRI	Share with blood bank	Indigent program
pga	0.166	−0.005	−0.039	−0.129	−0.525
	(0.172)	(0.189)	(0.228)	(0.281)	(0.237)
R^2	0.033	0.106	0.096	0.111	0.423
Mean dep. var.	0.155	0.145	0.456	0.675	0.508
Observations	370	370	370	370	370

C. Neighborhood characteristics, 1989

	Log pop.	Share below FPL	Share Hispanic	Share 5–17 years old	Log median income
pga	0.347	−0.030	0.026	−0.003	0.130
	(0.698)	(0.028)	(0.078)	(0.014)	(0.130)
R^2	0.745	0.296	0.514	0.454	0.459
Mean dep. var.	292,165	0.130	0.249	0.179	34,924
Observations	369	369	369	369	369

D. Growth in neighborhood characteristics, 1989–1999

	Pop.	Share below FPL	Share Hispanic	Share 5–17 years old	Median income
pga	0.025	0.287	0.090	0.056	−0.022
	(0.078)	(0.127)	(0.099)	(0.076)	(0.061)
R^2	0.412	0.402	0.351	0.347	0.564
Mean dep. var.	0.105	0.187	0.349	0.079	0.315
Observations	369	369	369	369	369

Notes: Dependent variables are from OSHPD's Hospital Annual Utilization Reports (panel A), OSHPD's Hospital Annual Financial Data (panel B), the 1990 Census (panel C) and the 1990 and 2000 Census (panel D). Dependent variables in panels C and D are based on zip codes within five miles of a hospital. All models include county fixed effects and a rural indicator. Except where used as a dependent variable, models also control for a hospital's license age and its square, the number of licensed beds in 1992 and dummies for 1992 ownership status. Standard errors are clustered at the city level to allow for spatial correlation in seismic risk. NICU = Neonatal Intensive Care Unit; FPL = federal poverty level; NFP = not-for-profit.

Unlike our main results, we generally find no significant correlation between seismic risk and our hospital or neighborhood characteristics. Panel A presents results for hospital characteristics in 1992. The correlation between seismic risk and the probability that a hospital is government-owned or not-for-profit is small and imprecise. The relationship between seismic risk and a hospital's age, the probability it had an emergency department, or its average length of stay is also insignificant. And the implied effects are small. For example, a 1 standard deviation increase in seismic risk, approximately 0.2 g, is associated with about 1.7 fewer license years off a base of sixty-one years. Moreover, a 1 standard deviation increase in seismic risk implies a 0.7 percentage point lower probability of having an emergency room, off a base of 70 percent, and 4 percent longer average length of stay. In results not shown here, we also tested for differences by ownership status by including interactions between pga and indicators for public and for-profit status (with not-for-profit the omitted category). We do this since we have found some differences by ownership in the way hospitals respond to the mandate (see Chang and Jacobson 2008). However, we find no evidence that baseline hospital characteristics differ significantly by ownership status.

For four of the five 1996 characteristics presented in panel B—the share of hospitals with a drug detoxification program, the share with a Neonatal Intensive Care Unit (NICU), the share with MRIs, and the share with blood banks—the correlation with seismic risk is similarly small and imprecise. The one exception is the probability of participating in a county indigent care program. A 1 standard deviation increase in seismic risk is associated with an 11 percentage point lower probability of participating in the program off a base of about 50 percent. The effects do not differ by ownership status.

Panels C and D provide results for the correlation between seismic risk and the characteristics of the neighborhoods surrounding a hospital. We find no significant relationship between seismic risk and the 1989 characteristics of their neighborhoods—the population, the share living below the federal poverty line, the share Hispanic, the share five to seven years old, and the log median income—regardless of ownership status. When we look at growth in these characteristics between 1989 and 1999, we find no significant relationship in four out of five cases. A 1 standard deviation increase in seismic risk is associated with almost 6 percentage points higher growth in the share living below the federal poverty line in the neighborhoods surrounding hospitals off a base of 19 percent. Estimates by ownership status reveal that the effects are concentrated in the neighborhoods around public and not-for-profit hospital. The effect is indistinguishable from zero in the case of for-profit hospitals.

Nonetheless, in eighteen out of twenty cases seismic risk is largely uncorrelated with hospitals' characteristics, both overall and by ownership status. Thus, we conclude that a hospital's underlying seismic risk is broadly unrelated to a host of pre-SB 1953 hospital characteristics, (such as not-for-profit status), and neighborhood demographics (such as median household income within a five-mile-radius of the hospital). Consequently, seismic risk, a key determinant of the cost of mandate compliance, will enable us to identify the implications of this regulation.

11.4.2   Regression Results

To the extent that SB 1953 increased the cost of capital, as hospitals compete for scarce financing resources, the mandate may have had the unintended consequence of increasing closures. For example, if equity and bond ratings decline for those with higher seismic risk (i.e., hospitals with higher leverage), some hospitals may have more difficulty financing their day-to-day activities and may choose to shut down.[16]

Hospital closures are not new to California and may be an important way for inefficient hospital systems to reduce capacity. For our purposes, the important question is whether SB 1953 had an independent effect on this process. We test this possibility in table 11.4 by modeling the probability that a hospital shuts down after 1996. Over our study period fifty-five hospitals, or almost 12.5 percent, closed. We present both linear probability and probit models overall (columns [1] and [3], respectively) and by ownership status (columns [2] and [4]). A shown in columns (1) and (3), seismic risk has a significant impact on the probability of closure after 1996: a 1 standard deviation increase in the ground acceleration factor increases the likelihood of closure by 6 to 7 percentage points off a base of 14 to 15 percent. This effect does not differ by ownership status.

The results in table 11.4 clearly indicate that seismic risk, an important predictor of the impact of SB 1953, increases the probability of hospital closure. To further test the validity of this conclusion, appendix table 11A.1 tests whether seismic risk is correlated with hospital closures between 1992 and 1996. Of the sixteen hospital closures during this period, six of them occurred in 1992 and 1993, before the Northridge earthquake that prompted the passage of SB 1953, while the rest occurred prior to the finalization of the details of the mandate. If seismic risk predicts these closures this would raise considerable doubt as to the causal effect of the mandate.

We find no evidence to suggest that seismic risk predicts pre-1997 hospital closures. In appendix table 11A.1, the correlation between seismic risk and closure is negative, small in magnitude, and indistinguishable from zero across both the ordinary least squares (OLS) and Probit models. Given the relatively low rate of closure over this period—just under 4 percent—the Probit model may be more appropriate. However, because closures were con-

---

16. In a 2009 California Hospital Association survey of hospital CFOs, 64 percent of those surveyed said that they were having trouble accessing enough "affordable capital" to comply with SB1953.

Table 11.4   The impact of seismic risk on the probability of hospital closures:
1997–2006

	OLS		Probit	
Seismic risk, pga	0.338	0.326	0.287	0.331
	(0.139)	(0.140)	(0.137)	(0.162)
pga · for-profit		−0.046		−0.093
		(0.268)		(0.199)
pga · government		0.090		0.053
		(0.209)		(0.210)
For-profit	0.118	0.141	0.060	0.071
	(0.053)	(0.150)	(0.051)	(0.053)
Government	0.001	−0.044	−0.027	−0.013
	(0.044)	(0.132)	(0.037)	(0.048)
Probability	0.134	0.134	0.163	0.163
Adj. R^2	0.048	0.043		
Observations	429	429	320	320

Notes: All models include county fixed effects. We also include controls for the number of licensed beds in 1992, the license age in 1992 and its square, 1992 ownership status (government-owned or for-profit, with not-for-profit status excluded), rural status, 1996 teaching status and 1996 multihospital system status. Teaching status and system status are measured as of 1996 because of data limitations. Standard errors are clustered at the city level to allow for spatial correlation in seismic risk.

centrated in a few counties and closures by ownership status varied very little within counties over this period, we are unable to estimate Probit models with interaction effects. Based on a linear probability model, we find no evidence of seismic risk effects, irrespective of ownership status. This suggests that the mandate is not simply exacerbating preexisting trends in hospital closures, which were concentrated in for-profit facilities (see Buchmueller, Jacobson, and Wold 2006). It also implies that local governments are not shielding their hospitals from the financial pressure associated with SB 1953. Finally, our results highlight the importance of weighing the benefit of having "earthquake-proof" hospitals against the cost of fewer hospitals overall. Whether policymakers were aware of this potential cost when they passed SB 1953 is unclear, but seems unlikely as the closures disproportionately affect hospitals with higher levels of seismic risk (i.e., the very hospitals policymakers wanted to be operational in the event of an earthquake).

We next consider the impact of seismic risk on hospital consolidations. We might expect consolidations to increase in response to SB 1953 as hospitals attempt to achieve economies of scale in service provision or other aspects of hospital operations (Cuellar and Gertler 2003). This would give them more financial flexibility to deal with the cost of the mandate. It may also improve their access to "affordable" capital, allowing one or both of the hospitals involved in the merger to more easily obtain financing. The results in table 11.5 suggest that these possibilities may indeed be important.

Table 11.5   The impact of seismic risk on the probability of hospital consolidations: 1997–2006

	OLS		Probits	
Seismic risk, pga	0.252	0.210	0.386	0.302
	(0.136)	(0.123)	(0.197)	(0.201)
pga · for-profit		0.133		0.078
		(0.274)		(0.260)
pga · government		0.102		0.238
		(0.261)		(0.328)
For-profit	0.071	0.064	0.080	0.036
	(0.053)	(0.111)	(0.060)	(0.169)
Government	−0.013	0.005	−0.030	−0128
	(0.048)	(0.150)	(0.060)	(0.105)
Probability	0.121	0.121	0.179	0.179
Adj. R^2	.205	.205		
Observations	429	429	291	291

Notes: All models include county fixed effects. We also include controls for the number of licensed beds in 1992, the license age in 1992, the license age in 1992 and its square, 1992 ownership status (government-owned or for-profit, with not-for-profit status excluded), rural status, 1996 teaching status, and 1996 multihospital system status. Teaching status and system status are measured as of 1996 because of data limitations. Standard errors are clustered at the city level to allow for spatial correlation in seismic risk.

A 1-standard deviation increase in the ground acceleration factor increases the probability of a merger by 5 to 8 percentage points. Estimates with interactions between seismic risk and ownership status are quite imprecise and do not allow us to reject similar effects of the mandate on consolidations across for-profit, public, and not-for-profit hospitals.[17] Assuming the effects are causal and drawing on prior research on hospital mergers, these results point to another potential unintended consequence of SB 1953—an increase in prices.[18] Whether prices actually rose is an area for future research.

In table 11.6, we assess whether hospitals that are financially squeezed by the mandate cut back on indigent care. When not differentiating by ownership type, we find small and imprecise negative effects of seismic risk on indigent care (not shown here). Breaking the effects out by ownership type, however, we find that government-owned hospitals unambiguously respond to seismic risk by changing their provision of uncompensated care. A 1-standard deviation increase in seismic risk is associated with about 330 fewer days of indigent care. This estimate, which is distinguishable from zero at the 10 percent level, is driven largely by GAC days (as opposed, for example, to psychiatric days). A 1-standard deviation increase in seismic risk is

17. We requested but have thus far not received pre-1997 merger data from the state to run a placebo test like the one performed for closures.

18. Dafny (2005) provides a nice review of the hospital merger literature as well as original evidence on the issue of price increases after hospital mergers.

Table 11.6   **The impact of seismic risk on changes in the provision of uncompensated care: 2002–2005**

	Total days	Total GAC days	ER visits	Clinic visits
Seismic risk, pga	408	259	321	691
	(363)	(345)	(542)	(881)
pga * for-profit	−183	−206	−179	−120
	(420)	(391)	(904)	(1,264)
pga * government	−2,069	−1,351	−2,300	−5,426
	(932)	(682)	(1,573)	(2,642)
For-profit	220	180	223	−389
	(212)	(195)	(430)	(770)
Government	1,100	725	1,278	1,938
	(556)	(411)	(894)	(1,150)
Mean days/visits	271	213	302	302
Adj. R^2	.030	.042	.103	.054
Observations	353	353	353	353

Notes: All models include county fixed effects. We also include controls for the number of licensed beds in 1992, the license age in 1992 and its square, 1992 ownership status (government-owned or for-profit, with not-for-profit status excluded), rural status, 1996 teaching status and 1996 multihospital system status. Teaching status and system status are measured as of 1996 because of data limitations. Standard errors are clustered at the city level to allow for spatial correlation in seismic risk.

associated with about 220 fewer indigent GAC days in public hospitals. High seismic risk public hospitals appear to reduce indigent ER visits, although our estimate is not statistically distinguishable from zero. They do, however, clearly cut free/reduced price clinic visits. A 1-standard deviation increase in seismic risk is associated with over 900 fewer visits. How hospitals reduce these visits is unclear from our data. They may, for example, limit operating hours, the number of patients per hour, or both.

That public hospitals with greater exposure to SB 1953 reduce uncompensated care suggests that the mandate has forced public hospitals to cut back on their altruistic goals, at least in the near term. We have found no evidence to suggest that policymakers anticipated this effect as a cost of insuring the earthquake safety of all hospitals in the state.

11.5   Discussion

Seismologists agree that the question of a major earthquake in California is not one of whether but when. Researchers at the Southern California Earthquake Center estimate an 80 to 90 percent chance that a temblor of 7.0 or greater magnitude will hit Southern California before 2024 (Chong and Becerra 2005). And earthquake risk is as high, if not higher, in parts of Northern California. Thus, California's desire to safeguard its health care infrastructure is eminently sensible.

While ex ante regulation is the obvious way to handle the market's failure to ensure access to care in the event of a serious earthquake, our results raise some serious questions about the wisdom of the current approach. Does the value of retrofitting or rebuilding hospitals to remain operational following an earthquake outweigh the cost of fewer hospitals overall? The potential for higher hospital prices raise additional issues.

Even putting these unintended consequences aside, the gain from ensuring every hospital's viability post-earthquake may not be worth the direct cost of retrofitting and rebuilding. The most comprehensive estimates of the construction costs imposed by SB 1953 range from $45 to $110 billion. Assuming a modest value of a statistical life of $2 million (see Viscusi and Aldy 2003), this would imply that 22,000 to 55,000 lives would need to be saved for the mandate to be worth the cost. Officials attribute sixty-one deaths to the Northridge Earthquake and some work suggests that an additional 100 cardiac arrests can be tied to the quake (Leor, Poole, and Kloner 1996).[19] A similar number of deaths have been attributed to the Loma Prieta Earthquake, which occurred five years earlier south of the Bay Area, and the Sylmar Earthquake, which occurred in northern Los Angeles County in 1971.[20] Thus, even assuming (a) the RAND cost estimates are overstated by an order of magnitude, (b) deaths are undercounted by an order of magnitude, and (c) earthquake-proof hospitals could have prevented all deaths, the benefits of the mandate hardly seem worth the cost.[21]

Obviously, this back-of-the-envelope calculation is a gross oversimplification. Injuries may be more common than deaths—the Northridge, Loma Prieta, and Sylmar earthquakes each caused several thousand injuries—and smoothly functioning hospitals may be indispensable for treating the injured and providing ongoing care to existing patients. Nonetheless, our work suggests that the costs of SB 1953 likely swamp the benefits.

11.6   Alternative Approach

Given the high risk of a devastating earthquake in California and evidence that private parties do little to insure against earthquake risk (e.g., see Palm 1981, 1995), the broad goals of SB 1953 and, in particular the move away from an ex post litigation approach, seem sensible. But more cost-efficient regulatory approaches may exist. For example, the state could pass a "functional" requirement that each GAC hospital "provide" a certain number of earthquake-proof beds. A hospital could provide these beds by retrofitting or rebuilding its own infrastructure according to SB 1953 standards. Alter-

19. Estimates of deaths attributable to the Northridge quake vary somewhat, although all are under 100. The number reported here is from the California Geological Survey: http://www .consrv.ca.gov/cgs/geologic_hazards/earthquakes/Pages/northridge.aspx.
20. See Nolte (1999) and http://earthquake.usgs.gov/regional/states/events/1971_02_09.php.
21. Many of the Sylmar deaths were caused by the collapse of a VA hospital. The VA hospitals are not subject to SB 1953.

natively, a hospital could contract with other hospitals within a defined area to provide those beds. In other words, to cover their burden, hospitals that faced a high cost of retrofitting could contract with hospitals that could more cost-effectively provide earthquake-safe beds. In this way, retrofitting would be concentrated among the hospitals in a market that could most cost-effectively do so.

This approach is akin to a carbon-trading system. Instead of permits to pollute, hospitals would have earthquake-proof bed obligations. The OSHPD would determine the number of beds each hospital is required to provide as well as the geographic boundaries of its market. Following the Acid Rain Program, the allocation could be based on the average of beds licensed and staffed by each hospital in a three- or four-year-period prior (e.g., 1993 to 1996) to the mandate. Hospitals could then trade bed obligations with other hospitals in the same market. In this way, hospitals that have a high cost of providing retrofitted beds would pay those with lower costs to provide them. The significant variation in underlying seismic risk (and therefore significant variation in the cost of new seismically safe construction), suggests that even in the absence of any economies of scale, there will be significant variation in the cost of providing seismically safe beds.

In markets with only one hospital, this trading system will not be feasible. For markets with at least two hospitals, however, this system would provide a more cost-effective means to ensure "operational readiness" in the event of a quake. The cost-efficiency should be greatest in markets with the most hospitals. Moreover, this system should prevent many of the closures and possibly mergers caused by SB 1953.

Lessons from the U.S. experience with environmental policy regulation suggest that this type of market-based policy instrument could be well-suited to ensuring hospital seismic safety (see Stavins 1998; Schmalensee et al. 1998; Ellerman et al. 2003). As in the case of pollution abatement, hospitals likely face very different costs of compliance, even within the same region. Some hospitals may have buildings that are close to the end of their life span and thus nearing a point to retrofit or rebuild even in the absence of the mandate; others may be in relatively new but still noncompliant buildings. Similarly, some hospital buildings may be on lots that—because they sit on the side of a hill or on relatively porous soil—are fundamentally costlier to retrofit. Allowing hospitals to contract amongst themselves would ensure the availability of earthquake-proof beds at the lowest cost.

California has built a large infrastructure to enforce SB 1953. We do not anticipate that the state will reverse course. The proposed system, however, can provide lessons for policymakers considering one-size-fits all regulation. In the most direct sense, this proposal could prove useful in Seattle, where the City Council is currently considering citywide seismic safety measures.[22]

---

22. See "New Seattle earthquake study targets up to 1,000 buildings," *Seattle Post Intelligencer,* May 14, 2008.

But areas prone to hurricanes, tornados, or other disaster scenarios may benefit from similar approaches to cost-effectively improve the performance of critical facilities in the event of catastrophe. More generally, using a cap-and-trade type system may be more efficient than a one-size-fits-all mandate in changing standards for an entire class of goods or services when there is heterogeneity in production. Thus, even where ex ante regulation clearly dominates ex post litigation, the specific form of regulation chosen can offer important efficiency gains.

Appendix

Table 11A.1   The impact of seismic risk on the probability of hospital closures: 1992–1996

	OLS		Probit
Seismic risk, pga	–0.013	–0.010	–0.004
	(0.080)	(0.071)	(0.005)
pga · For-profit		–0.056	
		(0.103)	
pga · Government		–0.056	
		(0.176)	
For-profit	0.064	0.036	0.060
	(0.026)	(0.095)	(0.051)
Government	0.033	0.061	0.010
	(0.026)	(0.072)	(0.008)
Probability	0.036	0.036	0.069
Adj. R^3	0.121	0.121	
Observations	443	443	231

Notes: All models include county fixed effects. We also include controls for the number of licensed beds in 1992, the license age in 1992 and its square, 1992 ownership status (government-owned or for-profit, with not-for-profit status excluded), and rural status. Standard errors are clustered at the city level to allow for spatial correlation in seismic risk. OLS = ordinary least squares.

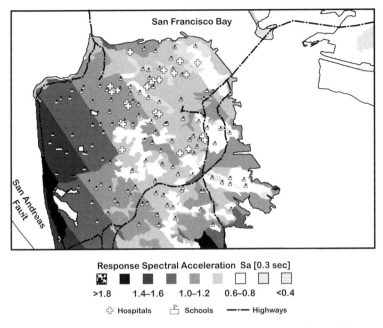

Fig. 11A.1   A map of expected ground acceleration in the event of an earthquake similar to the great quake of 1906

Source: U.S. Geological Survey.

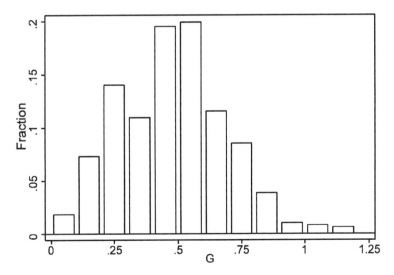

Fig. 11A.2   Frequency distribution of seismic risk among California hospitals

Sources: U.S. Geological Survey; OSHPD.

References

Alesch, D. J., and W. J. Petak. 2004. Seismic retrofit of California hospitals: Implementing regulatory policy in a complex and dynamic environment. *Natural Hazards Review* 5 (2): 89–94.

Buchmueller, T. C., M. Jacobson, and C. Wold. 2006. How far to the hospital: The impact of hospital closures on access to care. *Journal of Health Economics* 25 (4): 740–61.

Chang, T., and M. Jacobson. 2008. What is the mission of a not-for-profit hospital? Evidence from California's seismic retrofit requirements. Unpublished manuscript.

Chong, J., and H. Becerra. 2005. California earthquake could be the next Katrina. *Los Angeles Times,* September 10. Available at: http://www.latimes.com/news/local/la-earthquake08sep08,1,2126004.story?coll=la-util-news-local.

Cuellar, A. E., and P. Gertler. 2003. Trends in hospital consolidation: The formation of local systems. *Health Affairs* 22 (6): 77–87.

Dafny, L. 2005. Estimation and identification of merger effects: An application to hospital mergers. NBER Working Paper no. 11673. Cambridge, MA: National Bureau of Economic Research, October.

Davis Langdon, LLP. 2006. *Construction cost escalation in California healthcare projects.* Report prepared for the California Hospital Association, January.

Ellerman, A. D., P. L. Joskow, and D. Harrison, Jr. 2003. *Emissions trading in the U.S.: Experience, lessons and considerations for greenhouse gases.* Arlington, VA.: Pew Center on Global Climate Change.

Jones, W. 2004. Renewal by earthquake: Designing 21st century hospitals in response to California's seismic safety legislation. California HealthCare Foundation, March. Available at: http://www.chcf.org/documents/hospitals/RenewalByEarthquake.pdf.

Leor, J., W. K. Poole, and R. A. Kloner. 1996. Sudden cardiac death triggered by an earthquake. *New England Journal of Medicine* 334 (7): 413–19.

Meade, C., and R. Hillestand. 2007. *SB1953 and the challenge of hospital seismic safety in California.* Oakland, CA: California HeathCare Foundation.

Meade, C., J. Kulick, and R. Hillestand. 2002. *Estimating the compliance costs for California SB1953.* Oakland, CA: California HeathCare Foundation.

Nolte, C. 1999. After the fall. *San Francisco Chronicle,* October 17.

Palm, R. 1981. Public response to earthquake hazard information. *Annals of the Association of American Geographers* 71 (3): 389–99.

———. 1995. Catastrophic earthquake insurance: Patterns of adoption. *Economic Geography* 71 (2): 119–31.

Schmalensee, R., P. L. Joskow, A. D. Ellerman, J. P. Montero, and E. M. Bailey. 1998. An interim evaluation of sulfur dioxide emissions trading. *Journal of Economic Perspectives* 12 (3): 53–68.

Schultz, C. H., K. L. Koenig, and R. J. Lewis. 2003. Implications of hospital evacuation after the Northridge, California, earthquake. *The New England Journal of Medicine* 348 (14): 1349–55.

Stavins, R. N. 1998. What can we learn from the grand policy experiment? Lessons from SO2 allowance trading. *Journal of Economic Perspectives* 12 (3): 69–88.

Viscusi, W. K., and J. Aldy. 2003. The value of a statistical life: A critical review of market estimates throughout the world. *Journal of Risk and Uncertainty* 27 (1): 5–76.

Contributors

Tom Chang
Marshall School of Business
University of Southern California
Bridge Hall—308, MC-0804
Los Angeles, CA 90089-0804

John C. Coates, IV
Harvard Law School
Griswold 400
1525 Massachusetts Avenue
Cambridge, MA 02138

Philip J. Cook
ITT/Sanford Professor of Public Policy
Sanford School of Public Policy
Duke University
Durham, NC 27708-0245

Adam H. Gailey
RAND Corporation
1776 Main Street
Santa Monica, CA 90401-3208

Dana Goldman
School of Policy, Planning, and
    Development
University of Southern California
650 Childs Way, RGL 214
Los Angeles, CA 90089-0626

Joni Hersch
Vanderbilt University Law School
131 21st Avenue South
Nashville, TN 37203

Mireille Jacobson
RAND Corporation
1776 Main Street
Santa Monica, CA 90407-2138

Daniel Kessler
Hoover Institution
Stanford University
434 Galvez Mall
Stanford, CA 94305

Jens Ludwig
The Harris School of Public Policy
    Studies
University of Chicago
1155 East 60th Street
Chicago, IL 60637

Alison Morantz
Stanford Law School
Crown Quadrangle
559 Nathan Abbott Way
Stanford, CA 94305-8610

Stephen T. Parente
Carlson School of Management
University of Minnesota
321 19th Avenue South, 3-122
Minneapolis, MN 55455

Tomas J. Philipson
The Harris School of Public Policy
    Studies
The University of Chicago
1155 East 60th Street
Chicago, IL 60637

Richard A. Posner
University of Chicago Law School
1111 East 60th Street, Room 611
Chicago, IL 60637

Adam Samaha
University of Chicago Law School
1111 East 60th Street, Room 517
Chicago, IL 60637

Frederick Schauer
University of Virginia School of Law
580 Massie Drive
Charlottesville, VA 22903

Seth A. Seabury
RAND Corporation
1776 Main Street
Santa Monica, CA 90401-3208

Andrei Shleifer
Department of Economics
Harvard University
Littauer Center M-9
Cambridge, MA 02138

Eric Sun
Pritzker School of Medicine
University of Chicago
924 East 57th Street
Chicago, IL 60637-5415

W. Kip Viscusi
Vanderbilt Law School
131 21st Avenue South
Nashville, TN 37203-1181

Richard Zeckhauser
John F. Kennedy School of
    Government
Harvard University
76 John F. Kennedy Street
Cambridge, MA 02138

Author Index

Subject Index